JUDAISM AND THE WEST

NEW JEWISH PHILOSOPHY AND THOUGHT

Zachary J. Braiterman

JUDAISM AND THE WEST

From Hermann Cohen

to Joseph Soloveitchik

Robert Erlewine

Indiana University Press

Bloomington and Indianapolis

This book is a publication of

Indiana University Press
Office of Scholarly Publishing
Herman B Wells Library 350
1320 East 10th Street
Bloomington, Indiana 47405 USA

iupress.indiana.edu

Manufactured in the United States of America

Library of Congress Cataloging-in-Publication Data

Names: Erlewine, Robert, author.
Title: Judaism and the west: from Hermann Cohen to Joseph
   Soloveitchik / Robert Erlewine.
Description: Bloomington : Indiana University Press, 2016. | Series:
   New Jewish Philosophy and Thought | Includes bibliographical
   references and index.
Identifiers: LCCN 2016011857 | ISBN 9780253022257 (cloth : alk.
   paper) | ISBN 9780253022394 eb
Subjects: Jewish philosophy—Germany—19th century. | Jewish
   philosophy—Germany—20th century. | Judaism—History—19th
   century. | Judaism—History—20th century.
Classification: LCC B5800 .E75 2016 | LC record available at
   http://lccn.loc.gov/2015046060

1 2 3 4 5 21 20 19 18 17 16

To the memory of Alan Paskow, whose classes—and whose example—convinced me of the tremendous excitement of the life of the mind.

Contents

Acknowledgments

In many ways, this book marks a methodological departure for me. I have always thought of myself as a philosopher of religion who happens to work primarily with Jewish thinkers. However, as I increasingly engaged the work of intellectual historians and became more invested in the origins of religious studies, I found my own approach to Jewish philosophy changing. Issues and concerns that I once relegated to the background now stand prominently in the foreground, shaping the manner I elaborate the trajectory of modern Jewish philosophy. This book is very much the result of embracing the porousness of the disciplinary boundaries between Jewish studies, religious studies, intellectual history, and philosophy. I have found that attending to the intersections between fields and subfields that are too often kept separate provides inspiration and resources for reading modern Jewish philosophy in new and challenging ways.

I would like to thank the Provost and Dean of Faculty at Illinois Wesleyan University, Jonathan Green, for providing much-needed funds for the production phase of this project. A 2013 Illinois Wesleyan Artistic and Scholarly Development grant helped fund research on the chapters dealing with Martin Buber and Franz Rosenzweig. I would also like to acknowledge receipt of a *Re-centering the Humanities Grant* from the Andrew W. Mellon Foundation, which facilitated the writing of chapter 5, "Prophets, Prophecy, and Divine Wrath: Heschel and the God of Pathos."

Numerous colleagues and friends have helped me at various stages in this project. I would like to thank Dustin Atlas, Zachary Braiterman, and Bruce Rosenstock for reading various chapters and providing valuable feedback. I am also grateful to Adam Woodis for his help with many difficult translations. Martin Kavka and Aaron Hughes who, in different ways and in different capacities, have problematized the relationship between religious studies methodology and Jewish philosophy, have left an indelible mark on this monograph. Martin Kavka has patiently read many drafts of chapters and answered countless questions of mine, all with patience, generosity, and wit. Aaron Hughes, who was one of the reviewers of the book, not only offered a great deal of valuable feedback but also read subsequent drafts of the introduction and conclusion. His encouragement and his suggestions have helped me make the work bolder and more decisive.

During much of the time writing this monograph I worked as managing editor of the *Journal of Jewish Thought and Philosophy*. This brought with it the privilege of working closely with Elliot Wolfson, the editor-in-chief. In addition to the impact that his work has had on my own, our conversations about Continental philosophy, Jewish philosophy, and religious studies have left a deep impression on my thinking and have certainly found their way into this book.

Perhaps the single most important influence on the shape of this book is the work—and person—of Susannah Heschel. The more I engaged her scholarship on the significance of Jesus for modern Jewish thought and the manner in which the figure of Jesus linked Jewish and Christian thought in modernity, the more I came to see the embeddedness of modern Jewish philosophy in a network of discourses as central to its significance, rather than just a curiosity of mere historical importance. Above and beyond this, I am fortunate enough to count Susannah as a friend and mentor. Perhaps more than anyone else, she has pushed me to think about issues from points of view that were often quite foreign to my own training, and she has repeatedly exposed me to scholarly discussions that were previously unknown to me.

Family has also played an important role in the writing of this book. I would like to thank my parents and my brother for their willingness to listen to sundry details of this book project as it has developed. I am so grateful to my wife Molly for her companionship, commiseration, and support. Finally, I would like to thank my daughter Ada for all the trips to the zoo to see the sloth.

JUDAISM AND THE WEST

Introduction

Difference and Continuity in Modern Jewish Philosophy

Modern jewish philosophy is a subject that is often misunderstood—even by those whose job it is to study it. Scholars of modern Jewish philosophy scrutinize the works of philosophers in the canon because we see these thinkers as ultimately sharing the same set of problems and concerns as ourselves, even if we inhabit significantly different worlds.[1] We view these thinkers as engaged in an activity similar to the one with which we grapple—usually something like the struggle to harmonize visions of traditional Jewish teachings and beliefs with modern sensibilities. By studying these philosophers, we believe we can draw lessons for today; with enough tinkering we can refine their arguments about Judaism or the good, the true, and the beautiful into something that is tenable today. They are the sources with and through which we think and articulate our stances regarding Judaism and modernity.

By and large, contemporary approaches to the field of modern Jewish philosophy fail to attend to the distance and difference that separate current sensibilities from the major figures and works comprising its canon, and as a result they obscure something vital. The works of this canon demonstrate a ferocity and bellicosity toward Christianity that is all too often concealed or minimized by the philosophers who study them.[2] Rather than the clichés of futile, apologetic pleading for acceptance—or, in a more charitable assessment, the attempt to maintain dignity in the face of contempt—what we actually find in these works are active attempts to position Judaism as the beating heart of Western civilization at the expense of Christianity.

Perhaps it is because the canon looms so large in our own thinking that our discipline so rarely meditates on its distance or strangeness from us. To be sure, it is generally recognized that whereas today Jewish philosophy and Jewish Studies are accepted fields within the academy, our forebears philosophized about Judaism from a defensive position, working to counter the charges raised against it by its cultured despisers. And yet, the impact of this aspect of the canon is ignored or downplayed again and again because we assume that we share with these central thinkers the same fundamental understanding of the nature of modern Jewish philosophy.[3] By this I do not mean we necessarily assume that we share their metaphysical sensibilities or even share an understanding of how best to characterize Judaism. Rather, I mean that we assume that we share an understanding of what the task of modern Jewish philosophy consists in and that we need to simply continue in the footsteps of our predecessors. However, this is not the case.[4]

This book examines the work of five Jewish philosophers—Hermann Cohen (1842–1918), Martin Buber (1878–1965), Franz Rosenzweig (1886–1929), Abraham Joshua Heschel (1907–1972), and Joseph Soloveitchik (1903–1993)—over a span of roughly fifty years. The texts I study were published between 1914 and 1966, although my primary focus is on works written during the late 1910s through the 1940s. Using what I term the "world religions discourse" as an entering wedge into the respective philosophical projects of these thinkers, I highlight the critical, bellicose dimension of modern Jewish philosophy, particularly German Jewish philosophy. What I want the reader to take away from this book is the significance of the distance separating the canonical thinkers of the early to mid-twentieth century from us today. This distance is more than temporal and should be understood in terms not only of history and difference of philosophical methods and idioms but also in the larger sense of what precisely the task of modern Jewish philosophy is understood to be. Further, I want to emphasize that we overlook and minimize this difference if we read modern Jewish philosophy primarily as an internally Jewish activity, in which Jewish thinkers offer arguments about the timeless essence of Judaism or attempt to square traditional beliefs with modern sensibilities. Rather, a—perhaps *the*—central dimension of modern Jewish philosophy, at least from the vantage point at which I examine it, is its relation to the larger German, and indeed "Western," culture.

By prioritizing the search for better (however we configure this) arguments about how to think about Judaism, or by reading works by thinkers from the past explicitly in terms of our present concerns, we do violence to and distort modern Jewish philosophy on a very basic level. Although these thinkers offer much that is insightful and still relevant, it behooves us to acknowledge and emphasize the differences separating these thinkers from us today. We must recognize that the political, philosophical, and theological framework in which their respective works emerge and with which they engage are not ours, at least not straightforwardly. The questions that lie before us today have to do with pluralism, fragmentation, and the many challenges—moral and political—associated with state power, whereas the chief impetus for their thinking lay in contesting Christianity's assumed religious dominance as well as its cultural and political hegemony from the position of a disenfranchised minority.

These Jewish philosophers did not merely challenge Christianity in an abstract manner, on the level of doctrine or truth claims. Rather, they appropriated and engaged a dominant discourse at their disposal—nineteenth- and early twentieth-century comparative religion, or more precisely, *Religionswissenschaft*: what I refer to as the world religions discourse. I use this term intentionally to resonate with Tomoko Masuzawa's seminal work *Inventing World Religions*

(2005),[5] particularly its elaboration of the manner in which the burgeoning discipline of comparative religion and the "science" of religion were intricately bound up with fault lines in European identity.[6] In light of the political, cultural, and religious upheavals of Jewish life in the twentieth century, as well as the radical challenges to the notions of Europeanness at stake in the world religions discourse in the late twentieth and early twenty-first centuries, Jewish philosophy today operates with many different assumptions and concerns than did that of our predecessors.

Thus a rigorous study of modern Jewish philosophy must begin by appreciating its difference as well as continuity with our concerns and assumptions today. However, all too often we minimize difference for the sake of continuity. It is precisely because this book attends to the concerns and assumptions that distinguish our predecessors—at least those from the early to mid-twentieth century—from us today that it is well poised to both serve as an introduction to modern Jewish philosophy and to cast new light on figures grown all too familiar.

Disciplinary Issues: Religious Studies and Jewish Philosophy

Although modern Jewish philosophy was once largely housed within philosophy and history departments, in recent years, religious studies departments have served as sites of increased activity in the study of Jewish philosophy.[7] However, even though Jewish philosophy's home in the modern university currently tends to be in religious studies, for a variety of reasons—administrative, disciplinary, epistemological—there is a lack of interaction between the two fields. And yet this need not be the case. Attending to the historically situated nature of the study of religion—particularly as it operated in nineteenth- and early twentieth-century Germany—serves not only to illuminate previously undisclosed elements at play in modern Jewish philosophy but also to introduce the study of Jewish philosophy to, and facilitate a reconciliation with, the broader discipline of religious studies. One goal of this book is to show how fruitful and mutually enriching it can be to bring current discussions in religious studies scholarship about the origins and development of the category of religion into dialogue with the study of Jewish philosophy. That is, modern Jewish philosophy provides scholars of religion with concrete examples of how a specific, non-Christian tradition has appropriated and internalized into its own self-definition the terms of the Protestant study of religion. At the same time, the discourse about the category of religion provides resources for grasping the nuances of the historically circumscribed aspect of the arguments of German Jewish philosophy, enabling us to both better appreciate the subtlety of the arguments of our precursors and the differences between their primary motivations and assumptions and our own.

One of the chief features of contemporary research into the modern category of religion is its focus on its history and on elucidating the means by which this category was employed in the European study of religion from its inception into the present. Scholarship regarding the world religions discourse reveals that the concept of religion is inextricably entangled in the larger context of imperialism, colonialism, and Orientalism. This not only highlights the ways in which Europe is related or relates itself to non-Western cultures, but when sufficiently nuanced, these studies also bring to light that the world religions discourse emerges amidst a profound transformation regarding the theological and political inflected sense of "Europeanness."[8] Indeed, questions about the nature of the relationship between European Christianity and the religions of the ancient Near East and Asia are contemporaneous with an explicit challenge to the role Jews and Judaism play in Europe's present and future.[9] In this discourse, notions of identity, associated with proximity or the perception of shared history or sacred texts, become destabilized, as Buddhism comes to be seen to possess more in common with European civilization than the religion of Jews who had lived in Europe for more than a thousand years. It is in the midst of this crisis of identity—one particularly distressing for Jews—that modern Jewish philosophy, at least the particular strand of modern Jewish philosophy I examine here, emerges.[10]

At the heart of this transformation of Europeanness was a profound shift in the nineteenth century in how Europeans thought about the nature of religion. Central to these changing sensibilities was the emerging field of philology, which offered dramatic new possibilities for reconceiving and reconstructing the ancestry and origins of peoples and nations.[11] At that time, philology, which was not without racialist overtones,[12] drew a sharp distinction between Aryan and Semitic language groups. This linguistic distinction highlighted the innate spiritual or philosophical tension between Hebraism and Hellenism, strengthening a rift in sensibility and theology separating the Old and New Testaments that was already entrenched in German philosophy and theology. These changes in the way that language, identity, history and religion were understood brought increasing pressure on Christianity to shed its Semitic foundations.[13]

As the more traditional notion of Europe, understood as a synthesis of the legacies of ancient Greece and ancient Israel, threatened to unravel, theologians and historians studied the ancient Near Eastern context of the Old Testament in search of resources to help construct a Christianity shorn of Semitic influences.[14] Europeans, particularly in the German-speaking world, increasingly identified with religions of India, such as Buddhism, while continuing to valorize ancient Greece, at the expense of the Hebraic heritage of the Bible. Christianity's relationship to the Old Testament, Greece, the Middle East, and Asia more generally generated heated disputes among theologians, secular academics, and laypeople alike, given that it possessed significant implications for Germany's present.[15]

Unraveling the Greco-Hebraic foundations of Europe cast Jews as foreigners in Europe even though they had lived there for millennia. It undermined the basic categories by which European Christians and Jews had previously understood themselves as bound together.

What this new scholarship about the category of religion brought to light was the extent to which theological and scholarly questions regarding the taxonomies of world religions were inextricably bound up with racial and nationalistic ones. The implications of the world religions discourse were far-reaching and dramatic. Particularly in the German-speaking world, because of its preoccupations with *Volk* and nation, questions that touched on one's origins were permeated with contemporary significance.

Jewish philosophers, in different ways and to different degrees, not only engaged and contested the implications of the world religions discourse but also internalized and even appropriated its terminology. Yet, even as they adopted the concepts and terminology of this discourse, they did not accept its largely Protestant assumptions and actively contested its prevalent norms. They sought to challenge the racial and nationalistic implications of the study of religion and in many cases, to reorient the discourse on new foundations as a means of challenging the ongoing processes rendering Jews aliens in Europe.

As I mentioned earlier, examining the ways in which Jewish philosophers reconceptualized Judaism's relationship with Europe is relevant for religious studies. Indeed, Masuzawa notes the need to study the "process of mutually interactive development" between "European representations of non-Christian religions and, on the other hand, the native appropriation, reaction, or resistance to such representations."[16] In other words, to come to grips with the deep conceptual history of the modern category of religion, it is imperative to explore the manner in which non-Protestants—especially non-Europeans but also Jews, whose European identity in the shift to a paradigm rooted in "world religions" was suddenly undercut—engaged with and used the terms and concepts of religious studies. These terms not only shaped the manner in which the West perceived its others but also how the West's others perceived themselves.[17]

Indeed, attention to how Jewish thinkers appropriated elements of the world religions discourse in their own philosophies will add nuance to current discussions about the politics of Jewish Studies. At present there is tension between two approaches to scholarship, what Russell McCutcheon, a prominent commentator and theorist regarding the nature and role of religious studies in the curriculum, has framed as that between caretakers and critics.[18] A caretaker sees his or her task as describing or translating the insights of specific religious traditions such that scholarship remains "derived from, and fully inscribed within, the vocabularies and the belief systems of the groups [being] stud[ied]."[19] In contrast, the critic attends to the ways that human beings in different times and places "coordinat[e]

discourses on such things as nonobvious beings . . . absolute origins, and ultimate endtimes within highly rule-driven systems of practice," disclosing the
manner in which groups "create a system of enduring social and self-identities."[20]
Rather than looking to timeless metaphysical world pictures, the critic analyzes
the ways in which social conditions and institutions, including religious authority and language, construct reality. For McCutcheon, the scholar of religion is
tasked with being a critic and not a caretaker.

In light of the politicization of Jewish Studies, the prominent role of outside,
moneyed interests and organizations, and the blurred line between scholarship
and advocacy, McCutcheon's rather stark distinction merits attention.[21] And yet
it is also vital that there be clarity regarding the conceptual and philosophical
entanglements—some of which run quite deep—that render modern Jewish philosophy symbiotic with, and parasitic on, Western philosophy and conceptions
of European identity. Policing methodology can obscure important questions regarding who is using which method and for what end. For example, when seeking to demarcate "legitimate" theory from that which is more descriptive and
phenomenological (i.e., "caretaking"), McCutcheon obscures the structural and
political differences driving the work of a Jewish philosopher like Martin Buber
from Protestant theologians like Rudolf Otto or Paul Tillich. McCutcheon
laments "the dubious place of . . . Schleiermacher, Otto, Tillich, Buber, Wach, and
Eliade, to only name a few who, until now, have enjoyed prominent places in our
field's [i.e., religious studies'] pantheon."[22] Yet, as will become clear in the following pages, Martin Buber is situated very differently in regard to religious studies
and the world religions discourse than the other names on the list because as
someone rooted in Jewish traditions rather than Christian ones, he not only
has different religious sensibilities, but perhaps more importantly, his approach to
the field is informed by his desire to reform its philosophical foundations which
are bound up with the denigration of Judaism. If we—scholars of modern Jewish philosophy—find caretaking problematic today, this should not necessarily
diminish the work of our predecessors in our eyes, because they were faced with
a very different task.

In this book, I seek to highlight the contingent context in which a specific
discourse that comes to be called "modern Jewish philosophy" emerges and the
various conceptual tools it employs to empower itself to speak on behalf of Jews
and Judaism (often over and against Christianity). What are the ways in which
modern Jewish philosophy appropriates, engages, and contests the world religions
discourse? By answering this question, this work highlights the combative dimension of modern Jewish philosophy in which Judaism is privileged at the expense of Christianity, a dimension that is so often overlooked or downplayed in
subsequent accounts of the canon.

Scope

This book's focus is on that period of early to mid-twentieth-century German Jewish philosophy. I begin with Hermann Cohen's war writings and his methodological works on the study of religion, focusing on the manner in which they struggle with national belonging in the face of the world religions discourse. Cohen's work, in different ways, sets up the parameters and patterns that subsequent thinkers, even in opposing him, play out and deepen. Not only do subsequent thinkers respond to Cohen but like him they are also engaging with and responding to the developments in the world religions discourse that was quite prominent in Germany and had significant ramifications—both conceptual and political—for Jews. It also bears mentioning that although both Heschel and Soloveitchik, the final two thinkers I consider here, are scions of Eastern European Judaism(s) who gained fame in the United States, they wrote their dissertations in Berlin in the 1930s, and both take up in their work the same set of issues and concerns that motivate their their German Jewish predecessors, including engaging the larger world religions discourse. Indeed, another contribution of this book is to bring these two thinkers, often treated independently from the larger canon of modern Jewish philosophy, squarely into conversation with such prominent thinkers in the canon as Cohen, Rosenzweig, and Buber.

As I mentioned earlier, this book attempts to recapture the bellicosity, the ferocity, of modern Jewish philosophy in part by de-familiarizing it. That is, by exposing the manner in which modern Jewish philosophy is itself responding to the operating assumptions of the world religions discourse—assumptions we do not share or at least not in the same way—this work shows how this discourse was marshaled in various constructions of Judaism and in accounts of its relationship to other religions. Yet the attempt to navigate Judaism's relationship with European civilization and world religions can be seen in modern Jewish philosophy well before the predominance of the world religions discourse in the nineteenth century. In the eighteenth century, Moses Mendelssohn (1729–1786) frequently invokes what we might call world religions (Islam, Native American religions, Hinduism) in his critique of European imperialism and his metaphysical account of universal religious truths. In the nineteenth century, Abraham Geiger (1810–1874) and Heinrich Graetz (1817–1891) actively contested Christian narratives about Judaism and used their knowledge of Jewish texts to challenge the Christian quest for the historical Jesus, which—at least when they wrote—involved downplaying or an outright denial of his Jewishness. Indeed, there is a long, rich prehistory to the group of thinkers I examine in this book. However, focusing my reading of modern Jewish philosophy around Cohen and his legacy brings coherence and a unity to the study, while necessitating that I exclude important forerunners.

Additionally, there are a number of thinkers who are roughly contemporaries with Heschel and Soloveitchik that I do not discuss in this work. Leo Strauss (1899–1973), Emmanuel Levinas (1906–1995), and Emil Fackenheim (1916–2003) are all tied to the tradition of German Jewish philosophy beginning with Cohen and continuing through Rosenzweig and Buber. However, these thinkers are not as explicitly or immediately connected as Heschel and Soloveitchik with the world religions discourse, and thus more exposition would be needed to bring them within the ambit of this study. In addition, given the significantly different philosophical idioms of Strauss, Levinas, and Fackenheim, and given the considerable bodies of secondary literature around each figure, it would be virtually impossible to do justice to their work within the confines of the present volume. Instead, I begin with two chapters on Cohen's thought and devote individual chapters to Rosenzweig, Buber, Heschel, and Soloveitchik. I select these thinkers because, both individually and as a whole, they offer the biggest "bang for the buck" in relation to the world religions discourse.

Although no one issue or concern as manifested in the work of the thinkers included here defines or is constitutive of modern Jewish philosophy, one can nevertheless find a cluster of overlapping concerns. Perhaps most notably, these thinkers evince a need to ensure the distinctive or irreplaceable role of Judaism in world religions, its exemplarity, as well as an urgency in clarifying Judaism's relationship to Christianity, usually in such a manner as to cast the latter in a critical and unflattering light. Additionally, the status of Jesus's Jewishness, God's ontological relationship to the world, the relationship between the Old and New Testaments, the resurgence of the Christian heresy of Marcionism, and the philosophy of Kant are concerns that recur repeatedly in different iterations in the work of the thinkers discussed in these pages. Reading their respective philosophies in light of the profound shift in the manner in which Europeans understood the concept of religion and, as a result, of Europe's relationship to the world, brings fresh insight not only into these five thinkers but also into the central terms at play in modern Jewish philosophy in general, including ethical monotheism, God, revelation, prophecy, and halakha.

Chapter Overview

The first two chapters are devoted to the work of Hermann Cohen. His thought raises many of the major problems and issues that continue to occupy modern Jewish philosophy in some form or other. In chapter 1, "Exemplarity and the German-Jewish Symbiosis: Herman Cohen on War and Religion," I explore Cohen's much-maligned account of the complementarity of the conceptual and spiritual foundations of Judaism and Germanism (i.e., German culture conceived in terms of its highest ideals). Reading Cohen's writings on World War I, along with his more methodologically focused writings on religion, this chapter highlights the multiple levels through which Cohen attempts to maintain the cultural symbiosis between Judaism and Germanism. At the very moment when Christian theologians and historians were trying to eliminate any connections between German culture and Judaism, Cohen does not merely claim that Judaism is compatible with Germanism but also that it is the predominant basis of the latter's conceptual and spiritual foundations. For scholars of Jewish philosophy, this chapter emphasizes the rhetorical complexity of Cohen's nationalist writings and his work on the concept of religion thereby challenging many of the readings that have been used to dismiss Cohen and German-Jewish liberalism in general. For scholars of religious studies, this chapter illuminates not only the different ways in which, at the turn of the twentieth century, the concept of religion resonated differently with philosophers and theologians, Jews and Christians, but also how cultural and national concerns were intertwined with methodological disputes about its definition.

In chapter 2, "Symbol Not Sacrifice: Cohen's Jewish Jesus," I explore the Judeo-centric nature of Cohen's quest for a German Jewish symbiosis in more depth. Focusing on his posthumously published *Religion of Reason out of the Sources of Judaism* (1919), I describe how Cohen challenges a prominent German Protestant tradition that understands Jesus as essentially a Greek phenomenon rather than a Jewish one. I argue that Cohen not only deliberately distances Jesus from Greece, but that in this work Judea not Athens, becomes the standard bearer of rationality, at least of religious rationality. By setting up Judaism as exemplary in the manner in which it (by means of its literary sources) possesses the potential to rationalize itself and fulfills this potential, Cohen seeks to render the very framework of the world religions discourse irrelevant if not idolatrous. At the same time, his rationalist method entails the negation of philological and racialist modes of inquiry. He depicts the Greek world with an Orientalizing brush, highlighting the irrational and mythological aspects of Hellenistic thinking while emphasizing an account of Judaism rooted in sober, ethical rationalism. In this context, Cohen radically problematizes the traditional Christian notion of Jesus as messiah and agent of vicarious atonement, instead depicting him as a symbol of *teshuva* (repentance), the fulcrum of morality in his philosophy of Judaism. In short, I argue that Cohen renders Jesus as best understood as a Jewish phenomenon and presents a way to reinterpret Christianity such that it too can accord with reason and thus with Judaism. For scholars of modern Jewish philosophy, this chapter offers a new reading of Cohen's *Religion of Reason* that foregrounds its agonistic and polemical character. Scholars of religion should be interested in the ways in which the concept of religion is not only defined in terms of a rationalist philosophy but also is rather uncharacteristically put to the use of vindicating Judaism at the expense of Christianity.

Cohen's rationalism and liberalism mark him as very much a creature of his generation. By arguing that the concept of religion must meet criteria laid out by a rationalist philosophy, that it must correspond to a philosophical Idealism systematically conceived, Cohen uses the concept of religion in two discordant ways. On the one hand, by incorporating it into his philosophical system, he seeks to render it rational and thus as a means to delegitimize such irrational phenomena as antisemitism, vulgar nationalism, and racialism. On the other hand, he wants to use this same concept to vindicate not only Judaism's essential bond with Germanism but also to insist that these two cultures—ideally configured—represent the pinnacle of Western civilization. Religion is, then, supposed to be an agent of demythologization and yet simultaneously grant what can only be an ideological, not philosophically tenable, set of claims. He uses the concept of exemplarity to mediate these opposing tendencies within his concept of religion and, indeed, within reason itself.

The generation after Cohen, perhaps as a result of the traumas of World War I and rising antisemitism, had little faith in the rational grounding of culture and sought meaning in the lived, experiential dimensions of religion. Rejecting Cohen's call for reason to dictate the order of reality, their philosophies emphasize the indefinable, irrational flow of everyday existence. God now escapes the confines of reason, and religion transcends morality strictly understood. Nevertheless, as different as Rosenzweig's and Buber's respective sensibilities are from that of Cohen, both share his fears about ongoing efforts to de-Judaize Europe and Christianity, and both seek philosophical countermeasures to those efforts.

In chapter 3, "Fire, Rays, and the Dark: Rosenzweig and the Oriental/Occidental Divide," I focus on Franz Rosenzweig's *The Star of Redemption* (1921) in order to examine how he configures the relationship between Judaism and Europe. If Cohen uses reason as the means by which the category of religion is to be properly understood, Rosenzweig, eschewing abstraction, offers a theologically permeated political vision as the basis for grasping this concept. According to Rosenzweig, there exists a hidden and unbreakable theological bond between Judaism and Christianity, a filial relation that opposes every other world religion, particularly Islam and the religions of India and China. This chapter argues that Rosenzweig's notorious criticisms of Islam and of the religions of India and China are best understood as addressing elements of the role of the world religions discourse within the European imaginary rather than as criticisms of the religions themselves. For scholars of Jewish philosophy, this chapter challenges the prominent tendency to read Rosenzweig's *The Star of Redemption* as anticipating postmodern and poststructural turns of thought by highlighting the degree to which this work is historically circumscribed. For scholars of religion, aside from highlighting the methodological malleability of the category of religion at this period of time in German thought, this chapter illuminates some of the various ways in which Jewish thinkers attempted to use religious studies scholarship and the category of religion to create alliances—and oppositions—between Judaism and other religious traditions.

I examine Martin Buber's most famous work, *I and Thou* (1923), in chapter 4, "Redeeming This World: Buber's Judaism and the Sanctity of Immanence." Whereas Rosenzweig follows Cohen in offering a metanarrative of the West, Buber emulates Cohen insofar as he seeks to use philosophy to challenge the antisemitic tendencies then dominant in *Religionswissenschaft*, a prominent vehicle of the world religions discourse. This chapter treats *I and Thou* as a prolonged meta-physical meditation on human experience that was intended to serve as a foundation for the study of comparative religions. Unlike Cohen and Rosenzweig, Buber embraces the turn to world religions. However, he attempts to offer a new foundation for this discourse, based on spirit [*Geist*] and the living encounter. Indeed, in Buber's account, the dominant forms of the study of religion, like so much of European civilization, evince a crisis of spirit, in dire need of revitalization. For the scholar of Jewish philosophy, this chapter should de-familiarize Buber's work, challenging many of its common readings and, all too often, blithe dismissals of it. The scholar of religion should find interest in the manner in which this chapter reads *I and Thou* as a work attempting to reframe the world religions discourse in such a way as to oppose then prominent anti-Jewish philosophical and theological trends permeating it.

The last two thinkers whose work I explore are Abraham Joshua Heschel and Joseph Soloveitchik. In contrast to the other thinkers investigated here, Heschel and Soloveitchik are not only born in the twentieth century but are also not German Jews. Both were of Eastern European lineage, rooted and educated in Orthodoxy—albeit in distinct forms—and both immigrated to Germany in their early twenties to pursue secular studies because Germany was then at the center of a thriving intellectual and academic environment. Whereas Soloveitchik wrote his dissertation on Cohen's philosophy of science and Heschel wrote a phenomenological study of the prophets, the works of both thinkers are relevant to this broader meditation on the entanglement of modern Jewish philosophy with the world religions discourse.

Chapter 5, "Prophets, Prophecy, and Divine Wrath: Heschel and the God of Pathos," examines Heschel's dissertation written in Berlin and published in 1936 as *Die Prophetie*. Like Buber, Heschel follows Cohen in engaging and challenging *Religionswissenschaft*. However, unlike Cohen and Buber, who primarily focus on the philosophical foundations of religious studies, Heschel's *Die Prophetie* is an actual technical exercise in *vergleichenden Religionsgeschichte* or what we might call comparative religions, a subdiscipline of *Religionswissenschaft*. Heschel's study of prophetic consciousness, while employing historical and phenomenological methodology common in such studies, uses these same methods to challenge the norms and dominant assumptions of the "science" of religion and the world religions discourse. *Die Prophetie* emphasizes the radical uniqueness of the prophets, thereby undermining what Heschel sees as the tendency of comparative religions to homogenize all religious phenomena. Heschel's attempt to reclaim the unique character of the Bible implicitly challenges modern European sensibilities and adumbrates his later work regarding Jewish and Christian relations. For the scholar of Jewish philosophy, this chapter not only contextualizes Heschel's thought in the larger framework of German Jewish philosophy but also offers a study of a frequently overlooked but highly significant text. The scholar of religion should find interest in the attempt of a Jewish philosopher to overturn the tacit Protestant assumptions of biblical studies and comparative religion in the early twentieth century while remaining within their methodological confines.

Chapter 6, "Cultivating Objectivity: Soloveitchik, The Marburg School, and Religious Pluralism," explores the work of Joseph Soloveitchik, paying particular attention to his *The Halakhic Mind,* written in the 1940s but not published until 1986. This chapter situates *The Halakhic Mind* between Soloveitchik's dissertation written in Berlin in 1932 on the notion of pure being in Cohen's thought and "Confrontation," his famous essay on Jewish-Christian relations published in response to Vatican II in 1964. I argue that Soloveitchik follows Cohen in both offering a metanarrative of the West and critically engaging with the study of religion. Soloveitchik clearly has sympathy for Cohen's attempt to ground culture on science and to use a rationalist philosophical foundation to regulate the often violent elements that emerge in nationalism and irrational religiosities. However, he emphasizes the importance of recent developments in science—developments taking place after Cohen's death—which render Cohen's attempt to ground philosophy and culture on the foundations of the mathematical natural sciences no longer viable. These new developments—this epistemological pluralism, as he puts it—offer new freedom to study religion as something sui generis. Soloveitchik uses them to shift the focus of the philosophy of Judaism from texts and ethical norms to praxis and halakha. In this manner, Soloveitchik seeks to undercut the philosophical legitimacy of religious liberalism, whether Jewish or not, and to ensure that interreligious interaction can only take on political, especially democratic, grounds. For scholars of modern Jewish philosophy, this chapter not only contextualizes Soloveitchik's thought within the larger trajectory of German Jewish thought but it also reveals how congenial his thought remains to the commitments of the Marburg School of philosophy. For scholars primarily interested in religious studies, Soloveitchik's thought challenges many of the standard assumptions about the sui generis approach to the study of religion. Whereas traditional (Christian) proponents of the sui generis approach to religion have been criticized by the likes of Wayne Proudfoot and Russell McCutcheon as attempting to evade or to undercut the Enlightenment, Soloveitchik specifically invokes the Enlightenment legacy in his use of the sui generis method.

* * *

Although this book takes a critical perspective in regard to the study of Jewish philosophy, actively emphasizing the historical boundedness of the works studied, it is not intended to be anti-philosophical. Indeed, when we fail to appreciate the political and theoretical horizons in which the thinkers we study operated, we distort and often diminish their work. To truly inherit the works of the canon requires that we not only study the internal coherence of their respective arguments but we also grasp the larger discourse to which they were responding, to which their arguments were directed. We must grasp their distance before we can properly appropriate them and make them relevant for the present.

1 Exemplarity and the German-Jewish Symbiosis: Hermann Cohen on War and Religion

The Spurned Master

The work of Hermann Cohen offers an important place to begin in our exploration of how Jewish philosophers responded to the world religions discourse, to the unraveling of the once shared understanding of Europe's foundations as resting on the legacy of a synthesis of ancient Greece and ancient Israel. Hermann Cohen occupied a unique and controversial position in German culture as the only unbaptized Jew to hold a chair in philosophy prior to World War I, and he played a quite visible role in the cultural and political disputes of the day. Reflecting on Cohen's influence, Leo Strauss (1972) wrote, "I grew up in an environment in which Cohen was the center of attraction for philosophically minded Jews who were devoted to Judaism; he was the master whom they revered."[1]

And yet due to a variety of reasons, many not philosophical but rather sociopolitical,[2] neo-Kantianism in general and Cohen's thought in particular were eclipsed soon after his passing in 1918.[3] The "war" generation held significantly different sensibilities, both religious and philosophical, from those of Cohen and his generation.[4] Its members increasingly viewed as absurd Cohen's rationalist ideal of harmonizing Judaism and Germanism; they understood Judaism and Germanism to be incompatible and even categorically different conceptual structures.[5] Cohen was painted as someone who muddled bourgeoisie sensibility and Judaism; his vision of Judaism was seen as lacking authenticity.[6]

Politically, Cohen's adamant rejection of the growing movement of Zionism placed him at odds with subsequent developments in Jewish thought. Indeed, a major disagreement between Cohen and later Jewish thinkers concerned the role that Jews were to play in German culture. Cohen's "Deutschtum und Judentum mit grundlegungen Betrachtungen über Staat und Internationalismus" [Germanism and Judaism with Foundational Observations about the State and Internationalism] (1915),[7] in addition to supporting Germany's war effort in World War I, elaborates a notion of German-Jewish symbiosis.[8] This text elicited a great deal of criticism from both Zionists and antisemites, whose critiques overlapped significantly. Both groups believed that Jews could never be accepted in German culture and that a cultural symbiosis between them was untenable.[9] Even the non-Zionists among the following generation neither endorsed nor found credible the strong priority given by Cohen's generation to a cultural symbiosis between Germanism and Judaism.

Prominent in the critique of Cohen's argument was a sense of the futility of dialogue as a means for emancipation and assimilation.[10] This line of criticism found particular resonance in the wake of the Holocaust and the rise of the State of Israel. Those who take this view at present see Cohen as either a tragic or hopelessly deluded figure, his claims for a German Jewish symbiosis as "obsequious apologetics"[11]; they characterize Cohen as willfully repressing the "xenophobic, racist, and antisemitic elements of German political culture"[12] or as "act[ing] blindly in his German patriotism."[13] This line of critique resonates with Gershom Scholem's famous claim that although "the Jews attempted a dialogue with the Germans starting from all possible points of view and situations, demandingly, imploringly, and entreatingly, servile and defiant, with a dignity employing all manner of tones and a godforsaken lack of dignity," it was naught but a "cry into the void."[14] From this perspective, Cohen did not merely seek in vain for dialogue partners among his Protestant contemporaries, but he tragically embraced an insufficiently critical nationalism for the very nation that would give rise to Nazism a few decades after his death.

This way of viewing Cohen is anachronistic, deriving much of its force by projecting the Holocaust back in time and interpreting philosophical debates under its dark shadow. As Wendell Dietrich has correctly pointed out, "Cohen should be permitted to stand for what he stands for, no more and no less. In his time, a variety of historical options were still open for the development of the German nation and the situation of the Jews in Germany."[15] As we see later, Cohen does problematically privilege Germany for its special spiritual kinship with Judaism, giving rise to a bitter historical irony. However, what is too frequently neglected in this line of critique is that Cohen's claims are as much constructive as descriptive (or perhaps more so) and that his writings are rhetorically marshaled to counter the rising tide of antisemitism, of which he was very well aware.[16]

Cohen offers a vision of Judaism as a cornerstone of the West; it exemplifies—indeed, is constitutive of—Western civilization's highest values. Juxtaposing Cohen's war writings—namely *"Über das Eigentümliche des deutschen Geistes"* [On the Particularity of the German Spirit] (1914)[17] and "Deutschtum und Judentum" from 1915—with his more methodologically focused writings on religion, *Der Begriffe der Religion im System der Philosophie* [The Concept of Religion in the System of Philosophy] [1915][18] and the introduction from *Religion of Reason out of the Sources of Judaism* (1919),[19] highlights the multiple levels through which Cohen attempts to demonstrate the symbiosis between Judaism in German culture.[20] As this analysis makes clear, Cohen is no mere harmonizer. To be sure, Cohen, like many Germans of his time, maintains German culture as the pinnacle of rationality and ethics and thus considers it to be the epitome of European civilization, of the West. However, reading these texts together will allow us to trace how Cohen's thought is not merely compatible with Germanism but also that Judaism inhabits and even constitutes the foundation of Germanism.

Cohen relies on the notion of exemplarity—demarcating a particular identity or a pair of identities as manifesting the most fully developed instance of a universal value—to argue that all peoples and cultures can participate in Germanism and Judaism. Cohen thereby disentangles culture from religion and race. In this same vein, he argues that the ideational cores of Judaism and Germanism are profoundly and inextricably bound up with one another. Cohen shows great ingenuity in using one of the tropes of cultural imperialism—that Germany is the pinnacle of Western culture—as a means to undermine racialism. However, this approach—the privileging of certain identities against all others—can only be justified through circular reasoning.

To make his claims, Cohen combines two different strategies with which later thinkers will wrestle and develop. He both seeks to ground his thought in an overarching philosophy of the West, a philosophical *Geist* of European civilization, and to engage and critique the comparative study of religion through the use of philosophy. However, where Cohen uses both strategies, later thinkers—at least in the works we investigate here—will privilege one path over the other (Soloveichik will be the exception, in that he, like Cohen, uses both methods, albeit to very different ends). Indeed, although Cohen's thought is roundly found insufficient or no longer relevant by later thinkers, his work provides the point of departure—whether explicitly or tacitly—for those philosophers discussed here. That is, it is essential to begin with Cohen to understand the subsequent accounts of Buber, Rosenzweig, Heschel, and Soloveitchik regarding the relationship between Judaism and the world religions discourse. Not only do these later thinkers consciously see themselves as following in Cohen's wake, but also in many ways, given his towering presence on the philosophical, German, and Jewish cultural scenes, as well as the rigor and ingenuity of his thought, they could agree or disagree, appropriate or repudiate, but they could not ignore his work.

"Deutschtum und Judentum"

"Deutschtum und Judentum" is a notoriously difficult, dizzying, even esoteric text.[21] Cohen's wartime writings play on the notion then prominent in German nationalism that Germany was the educator of Europe and thus the world. However, in the process of "establishing" German cultural and ethical superiority over the other nations of Europe as a justification for its role in the Great War, he simultaneously disentangles culture from race and secures a prominent place for Jews in German culture.

Throughout his wartime writings (and other later works) Cohen uses broad, vague terms such as "Germanism" and "Judaism," but not to designate anything either metaphysical or empirical. Although he speaks of a German and Jewish spirit, Cohen is certainly not invoking anything metaphysical such as Hegel's *Geist,*[22] nor is he referring to race or ethnicity.[23] Commentator Steven Schwarzschild helpfully points out that too often people "take it for granted that by the term 'Germanism' [Cohen] meant to refer to empirical Germany, or at least to actual, historical German culture—and then [proceed] to refute his thesis of an identity or symbiosis by simply pointing to the blatant discordancy between the two entities."[24] Such a view, which fits quite nicely with the typical critique of Cohen, fails to take into account Cohen's philosophical methodology, which never simply accepts the state of affairs or entities like a nation as they are, but instead seeks to idealize them and envision what they could be, a method Michael Zank refers to as a "hermeneutics of optimization."[25]

Indeed, when Cohen speaks of Germanism or Judaism he is using his methodology of idealization.[26] That is, Cohen is at once positing an ideal—what Germany ought to be—and then uses it as a standard by which to measure the deficiencies of the present.[27] Cohen uses this idealizing—and mystifying—method to reconstruct the German-Jewish symbiosis. According to Cohen, the spirit of Judaism and the spirit of Germanism are bound together by their profound rationalism. Instrumental in Cohen's account of this link—and indeed, its historical realization—is the famed German Jewish philosopher, Moses Mendelssohn. However, Cohen does not celebrate Mendelssohn for his philosophical achievements,[28] but instead for reforming Judaism by exposing it to the spirit of Germanism. Cohen writes, "From the *unity* of his German and his Jewish essence accrued in him not only the force, but also the restraint and the modesty, to help the *German* Jews, to raise them into the sunlight of German culture and literature, and to free them from, and inoculate against, the jargon of World Judaism." Cohen's German chauvinism is clear here in that it is not just any language that is "to be the means salvation [*Erlösung*] from the Ghetto." Rather, the "German language" is "the remedy of Judaism."[29]

As Cohen understands it, by writing in German and engaging in the broader culture, Mendelssohn facilitated the cultivation of Germanism for the Jews of Central Europe. Thus, Mendelssohn's legacy frees—or at least instantiates the process of freeing—Jews from the fetters of backwardness and makes Germany the spiritual homeland of all Jews. It is not that German culture implants something new in Judaism; instead it helps regenerate the rational elements of Judaism that had been suppressed and atrophied by years of persecution: it helps restore rationalism as the proper core of Judaism and allows the jettisoning of superstition and mysticism as aberrations and pathologies of persecution. Cohen is offering a normative vision of both Judaism and Germany here. He insists that authentic Judaism is rationalist Judaism, a Judaism free of any mystical or superstitious commitments. In turn, authentic Germanism is cosmopolitan, the language and culture of the highest human ideals, of the culture of Kant, Goethe, and Beethoven. If there are tensions between extant instantiations or iterations of Judaisms and Germanisms, their ideal forms are perfectly compatible, indeed complementary.

In Cohen's estimation Mendelssohn's most significant contributions were his translations of the Pentateuch and the Psalms. His use of German language did not introduce anything foreign, but rather the "German words and writing and at the same time the German religiosity flowed over into the Jewish, and both recognized each other in their affinity" [*beide erkennen sich in ihrer Verwandtschaft.*]"[30] In less obscure language, Mendelssohn's translations of the Pentateuch and Psalms brought together two different thought worlds through language, revealing that these two seemingly different worlds are actually conjoined in their depths or, at least, express a profound complementarity.

Cohen seeks to account for this deep "affinity" between Judaism and Germanism by means of the relationship of both cultures to Greekism [*Griechentum*]. Not only does the complementarity of the thought worlds of Germanism and Judaism come to light through German translations of the Hebrew Bible, but more significantly, Cohen argues that Judaism and Germanism are profoundly linked by means of sharing a relationship with Greekism. In regard to the connection between Judaism and Greekism, Cohen celebrates the diasporic existence as bringing new life to Judaism. He writes, "The new freely willed exile in *Alexandria* lifted Israel to its world mission."[31] Indeed, Israel's peculiarity [*Eigentümlichkeit*] is tied exclusively to its world mission, not to its power. Cohen mentions "the Alexandrian Jew, Philo," who in his attempts to blend Judaism with Platonism paved the way for Christianity by introducing such terms as Logos, which serves as a mediator between God and humans. Cohen claims that Philo, in regard to his beliefs and writings, is more of a follower of Plato than a Jew. Nevertheless, although Greekism had a role, is even a "fundamental source [*Grundquelle*] of Christianity," it is essential to recognize that "Judaism is the main source [*Hauptquelle*] of Christianity."[32] And Christianity is a key element of German identity, because Germanism is defined by its particular brand of Christianity, Protestantism (i.e., Lutheranism). If Judaism is the main source of Christianity and Christianity is constitutive of Germanism, then it stands to reason that Judaism is not only inextricably bound to Germanism but is one of its most primordial sources.

However, before we delve into this foundational relationship, it is useful to turn to "Über das Eigentümliche des deutschen Geistes," a piece of wartime literature that Cohen wrote one year before "Deutschtum und Judentum."[33] In this text, Cohen asserts that there is a special affinity between the Germans and the Greeks, a particularity [*Eigentümlichkeit*] that marks both the Greek and German spirit as distinct from others: This shared particularity is, paradoxically, their universality. That is, the two spirits are bound up in modes of thinking whose classical expression may be associated with specific geographical locations and particular cultures, but whose validity is universal; it is applicable beyond temporal and spatial boundaries. Indeed, it is precisely through their universality and accessibility to other cultures that their respective spirits transcend historical and cultural specificity, a feature that distinguishes them from all other national spirits.[34]

According to Cohen, Germany and Greece share a "universalism" in which other nations can partake or even express to a more or less adequate degree. However, it is the purity or perfection of the universality embodied by Greece and Germany that distinguishes them from all other cultural or spiritual forms. It is precisely this universalism—rooted in science—that Cohen claims distinguishes Greece from "Egypt and Babylon" even though the "the Greeks had learned much from the Egyptians and from the Babylonians."[35] If Greece, this embodiment of occidental rationalism, did in fact borrow from and thus is indebted to the wisdom of the Orient—the religions of the ancient Near East, Egypt, and Babylon—such borrowings did not have anything to do with its essence. Thus, Cohen is critiquing, at least tacitly, the claims of those taking part in what Suzanne Marchand refers to as "the furor orientalis." This movement, taken up by those coming after Cohen to challenge the liberal priorities of his generation, sought to relativize and de-center Greece as the spiritual center of the West. Its proponents attempted to do so by demonstrating, through archaeological and philological methods, that other nations such as Babylon and Egypt had achieved great accomplishments before Greece and therefore most likely influenced it.[36] However, at least according to Cohen, it is not Greece's age that merits distinction, but rather that Greece, and Greece alone (at least in the ancient world), was able to achieve a particular sort of universality, a universality that is an exemplarity.[37] It is important to note that Cohen's defense of Greece is bound up with a notion of exemplarity, a notion whose universality is due to reason and ideas, not language and race.

Derrida, in his insightful if not entirely unproblematic reading of "Deutschtum und Judentum"—"Interpretations at War: Kant, the Jew, the German"—suggests correctly that Cohen is part of "a German tradition which survives as far as Heidegger," where "the German holds an absolutely privileged relation to the Greek-descent, *mimeses*, and rivalry with all the consequent paradoxes."[38] However, one might ask (although Derrida did not) whether Cohen and Heidegger relate to this tradition in the same way. Heidegger never had to justify his German *Gesinnung* to his colleagues; thus privileging the German-Greek relationship was purely part of a German tradition that he felt to be his for the taking.[39] To be sure, Cohen's work is not disconnected from this notion of a privileged connection between Greece and Germany, but as a Jew, he could not simply assume that his colleagues would grant—and they very often did not—his Germanness. For example, the Freiburg neo-Kantian Heinrich Rickert notoriously stated that Cohen's work was "more race than philosophy."[40] Cohen's outsider status as a Jew makes his appeals to Germanism and Greekism all the more relevant for our inquiry, because he uses the exemplarity of these traditions to undermine racialist claims on culture.

Cohen argues that we find the same *Eigentümlichkeit,* the same exemplarity, the same conjunction of universality and particularity, in the German spirit, which alone maintains this special *"analogy with the Greeks."*[41] But Germanism is not the same as Greekism. For Cohen, "that which the Greeks began [namely, the scientific quest for certainty through mathematics and the hypothesis], the Germans have continued with congeniality: that is their peculiarity" [*Eigenart*].[42] Indeed, the Germans do not simply reproduce the strict rationalism that the Greeks initiated, which presumably all Western cultures do to a greater or lesser extent, but they "alone refine it to its fulfillment, to Idealism."[43] Indeed, as we see, *pace* Rickert (and the world religions discourse in general), race has nothing to do with Germanism and Greekism for Cohen, which are about a set of ideas and cultural practices that, although expressed by a particular culture, are universally accessible by all human beings regardless of ethnicity. Germanism and Greekism derive their force, their legitimacy, from rationality and ethics, not from anything like destiny or *Volk*.[44]

Germany—and German Idealism, as the inheritor and fulfiller of the Greek quest for science—is central to the manner in which Cohen situates Germany and its position within Europe. For Cohen, Germany is the epitome of European civilization because of its Idealism that in his understanding is inextricable from science, which in turn is tied to its status as the pinnacle of rationality and ethical culture. Indeed, Cohen believes that a philosophical system—including ethics, aesthetics, and later religion[45]—grounded on the transcendental foundations of science will extirpate eruptions of irrationality that lead to violence and antisemitism. Rationalism and science are key to the ethical refinement of culture.[46] The highest task of philosophy is to maintain the ideal nature of culture, to prevent errors that lead not merely to epistemological mistakes but also to cultural and political ones. Religion in particular must be domesticated and grounded in ethics, which is in turn rooted in logic. Thus, (Critical) Idealism is a high achievement of culture made possible, according to Cohen, by the German integration of the Greek universalistic impulse into modern scientific thinking and the development of it into Idealism, in regard not only to theoretical but also to practical reason.[47]

Returning to "Über das Eigentümliche des deutschen Geistes," we see that for Cohen it is the Germans, not the Greeks, who are infused with the idea of humanity. Because the German philosophers have brought Greek thought to its fulfillment, they have reached a greater notion of universality than the Greeks. Cohen writes, "The [idea] of Humanity [*Menschheit*][48] appears to above all correspond to the *cosmopolitan disposition* [*weltbuergertumlichen Gesinnung*] of German humanism, even if it leads as a methodological idea to the direct illumination of the human individual."[49] As we see, respect for the individual and recognition of the unity of the human race are inextricably correlated. Although Cohen most often celebrates Kant as emblematic of this German humanistic tradition, Luther also plays an indispensable role.[50] Cohen sees Luther's notion of faith [*Glaube*] and his polemics against the church functioning as a kind of "Idealism against the given of reality of the church" [*Idealismus gegenüber den gegeben Realitäten der Kirche*.][51] With Luther's notion of justification through faith, "religion takes on a new sense of *truthfulness* [*Wahrhaftigkeit*], which constitutes the determination of the German spirit."[52] Germany is bound up to the Greek spirit, but it is also its own world-historical phenomenon, a step forward for humanity as a whole.

Cohen is not suggesting that Germanism is Greekism, but rather that Germanism fulfills the highest aspirations of Greekism. He expresses this claim with particular clarity in "Deutschtum und Judentum." With the Reformation serving as a form of Idealism—in Cohen's mind these two phenomena are part and parcel of the same intellectual process of development—Germany fulfills and surpasses the aims and promise of Greece. In a rather Hegelian turn, Cohen claims, "*With the Reformation the German Spirit moves to the center of world history.*"[53] The Reformation is not merely a German phenomenon but also a Western one. Not only do both Jews and Catholics now find themselves adopting, or at least recognizing that they should be adopting, the Protestant notion of freedom of conscience[54] but also, and more importantly, Germany is the new exemplar, the new heart of the West.

One of the great accomplishments of the Reformation that Cohen champions is its creation of a new notion of truth, one separate from theoretical reason; practical reason now lays the ground for religion and culture. Although Cohen certainly has an idiosyncratic reading of the Reformation, it provides important conceptual resources for his larger argument. For Cohen, what is of central significance about the Reformation is that it had nothing to do with race or ethnicity but rather was purely concerned with the universality and purity of thought and culture.[55] This claim is striking for two reasons. First, universality of culture and purity of thought are intangibles—one's ethnicity is irrelevant according to these standards. Thus a Jew is German depending on his or her culture, on his or her disposition, not according to such vulgar standards as race. Indeed, a Jew from Poland can profitably study German Jewish *Wissenschaft*,[56] and by so doing, Germany can become—or, for Cohen, is—the spiritual homeland for Jews all around the world. Second, by making the Reformation central to world history— or, more precisely, Western or European history—Cohen is intimating that the essence of the West, of Europe, which was increasingly being interpreted in racial terms, is actually purely spiritual and rational, if understood properly. If the Reformation and thus the true essence of the West are properly understood, then notions such as ethnicity and race are merely vulgar distractions.[57] What the Greeks brought in terms of science and mathematics, the Germans have extended and fulfilled in Idealism.

Therefore, if Germany is the new spiritual and cultural heart of the West, it is essential to understand what role Judaism plays in Germanism. Cohen claims that because Judaism is the "historical fundamental force" [*Grundkraft*] of Christianity and therefore of Germanism. As a source it can never be depleted, "but rather the native force of its source [natürliche Quellkraft] is always relived in the steady course of national history." Cohen claims, "through Christianity the relationship between Germanism and Judaism is mediated perhaps several times at the *inner turning points in the history of the German spirit*."[58] In other words, Judaism is inextricable from Germanism, and in every central moment where the German spirit unfolds and expresses itself, there also is the Jewish spirit unfolding and expressing itself.

However, there is another element to this claim, one that remains unspoken in "Deutschtum und Judentum" but is expressed more explicitly in its "Kritische Nachtrag" [Critical Postscript] (1916). Cohen writes, "Who however does not recognize the life force of Christianity in Greek mythology but rather can recognize it in the root of the Prophets and the Psalms, can nevermore spiritually dissociate themselves from the Jews." In other words, Protestants, given their attachment to the Old Testament, must also recognize—at least if they are to have intellectual integrity—their spiritual kinship to the Jews. Cohen demands "respect and sympathy for the *Urvolk*" who have served as martyrs throughout world history to protect this "highest good of humanity."[59] Both Judaism and Christianity are profoundly related to Greece or, more specifically, to Greek philosophy. However, when it comes to rational religion, it is Judaism—in particular, prophetic Judaism—that is the exemplar, not Greece. Just as German Idealism has surpassed Greek philosophy, so too has Jewish monotheism surpassed Greek religion and culture.[60] German Protestantism is more of a product of Judaism than it is of Greece, and it should recognize itself as such. Indeed, Cohen claims that the Reformation has "fulfilled Protestantism's rapprochement with Prophetism."[61] Cohen triangulates Judaism, Greekism, and Germanism to claim that, in the historical moment of the Reformation, itself bound up with Jewish not Greek sources, Germanism surpasses and fulfills its Greek heritage. As a result, Judaism's place in Germany and Germanism is secure without problematizing Protestantism.

Thus, to return to Derrida's claim about the German tradition that privileges the relationship between Greek and German philosophy, we see that Cohen is in fact working to elucidate a notion of Germanism, with its ties to Greekism, that has an intellectual and cultural valence, rather than a racial one.[62] At the same time as Liberal German Protestant theologians were busy trying to de-Judaize Christianity, Cohen insists that the very notion of Germanism is as unthinkable without Judaism as it is without Protestantism. At least when it comes to the ideal as opposed to mere empirical history, Judaism is to be the inner guiding force of German history. As a result, Judaism is not only an equal, complementary nationality within the German nation but it is also deeply imbricated in the underlying conceptual history of Germanism.

Of course, we must not lose sight of the fact that "Deutschtum und Judentum" is primarily a tract justifying Germany's involvement in World War I. Cohen grounds his defense of Germany with his highly idiosyncratic reading of German literary history that culminates with Kant's philosophy, for which "*humanity* [Menschheit] *is the fundamental concept of his ethics.*"[63] The "idea of humanity roots out [*entwurzelt*] all *sensualism*, all *eudaeominism*, and all *egoism* in the moral [*sittlichen*] concept of man."[64] In short, the idea of humanity is essential in idealizing (morally purifying) the idea of the human being. No longer are we concerned with the " 'I' in the empirical sense but rather one is treating the 'I' of humanity in the ideal sense."[65] Now relations between people are not bound by their "corporeal, racial [characteristics], nor by their historical isolation, but rather only as carriers of the eternal, world historical idea of humanity."[66] Humanity is an ideal; no one possesses it, but rather all strive to live up to it, as an eternal task. Indeed, "humanity is the principle of all that is human, in the individual, in the state, as in world history."[67] Humanity as an ideal then pertains to all aspects of human endeavor and thus of necessity transcends Germany; more precisely, the ideal of humanity demands that Germany be involved in world history. Paradoxically, it also demands that Germany fight to defend itself and its cultural legacy because it alone truly recognizes the universal value of humanity.[68] One can reasonably charge Cohen here with circular reasoning. Derrida sees Cohen as saying something akin to the following: "There will be no understanding and no peace among nations unless our example is followed . . . our example (Beispiel) must be followed as an example (Vorbild) in order to acknowledge our *Vormacht*, German hegemony or preeminence."[69] However, Cohen is offering a defense to charges of German barbarism, and it is equally plausible that he is also taking this occasion to elucidate an ideal of what Germany ought to be. Not merely a manifesto of why Germany must win the war, this text is also an assertion of what Germany ought to be—the embodiment of the German humanistic tradition—and, as only thus, why it should, win the war.[70]

Cohen links Jews and Germans (or should we say German Protestants and German Jews, because both groups are Germans)[71] in their shared commitment to the universally valid ideal of humanity. But he goes further by insisting that this "basic concept [*Grundgedanke*] of German [and German Jewish] spirit" is precisely what is at stake in the war and the crises of his time. It is this concept which justifies the philosopher to adumbrate "the incalculable future of our history" [die unabsehbare Zukunft unserer Geschichte].[72] Indeed, by examining this idea, one that is universal in its validity and significance even if it is arrived at by a particular people, the philosopher Cohen can "anticipate the future of [the German people's] world-mission."[73] In short, the idea of humanity in all its different dimensions demands nothing less than that the Germans take up a world mission. "That we must recognize in the German spirit the *pedagogical spirit of the nations* [Erziehungsgeist der Völker] and with all due sobriety and historical modesty, recognize our historical vocation as schoolmaster [Zuchtmeister] of this world."[74] Derrida helpfully elucidates that Cohen's recourse to Germany's duty in regard to the education of the nations of the world is a particularly toxic iteration of Cohen's notion of the German-Jewish symbiosis:

> The German state is supposed to be in its modernity both priestly and messianic. This is recognizable in its social policy, more precisely by the fact that social policy is recognized by it as a duty: an ethical duty prior to being a political one, a duty already prescribed by natural law. Socialism is not a policy among others, and it is the German policy par excellence, by essence. Socialism is national and it is German. . . . This socialist policy, this morality inspired by universal priesthood, serves a fundamental messianism: Jewish-German messianism.[75]

Although it is beyond the limits of Derrida's essay, it is interesting to consider Cohen's emphatic pacifism and emphasis on martyrdom in *Religion of Reason*, written after the war and these war tracts. This topic is addressed in more depth in the next chapter.

Given that the uniqueness of the German nationality consists of its universality, it is its cultural productions—its art, literature, and most of all, its philosophical Idealism—that ground its identity, an ethical identity, not one constituted by race or any other biological factor. Even though all the other peoples of Europe, so Cohen claims, are making spurious charges of German barbarism, "*the German [concept of] humanity alone rests on the ground of an ethics*" [*Die Menschheit des Deutschtums allein ruht auf dem Grunde eine Ethik*].[76] One of the central arguments of Cohen's essay—which of course, goes hand in hand with a certain German imperialist vision—is that German identity is ultimately grounded not in any sort of given empirical data, but rather in an ethical ideal. To be sure, the literary and cultural history of the Germans, which is itself rooted in the empirical peoples living in the German-speaking worlds, provides the material from which the ideals are derived, but it is the ideals themselves that are the ultimate grounding. In short, Cohen's justification of the war rests on an idealized Germany.[77] And this ideal Germany is justified in taking up arms to defend itself, its culture, and indeed its mission; it is the elect nation precisely because it is the epitome of the values of European civilization.[78] Judaism is at the core of Germany's elect status, providing a religious dimension to its war effort and undercutting any notion of biology being the primary foundation of its culture/nation.

The Concept of Religion and the Philosopher as Interpreter

Where Cohen's war writings illustrate a distinct vision of European civilization whose pinnacle is embodied by the German-Jewish symbiosis, his writings on the study of religion attempt to secure this vision against methodologies for the study of religion that seek to de-Judaize Germany and Christianity. At the very moment Cohen was trying to articulate the centrality of Judaism to the essence of the West, numerous theologians and scholars attempted to downplay, if not eliminate outright, Judaism from Germany's culture. New discoveries in archaeology and new methodologies in the study of religion provided resources for contesting established histories and for reimagining Germany's origins. As Susannah Heschel points out, prominent scholars and historians used these new techniques "to interrupt . . . the direct transmission of Judaism to Christianity," believing they "provided a genealogy for Germany and its putative Aryan origins."[79] These new discoveries and insights fed into, were driven by, and drove rising antisemitism and *Volkish* modes of thinking.

A brief discussion of the work of Adolf von Harnack, a prominent historian-theologian often associated with the history of religions school [*Religionsgeschichtliche Schule*] provides a context for Cohen's concerns. Protestant theologians like Harnack actively sought to reconfigure Christianity to meet the needs of the time. According to Marchand, "these men saw themselves not just as scholars but as educators with a crucial cultural mission."[80] Their mission, to modernize Christianity, almost inevitably involved denuding Christianity of its Jewish roots. This mission allowed scholars/theologians in the history of religions school a free hand with the facts. Indeed, Harnack explains, "with respect to the past, the historian assumes the royal function of a judge, for in order to decide what of the past shall continue to be in effect and what must be done away with or transformed, the historian must judge like a king."[81] In his wildly famous lecture series published as *Das Wesen des Christentums* [What Is Christianity?] given in

1900, Harnack wastes little time in separating the kernel of Jesus's thought from the husk of the "Jewish nation."[82] He writes,

> Take the people of Israel and search the whole history of their religion; take history generally, and where will you find any message about God and the good that was ever so pure and so full of strength—for purity and strength go together—as we hear and read of in the Gospels? As regards purity, the spring of holiness had, indeed, long been opened; but it was choked with sand and dirt, and its water was polluted.[83]

Thus, although he concedes that Jesus is rooted in the culture of Second Temple Judaism, Harnack nevertheless insists that the connection between Jesus Christ's teaching and Judaism is "only a loose one."[84] Scholars such as Heschel and Christian Wiese have pointed out that Harnack's account of Jesus's life was driven much more by challenges facing Christianity in the present than attention to the facts.[85]

Cohen was aware of the connection between historical scholarship and political developments. Indeed as Wiese explains, "The negative image of the Jewish tradition, historically justified by well-known exegetes, seemed to [Jewish scholars] a dangerous questioning of present-day Judaism's right to existence and as a bridge to anti-Semitism."[86] In his programmatic text, *Einleitung mit kritischen Nachtrag zur F. A. Langes' 'Geschichte des Materialismus'* [Introduction with Critical Supplement to F. A. Langes' "History of Materialism"] (1914), Cohen charges his Christian contemporaries with perpetrating a "religious injustice against the Old Testament," an injustice that results in the contemporary Jew being painted as consumed with a tribalism that amounts to wishing to "remain foreign to the national whole," regardless of his or her actual participation in the national culture.[87] Thus, where Cohen seeks to present a notion of Germanness that could be inclusive to Jews because it is grounded in cosmopolitan reason, many of his Christian contemporaries present Jews as un-German precisely because they willfully exempt themselves from this inclusion and universality.

Cohen is particularly troubled by the "comparative interest" in religions among his Christian contemporaries spurred by their diminishing concern for the Old Testament. In regard to the growing interest in comparative religion, Cohen writes, "Where the horizon is most in need of furthering [is] not with the savages [*Wilden*] but with the old and still presently neglected wandering Jew. The greatest philologists make schoolboy blunders, where a position and tenure allows him to explain away his mother religion [i.e., Judaism]."[88] Thus Cohen perceives a correspondence between the interest in world religions among his German Protestant contemporaries and the process of de-Judaization.

Much of Cohen's *Der Begriff der Religion im System der Philosophie* articulates a philosophical rationale for the study of religion as a means of critiquing the methodologies and conclusions prevailing among his prominent contemporaries, such as the members of the history of religions school.[89] Cohen marshals resources from philosophy to counter the Christian hegemony in the study of religion.[90] Bringing the resources of his system of Critical Idealism to bear on the study of religion, Cohen seeks to create a counterforce to the increasing allure of the world religions discourse. Cohen cannot ignore these developments not only because they contradicted his own philosophy of Judaism and its relationship to Germany but also because the social and political stakes were so high. In what follows, I focus on the methodology for the study of religion that Cohen lays out in *Der Begriff* and *Religion of Reason out of the Sources of Judaism*.

Cohen brings his Critical Idealism to bear in the study of religion as a way to break the tendency of the discipline to privilege descent, transmission, and linguistics and thus facilitate a racialist turn.[91] In a sense, in *Der Begriff* Cohen is recovering Kant's distinction between the philosopher and the biblical exegete. Cohen posits that religion must be understood as a part of culture. Indeed, he distances himself from his oft-quoted claim in *"Religion und Sittlichkeit"*(1907) that "the direction of Religion is sublated [*aufgehoben*] into that of ethics."[92] In Cohen's *Der Begriff*, written eight years later, his concern is to pose the "cultural fact of religion" as a "transcendental question."[93] That is, if religion is a part of culture, then it must be presumed that reason dictates its underlying structure.[94] To be sure, this requires that religion be bound up with the rest of culture and ultimately rooted in logic, as the full title of the work, *Der Begriff der Religion im System der Philosophie* would indicate.[95]

Cohen's method therefore is to subordinate the empirical element of historical research to the philosophical task of constructing ethical culture. Insofar as religion is part of human culture and human culture is permeated by human reason, then philosophy is tasked with serving as a continual corrective to culture.[96] It is the philosopher, not the historian, who has the ultimate authority in the study of religion.[97] Cohen's method begins with the empirical or historical fact and proceeds to rationally reconstruct its a priori conditions. Thus, in a bit of hermeneutical circle, it is only through transcendentally reconstructing religion that Cohen can justify his hypothesis that religion is a fact of culture.

Cohen mounts a defense for the philosophical notion of religion and critiques the historian-as-scholar-of-religion for proceeding too hastily to empirical research, because the notion of religion qua fact of culture is normative. Cohen does not dispute the goals of the historical theologians of his day, who were very much trying to harness their "research" in the hopes of rejuvenating German society, but he disagrees with their method. Lacking a rigorous concept that guides and orients the organization of the material, they proceed in a haphazard and subjective manner. If religion is acknowledged to be a fact of culture, then it is more than empirical data collected about what people do; culture has normative implications. Cohen refers to ethics (he specifically seems to have in mind ethics as it is configured in his *Ethik des reinen Willens*), in particular the "relationship between ethics and sociology," to help illuminate the relationship between the normative notion of religion and the information collected by historians.[98] Ethics is not independent of the facts that sociology collects, but rather abstracts from these concrete facts to determine its ideal grounds. It is the ideal, not the factual—the "ought" not the "is"—that drives ethics. Sociology provides the raw data from which the ideals of ethics are derived, but it itself does not constitute ethics. Sociology is a necessary but not sufficient condition for ethics because sociology only treats the human being as a biological entity, as a creature of linear causality. Ethics, however, operates with a conception of the human as teleological in nature, as an ideal being.[99] Cohen writes,

> And therein lies the analogy [with ethics]: that the problem of the concept of religion [Problem des Religionsbegriffs] grasps the whole broad material the history of religions [Religionsgeschichte] just as much as its preconditions, just as the ethical concept [Begriff] of society [grasps] the entire material of sociology. . . . *The material is the negative precondition, the concept however is the problem of positive creation [positiven Schöpfung.]*

Just as ethics requires existing sociological conditions from which to derive the material to construct an ethical ideal, so too the concept of religion cannot be generated without reference to any actual data. Just as in ethics, for religion, "the data [*Tatsachen*] can never and nowhere produce the concept [*Begriff*] which is itself much more its own spiritual bond—no, simply its own spiritual creation [*Erschaffung*]."[100] That is, the concept of religion is both derived from and yet also guides one's inquiries into the sources of a religion. In other words, we must not think that, because the idea is abstracted after the data is gathered, it is somehow secondary or comes later. Rather, the rational, ideational structure is inherent in the data, even if it is only discerned after all information is gathered. The idea actually precedes and must (as in ought to) structure the data. Without the idea that is deduced from the data and that guides the data's interpretation, "all research remains a blind groping."[101] Or worse, without proper methodological foundations, the researcher can be led astray by his or her own biases, as Cohen claims is the case with his Christian contemporaries in their reading of Jewish sources.[102]

In the introduction to *Religion of Reason out of the Sources of Judaism*, which is centered on methodology, Cohen writes, "Obviously *reason* is meant to make religion independent of the descriptions supplied by the history of religion. We do not shrink from the argument that reason must rule everywhere in history. However, history in itself does not determine the concept of reason. The concept of reason has to engender the concept of religion."[103] Cohen charges his historian contemporaries with approaching the Hebrew Bible as "a primitive artifact of literature" [*ein primitives Literaturprodukt*].[104] They are willing to trace the development of the names of God and different stages of the text, but fail to draw the important philosophical conclusion that what we see is an abstract thought working its way to development. Exegesis, at this point, requires a philosopher, not a historian. Or as Cohen puts it, "For the problem remains neither the essence of God, as a demon, nor of man whose being is subordinated to fate or to the will of the gods." What is required is the "abstract idea" of religion in which the hitherto separate ideas of God and human being come together.[105] Rationality—philosophy—is to be the guide for the reconstruction of data collected by historians.

On the one hand, Cohen, like the figures of the history of religions school, rejects the authority of tradition as the guiding hermeneutical principle. Or as he famously puts it, "Even if I am referred to the literary sources of the prophets for the concept of religion, these sources remain mute and blind if I do not approach them with a concept which I myself lay out as a foundation in order to be instructed by them and not simply guided by their authority."[106] The sources of a tradition cannot speak directly to us in a meaningful sense. However, Cohen rejects the privilege that Harnack grants to the historian: to make judgments "like a king."[107] Rather, Cohen gives authority neither to tradition nor to the individual historian but rather to the transcendental method, which takes the literary sources of the tradition as its data. The task then is to work through the data in order to discern a guiding, rational concept. This is the work of a philosopher/ exegete, not a historian. That is, the exegete turned philosopher—or, even better, the philosopher turned exegete—must reject the independence of the texts and the autonomy of their sensibilities and forms of thought. He or she must not grant the local logic of the text autonomy, but rather must situate and read the text by means of an already established foundation of reason: "Reason is the rock out of which the concept originates and out of which it has to originate for the sake of systematic examination." Indeed, Cohen goes further, arguing, "What holds true for every science holds no less true for religion. Insofar as religion, too, consists of concepts and is based on concepts, its ultimate source can only be reason. This connection with reason determines and conditions its connection with philosophy, understood as the universal reason of human knowledge."[108] This means, as Cohen repeatedly points out, that religion is an *Eigenart* of the system of philosophy; it is not *selbstandig* or sui generis.[109]

In contrast to the openly biased, and therefore unreliable and unscientific, judgments rendered by Harnack's vision of the historian, Cohen vouches for his account of religion by grounding it in his system of philosophy. For Cohen, philosophy is more primordial than religion, because the foundations of reason are to be found in even the most primitive religious constructs.[110] Thus, Cohen conceives of religion as an *Eigenart*, as part of the system of philosophy and not something autonomous and outside of its reach: "The concept of reason has to engender the concept of religion."[111] Because reason is universal, "the religion of reason cannot be the religion of a single people."[112] In regard to the challenge of historicity, Cohen acknowledges that "there is only one mathematics, but there are many religions. At least it seems so."[113] One must not be misled here; all of the weight of this passage is in the second sentence, which calls into question the second clause of the first. Although the historical study of religions might do justice to the tremendous variety of customs, institutions, and forms of expression, it cannot make sense of it or bring unity to it. Any sort of *Religionswissenschaft* that seeks to be a descriptive study of religion focuses solely on induction. It tries to build pictures based on what it finds. Cohen finds this to be a necessary but not sufficient condition for the generation of the concept of religion; induction is "only a preparatory step."[114] Induction is an essential step for gathering data, but if one stops there, then there is no capacity to "find a common concept of religion"; more importantly there is no ability to apply reason to secure and assess religions from any sort of normative dimension, from the dimension of culture. The purely historical approach to the study of religion, even if it did not seek to privilege Christianity and denigrate Judaism, would condemn the study of religion to be merely descriptive. According to Cohen, the historical study of religion "has no means whatever of securing the legitimacy of religion."[115] Only reason can secure the concept of religion: no amount of data, which is only a pile of facts, can provide such a foundation. In short, only philosophy (i.e., Critical Idealism), not history, can legitimately ground the study of religion.

It is helpful to juxtapose Cohen's account of the concept of religion with that of Harnack. In a speech given in 1901 titled *"Die Aufgabe der theologische Fackultäten und die allgemeine Religionsgeschichte"* [The Task of Theological Faculty and Universal History of Religions], Harnack asserts, "We wish, that the theological faculties remain for the research of the Christian religion, because Christianity in its pure shape is not *a* religion next to others, but rather *the* religion."[116] Harnack, whose philhellenic tendencies were well known, was no friend to the radical Orientalists.[117] He wished to maintain the supremacy of Christianity and thus eliminate the growing tendency to research other cultures, a trend that brought with it continuing demands to redefine and, at times, to cast off Christianity in the process.[118]

When examining Cohen's account of religion in light of Harnack's formulation, at first glance, the differences seem stark. Cohen claims that despite obvious cultural and religious diversity, "all people, even those in the most primitive conditions of culture, have their share in religion."[119] Reason, for Cohen, serves as the "distinctive mark and the systematic criterion" of his investigation. Despite the significant ostensible differences between religions, when it comes to the concept of the religion and its normative form, the religion of reason, Cohen states,

The religion of reason cannot be the religion of a single people, or the bastard offspring of a single age: reason must be uniform in all those men and peoples who have become conversant with science and philosophy. This uniformity gives to religion the original imprint of universal humanity, the only indispensable limiting condition being the degree to which humanity has reached the stage of articulation displaced in scientific culture.[120]

Cohen's emphasis on the universality and inclusivity of reason seems to stand in stark contrast with Harnack's exclusivism. Cohen seems to be claiming that the products of reason are homogeneous or at least translatable, regardless of their linguistic or cultural context.

Cohen continues, "It would have been an irreparable mistake in our arrangement if we were to limit and confine the religion of reason to the Jewish religion because of its literary sources. This limitation would be an insoluble contradiction to the signpost of reason."[121] However, he then immediately proceeds to undermine his posture of a rational inclusivism, in what appears to be a train of speculative musings filled with requisite "if" clauses. It is not a contradiction to reason "if in Judaism the concept of a *source* were to have a peculiar significance and a peculiar methodological meaning with regard to the religion of reason." "If this is the case," then Judaism is the source of "other religious monuments"—indeed is the "original source for other sources—which latter in turn would still retain our undiminished recognition as sources of the religion of reason."[122] Cohen tacitly concludes from these musings that granting Judaism the status of the original source for other religions is not in contradiction with the universality of reason. He writes, "Only insofar as the original source has as such an undeniable spiritual and psychological advantage must this supremacy of reason in the primary origin [*Ursprünglichkeit*] of the sources of Judaism remain indisputable."[123] Thus even though rationality cannot be limited to any particular religion, Judaism is the most primordial in terms of rationality and rationalizing.

How are we to make sense of this strange claim? In part, Cohen is likely mimicking or unconsciously appropriating the Orientalist strategy of granting prestige to that which is oldest and most primordial—Judaism. But more is at stake here than this. Steven Schwarzschild echoes Cohen's triumphalism in his explanation:

Other historical religions and cultures also partake of that universal, rational "ethical monotheism" (as nineteenth-century Jewish philosophers favored speaking of Judaism), but they attained it with neither the same philosophical purity nor the historical immediacy that distinguishes Judaism. . . . In order to crystallize the universal "religion of reason" out of their respective sources, these other religions consequently are compelled to work harder at shedding the mythological, immoral, pagan, irrational, and other barnacles that they accumulated on their voyage through history . . . and they were well advised to use Judaism as their (relatively) ideal model in performing this task.[124]

And yet, Schwarzschild's explanation conceals as much as it reveals. For what religions do Judaism and its literary sources (broadly speaking) serve as an original source?[125] At best these can only be Islam and Christianity (and perhaps Bahai, if Cohen was even aware of this religious tradition). Cohen is not offering a sort of pluralism or inclusivism rooted in reason and scientific culture rather than in religious doctrine.[126] Rather, he is establishing the Western monotheisms grounded in Judaism as the site of reason. To be sure, Cohen's reverence for the Greeks is sincere. However, he is emphatic that the religious environments of the ancient Near East and the Orient, including Greek mythology and the Greek mystery religions, were not constitutive of the core of Christianity. Rather, Germanism has achieved the stage of Idealism in regard to religion only to the degree that it has absorbed the prophets and the Psalms (i.e., its Jewish influence).[127] This might be rephrased somewhat paradoxically: Germanism is only Germanism to the degree it is Jewish in its Christianity.

Conclusion

I want to conclude this chapter by pointing to a controversy between Hermann Cohen and Ernst Troeltsch that highlights the close connection between Cohen's religious thought and his nationalist vision. In 1916 Ernst Troeltsch, the famed theorist of the History of Religions School, published an essay, "Glaube und Ethos der hebräischen Propheten" [Faith and Ethos of the Hebrew Prophets],[128] which elicited an impassioned response by Cohen in 1917, "Der Prophetismus und die Soziologie" [Prophetism and Sociology].[129] In "Glaube und Ethos," Troeltsch suggests that the prophets were not really concerned with ethical universalism. In fact, the morality for which they are celebrated was not so much a result of innovation but a reversion to "the intimacy and mutuality" inherent in "simple neighborhood ethics" [*einfachen Nachbarschaftsethik*].[130] Troeltsch claims that the prophets were rural folk with rural views who came to prominence when the cosmopolitan cities collapsed in the wake of political calamity.[131]

It is not hard to understand why Cohen feels it necessary to respond to this essay. First, Troeltsch mentions him by name and suggests that his approach to the study of the prophets has no historical grounding and is of questionable cultural merit.[132] Second, Cohen's philosophy of Judaism,[133] not to mention his justification of the prominent place of Judaism in German culture, is grounded in the supposed universalism of the prophets' ethical teachings. In his response to Troeltsch, Cohen not only questions the soundness of sociology (Troeltsch's preferred methodology) but he also asserts the profound correspondences between Kant's philosophy and the teachings of prophets—"There is a difference between the religion of the prophets and the ethics of Kant only in the logical justification [*Begründung*] but in no way in the content of ethical teaching" [*Inhalt der sittlichen Lehren*].[134] Cohen declares that a universal religion, "however, can only be the religion of a pure morality."[135] Judaism, then, fulfills the concept of religion as established by philosophy because it is a religion of pure morality. Or as Cohen puts it, "Israel becomes 'the Servant of the Eternal' through Prophetism." And lest we think we are dealing with a parochial notion of God, Cohen immediately explains that the *Shema* prayer—so central to Judaism—refers to "the unique God as the God of all human beings and peoples."[136] Troeltsch's essay casts the prophets as a mere national phenomenon tied to a tribal God [*Stammesgott*] (which only transforms into a genuinely universal God in Christianity),[137] undercuts their ethical genius, and thus rejects their universality.[138]

By downplaying the importance of the prophets, Troeltsch's methodology seeks to situate and therefore relativize their teachings against the broader background of the ancient Near East. As we see in the next chapter, Cohen's philosophical reconstruction of Judaism rests on the claim that a particular religious tradition, Judaism, embodies or manifests, more perfectly than any other, concepts that possess universal significance. His claim that Judaism is a universal religion is grounded precisely in privileging the teaching of the prophets as *Quellen* for the construction of a religion of reason. Troeltsch's methodology casts doubt on the uniqueness of the prophets, the precise assumption on which Cohen builds his entire philosophy of Judaism. The prophets serve as the point of transition between concept and history for Cohen. If Judaism's identity is grounded in exemplarity, it is the prophets who instantiate the link between the particular Jewish tradition and universality, ethical politics, and messianism. For Cohen, it is precisely the universality of the God concept of the prophets that leads to their ethical significance, which in turn facilitates their correlation with the universality of the Greeks and thus their compatibility with Germany.

Troeltsch's essay touches a nerve; it exposes the precarious foundation on which Cohen's account of Germanism and Judaism rests. Although there is not space to adequately discuss Troetlsch's motivations or the success or failure of his endeavor, it must nevertheless be acknowledged that the issue of pluralism presents a significant problem for Cohen's attempt to secure the place of the Jew in German culture.[139] Cohen seeks to secure that place through the logic of exemplarity, by making Judaism the bastion of reason. However, this means that all other traditions are inferior, deficient, at best imperfect copies, and, at worst, errors and idolatrous vanities. Troeltsch, by downplaying the significance of the prophets, reveals the exceptional status that Cohen grants to a particular tradition of thought but denies to others. In doing so, he shows that the logic of exemplarity lies at the core not only of Cohen's notion of the German-Jewish symbiosis but also of his very account of Judaism's significance.

2 Symbol Not Sacrifice: Cohen's Jewish Jesus

In the previous chapter, Cohen's wartime writings were juxtaposed with his philosophical interventions into the study of religion to reveal the complexities of his notion of the German-Jewish symbiosis. This symbiosis is central to Cohen's metanarrative of the West in which Germany—or, perhaps better, Germanism—embodies and exemplifies rationality and culture. And Judaism is a central component of and, indeed, is foundational to his conception of Germanism.[1]

In this chapter, we delve further into the German Jewish symbiosis. Focusing on Cohen's posthumously published *Religion of Reason out of the Sources of Judaism* (1919), this chapter explores how Cohen Judaizes the figure of Jesus, claiming that his passion and martyrdom are distinctly Jewish. Cohen's account of Jesus is an explicit challenge to a distinguished German Protestant tradition that understands Jesus as essentially—that is, in his thoughts and consciousness—Greek rather than Jewish. Exponents of this tradition are such luminaries as Immanuel Kant, Friedrich Schleiermacher, and Adolf von Harnack. I argue that Cohen's engagement with Christianity is foundational to his very elucidation of Judaism. By casting Jesus as a Jew, Cohen not only uses Christianity as the mythical and irrational foil against which to illuminate and elaborate his concept of Judaism but he also undercuts Christianity's theological foundations. Cohen uses the Judaized Jesus both to bring about transformations within Protestantism—to guide it toward rationality, to make it more Jewish, as it were—and to increasingly displace Greece as the arbiter of rationality.

In reconstructing Judaism in Christlike terms and in offering a reconstruction of a rational Jesus, Cohen deliberately distances Jesus from Greece. Judea, not Athens, becomes the standard bearer of rationality, at least religious rationality. In a moment of shifting idioms and terminology, when race and linguistics were eclipsing classical theological motifs among European Christians, Cohen insists not only that Europe is defined by its possession of rationality and not by race (and philologically determined language families) but also that Judea, not Greece, is its true foundation. Judaism is the ultimate embodiment of rationality and thus is or should be the ideal orienting Europe.

The Jewish Jesus

Susannah Heschel, more than any other scholar, has clarified the profound role that the figure of Jesus plays in modern Jewish philosophy: "A crucial image for modern Jewish thought is the figure of Jesus as a pious, loyal Jew.... The modern Jewish understanding of Christian origins is not merely a matter of Jews wishing to 'set the record straight.' Rather, it demonstrates a Jewish desire to enter into the Christian myth and thereby claim the power inherent in it."[2] Heschel postulates that the Jewishness of Jesus functions as a core element of German-Jewish philosophy.

Cohen uses his concept of religion qua fact of culture, and thus as philosophically grounded in "purified" reason, to transform the very idiom of the dominant Protestant culture into something Jewish. In *Religion of Reason out of the Sources of Judaism*, Cohen amplifies—or at least makes the implications more explicit— his earlier claims about Judaism's role as the main source [*Hauptquelle*] of Christianity.[3]

It is therefore imperative to read Cohen's account of Judaism as demonstrating, again citing Heschel, "a Jewish desire to enter into the Christian myth and thereby claim the power inherent in it."[4] Where other Jewish scholars from Abraham Geiger to Leo Baeck argued that Jesus was really a Pharisee and understood himself as such, Cohen does not talk about his teachings, but rather focuses squarely on his passion, his crucifixion.[5] Two of *Religion of Reason's* most intriguing and infamous elements are its celebration of suffering and its appropriation of this Christological trope for Judaism. Cohen celebrates passages from the Bible such as the servant songs in Deutero-Isaiah that have long been invoked by Christians as foreshadowing the notion of vicarious atonement and Jesus's martyrdom. Cohen recognizes Jesus as a suffering servant, as "an imitation of the messianic imagination of Deutero-Isaiah."[6] Indeed, for Cohen, it is precisely in his function as a suffering servant that Jesus is a Jew.

Cohen draws attention to Jesus in his role as martyr. And martyrdom takes courage, a specifically religious virtue for Cohen. Indeed, he references the talmudic injunction to the Jew to martyr him- or herself rather than engage in idolatry.[7] As a result, all Jews live constantly under the threat of martyrdom or, as Cohen puts it, "the sword of Damocles has hung over the Jew throughout his history." The enormous pressures to engage in idolatry and to deny pure monotheism— that is, to abandon Judaism—placed on Jews just by their living as a minority in a dominant Christian culture are sufficient in Cohen's eyes to maintain that "the historical life of the Jew [is] the life of courage."[8] Martyrdom becomes the central link between Jesus and the historical Jew in the Diaspora.

The story of Jesus, then, is a very Jewish story of martyrdom for the love of God, a self-willed, autonomous giving of oneself to bear witness to the ideal of God. As Cohen writes,

> It is truly an unparalleled irony of history that the story of Jesus Christ's life, sealed by his death, should have become the source of the main difference between Christianity and Judaism. The history of this passion is an imitation of the messianic imagination of Deutero-Isaiah . . . anticipating the history of the "remnant of Israel." And hence, according to this original poetic image, the history of Christ is actually the history of Israel.[9]

This is a striking reversal of Christian triumphalism, where Jesus serves as an anticipation, a prefiguration of the righteous remnant, of the diasporic Jews suffering among the nations. It is also a steadfast rejection of all those claims, whether from Harnack, Schleiermacher, or Kant, that the figure of Jesus is not really a Jewish phenomenon. Indeed, Cohen is incorporating Jesus into the dominant Jewish understanding of the servant songs of Deutero-Isaiah—that they describe the Jews as God's suffering servants, as God's light to the nations. Cohen suggests then that Jesus not only anticipates the diasporic condition of the Jews rather than Christianity but also that Christians fundamentally misunderstand God and therefore subsequently misunderstand Jesus, morality, and the very nature of the human being. Such a misunderstanding is not to be taken lightly. As Cohen puts it, "Errors in men's concepts of God are the greatest afflictions of man, and perhaps the cause of the greatest suffering which men bring upon themselves again and again. Moral offenses have their deepest origin in these fundamental notions of men about God."[10]

By linking the concept of God so closely with morality, Cohen is developing a kind of ethical natural theology. By postulating ethics—indeed, a certain monotheistic ethics—as foundational for the ethical conception of the human being, Cohen seeks to undermine the world religions discourse by undercutting the historical/linguistic basis of comparative religions. By so doing, comparative religion is reduced not only to an antiquarian interest but also becomes an idolatrous distraction. There is no possible pluralism, because there is only one criterion by which to judge—namely, reason—and this criterion is most fully and purely realized in the Jewish tradition. If the Jews lack power in the empirical world, Cohen is rendering the ideal world inimical to all non-Jewish religions. The ancient Near East, including Greece, functions as the matrix of mythology, insufficient rationality, and morality, in which Christianity remains mired. Cohen's Idealism offers a vantage point by which to assess, critique, and provide methods for transforming other religions—most particularly Christianity. Given the pressing concerns of his time, Cohen is not genuinely interested in contemporary non-Western religions.[11] Indeed, even with regard to the ancient world, his primary focus remains Greece, which he increasingly depicts in Oriental terms, full of magic, idolatry, and the irrational, and thus quite at odds with the dominant manner in which Europeans traditionally understood Greek civilization.[12]

At its most basic level, Cohen claims that Christianity fails to properly conceptualize the relationship between existence and the ideal. To help understand the theoretical underpinnings of Cohen's ensuing critique it is helpful to turn to Cohen's *Logik der reinen Erkenntnis* [Logic of Pure Cognition] (1902/1914).[13] In a core passage near the end of this work, Cohen explains how his logic transforms the notion of substance in Western thought beginning with the Greeks. Indeed, the very notion of being [*Allgemeines Seins*] as substance is radically undermined, or better, reformulated in Cohen's thought. Cohen offers a new notion of substance grounded in the concept of motion [*Bewegung*] central to the mathematical natural sciences [*mathematischen Naturwissenschaft*] that have emerged in modernity. This new account of substance "destroys the prejudice of *absolute substance*" [*Vorurteil der* absoluten *Substanz zerstört*].[14] As a result, Cohen renders dynamic the Eleatic notion of substance, which is eternal and unmoving.

In *Religion of Reason*, Cohen acknowledges that Judaism does not create science, but that because it is rational, it is commensurate with it. Indeed, Judaism lends itself to what we might call metaphysical reflection even if this was not its originary form of expression. Cohen argues that Judaism holds that "the unique God can have no actuality [*Wirklichkeit*]. For actuality is a concept relating thought to sensation. This relation to sensation is, however, excluded from the concept of God."[15] Human beings can only relate to God via the realm of action, via emulation of God's attributes of action as ideal "archetypes for action" that function as "models for the actions of reasonable beings." However, God and human beings remain radically distinct.[16]

Greek philosophy, according to Cohen, is unable to conceptualize God's uniqueness because it does not sufficiently separate God from nature. That is, it is rooted in the problematic notion of absolute substance that Cohen's own philosophy undercuts.[17] Greek thought, which does reach a notion of oneness, of monotheism, either thinks of it in terms of the unity between God and nature, an "ontology, which . . . contains no safeguard against *pantheism*,"[18] or, following Plato in the *Timaeus*, introduces the notion of a mediator between God and existence. Cohen sees both alternatives as errors that blur the distinction between God and nature/human beings, or between being and existence/actuality. In short, Greek philosophy does not radically distinguish God from the world, in contrast to Cohen's account of biblical monotheism that ascribes being to God and mere existence and becoming to all else.[19]

According to Cohen, Christianity runs into theological problems because it deviates from biblical ontology in order to follow Greek philosophy. In so doing, Christianity blurs the boundaries between actuality and ideality, between God and human. It does so in two inherently related ways. First, regarding human beings, Christianity "overrates the importance of *existence* [*Dasein*] with regard to nature and the human spirit."[20] This becomes evident with the idea of the immortality of the soul, which undermines the purity of monotheism in that such a notion implies that "man should possess eternal and therefore true being."[21] Second, in relation to God, Christianity seeks to conceive and portray God's essence and to make God an actor in the lives of human beings. If Judaism distinguishes between God and the human being such that the status of the human being resides between actual existence and the ideal, striving to realize the ideal but still tied to the actual, Cohen claims that Christianity, with its notion of the eternal soul, contends that the human being is eternal, is made of the same stuff as God. Where Judaism strives to preserve a radical separation of God and the human being, Christianity blurs this distinction.

It is at this juncture that the problematic nature of Jesus Christ must be considered. According to Cohen, Christ is an image of God, and like "every plastic image" this "Christ . . . is in contradiction of monotheism." God as an idea, as true being, cannot be represented by anything plastic, by anything this-worldly, not even a human being. For Cohen, there is nothing that fundamentally separates Christ from other images of God and from the making of images, which the prophets see as the root of idolatry.[22] Cohen is emphatic on this point: "The man who is God can be thought of only as a symbol, and the finest idealization is able only to make the Trinity, the divinity of Christ, understood as a symbol. Every symbolism, however, that concerns the concept of God himself is an obstruction to the truth."[23] There is no manifestation of God beyond the realm of ethics, which is a process always in flux, always to be realized. Logically speaking, for Cohen there can be no substance, no corporealization of God. God's radical otherness, God as true being, must be univocal. God never becomes actual and is thus "accessible" only through emulation and approximation—which means recognizing that God's being remains ultimately unattainable by human beings.

Cohen's *Logik* has important implications for and operates with normative assumptions about the distinction between logic and ethics, nature and morality, the "is" and the "ought." The *Logik's* transformation of substance forces rejection of the notion of the self as there, as given [*Gegeben*], as a substance. Rather, the self is a project, engaged in a task to perpetually create itself through action. Or as Cohen puts it, "The subject is not the absolute soul substance [*nicht die absolute Seelensubstanz*], but rather it is stretched between a correlation, in which physical motion corresponds to *moral action*" [*sittliche Handlung*].[24]In Cohen's system, the "ought" is an ideal that the self perpetually holds in front of itself as it creates itself. It inevitably falls short, but continues to strive toward it.[25]

In the language of *Religion of Reason*, this new notion of the self manifests in the radical chasm between God and the human being. Cohen even refers to the recognition of this unbridgeable disparity as "the correct *preparation* for morality." He continues, "If nature and man should be able to attain any worth at all, it could only be derived from the unique worth of God's being."[26] Human beings have no intrinsic worth, or in the language of the *Logik*, their selves are not "absolute soul-substances," but instead are projects in the making. God or rather God's attributes of action provide models to emulate in the perpetual construction of the self, but there is no noun there (i.e., there is no metaphysical substance giving the self an identity beyond that of the task of perpetually creating itself).

The Christian Jesus

According to Cohen, the Christian notion of Jesus, based on Greek ontology, is incompatible with a notion of a radically unique God, of a God distinct from all sensibility. Even if one were to merely understand Jesus as a symbol of God, he is a symbol of that which cannot be symbolized. Cohen claims that the diminishment of God's radical uniqueness in Christianity can be seen in the very figure of Jesus. Not only does this figure claim to be a symbol of that which can have no symbol but also this symbol itself is understood mythically, as primarily a sacrifice. Indeed, Cohen argues at length that, as Judaism has developed, ritual sacrifice was not only diminished in significance but also its very meaning changed. It ceased to function as a means of mediation between God and human beings, of immediately releasing one from sin, but instead became a symbol of atonement, a call to ethical action, to the perpetual nature of the task of self-perfection.[27]

Cohen argues that the prophets waged war against sacrifice and its dangers. Only Ezekiel preserved sacrifice, and he relativized its importance. Cohen writes, "Among the wonders that are pertinent to the historical understanding of the wonder of monotheism, the fight of the prophets against *sacrifice* occupies perhaps the first place. The entire classical world is attached to sacrifice; the idea of sacrifice is also the foundation of Christianity."[28] According to Cohen, the prophets alone "recognized in sacrifice the root of idol worship"[29]

It is hard to miss the polemical tone of Cohen's hard and fast assertions about the uniqueness of the prophets' equation of sacrifice and idolatry, which allow for little ambiguity and nuance. On the one hand, Cohen disputes the claim made famous by Julius Wellhausen that the prophets are proto-Christians and thus far removed from the "legalistic character" of the Pentateuch.[30] Cohen's reading of the prophets reverses the widely held Protestant assumptions of a moribund, morally decrepit Judaism and a spiritually ascendant Christianity.

At the same time, Cohen challenges dominant conceptions of the "classical world." He casts the world of the ancient Near East—including Greece but extending beyond it, most likely reflecting the burgeoning interest in Assyriology among his contemporaries—as one rife with sacrifice and myth. As we saw earlier, for Cohen, Greek philosophy is bound up with an erroneous metaphysics that prevents it from grasping true monotheism. In this view, to the degree that Christianity remains Greek, it is at odds with prophetic monotheism and thus mired in error. Cohen is thumbing his nose, as it were, at the German tradition that seeks to rationalize Christianity, to make it the religion of modernity through Jesus's access to the spirit of Greece. Greece is at once bound up with mythology, the mystery religions and the jealousy of the gods, and irrationality, and its celebrated philosophy is increasingly shown to be a source of error that also facilitates myth by justifying some version of pantheism.

Cohen, his notion of religion as functioning normatively, maintains that sacrifice, unless it becomes merely a symbol, is not only premised on a faulty conception of the human being and sin but also undermines human autonomy by bringing a mediator between the human being and God.[31] In stark contrast to Christianity, Jewish cultic law has replaced sacrifice,[32] and as a result, redemption is acquired through atonement whose focus is injustice, not appeasement through offerings. With this shift in emphasis, Judaism has departed from the ancient world of myth, which is haunted by the idea of the envy of the gods. Judaism recognizes that forgiveness of sin is part of the process of atonement, which is inextricably bound up with self-reflection and self-reform (i.e., striving to bring oneself into line with the ideal). This shift in Judaism, Cohen argues, is largely a result of the prophets, whose "zeal . . . against sacrifices is sufficiently explained by their opposition to the false gods who could accept atonement apart from human morality. For [the prophets], therefore, no concession should be permitted, with regard to sacrifice, which is the absolutely dangerous symptom of the worship of false gods."[33]

Christianity—not unlike the mystery religions of Greece or the ancient religions of the Near East—however, continues to be rooted in the logic of sacrifice. Cohen blames Paul not only for turning Christianity away from ritual law but also for creating a situation where "moral law . . . is opposed to faith in Christ's death and resurrection," which alone "afford[s] the salvation of man from sin and its recompense in death." Cohen claims that Christianity sharply breaks with Judaism (or Cohen's normative notion of Judaism) on the notion of atonement. By creating a bifurcation between moral law and faith, and then prioritizing the latter, the emphasis on atonement in Christianity is "transferred from man's horizon to that of God." Where Judaism renders atonement as the fulcrum of human ethics, Cohen claims that for Christianity atonement is a matter of "God's authority and arrangements, which God causes to be fulfilled in his own being and in the depiction of his being in sacrifice."[34] One can conclude from this that, for Cohen, Christianity remains bound up with myth and God continues to be the principal actor. God is the agent of redemption, the key actor in the drama of salvation; morality, which is in the domain of human beings, is relatively unimportant.

According to Cohen, Greek metaphysics and culture have led Christianity to misunderstand religion and God. It is only the Hebrew Bible, in particular the prophets, who offer the proper tools for correctly grasping monotheism, not Greek philosophy. Cohen also loosens the bond between Christianity and the Greeks through his selective reading of the philosophical significance of German Protestantism. By emphasizing the Reformation and Luther's return to the Hebrew

Bible, Cohen casts German religion and philosophy as bound up with the religion of reason.[35] For Cohen, it was not surprising that it was the German philosopher Kant who posited a separation between practical and theoretical philosophy, a distinction that requires the idea of the unique God. The Lutheran heritage, the appreciation of the Hebrew Bible, and the break from Christian scholasticism made such a discovery possible.

The Christian notion of Jesus as the God-man results in two decisive errors. First, as we have discussed, any symbol of God, even Jesus, is fundamentally mythical because symbols only pertain to the human realm and certainly cannot disclose aspects of God's being, which is forever unknowable to us beyond the extent that it translates into ideals for emulation, into plans for action. Second, symbols are meant to be reminders, signs that one ought to autonomously recommit oneself to the ethical ideal, to work for repentance. However, Christianity inverts this paradigm. Christ, the symbol, is a sacrifice that takes on metaphysical significance; he is no mere reminder or call to repentance, *teshuva*, or ethics. Instead, Christ as sacrifice from God redeems the individual rather than calling on the individual to autonomously redeem him- or herself. Christianity takes the symbol—of that which cannot be symbolized no less—literally.

The sacrifice of Jesus causes the link between God and human beings to be thought of materially, metaphysically, rather than formally, thus distorting the methodology of the correlation, in which God serves as the moral archetype for human beings. It fundamentally undermines the logic of correlation—where two terms exist in relation without merging. As mentioned earlier, in his *Logik* Cohen rejects traditional notions of substance, and his ethical thought, as formulated most fully in *Ethik der reinen Willens* (1904/1907), elucidates the notion of a self that is continually in flux and is perpetually directed toward an infinite task, such as morality, action [*Handlung*], the process of continually reforming oneself in relation to the ideal.

Whereas philosophical ethics (by this Cohen means his ethics, and perhaps Kant's ethics as he reads them) and Judaism demand that the notion of the self be thought of as being in flux, as an ongoing task, Christianity takes the self or soul as a substance, a material entity. In Christianity, immortality of the soul is not a function or method for formulating the ethical task, but instead is meant literally. If one understands the self as a substance, as Christianity does, then the self is not merely reified, but is also thought of as an eternal soul.[36] Thus Christianity construes at least part of the human being—the soul—out of true being, thereby ascribing it the same status as God. Redemption is not primarily an activity on the part of the self—the perpetual re-creation of the self in light of the ideal—but the result of an action, on the part of God no less, which removes an innate stain from the soul. If the soul is an eternal substance and it possesses an inherent flaw—original sin—only an action on the part of the divine can cleanse it.

Thus Cohen offers a polemical account of Christian sacrifice to draw a distinction between the two very different sorts of symbolism: One we might say is "kosher" and one not. In Jewish law, Jews are commanded to wear fringes [*tzitzit*] affixed to their garments as a symbol of the law. *Tzitzit* are a symbol in that they remain in the human sphere, and they remind the wearer to follow the law. Wearing *tzitzit* is about emulating God's actions (i.e., about the importance of God's ethical attributes, not God's being). One cannot claim that taking communion at mass functions the same way, because that ritual involves a sacrifice, indeed one taking place from the side of God. Partaking in mass is not only about the immortality of the soul but also transubstantiation, which even if only seen as symbolic, still involves "the depiction of an action in God's being."[37]

To be sure, Judaism recognizes God's forgiveness, but in a way that neither involves speculations about God's being nor compromises the integrity of human autonomy. As Cohen puts it, in Judaism "it is not a diminishing of the dignity of man that his sin is forgiven him; for this forgiveness through God depends on the self-sanctification of man."[38] As mentioned earlier, Cohen is emphatic that there must be a strict separation between God and the human being. Repentance and observance of the law involve the human being turning away from his or her sins and striving to rise to the ideal of God's attributes—a task that can never adequately be achieved. The inherent failure or falling short of the ideal is a necessary part of this task; the boundary between God and the human being must be preserved. In this vein, any mediation would undermine the process of autonomous striving and thus compromise human dignity and the human as ethical agent. Whereas Christian theologians and philosophers, including Kant, argue that the halakha necessarily involves heteronomy, Cohen reverses the charge by shifting the debate to sacrifice and thus mediation.[39] It is not law, which one freely takes on oneself, but rather the sacrifice of another for one's own account, that undermines autonomy. In other words, it is Christianity's notion of Christ and vicarious atonement, not the halakha, that undermines autonomy and thus morality.

Indeed, Cohen's account of the election of the Jews posits that they are an elaborate symbol of humanity. In fact, the Jews as elect serve both as a stark contrast to and yet a continuity with the figure of Jesus in Cohen's work. Cohen frequently juxtaposes the Jewish people as martyrs for God's truth over against the Christian understanding of Jesus as God's son who is sacrificed for the sins of the world and provides vicarious atonement to those who accept him. "Monotheism fundamentally severs forgiveness (סליחה) from the wholly mythological, original form of atonement."[40] Unlike mythical thought, which requires a sacrifice to appease or take away a god's anger at the offense, genuine monotheism reads sin as the necessary pivot to the process of redemption. That is, monotheism (i.e., Judaism here) requires autonomous striving after a goal that drives the process of redemption and forgiveness; in this process the sinner turns away from the past and recommits to the ethical ideal. Christianity, however, according to Cohen, remains rooted in myth, antiquity, and paganism precisely because it is God who intervenes to extinguish the sins of the individual.[41] Genuine monotheism insists on the correlation between God and the individual, but only in a way that distinguishes between the human and divine.[42] Christianity, in contrast, blurs this correlation with a form of pantheism that mixes the divinity within the human being with the ideal self generated through moral work. As a result, "not only does the concept of God thereby lose its transcendence and univocity [*Eindeutigkeit*] but also the ethical concept of man is rendered imprecise at this boundary-point insofar as the moral competence of its ethical work is impaired."[43]

Cohen maintains that the chosenness of the Jews avoids the problems arising from vicarious atonement through Jesus, even as he shapes this election/bearing witness in strikingly Christlike terms. To be sure, there is a dialectical tension between the particularity of the Jewish people and the universalism of the monotheistic message. Cohen seeks to resolve this tension through messianism or, more specifically, the process of testifying to the messianic ideal, of bearing witness to the universal ethical ideal. In messianism, "the chosen people becomes the chosen mankind." In short, "Israel itself now becomes a symbol. Man, a people may become a symbol; only the unique God may not, and with the people of Israel, its entire national history becomes symbolic."[44] Israel serves as a symbol because it is a call for all people to embrace the ethical ideal, to become "Jews" in the ideal sense.[45] Thus, at its most profound point, the distinction between Jew and non-Jew is rooted not in ethnicity but in the recognition and adherence to the ethical ideal. In the ideal sense, all are potentially Jews, and no one is fully so.[46] Again, Cohen is relying—for better or worse—on the logic of exemplarity, as we discussed in the last chapter. Judaism, then, like Greece in "Über das Eigentümliche des deutschen Geistes," is characterized by exemplarity; it is particularly distinguished by the purity of its universality. It is no longer clearly an ethnic or even a cultural marker, but functions increasingly as an ethical/political one.[47]

Indeed, as exemplary, the Jews appropriate the mantle of the Christ, as Cohen depicts them as the ones who suffer vicariously for others. Yet, they cannot atone for others, because atonement means *teshuva*, the autonomous turning away from one's old life to a commitment to the ethical ideal. Thus, although "all the peoples are slaves to idol worship and they glitter and blossom in history," in a Christlike fashion,

> only Israel suffers from the persecutions of the idol worshippers, and Israel has the calling not only to maintain the true worship of God, but also to spread it among the peoples. Such a contradiction in historical imagery between past

> and future history does not permit any other solution but the following: *in suffering for the peoples Israel acquires the right to convert them.*[48]

This is a complex passage. Cohen articulates the mission of the Jews in terms of Deutero-Isaiah's suffering servant, as bearing witness to the divine. Their mission is to testify against the forces of the empirical world to a higher order, to the messianic, when *is* and *ought* are one. But there are two things to bear in mind. This messianic world is in the future, indeed in a future that will never be present. It is also essential to recognize that conversion means that all human beings will cease to worship idols. Idolatry, in this case, is not about the worship of objects instead of God so much as the failure to recognize the ethical dimension that ought to guide history. However, because ethics is rooted in knowledge there can only be vicarious justice and vicarious suffering, not vicarious atonement. Atonement, again, requires self-knowledge and self-transformation: it is *teshuva*.

The Jews suffer for the Other; they suffer so that the Other might learn. But the Jew cannot do the work of learning for the Other. If the Other is to embrace the one true God, the Other must do so on his or her own. The most the Jew can do is testify—indeed, testify with his or her own life. "Consequently, the conversion of the peoples is thought of by the prophet as self-conversion, as the recognition of the nothingness of the gods."[49] Conversion is still autonomous, in that it is about an individual recognizing the truth, the falsity of the gods; it is about rejecting the desires of the world of actuality in favor of the ideal and choosing to make the concomitant moral changes in him- or herself.

Christianity, according to Cohen, thinks materially (in terms of soul substances) rather than with idealistic rigor, and as a result the idea of Christ becomes most prominent, causing concern for humanity, for human beings, to recede. In contrast, the Jew willingly suffers out of concern for other human beings, willingly endures their torments because he or she recognizes that sin is ultimately not real, but is a moment in a process of redemption. Sin cannot be a barrier to seeing the Other as a human being, to being capable of redemption. As a result of its material thinking, because it requires humanity to be ultimately sinful and unable to redeem itself, Christianity, Cohen claims, is methodologically speaking incapable of foregoing war and oppression and indeed, seems to generate a certain apathy to the suffering of others: it has not broken with the causal relationship between sin and suffering. For Cohen, so much present misery stems from this erroneous idea of God that is still rooted in myth and that continues to persist in Christianity.[50]

One can and should critique Cohen for the heavy-handedness with which he makes his argument. Given the inherent mystification bound up with the logic of exemplarity, his argument does not even consider other religions and traditions. However, this should not blind us to the significant developments in Cohen's position regarding the metanarrative of the West and the role of the Jew therein. In *Religion of Reason* Cohen returns to the theme of the education of the human race, which surfaced rather chillingly in our discussion of "Deutschtum und Judentum" in the last chapter, but changes its emphasis. This education comes not through the military might of the German nation but through martyrdom, by means of the Jew bearing witness as the suffering servant. It is no longer the German nation per se but the Jews alone who bring this enlightenment. The Jews, in all humility, are the educators of the world. Indeed, their exemplarity as the suffering servant is now the ultimate arbiter of Western rationality, not Greece and perhaps not even Germany.[51] No longer emphasizing the notion of a just war, but still embracing the argument of exemplarity, of a particularity imbued with universal significance, Cohen now locates true and ultimate universality, the beating heart of the West, in the Jew. Cohen's thought here does far more than merely respond to the world religions discourse; it does more than attempt to maintain a triangulation between Judaism, Greekism, and Germanism. Cohen, with an evangelical zeal, is basically asserting that it is Judaism, not Greece and certainly not any other tradition, that constitutes the authentic foundations, the only true moral grounding, of European—indeed, world—civilization.

Reconfiguring Jesus

Cohen's critique of Christianity is systematic and deep rooted; indeed he increasingly maintains that reason emerges from Jewish sources alone. As a result, he simultaneously rejects the presumed privilege of German philosophy, which understood itself as the uniquely distinguished inheritor of Greekdom. Cohen implies that German thought remains too Christian and thus too Greek, which is tantamount to saying that it is too mythical to be rational. However, another way to read this is that Cohen is actually rationalizing Christianity and thus Germany. That is, he is highlighting and critiquing the mythology of German Christianity— the exemplar of the Christian West—to enable it to become more rational and thus more Jewish. Indeed, in *Der Begriff* and in his essay written two years later, "Der Jude in der christlichen Kultur" [The Jew in Christian Culture] (1917),[52] Cohen offers a vision of a "rational" Jesus or a notion of Jesus that is compatible with prophetic Judaism. In "The Jew in Christian Culture," Cohen is ostensibly explaining why Jews do not need to convert in order to partake in German culture. *Der Begriff* proclaims itself to be a strictly philosophical and methodological study of the concept of religion. However, in both pieces, one can find earlier iterations of the same subversive elements fully developed in *Religion of Reason*. In *Der Begriff* Cohen aligns philosophy and Judaism, and in "The Jew in Christian Culture," he makes Judaism the spiritual center of Christianity. In both works, Cohen ascribes to Judaism a role from which to dictate or guide Christianity in revising and reforming itself along the lines of pure monotheism and rationality. At the center of this project is a new notion of Jesus.

To understand Cohen's account of Jesus, we must appreciate one of the primary developments that emerges from Cohen's notion of religion. Religion is an *Eigenart* rather than a fully independent element of Cohen's system of philosophy that consists of a logic, an ethics, and an aesthetics. Although religion is bound to all of these structures, it maintains a special relationship with ethics.[53] In particular, it builds on the notion of the individual developed in Cohen's ethics. As Cohen later explains in *Religion of Reason*, in ethics "*the I of man becomes the I of humanity,* and only in humanity is that true objectivization of man achieved which can secure the ethical concept of the human subject"[54] In other words, the human being is an individual as a member of humanity, of the whole, of *Allheit.* To be sure, in *Ethik des reinen Willens* Cohen invokes God as a precondition for ethics needed to secure the relationship between ethics and logic, such that the ethical endeavor is not futile. Or as Cohen puts it, "God signifies that nature has stability so morality is eternal."[55] However, the individual has no relationship to God as such, except insofar as God serves as a transcendental condition for ethics, which applies to all individuals universally and collectively.

Cohen's notion of the role of God changes from *Der Begriff* to *Religion of Reason.* In these works, Cohen elaborates the correlation between the individual and God, such that God takes on a new function in relation to sin and forgiveness.[56] As we have discussed, sin, far from being a metaphysical stain or curse, is rather "nothing more or less than a first principle." It provides an alternative methodological route to God, outside of God of ethics (i.e., God as a transcendental condition). It is a point of "transition" whose consequence is a new notion of the self, of the "I."[57] "Through sin man is to become an individual." Ultimately, for Cohen, sin reflects and discloses "human frailty."[58] He continues, "For without finding one's way through all of human frailty, man cannot find his way to God."[59] However, this account of the relationship between the human being and God, this correlation, is quite distinct from the indirect relationship in ethics. Cohen explains: "As soon as the knowledge of sin itself enters into his consciousness the individual recognizes and discovers his personal relation with God."[60] The God of ethics is radically transcendent, indifferent to the individual; God functions as the transcendental condition for the coherence of the moral enterprise. Indeed, that world of human beings is not solely oriented by linear causality, but is ultimately primarily determined by teleology. In religion, however, God is concerned with the individual who struggles to meet the ethical ideal and falls short. As Cohen writes, "But I remain isolated by myself in my individuality with my honest efforts to achieve, recover and resume my morality. The God of mankind [i.e., the God of ethics] doesn't verify my efforts."[61] God serves as a warranty that nature will not undercut the ethical endeavor, not that the ethical endeavor itself will be fulfilled. From the point of view of the individual, this means one is always doomed to fall short, to be insufficient, and to fail. Religion proposes a notion of God that acknowledges and responds to this inability of ethics to respond to the need of the individual. It provides the correlation between the individual, the sinner cognizant of his or her sin and God. Or as Cohen puts it, "My own God is the God of religion."[62]

However, far from a shift to existentialism, the relation to God remains carefully delimited by the system of philosophy and the conceptual constraints on religion. And Cohen, as before, is using his methodology to problematize Christianity. For instance, he writes,

> The correlation is fitted to, and concluded between, man and God, and no other link can be inserted. As man is to become an individual conscious of himself, so God proves himself in this correlation, and also in his unity, which excludes any co-redeemer. Any collaboration of anyone else destroys God's uniqueness, which is even more necessary for redemption than for creation.[63]

Sin and redemption are the fulcrum around which the correlation between the individual and God pivot. Cohen clearly emphasizes the autonomy of the individual and problematizes any intervention or mediation. And because for Cohen autonomy is achieved in the Jewish (and thus *not* Christian) tradition, redemption itself must follow the path laid out by the rationalization of *teshuva*. Sin is the occasion for repentance, for autonomously turning away from the life of sin and recommitting oneself to the ethical ideal.

Even if there is no room for a mediator between God and the individual when it comes to sin and redemption or atonement, Cohen does not think Jesus has become irrelevant. However, Jesus must be rationalized—one is tempted to say "made Jewish"—to be commensurate with his system of philosophy. Yet Cohen is also concerned to undercut the methodological underpinnings of the Protestant search for the historical Jesus. This Christian endeavor, despite its neutral sounding name, was quite theologically invested, predicated as it was with the paradoxical attempt to both contextualize Jesus and to preserve his radical uniqueness.[64] As I have mentioned, Cohen also accepts the works of Abraham Geiger and other Jewish scholars that claim that there is nothing unique in Jesus's teachings. Again, for Cohen it is not Jesus's teachings or his supposed abrogation of the Jewish law in which his significance lies, but rather it is his suffering. Cohen mounts a philosophical critique of liberal Protestantism and, on the basis of reason and philosophy rather than theology (or a theology seeking to incorporate history and philology into itself), seeks to reverse the anti-Jewish tendencies of the world religions discourse; indeed, by grounding his defense of Judaism in philosophy, he seeks to repudiate the very tenability of the world religions discourse without undermining Protestantism per se.

Jesus could not be reconcilable with reason if he is understood as either a mediator between the individual and the divine or as a historical figure or literary character to whom authority is attributed. Cohen finds in Luther's meditations and indeed in his Reformation the radical freedom from dogma and thus the capacity to idealize Jesus away from dogma, text, and history.[65] In both *Der Begriff* and "The Jew in Christian Culture" Cohen praises Jesus as a symbol. Yet, there is no inconsistency with the *Religion of Reason*, because these works consider Jesus as a symbol that does not transgress reason: The symbol of Jesus does not necessarily involve depicting the essence of God nor require the prioritizing of mythic rituals of sacrifice over the ethical maturity of *teshuva* and autonomous repentance. Rather, Jesus serves as the symbol of human suffering. Like the book of Job, the stories of Jesus are "profound poetry of suffering as the highest value of human existence."[66] Once demythologized, we see that Jesus is an idea grounded in reason. Or as Cohen puts it, "This Christ, although drawn from the materials of the Gospels and taken freely from the prophets and the psalms, is, however, actually a creation reason."[67]

Indeed, Cohen claims that Christianity has the resources to facilitate a correlation between the individual and God through Jesus. Jesus in his struggles can serve as a model for the self. For Christians, then, Jesus becomes a conduit to the correlation with God. He represents "the ideal of a person, not the human race in its historical universality, but the individual with knowledge of its isolation, its necessity in his infirmity; but also his worthiness for redemption."[68] Jesus is a model of the individual person, who despite his sinfulness, has his "human limits" "transfigured by his confidence in redemption . . . of a God who is not man, but for whom the sinful man is sufficient."[69] For Immanuel Kant, Jesus is a heroic exemplar of morality, in relation to which an individual "must consider himself unworthy of the union of his disposition with such an idea, even though this idea serves him as an archetype."[70] For Cohen, Jesus also involves knowledge of our ethical shortcomings, and against Kant's rigorism, Cohen's Jesus brings a trust in the God who redeems despite our ethical failings; recognition of our ethical fragility is part of the process of redemption itself.

Indeed, for Cohen the most profound moment of Christianity, where it truly diverges from the mythology of the ancient Near East, is precisely where it breaks with the sphere of the aesthetic. Indeed, the "devaluation of all art is the sublimity of the Christian religion. The suffering of man is its subject." To be sure, Christian culture makes use of art, drawing heavily on Greek tragedy. However, where the "suffering heroes" of Greek tragedies "do not simply think as individuals, but as the scion of their ancestors," in Jesus we see "an individual" who "can be thought precisely as a single individual because he is supposed to represent in his sorrow, man, whose individuality God alone is associated with. This is the deepest meaning of Christian mythology, which is transformed into religion."[71] Christianity, with the notion of the suffering Christ who trusts God in his despair, overcomes the mythical view of tragedy and represents the correlation between the individual and God. This is genuine religion, and thus, Christianity—methodologically speaking, in light of the concept of religion—is reoriented, rationalized, and, one could say, made more Jewish.

Jesus, in Cohen's configuration, is de-Hellenized, returned to the Jewish people. Jesus represents the single individual who recognizes his inability to fully realize the moral ideal and bring about redemption to the world, and thus also the need for redemption from God. As a Jew, Jesus has full faith that God will redeem him. Additionally, Jesus the Jew takes on a supererogatory responsibility, becoming a witness in his very suffering, testifying to the moral order beyond the *Realpolitik* of the world as it is now. "The people of Israel, as God's servant, according to the Talmud, has already received in its bosom 'the pious of the peoples of the world.'" Other religions "have their entitled share in this messianic suffering" freely undertaken by the Jewish people.[72] With his Jewish Jesus, Cohen seems to be offering the passageway for Christians into the rationalized notion of the remnant of Israel testifying to the messianic ideal.

* * *

Near the beginning of *Religion of Reason*, Cohen writes as follows:

> The Greeks bestowed upon philosophy a peculiar character that distinguishes it from the speculation, however profound, of other peoples. Similarly, the Greeks stamped upon the sciences, which they borrowed from the Oriental peoples, the stamp of the specific method of science, their philosophy. This science, and especially this philosophy, became the common property of all civilized peoples. Although the Jews resisted Greek science, they could not resist their philosophy. Indeed, they produced the religion of reason, and to the degree that the share of religion in reason brings with it positively the essence of reason, this homogeneity unavoidably demands that religion be connected, if not with science, yet with philosophy.[73]

In this passage, at first glance Cohen seems to be explaining that Greece is exemplary, that its particular mode of thinking—philosophy—bears universal significance. It is exemplary because, though produced by Greeks in their particularity, its philosophy can be taken up and used by other people. Indeed, Greek philosophy, not to mention science, becomes the possession of "all civilized peoples," by which Cohen presumably means the peoples of Europe. Other modes of thought, including that of the Jews, find themselves compelled to adapt to Greek modes of thinking. Thus, if Judaism is to be a religion of reason, even though it is not Greek, it must pass muster with Greek thought. This is a crucial component of Cohen's metanarrative of the West, as we saw elaborated in chapter 1.

Indeed, we see this same conception of Greece as the standard bearer of Western rationality a bit later in Cohen's chapter on "God's Uniqueness" in *Religion of Reason*. Here, Cohen spends significant energy on etymology and textual criticism of passages from the Hebrew Bible. He also devotes attention to the Greek philosophers who conflate nature and being, thus thinking of God's oneness in terms of unity rather than uniqueness. The Jews' notion of uniqueness means something else—a God that is radically separate from this world and without a mediator. In light of Greek thought, and before his discussion of its inheritance by the Christians, Cohen makes an interesting remark. He says that if "the Jews were not to fall into the Persian error of the two powers in the world,"[74] then reason itself had to become the means of correlating human beings and God. That is, reason is something God and human beings both possess, albeit differently.

What is of interest is the reference to Persia. At the time, Persians were considered to be Aryan like the Greeks and Indians. Cohen never explores Manichean sources or even considers the possibility that they might contain reason. One suspects that for Cohen these sources are not worth exploring because, even if their wisdom did inform Greece—as we see from the lengthy quote at the beginning of this section, Cohen is quite willing to grant that "Oriental" wisdom informed Greece—the wisdom of the Orient, "the speculation of other peoples, however profound," lacks the "peculiar character that distinguishes" philosophy from mere speculation.[75] If we recall from the last chapter, the exemplarity of the Greeks lies not in their originality, but in the manner in which their thought and culture finds expression, a manner that paradoxically transcends cultural and geographic specificity.

And yet, as *Religion of Reason* proceeds, Cohen increasingly denigrates and chips away the position of Greece as standard bearer of rationality in the West, as the exemplar of exemplarity. In the beginning, Cohen does not merely concede that he must hold up Judaism to the teachings of philosophy: he demands it. However, as he proceeds, he increasingly associates Greek ideas with mystery cults and antiquated metaphysics—with the problems haunting Christianity— and Judaism with his new, critical philosophy grounded in modern physics, where theories of motion undercut antiquated notions of absolute substance. Without saying it explicitly, Judaism displaces Greece as the standard bearer of European rationality. The figure of Jesus embodies this transformation. In contrast to the German Protestant philosophical and theological tradition that holds that Jesus was essentially Greek, not Jewish, in Cohen's hands Jesus becomes a representative of rationality precisely where he diverges from the classical world.[76] If Europe as a "synthesis" of the legacies of ancient Greece and ancient Israel was unraveling as a result of philology and the world religions discourse, then Cohen insists that, contrary to common assumptions, it is ancient Greece or at least its irrational tendencies that have no place in contemporary Europe. Judaism is depicted as having surmounted the mythical, Oriental world of the ancient Near East, to have grasped reason, and thus, it constitutes the core of European identity.

3 Fire, Rays, and the Dark: Rosenzweig and the Oriental/Occidental Divide

Although rosenzweig belongs to the generation after Cohen, the two share a concern with the challenges that the world religions discourse poses to Judaism's place in Christian Europe. That is, however else we might read Rosenzweig, he is grappling with the increasing displacement of Judaism no less than did Cohen. Like Cohen, he puts forward a philosophy of history that is itself a metanarrative of the West, one in which Judaism occupies a primary place. However, where Cohen employs reason to ensure Judaism's symbiosis with Germanism, Rosenzweig not only rejects rationalism but he also argues that suprarational foundations of Revelation conjoin Judaism and Christianity. [1]

Although this study reads both Cohen's and Rosenzweig's works in light of the rising tides of antisemitism in early twentieth-century Germany and especially their ideological undercurrents, it is apparent that this phenomenon's particular manifestations and impact significantly differ for the work of these two thinkers. For Cohen, antisemitism is linked to the growing threat to German culture caused by its failure to live up to its ideal and embrace its authentic essence, which is rationalist and cosmopolitan. As such, it is a dire threat for Jews, Germany, and Europe itself. For Rosenzweig, on the contrary, the presence of antisemitism among Christians does not threaten, but rather confirms the status of Jews and Judaism in world history in a metaphysical and metahistorical sense. Indeed, according to Rosenzweig, antisemitism is not a sign of the foreignness of the Jews to Europe, but instead is foundational to the relationship between Jews and Christians, and thus to the West. Rather than threatening Jews' status it reveals the integral role Jews play in the inner struggle among Christians (Europeans) to reject their inner paganism and to live up to their Christian responsibilities. [2]

Although there are some signs of change, Jewish Studies scholarship in the United States has largely rebuffed Cohen because of his wartime writings—read more often than not without sufficient nuance—and because his notion of a German Jewish symbiosis is seen as intolerable and hopelessly naive in the wake of the Holocaust. [3] However, Franz Rosenzweig has been embraced by Jewish Studies scholars like no other figure in modern Jewish thought, [4] as has his work *Der*

Stern Der Erlösung [The Star of Redemption] (1921).[5] Michael Oppenheim is no doubt overstating the case when he states, "In the context of the modern Jewish philosophy, it stands as a unique classic, occupying a corresponding place to that of Maimonides' *Guide for the Perplexed* in its setting within Medieval Jewish Philosophy."[6] Yet, even though Oppenheim's claim is an exaggeration, it makes an important point: Rosenzweig's thought continues to attract more attention and followers than that of any other modern thinker, perhaps with the exception of Emmanuel Levinas.[7]

Given the prominence of Rosenzweig's thought, the degree to which Rosenzweig's Orientalism remains unexplored, often unacknowledged, and insufficiently addressed is something of a scandal.[8] Although the desire to find a way to make Rosenzweig relevant to present discussions is commendable, the tendency to dismiss his remarks about non-Western religions as a mere prejudice of bygone times and antiquated ways of thinking is untenable.[9] There is no avoiding the fact that, in the words of Leora Batnitzky, "Rosenzweig does not believe that all communities are equal to the task of creating eternity in time."[10] Indeed, it is necessary to go further than Batnitzky's claim and posit that for Rosenzweig not only are all communities unequal in regard to eternity but also certain communities—that is, Jewish and Christian communities—foster the creation of eternity in time, whereas others, namely Islam and the religions of India and China, stifle this possibility.[11] As troubling as this view may be to our multicultural sensibilities, Rosenzweig's vision must be recognized for what it is. Indeed, it is imperative that we take stock of his actual position before we rush to reconstruct it in ways that are more palatable to our contemporary sensibilities. My study, rather than dismissing, avoiding, and repudiating Rosenzweig's account of non-Western religions,[12] seeks to engage it.

The interesting question is not whether Rosenzweig is Orientalist in the pejorative sense of the term—he certainly is—but rather what motive or motives drive his Orientalism. Perhaps even more significant is this question: How does Rosenzweig's Orientalism shape his notion of the Occident? The religions of Greece, China, and India, as well as Islam, functioned for Rosenzweig primarily as cultural figments in the European imaginary,[13] and thus whatever else his comments about these religions amount to, they are also commentaries about his fellow Europeans and their fascination with the East. The various manifestations of the religions of India and China, and of Islam represent two different foils for illuminating the theo-political religiosity at play in Rosenzweig's idiosyncratic account of the Jewish-Christian dynamic in Europe. Where the religions of India and China represent abstraction from factuality, which Rosenzweig explicitly links to a flight from God's countenance, Islam represents religious rationalism and the attempt to determine the indeterminable, to ground religion in terms of (human) rationality, thus constraining God's freedom. Central for Judaism and

Christianity, which according to Rosenzweig are genuine religions of revelation, is the dialogical experience of God's love as the basis of the redemption of the world;[14] the Orient embodies different ways in which this relationship is distorted and thus serves as both a foil and as opposition that must be overcome by the Occident (i.e., Judaism and Christianity) in history. It is imperative to recall the prominent role of the Orient in the European imaginary.[15]

Both the religions of India and China, and of Islam do not allow God's act of love to be the foundation of redemption, as disclosed in the genuine path of revelation, and the fruit of Rosenzweig's "New Thinking" in *The Star of Redemption*. His schematic treatment of these Oriental religions is not so much an expression of disdain for exotic, foreign traditions, as much as the flip side of his systematic attempt to blend the philosophy of history and *Heilsgeschichte* [salvation history] in his system.[16] The non-Western religions of the Orient are the dark background against which the fire and rays of the divine countenance—the famous vision from which he derives the title of his opus—shine forth. If the religions of the Far East, India, and China represent a flight from human responsibility before God, Islam represents the prioritization of human agency at the expense of God. Thus all these religions negate God's agency, thereby stifling revelation and genuine faith—the characteristics of Judaism and Christianity in his polemical account of the spiritual Occident.

Modernity, Heresy, and the Orient

In a letter dated November 16, 1916, Rosenzweig's friend and interlocutor Eugen Rosenstock-Huessy,[17] himself a philosopher/linguist/jurist, wrote to Rosenzweig that "the Western world" has come to a point "when it can forget the Old Testament. And what is worse . . . it will forget its Old Testament."[18] According to Rosenstock-Huessy, "Israel's time as the people of the Bible has gone by. . . . The epoch of the eternal Jew has come to an end."[19] Alluding to the cultural phenomenon that Suzanne L. Marchand would later name the "furor orientalis," in which scholars in a broad range of disciplines sought to displace the prominence of the ancient civilizations of Greece and Israel through recourse to the "Orient,"[20] Rosenstock-Huessy writes, "The more one excavates Sumerians and Akkadians, the more completely and quickly will Europe forget Moriah, Marathon, Brutus: and I add, it will be allowed to forget them."[21] Thus, the more that scholars recover the cultures of the ancient Near East, the more that Greece and Israel (as well as Rome) will lose their metaphysical significance; they will eventually become nothing more than merely national, *Volkish* expressions.

Rosenzweig, responding in a letter on November 30, 1916, agrees with his correspondent that the traditional relationship between Christianity and Judaism has ceased to exist. Jews do not constitute a threat to Christianity.[22] Instead that threat comes from Orientalist politicians such as Wilhelm II and Constant d'Et-erounelles or from intellectual, cultural, and religious figures from the Orient such as "Mohammed that so and so, or Rabindranath Tagore."[23] It is not insignif-icant that Rosenzweig saves his strongest language for the prominent Christian theologian, Ernst Troeltsch—whose own conflict with Cohen we discussed at the end of chapter 2. Rosenzweig likens Troeltsch to the "Antichrist"[24] presumably because his historicist methodology leaves no room for a relationship with eternity. What Mohammed and Tagore presumably have in common with Troeltsch in Rosenzweig's view is that all three testify against the revelations—which, accord-ing to Rosenzweig, alone give orientation in the face of the crisis of historicism—of Judaism and Christianity.[25]

However, Rosenzweig expresses confidence that the threat to the Jewish and Christian traditions from the Orient or, rather, the world religions discourse is not genuine. He writes, "Sumerians and Akkadians will not neutralize Moriah, Marathon, Butros," and "Jews, Greeks, and Romans will remain the everlasting history because they are the *Ioudaioi, Hellēnes, Romaioi* of Paul."[26] Rosenzweig insists that the classical ideal of Greece is not in danger, but that its legitimation comes not from historians and theoreticians but from "teachers of religion."[27] In short, it is religion—or, more specifically in *The Star of Redemption*, Judaism and Christianity—that will ensure the eternal value of Greece and Rome and of the West in general. Philosophy, bound as it is in Rosenzweig's understanding to a metanarrative of the West, is unable to preserve the special significance of Christianity and Judaism. Yet the new scholarly technologies associated with the world religions discourse are threatening to undermine the historico-teleological basis on which this metanarrative of the West was founded. Rosenzweig's response to this threat is simple and radical. It is not Western culture in general, but the re-spective relationships between the transhistorical communities of Judaism and Christianity and eternity that give these religions meaning.[28]

In *The Star of Redemption*, Rosenzweig addresses the question of the con-tinuing relevance of the Old Testament raised five years earlier by Rosenstock-Huessy. Probably in reference to the heresy of Marcionism, which had been given fresh credence by Adolf von Harnack's widely read work, *Marcion: Das Evange-lium vom Fremden Gott* [Marcion: The Gospel of the Alien God][29] (1920/1924), Rosenzweig mentions that one of the perpetual threats of re-paganization that Christianity faces is the "spiritualization of God" [*einer Gottvergeistigung*][30] that severs God from the world. The threat of the pagan, spiritualized God reasserts itself in Christian anti-Judaism, in the old Gnostic resentment of the Law. For Rosenzweig, the authentic figure of Jesus necessarily stands in opposition to the ways that nationalisms co-opt Jesus as an idea for their own purposes. However, the Marcionite heresy, which presents God as distinct from the world, as purely spiritual, is in fact much more amenable to the nationalistic mindset: "That spiritual God, in his spirituality, is a very pleasant partner; and he leaves the world at our freest disposal, which is really not 'purely spiritual' [*rein geistig*] and therefore not from him and hence very probably from the Devil."[31]

If God is divorced from the world, then the human being has no obligation to be God's partner in redemption and thus is free to immerse him- or herself entirely in worldly affairs—the affairs of history—without any concerns for eternity. In regard to "this world itself," a natural response seems to be that "we would like to regard it as a universe and feel marvelously irresponsible in it, like a 'speck of dust in the universe.'" However, in truth we are "its responsible center around which all things turn or a pillar upon whose solidness it rests."[32] That is, as Alexander Altmann puts it, "The Christian soul is divided between nation and Church, between 'Siegfried' and Christ, between myth and revelation."[33] However, the Marcionite heresy dissolves this tension so that one can embrace nationalism—the "Siegfried"—without any dissonance from also embracing the Christ. As we see, the manner in which Marcionism's account of a "purely spiritual" God relieves one from actual responsibilities for redemption is fundamentally similar to the "spiritual religions of the far East'" [*Geistesreligionen des fernen Ostens*][34] that Rosenzweig read as a flight from the divine countenance.

Recall that Cohen critiqued the neglect and disparagement of the manner in which the faculties of higher education treated the Old Testament, presenting it as an object of study for Christians by Christians in a manner from which Jews were largely excluded.[35] Cohen's overpowering presence in the Jewish intellectual scene in the early twentieth century is well attested,[36] as is his own profound influence on Rosenzweig. However, Rosenzweig's own account of Judaism's relationship to Christianity is profoundly antithetical to Cohen's account of a German-Jewish symbiosis.[37] Rosenzweig sees the Old Testament as no longer relevant to the relationship between Judaism and Christianity, which he asserts had changed in modernity. Indeed, in his letter to Rosenstock-Huessy in 1916, Rosenzweig states that Christianity is not so much focused on the church of old as on the life of the individual,[38] and Judaism is no longer condemned to be viewed through the lens of Christian theology. Instead, there is now the "naked Jew, without Old Testament,"[39]—understood not in reference to the New Testament's supposed supersession of the Hebrew Bible but only in him or herself, only as this Jew, freed from the fetters of Christian theology, is "the Jew of Christianity."[40] Perhaps in a reference to Cohen's efforts to defend the integrity of the Old Testament, in *The Star*, Rosenzweig insists that this "mere book"—the Old Testament—cannot save Christianity from idolatry. He eschews Cohen's attempts to change culture through ideals or intellectual synthesis.[41] Rather, far more effective is the actual (i.e., concretely existing) Jewish people, who testify to the genuine God of revelation: "Whether Christ is more than an idea—no Christian can know. But that Israel is more than an idea, he knows it and sees it. For we are living. We are eternal, not as an idea may be eternal . . . . About us the Christians cannot be in doubt. Our existence [*Wirklichkeit*] guarantees for them their truth."[42] Where Cohen privileges the ideal over the actual or actuality [*Wirklichkeit*], Rosenzweig and Buber as well celebrate the actual. Where Cohen asserts that the Jews exert cognitive, intellectual, and thus spiritual influence on the Christians, Rosenzweig insists they are empirical, living, breathing witnesses to the God to whom the Christians profess.

Historical Enmity and Messianic Friendship

Rosenzweig is famously characterized as a thinker of Judaism and Christianity, or of Jewish and Christian partnership.[43] In the wake of the Holocaust, Jewish and Christian theologians seeking to rebuild what was rent asunder eagerly embraced some of his claims such as the following: "Before God therefore, both, Jew and Christian, are workers on the same task. He cannot dispense with either."[44] In her article, "Dialogue as Judgment, not Mutual Affirmation: A New Look at Franz Rosenzweig's Dialogical Philosophy," Leora Batnitzky points out that such an appropriation ignores the fact that Rosenzweig envisions this dialogue as a form of mutual critique, rather than a process of bridge building. Indeed, as Batnitzky highlights, Rosenzweig predicts perpetual enmity—at least for the duration of history—between Jews and Christians.[45]

Even if, according to Rosenzweig, "between the two [i.e., Judaism and Christianity], [God] set an enmity for all time," God nevertheless "binds them together in the narrowest reciprocity." The Jews possess "eternal life" by means of "igniting in our heart the fire of the Star of his truth." Christians, in contrast, are "on the eternal way," hastening "after the rays of that Star of his truth in all time until the eternal end." Jews turn inward, and Christians turn outward, but both reflect the eternal: "The truth the whole truth, belongs therefore neither to them nor to us."[46] Both Jews and Christians, in their enmity and—despite themselves— their cooperation, "have only a share in the whole truth." Rosenzweig is quick to emphasize, as he does throughout the book, that human beings remain human, and thus "immediate sight of the whole truth comes only to him who sees it in God. But this is a seeing beyond life."[47] Although his claim to grasp the whole, the vision beyond life while in life, is enormously complex,[48] it is important to recognize that Rosenzweig is not merely commenting on creatureliness nor that truth remains partial, rooted in tradition.[49] Nor is he simply trying "to work out the question of how to make the eternal come into time."[50] Instead, he is specifically talking about Judaism and Christianity and the manner in which these two religions are inextricably bound up with each other. Indeed, it would seem that a major factor bringing Judaism and Christianity together is their shared opposition— configured metaphysically—to Islam and the religions of India and China.

It is instructive to juxtapose the manner in which Cohen and Rosenzweig understand the relationship between the world religions discourse to antisemitism.

Recall that Cohen saw antisemitism and world religions discourse as bound to-gether. The interest in comparative religion, for Cohen, was evidence of a German effort to break with the rationalism and humanism, which he perceived as the classical essence of Germany. Evidence for this conclusion was the close link be-tween the Protestant fascination with so-called world religions and its desire to reject its Jewish origins. Given that, for Cohen, Judaism is the most rational of all religions, antisemitism, then, reflects nothing less than the most intellectu-ally and morally sophisticated culture of Europe abandoning its task of embody-ing and exemplifying the cultural ideals of the West; it is a degeneration of Germanism into vulgar nationalism.

Rosenzweig, however, sees Europe as bound up with paganism; indeed, pa-ganism is inherent in Christianity. The antisemitic element of the burgeoning world religions discourse is but a manifestation of Christianity's paganism and its jealousy of Judaism's closeness to eternity. Where the world religions discourse is inherently threatening to Cohen, for Rosenzweig it shores up the unity of Judaism and Christianity—a unity persisting despite enmity—against the rest of the world (i.e., all those who lack Revelation). Indeed, if Cohen sought to preserve, or to create, a harmonious Jewish-German symbiosis, Rosenzweig offers a Jewish-Christian front,[51] but one whose harmony is rooted in the future and whose present form exists as tension between the two parties. The "Oriental" religions, especially Islam and the religions of India and China, illuminate the identity of the West, particularly Christianity's own internal struggle during history. In-deed, because Christianity remains stubbornly bound up with paganism—albeit in the "higher" form of the paganisms of Greece and the ancient Near East—Rosenzweig seems to think that it is especially in need of demarcation from non-Western forms of religion such as those of India and China, which he thinks are particularly dangerous temptations. Islam, which in Rosenzweig's account re-sembles religious liberalism and rationalism, offers another subtler temptation, in that it represents the rationalized counter-image of the monotheisms. Rather than making possible a flight from God, Islam is an attempt to domesticate God, and thus it is the foil against which Rosenzweig seeks to illuminate "genuine" reli-gions of revelation. However, these religions are deeply imbricated in the system that Rosenzweig crafts and thus must be understood as part of his larger philo-sophical vision.

The Primordial Elements: God-World-Man Being

At a time when the generation of the furor orientalis was disparaging Greece and Israel in favor of the religions of the Orient, Rosenzweig aligns Greece with the West and defends it against "the favorites of modernity, the 'spiritual religions of the far East.'"[52] Indeed, Rosenzweig writes, "It is no coincidence that the Revelation when it went out into the world, did not take the path of the East but that of the West."[53] However, Rosenzweig is doing more than just voicing his opinion about the Occident and the Orient; he seeks to demonstrate this claim about Revelation by building it into the philosophical structure of *The Star* itself. Rosenzweig's critique of the religions of Asia mirrors his account of the heresy of Marcionism insofar as he perceives in these religions a systematic attempt to escape the responsibility for factuality [*Tatsächlichkeit*] i.e., the interrelationship between the elements of God-World-Man. Thus, he sees these religions, like Marcionism, as facilitating a flight before the decisionism that a living God of Revelation demands.[54] Unlike paganism that recognizes these elements but refuses or is unable to bring them together into factuality, these religions dissolve the elements themselves.

Rosenzweig begins *The Star of Redemption* by talking about death. According to Rosenzweig, the individual realizes that "philosophy" ignores the real concerns of actual people.[55] Or as Rosenzweig puts it, "Philosophy commenced only when thinking united with being. It is precisely philosophy, and precisely here, that we refuse to follow. We are seeking a permanence, which has no need of thinking to be." Philosophy avoids "that empty being, being before thinking," equating it with "nothing."[56] Because Rosenzweig claims that philosophy is characterized by the equation of thinking and being, it reduces that which preexists thought—"being before thinking"—to nothing. However, as Rosenzweig puts it, "the nothing is not nothing, it is something."[57] Thus such things as the individual and his or her death are not genuinely nothing despite the claims of philosophy. Concern for them cannot and should not be extinguished. In the equation of thought and being, philosophy loses the factuality of existence. And this factuality cannot be grasped straightforwardly or generated by reason.

Rosenzweig argues that there are three primary elements that constitute factuality: God-World-Man. Philosophy or rather Idealism cannot capture these three elements; something, or rather "nothing" remains left over when Idealism tries to equate thought and being: "The nothing of our knowledge is not a singular nothing, but a threefold one."[58] In other words, these elements are all irreducible to one another, and therefore each must first be derived in its individuality. At this juncture, Rosenzweig turns to Cohen's use of infinitesimal mathematics, in particular the differential, which does not embrace "an empty nothing." Instead "the differential combines in itself the properties of the nothing and of the something; it is a nothing that refers to a something, to its something, and at the same time a something that still slumbers in the womb of the nothing, for producing something from nothing."[59] That is, Rosenzweig finds in Cohen's thought the generative nature of the nothing, that it is not an empty nothing. This is helpful for Rosenzweig, because the nothing he is talking about is only nothing from the point of view of philosophical abstraction; for real life it is not-nothing.[60] As a result, this nothing that is not-nothing is what, according to Rosenzweig, gives us access to the pre-factual.

There are two paths of determining or bringing something out of the nothing that is not-nothing: the path of affirmation and the path of negation. Or as Rosenzweig puts it, "The No is the original negation of the nothing."[61] Whereas the "Yes," the path of affirmation, "is repelled by the nothing" although it falls back into it, "the No is most intimately intertwined body to body with the Nothing."[62] According to Rosenzweig, the path of affirmation pertains to the "sought after . . . the not-nothing," whereas the path of negation pertains to "what is presupposed, the nothing."[63] Thus these two paths attend to the bivalent nature of the differential. They differ from one another and "do not converge in a sort of identity with that which was previously called the 'sought after,' but they are different among themselves . . . like Yes and No." The result is that the something has a "twofold figure and in a twofold relationship to the nothing: on the one hand, it is its inhabitant, and on the other hand, it escapes from it."[64] The Yes and No are joined by a third term, an And. The three terms together form a root sentence: "Yes and No, so and not-otherwise."[65]

Rosenzweig offers rather schematic accounts of the religions and cultures of Greece, India, and China to illustrate the structure of the pre-factual world, the world prior to Revelation.[66] However, more is at stake here than Rosenzweig's preference for Greece over India and China. By juxtaposing the religions of India and China with Greece, Rosenzweig not only illustrates the properly fulfilled constellation of Yes, No, and the And but he also demonstrates that Greece, which he sees as part of the *Heilgeschichte* of the West, is metaphysically fulfilled in Judaism and Christianity and thus metaphysically distinguished from the religions of the Orient. Unlike the religions of India and China as Rosenzweig depicts them, "[Greek] antiquity certainly possessed the factuality of man, the world, and God."[67] That is, Greece achieves God, Man, and World, but it never achieves the interrelationship of these elements. The ancient Greeks represent the proper fulfillment of each of these entities in their pre-factual state, but factuality only emerges from the interrelationship of these three elements, which occurs in the wake of Revelation.

We must understand that Rosenzweig is not doing mere—albeit problematic—philosophy here. His celebration of the Greeks and the ire behind his bleak assessment of the religions of India and China are motivated by their present relevance for Europeans.[68] As Bruce Rosenstock has shown, for Rosenzweig, World War I "dealt the pagan fusion of philosophy and the state its death blow" and thus created the conditions for "Revelation" to spring forth in history."[69] The paganism of 1800, as embodied by Hegel and Goethe, remains a live choice. As Rosenstock explains, "each person must return to 1800 and stand before the existential choice posed by Hegel and Goethe in order to hear the word of God once more."[70]

Paganism—this conflation of the Greeks, German Idealism, and culture that culminates in 1800—is an essential component in the Johannine epoch of Christianity. Each Christian must pass through it and make the existential choice for Christianity to be able to hear Revelation. Yet, the religions of the Orient precisely obfuscate or prevent the conditions of paganism and, thus, Christianity from emerging. Therefore, although Rosenzweig confronts philosophers such as Hegel and Nietzsche who are deeply influenced by Greek culture and thought, he is much more negative in his assessment of German thinkers influenced by Asian sources such as Schopenhauer.[71]

The difference between Greece and the religions of India and China, Rosenzweig claims, is that whereas the latter "remain on the porch of Yes and No," the Greeks moved further; they "progressed to the And, to the completed figure."[72] Although this shift may seem to be a matter of mere technical detail, it possesses grave existential importance. Rosenzweig maintains that pagan prayers, even in monstrous child sacrifice, "cannot have been unheard and could not have remained unseen." Rosenzweig follows this by asking rather indignantly, "Or should God have waited for Mount Sinai or even Golgotha? No, as little as paths lead from Sinai or from Golgotha, on which he can be reached with certainty, so little can He have denied himself the [possibility of] encountering even the person who sought Him on the trails around Olympus."[73] And yet, in sharp contrast, Rosenzweig maintains that those who fail to maintain the genuine distinction between the three elements God-World-Man are essentially closed off to God.[74] "And if there were a 'godly' man—as an enthusiastic German professor under the impact of Rabindrath Tagore's teaching proclaimed—then this man would actually find himself barred from the path to God, which is open to every human being who is human. So important is the presupposed separation of 'being.'"[75]

God is the first element that Rosenzweig isolates in its pre-factual dimension. Rosenweig begins with the path of affirmation, the Yes. This approach, affirming God's not-nothingness, leads Rosenzweig to "God's infinite essence, his infinite factuality, his nature."[76] The path of negation, the No, deals with God's "self-negation," which manifests itself as freedom. God is not simply a divine plenum, an "infinite sea," but rather "an inexhaustible source," one that "rises up" and expresses a "divine freedom . . . the finite configuration of action, an action whose might is inexhaustible."[77] God is not an absolute substance, but an actor. For Rosenzweig, God possesses an absoluteness and yet also an arbitrariness, such that the two are bound up together, resulting in God as both all-powerful and hidden within God's own self.

According to Rosenzweig, the "gods of antiquity," those of ancient Greece, represent the most fully realized conception of the element of God in its isolation in the pre-factual world.[78] The Greek gods are alive and immortal, but yet are cut off from the world of the living. Their actions and their relationships with things are purely arbitrary; they are driven by passions that have no grounds, no rationale. In Rosenzweig's reading, these gods are fundamentally isolated from the world and human beings for the primary reason that "the gods live among themselves."[79] This manner of grasping the divine is not so much wrong as insufficient; it only reaches God insofar as God remains an isolated element, disconnected from Man and World.

In contrast to Greek mythology, according to Rosenzweig, "[t]he godheads of China and India are immense edifices built from the blocks of ancestral times; like monoliths, they still tower up to this day in cults of the 'primitives.'"[80] For Rosenzweig, the God of India represents the God of the Yes, the path of affirmation, whereas China is the No, the path of negation. Unlike Greek myths' expression of the vital, living divine, the religions of India and China are a way of taking flight "before the countenance of the living God into the dense fogs of abstraction."[81] Neither proceeds to factuality. India's God is "on the road between the nothing and the pure, all-penetrating silence of the essence, of the divine nature."[82] Similarly, China's heaven is "world-embracing" of "divine power" without "divine essence" and without "divine vitality,"[83] and as a result it is confined to sheer arbitrariness, threatening to "disappear in pure nihilism, free of any particular tie to God and the gods."[84] Thus, if the Greeks, according to Rosenzweig, adumbrate the God of Judaism and Christianity insofar as their myths show a "God not merely worthy of being loved, but who loves, independently of the love of men,"[85] the religions of the East reveal something very different. Rosenzweig casts the religions of China and India as "securus adversus deos [security against God] as well as adversus Deum [against the gods]."[86] For Rosenzweig, these notions of God are nothing but a flight from the living God. All mythologies are not created equally, and indeed, Rosenzweig now casts the pagan religions that Christians historically critiqued as forerunners of Christianity.

Next, Rosenzweig turns to the World. The path of affirmation, which leads to the world of thought, the logos, is "that which is universally valid."[87] Here the Yes opens the World to thought, which operates according to the categories of universality and necessity. As Rosenzweig puts it, "The infinitude of the affirmed not-nothing of the world appears as infinite possibility of application of the worldly logos."[88] For Rosenzweig, this everywhere and always is the "logos," the being of the world according to (old) philosophical thinking.[89] The path of negation reveals that there is "something always new, pressing, imposing" beyond measure.[90] Where the path of affirmation leads to universality, the path of negation leads to the particular that is born anew.

As with God, with the World there is also a Yes, No, and an And that unites the paths of affirmation and negation. Rosenzweig juxtaposes the "phenomenon" [*Erscheinung*] against 'the given' to illuminate new thinking from traditional philosophy. The "phenomenon . . . the ever new—the miracle of the world of the spirit"[91] represents Rosenzweig's new thinking, the thinking grounded in the interrelationship of God-World-Man. On the other hand, the "given," a term associated with traditional philosophy, is grounded solely in the world rather than in the relationships of God-World-Man. And unlike the phenomenon, which is always new, the given is "'once and for all,'"[92]

Rosenzweig directly equates philosophy or, more specifically, Idealism with Greek paganism. According to Rosenzweig, the Greeks grasp being as thought and the nature of cognition in the World in isolation, thereby setting the tradition that Idealism follows. However, they fail to grasp the greater reality: the interaction of the elements of God-World-Man. As a form of Idealism—the equation of thinking with being or with the world—this type of "thinking must console itself with the unity of its point of application inside the hermetic walls of the world."[93]

Rosenzweig again favorably juxtaposes the Greeks against India and China in regard to the notion of World. He casts India as the path of affirmation, as affirmation without negation. As Rosenzweig tells it, "Indian thinking" undermines all singularity, all determinability with its notion of Maya. All particulars are dissolved into the world, even the gods and the human worshippers who daily seek to "dissolve" their selves "anew in the oneness of the Brahmin."[94] In this schematic, China functions as the opposite to India. It lacks the path of affirmation and thus is without universality and only grasps particulars. According to Rosenzweig, for China everything is "concrete, particular," such that even the spiritual world is bound to individuals, to one's ancestors.[95] Rosenzweig casually dismisses the religions of India and China in regard to the World: "The cool emptiness of flight from the world, the intimate depth of love for the world—again, here as there, India and China, the people that dreams with eyes closed and the people that dreams with eyes open—are the heirs of man of primitive times who take refuge in the delirium of the world because he lacks the courage to observe the world."[96] As a result, "once again the Greeks, the people of discoverers, are the guides of our breed on the road of clarity."[97] That is, even if for the Greeks cognition (Idealism) never transcends the World, they nevertheless grasp it in its fullness such that it does not dissolve one-sidedly into the Yes or No.

The third element in Rosenzweig's scheme is Man. The route of affirmation leads us to the human being's "essence," as it has with the other elements. Human beings or here "man" is defined as "ephemeral."[98] This notion of the ephemeral illuminates man as a particular, but as a particular defined affirmatively, as himself: "a singular then, which knows nothing of other singulars beside it."[99]

The route of the negation leads to free will. Rosenzweig is keen to differentiate human free will from divine freedom. Human free will, although unconditional, is bound up with human finitude. Thus, in contrast to Rosenzweig's account of God, "it is not freedom for action . . . but a freedom for willing, not free power, but free will."[100] However, human free will resembles divine freedom insofar as it possesses an infinite, unconditional element. The And, which links the Yes and No of the "Man," is for Rosenzweig, the notion of the Self. What is uniquely itself as the "Self" cannot be compared: "[I]t is incomparable" and has "no plural."[101]

In regard to human beings, or the element of Man, it is the Greeks who reached the limit of the pre-factual, the "metaethical," for whom "metaethical man was a living figure."[102] This is revealed most clearly in Greek tragedy.[103] In these narratives, we see the notion of the Self—the And that unites Yes and No— expressed through a tragic muteness, an inability to speak that separates the singular, incomparable Self from the worldliness of others, of personalities. Rosenzweig explains, "By being silent, the hero dismantles the bridges that link him to God and the world, and he tears himself away from the landscapes of personality, which, through the spoken word, marks out its limits and individualizes itself in the face of others in order to climb into the icy solitude of the Self."[104] The Self cannot speak, because the "Self is Self only as long as it is alone."[105] Here we have Man alone, apart from World and God.

As with his account of God and World, Rosenzweig depicts the Greeks as having the most dialectically fulfilled notion of Man, with the Indian and Chinese as points of comparison. Whereas the Greeks achieved "the tragic hero of antiquity,"[106] which is "nothing else than the metaethical self," Rosenzweig claims that "India and China, which stopped on the way before reaching the goal, achieved the tragic neither in dramatic work of art nor in the prefiguring of the folk-tale."[107]

As is characteristic of the conclusion of each section on the elements of the proto-cosmos, Rosenzweig now disparages the religions of China and India: "India and China have shown the only two ways in which man can at all times turn away before his Self. When he does not have the courage to become tragic."[108] Rosenzweig claims, rather dubiously (unless one accepts his "revealed" criteria), that the evidence for the failures of India and China is their lack of the notion of the tragic. India never recognizes the Self because it fails to recognize negation; it does not recognize the And because there is only the particularity of the given circumstances. As Rosenzweig puts it, "There is no human ideal which stays as much a prisoner to all articulation of the natural character as does the Indian ideal." For Rosenzweig, Indian religion cannot escape particularity, because all duty is bound to particularity, all is conditioned.[109] In contrast, whereas India remains utterly bound up with particularity and character, China is lacking in this connection. Rosenzweig writes, "Whereas here the world is rich and too rich in individuality, man however, at least to the extent he is not outwardly seen as part of the world, is thus the inner man, that is to say without character."[110] According to Rosenzweig, Chinese religion cultivates the hollowing out of interiority and is characterized by its impersonality. The figures of both Indian and Chinese religions, according to Rosenzweig, fail to produce the conditions necessary for Greece's tragic hero.

What are we to make of these rather grotesque depictions of the religions of China and India?[111] For one thing, Rosenzweig's hierarchical juxtaposition of Greece alongside the religions of India and China reveals the problematic nature of his attempt to treat theology in a serious philosophical manner. His criteria of the Yes, No, and And are hardly convincing, their fulfillment in Greece all but inevitable.[112] For example, in regard to Man, how can we possibly ascertain that the tragic is the legitimate criterion and is thus superior to an ascetic ideal? There is no necessity to Rosenzweig's criteria except what he claims to derive from Revelation, which is conveniently accessible only by Jews and Christians. Rosenzweig's notion of Revelation—apparently derived from experience, in particular the ostensibly different modes of experience in which Jews and Christians experience it—is, at bottom, philosophically arbitrary.[113] It demonstrates precisely the problem with trying to integrate theology and philosophy: One incorporates assumptions particular to a specific tradition or traditions into one's philosophical analysis, which is supposed to be free of such biases. Despite the fanfare Rosenzweig has and continues to receive in Jewish Studies, it is hard to take these accounts seriously in any philosophical sense.

However, it would be a mistake to read and judge Rosenzweig solely on the tenability of the categories of his thought. Indeed, if we shift our attention away from rigor to the rhetorical or to the structure of the work, it becomes clear that the schematic caricaturing of these religions plays an essential role in *The Star of Redemption*. It produces the divide between the Orient and the Occident that in turn creates the conditions for privileging his idiosyncratic accounts of Judaism and Christianity.

In Rosenzweig's philosophical-theological account of *Heilsgeschichte,* paganism—a concatenation of Greek and German philosophy and culture—plays a decisive role in the current, Johannine epoch of Christianity. As Bruce Rosenstock shows, Rosenzweig is attempting to bring to his readers' attention the two choices they face: either to revert to pre-1800 paganism or to accept Revelation. In a similar vein, Benjamin Pollock recently suggests that in *The Star* Rosenzweig is not just attempting to offer an account of the whole but also empowers the reader: "As a human being who stands in the 'middle' of the realization of the system of the One and All, who grasps the system as it hovers between hiddenness and revelation, I have a choice." That is, the reader—as one on whom the Absolute is dependent and one who can effect "the ultimate systematic unification of all that is"—thus "faces a decision" about "whether to take up the call of revelation."[114]

We have not yet discussed Revelation, which is the central theme of Section II of *The Star*—and arguably the central theme of the entire book—because a full understanding of it requires that the three elements of the primordial, pre-factual world be fully developed. Pollock's suggestion that Rosenzweig's system is itself bound up with an existential choice helps us see that not only do the religions of India and China serve as the dark background against which Greece, paganism proper, stands forth but they also insinuate a critique of the efforts among Rosenzweig's contemporaries to redefine the nature of the West via the Orient. Rosenzweig depicts these religions as attempts to flee God, as expressions of a sort of existential cowardice. There is no question that Rosenzweig paints these religions in an unflattering light. Yet we must bear in mind that his critique came at a time when, as Tomoko Masuzawa points out, something of a "sea change in the European relationship to the rest of the world,"[115] by means of history and comparative linguistics, made possible a radical new de-Judaization of European culture:

> The idea of Aryan Christianity was apparently intriguing to many, so much so that there appeared a number of sensationally successful treatises in the latter half of the nineteenth century advocating that the true origin of Christianity, qua religion of Europe, should be sought not in the Hebrew Bible, but in some late Hellenic, possible Indo-Persian, or even Buddhist traditions.[116]

Rosenzweig's work, if overly schematic, adamantly rejects this possibility. To return to the Marcionite heresy discussed earlier in the chapter, within the Christian, the "blond and blue eyed" "Siegfried," the nationalist, struggles against the "figure of the crucified man,"[117] seeking alternative foundations for his or her identity, ones that do not require a forfeiture of mythic origins. India and China, the religions of the East—at least in the way they existed in the modern European imaginary—are nothing short of idolatry. They are flights from God, because they threaten what Rosenzweig claims is the true core of the Occident—genuine Revelation—of which Judaism, and Judaism alone, is the great witness.

Thus, if we step back from trying to justify Rosenzweig's account philosophically/theologically or attempting to defend his claims by locating the fault in the constraints of his system, we can see that his sharp caricatures are part and parcel of the larger concern with German Orientalism. Where Cohen charged his contemporaries looking for new origins of Christianity with committing a "religious injustice against the Old Testament,"[118] Rosenzweig provides a theology/metaphysics that renders the religions of the Orient deficient. With Revelation as the measuring stick, only Greece (in Rosenzweig's idiosyncratic account of it) continues to have relevance: All other Oriental religions are merely historical, and what is more, they deflect one's attention from the divine.

Revelation and Islam

If the religions of the East, namely, India and China, reflected those religions that had not attained factuality, Rosenzweig turns to a different Oriental religion, Islam, to exemplify and embody another deficient mode of religiosity. That is, if the religions of China and India represent a failure of nerve before the decisionism that *The Star of Redemption* seeks to foster in its readers, then Islam represents the result of the wrong decision (i.e., the choice in favor of paganism). As I mentioned earlier, while many contemporary scholars acknowledge the inadequacy of Rosenzweig's account of Islam, they would prefer not to acknowledge how deeply intertwined it is with the fundamental philosophical project of *The Star*,[119] Rosenzweig uses Islam as a cipher that allows him to reject the dominant mode of Jewish thought, rationalism, in the generation prior to his own.[120] Through his rejection of Jewish rationalism, which often maintained antagonistic relationships with Christian culture, Rosenzweig redefines the Occident in terms of Revelation.

Rosenzweig's rejection of Jewish rationalism—which was bound up with Jewish liberalism—manifests itself through the cipher of Islam. Susannah Heschel has recently argued that German Jewish thinkers sought to establish a filial relationship with Islam. As Heschel notes, these scholars constructed "an alliance with Islam" and in the process sought to marginalize Christianity "theologically" for its "dogma contrary to reason, miracles, and the supernatural."[121] Heschel suggests that German Jewish scholars read religious rationalism and liberalism into Islam and used it as an ally to render what they perceived as the conservative and dogmatic nature of Christianity to be the exception rather than the rule. For example, whereas Hermann Cohen rarely commented about any religion other than Christianity—which he mostly disparaged or radically and idiosyncratically reinterpreted—he wrote in respectful terms about the "intimate relationship between Judaism and Islam."[122] Similarly, the legendary Islamicist Ignác Goldziher (1822–1921) maintained strong ties to the Haskalah, the Jewish Enlightenment, and, as Lawrence Conrad points out, was a "a bitter critic of Christianity for" among other things, "what he saw as its absurd doctrines [and] intolerance."[123] Yet, in contrast to liberal rationalists like Cohen and Goldziher, it is precisely by means of the recovery of mythology, dogma, and miracles—all elements associated with Christianity, not with rationalized Islam—that Rosenzweig makes the basis of his account of Judaism. Rosenzweig's break from rationalism therefore reverses the Jewish turn from Islam to Christianity.

If rationalism is cast as pagan, and the new grounding of Judaism is to be supernatural Revelation (as opposed to Cohen's rationalized, demythologized account of it), then (Jewish) scholarship on Islam proves a ready-made tool for Rosenzweig to use in refashioning the Occident (i.e., the fraternal, if antagonistic, relationship between Judaism and Christianity). Rosenzweig links this rationalized Islam with Idealism, a mode of thinking he associates with paganism, an approach to life that is cast as lacking access to genuine Revelation. To be sure, Rosenzweig makes tendentious claims such as comparing Allah to an "Oriental

Despot" or calling Islam a case of "world-historical plagiarism."[124] These give the appearance of a simplistic Eurocentrism that belies the complexity of what is at stake in his alignment of Judaism with Christianity rather than Islam.

Indeed, despite his claims of Islam's theological despotism, the manner in which Rosenzweig actually discusses Islamic theology/philosophy reveals a link to the ethical Idealism of Kant and Cohen. Yossef Schwartz suggests the following:

> Between Islam and philosophical idealism—because these two streams of thought suggest world interpretations—Rosenzweig understands a fundamental analogy that has influenced the classical heritage of pagan philosophy up to the modern era. The belittlement of Islam would imply a belittlement of idealism, and Rosenzweig uses the foreign religious faith in order to reject the more familiar philosophical faith.[125]

Schwartz is correct to link Islam and Idealism, but I want to suggest that Rosenzweig's linkage of Islam and Idealism functions in the opposite direction as well. By rejecting Idealism, Rosenzweig is rejecting the basis on which Jewish scholars had sought to link the two religions: demythologization and rationalization. Instead revelation and theology become the basis for joining Judaism with another religion. By overturning the priorities that made Islam seem like an ally for liberal, rationalist Judaism, Rosenzweig reverses course, casting Judaism and Christianity as siblings in Revelation against Islam and the Orient more generally.

Therefore Islam plays a significant role in all three books of part II of *The Star*, where experience rooted in the lived encounter with Revelation brings the sharpest break between Rosenzweig and the Idealism of "Old Thinking," including the work of Cohen. Part II of *The Star of Redemption* marks the shift from the protocosmos of the elements, God-World-Man, in their individuality, to factuality, the interaction of these elements.[126] Most importantly, it is here that we find the living God who is bound up with the World and Man through Creation, Revelation, and Redemption. However, both Creation and Redemption are disclosed and accessed through Revelation, which is the main focus of this part. This "new concept of God that Revelation brings . . . establishes God's relationship to the world and man with an unequivocalness and unconditionality totally foreign to paganism."[127] Islam, then, serves as the dark background against which Revelation shines forth. Conversely, to understand Islam, we must first understand Rosenzweig's account of Revelation.

Genuine Revelation: God's Beloved

Rosenzweig seeks to ground his methodology in the experience of Revelation, which has at least two meanings for him.[128] The first manifests itself in Creation, and the second, more narrow, meaning is Revelation proper. Revelation in its broader sense is bound up with Creation because Creation cannot be understood in a straightforward causal sense, as God having created the world "once and for all"; instead Creation consists of the "continuous Revelation [of the world] as creature. For the world it is therefore not its appearance as Creation, but as Revelation."[129] The God of the proto-cosmos was hidden; he was the God of myth. "But God the Creator is in the beginning,"[130] in the sense that Creation occurs after the configuration of the world. Creation is "the breaking in of the consciousness," the sense of "of being a creature, of its consciousness of being constantly created." That is, for creatures, Creation is the "consciousness of being constantly created."[131] Creation here is understood phenomenologically (although not in the sense of the Husserlian tradition), rather than in a cosmological sense.

Rosenzweig's new methodology is characterized by a marriage of philosophy and theology, or philosophy driven by the experience of Revelation, which is not about "content" but "event"; more precisely, Revelation is not so much "life . . . as lived experience—the preconditions [for which] are not conceptual elements, but existing reality."[132] In *The Star*, Rosenzweig makes the transition from the proto-cosmos, detouring through the nothings, to the realm of experience where through Creation, Revelation, and Redemption, the three elements, God-World-Man, come into relationship with one another. Islam (as well as Idealism) is used as the example of that which remains pagan, of that which does not make this transition from the proto-cosmos such that the elements interact with one another.

Creation, initiated by the inner transformation on the side of God, breaks forth from the protocosmos such that God and World are no longer isolated elements but now are inextricably bound up with one another. To account for the relationship between God and World Rosenzweig uses Cohen's notion of correlation [*Korrelation*], where two terms are in relationship with each other without either being sublated to the other. As Cohen puts it, "*A change does not occur*: *Rather a preservation [Erhaltung] at the same time of separation [Sonderung] and unification [Vereinigung]. In the separation the unification preserves itself, and in the unification the separation preserves itself.*"[133] The notion of correlation allows both for a relationship among the elements and for the elements to maintain their integrity. For Rosenzweig this means that all three elements, God, World, and Man, maintain their ontological independence even as they transcend the isolation of the protocosmos in their interrelationships with one another.

For Rosenzweig, Revelation proper is a second, narrower notion of Revelation that follows on the sense of Revelation inherent in Creation. It "must be a Revelation that 'does not posit' anything," that is, "it is quite essentially Revelation and nothing else."[134] Revelation, "the illumination of such a blink of the eye," of course, is bound up with Creation because "every thing represents . . . a testimony [to God] already because it is a created thing and the Creation is already itself the first Revelation."[135] That is, this second notion of Revelation builds on and reaffirms the notion of Revelation inherent in Creation.

According to Rosenzweig, in genuine faith (that which is present in Judaism and Christianity), Revelation is an event; it is momentary, purely present. In Revelation, God and Man, two primordial elements, now externalized out of themselves, enter directly into a relationship. The primary content of this Revelation is love. God loves the human being, who in this moment of receiving God's love becomes the beloved of God. God loves the human being as human being, thus preserving the individuality of the human, of the beloved. "The faithful belief of the beloved acquiesces to the love of the lover, bound to the moment, and reinforces it so far as to make it a lasting love . . . The faith of the soul testifies, in its faithfulness, to the love of God, and it gives to it permanent being."[136] God's very existence, Rosenzweig suggests, is bound to human recognition: "If you testify to me, then I shall be God, and otherwise not—these are the words that the Master of the Kabbalah puts into the mouth of the God of love. The lover who surrenders himself in love is recreated in the faithfulness of the beloved, and the beloved from then on, it is forever."[137] This is a prime example of how seriously Rosenzweig incorporates Cohen's notion of the correlation; God and Man become not merely irreducible to one another but also cannot fully exist without the other.[138]

There is something anarchic and exclusive about love. "God always loves only whom and what he loves." And yet this love is always expanding:

> What separates his love from an "all-love" is only a "not yet"; it is only 'not yet' that God loves everything besides what he already loves. His love traverses the world from an always new impulse. It is always in the today and entirely in the today, but every dead yesterday and tomorrow are one day swallowed into this triumphant today: this love is the eternal victory over death.[139]

God's love does not proceed in all directions; it is not predictable and is completely unforeseeable "except for the one certainty that the love will one day seize even that which has not yet been seized."[140] Creation and Redemption, two states that possess totality, the "all at once," constitute the past (Creation) and the future (Redemption), but the present—love, Revelation—lacks this completeness; it is characterized by a "not yet." The present is still in motion, still under construction.[141]

The beloved, according to Rosenzweig, returns God's love, not directly to God but through the neighbor. The neighbor is not valued for who he or she is but only as "a representative; he is not loved for himself, he is not loved for his beautiful eyes, but only because he is just there, because he is just my neighbor. In his place—in this place that is for me the one neighboring on me—there could just as well be another person."[142] The neighbor is merely a "place keeper" to whom one is directed by love, until finally one covers the world with love. "So action is oriented toward the world; the world is the other pole toward which the love of neighbor strives."[143] There is a striking lack of ethics here; instead the work of redemption is oriented toward one's duty to God, not to the Other.[144]

Redemption is oriented toward the future, which "is experienced only in the waiting. Here the last must be the first in thought."[145] This is a peculiar notion that Rosenzweig elaborates a bit in the following passage about the Kingdom of God, which he equates with the future[146]:

> The Kingdom, the vitalization of existence, comes from the beginning; it is always coming. So its growth is necessary. It is always in the future—but in the future it is always. It is just as much present as it is in the future. Once and for all, it is not yet there. It is coming eternally. Eternity is not a very long time, but a tomorrow that could just as well be a today that would be conscious of being more than today. And to say that the Kingdom is eternally coming means that its growth is no doubt necessary, but that the rhythm of this growth is not definite, or, more exactly: that the growth does not have any relationship to time. An existence that has once entered into the Kingdom cannot fall back outside again; it has entered under the sign of the once-and-for-all, it has become eternal.[147]

The perpetual possibility that the Messiah, the future, will arrive is precisely what keeps one directed forward. Redemption is unlike Creation and Revelation in that it involves all three elements, i.e., God, World and Man. "To man and the world, only One Third Party is added, only One can become their Redeemer."[148] That is, Redemption involves God simultaneously relating to Man and World, or rather, Redemption is the ever present promise that this will take place even if it has not yet. To be sure, one can make progress toward the Kingdom, incorporate something into the once-and-for-all, but as to when the once-and-for-all will reign over the world, that moment always remains not yet. In Redemption, experienced proleptically, the All is experienced here and now, and yet it is experienced only as a trace. Not as present. As Alexander Altmann points out, "Eternity is presentness and future at the same time. It is a dimension of existence rather than a fixed point to be reached. The 'waiting for the Messiah' is not mere passive expectancy but means entering into eternity, living in the Kingdom, and giving birth to the Kingdom."[149] Eternity is an existential term, and yet, even though it interacts dialogically with history, can never be incorporated with history.[150]

Rosenzweig's account of Creation, God, love, Revelation, and Redemption stand in stark contrast to the prominent rationalist understanding of such notions held by those in the previous generation. That earlier generation, of course, was largely dominated by the thought of Hermann Cohen, along with the scholars of the *Wissenschaft des Judentums* who rejected the supernatural, "living" God. Kant, not Schelling, was the order of the day. Rosenzweig's rejection of the values of his parents' generation, of religious rationalism and liberalism, can be seen in his account of Islam.

Islam: The Pagan Alternative

Rosenzweig critiques Islam, as he does Idealism, for failing to preserve the integrity of all three elements—God-World-Man—in its account of the ordering of the whole. Idealism is identifiably Greek in its origins, reducing everything willy-nilly to the World. Islam, in contrast, radically prioritizes God over the other elements, Man and World, such that there can be no genuine interrelationship between them (i.e., no Creation, Revelation, Redemption in the sense in which Rosenzweig defines these terms). However, Islam is not identical to philosophy, which as we recall is traditionally grounded in the priority of the World. Yet, like the Idealism he critiques, Islam fails to provide for the factual accounts of God-World-Man, but rather retains them in their pre-factual, pre-reversed, state. As a result, he avers that Islam can claim the relationships of Creation, Revelation and Redemption in name only. Because God stays hidden, does not undergo the reversal that takes place in becoming actual, there is a lack of any causality beyond that which is accessible to reason (i.e., Idealism). Thus, although it claims Revelation for itself, Islam never undergoes "the inner reversal of its direction" out of the naught to something.[151] As a result, Rosenzweig refers to Islam's notion of Revelation as a "remarkable case of world historical plagiarism," which allows us to see "what a belief in Revelation would necessarily look like when springing directly from paganism so to speak without God's will, without the plan of his providence, that is, in 'purely natural' causality."[152] For Rosenzweig, Islam is as pagan as Idealism, except that where Idealism prioritizes World it prioritizes God.

Islam is unable to maintain the correlation between God and World because it overemphasizes God at the expense of the World. In Rosenzweig's account, Islam depicts God as so radically superior to and independent from the World that human beings can have no real relationship with the divine. By attributing such absoluteness to God, "God's creative self-emergence is made into a mere unessential factuality for him, and God's essence is thrust into a height that is foreign to the world, raised above the world."[153] God is the creator in Islam, but "like an oriental despot" God creates on a whim and could have created otherwise.[154] Creation, the relationship between God and World, is thus fundamentally arbitrary. There is no sense of necessity, but rather, each moment is isolated and fails to connect with all others. In other words, the divine is radically separate from the World and Man, just as in paganism.

Rosenzweig claims that Islam's account of Revelation "emerged without mediation from out of the living God of myth without the reversal of the Yes and No."[155] Islam's notion of Revelation is much more similar to faith's notion of

Creation, which is characterized by the past tense and its all-at-once nature, than its notion of Revelation. What this really means is that whereas faith's notion of Revelation is spontaneous or, rather, depends on time and is unpredictable—God chooses whom God chooses—Islam emphasizes the universality of God's love and of the duty of the human being, or in Rosenzweig's parlance, Man, to God. The rationalist echoes are unmistakable.[156]

Where Rosenzweig casts Revelation according to faith (i.e., in Judaism and Christianity) as piecemeal and unpredictable, in which God's love is characterized by the "not yet" and thus is opposed to the notion of the "all-love" of the future, of Redemption, "Allah's essence is that 'all-love,' which does not boundlessly, in every moment, give itself away to love." That is, rather than Revelation being given as a purely arbitrary gift that arises in the moment in a purely unpredictable event, Islam offers "Revelation to humanity like an objective gift from out of itself." This gift comes not from love but from mercy, because "God is the God of Mercy, every Sura in the Koran says it: Mercy is his attribute, it shines from its essence upon all men, upon all peoples." That is, there is no exclusive or unpredictable element in this mercy. It is necessary and universal, much like the reasoning of the idealists. Rosenzweig contends that "the Koran rejects from the concept of God the idea of a partisan preference, in favor of a people, for instance. To every people, and, not only to the Arabs, Allah has sent a prophet." However, in Islam's view, it is the unfortunate case that not every people has heeded these prophets.[157] Islam's notion of Revelation resembles Kant's and Cohen's vision of the religion of reason in that it requires that all human beings have access to it, whereas for Rosenzweig, genuine Revelation will move beyond the communities of Jews and Christians or, rather, all non-Jews will be incorporated into Christianity only when Redemption comes.

Whereas Rosenzweig characterizes "genuine" Revelation by love, Islam's notion of Revelation is characterized by mercy. There is no mutuality in mercy. It is unidirectional, from God to man. Where faith's notion of Revelation is piecemeal, Islam's notion of Revelation "is complete from the beginning: to Adam, and to all the prophets who followed, God ordained 'Islam'!" Indeed, where "faith" believes in a God who loves, in an exclusive God who loves some people more than others or sooner than others, for no discernible reason, for Islam the relationship between God and human beings is grounded in merit. "The Patriarchs, the Prophets, Jesus: all are 'believers' in the full, theological and received sense of the word. Mohammed's superiority comes from his personal qualities, and not, for example, from the fact that he would have received the greatest quantity of divine love." Mercy does not have the character of an event. God's love is "simple once and for all, it has been given to the world; there is no increase in it."[158] There is a rationalizing of God in Islam, a denuding God of choice, such that merit is made the basis of relationships that Rosenzweig seeks to depict as lifeless in comparison to the

"God of faith." He writes, "Contrary to the God of faith, Allah could not tell his own to their face that he chose them before all others, in their sins, and was calling them to account for their sins."[159] Allah does not love sinners, which Rosenzweig claims is the foundation of faith. Thus Rosenzweig depicts Allah as lacking "divine humility,"[160] but he also tellingly likens this quality to reason; as I mentioned earlier, he even titles one of his subsections of Islam, "Islam: Religion der Vernunft,"[Islam: Religion of Reason] which clearly calls into mind the conceptual, moral, and non-passionate depictions of God by figures such as Immanuel Kant and Hermann Cohen. Indeed, in many ways, this depiction of Islam resembles German Idealism, especially its manifestation in the work of Kant and Cohen.[161] As mentioned, Cohen holds that God forgives individuals for their sins only in the sense that they repent and work to make themselves worthy of this forgiveness. Forgiveness is purely a task initiated by the human being. God is an ideal or unchanging figure, and it is the self that must change, not God.

In contrast to the immediacy of the event of Revelation for Judaism and Christianity, apparently in Islam, "one can see it like a sign in Revelation that it is here from the very beginning, that which, in faith, even for its own consciousness, is only gradual and never completely finished."[162] Indeed, Rosenzweig harshly decries the conception of Revelation being merely a book: "The Book sent down from heaven—can there be any greater distortion of the notion of God himself 'descending,' giving himself to man, of surrendering to him? He is enthroned in his highest heaven and given to man—a Book."[163] Again, the problem appears to be that the content or experience of Revelation occurs all at once, rather than taking place through time.[164] If it takes the form of a book, all that one needs to know is there, and there is no direct contact, no command from God to the human being to "love me."[165] Rather, Revelation is the content of a book, and thus there can be no genuine contact between God and human being except through emulation.[166]

What troubles Rosenzweig so much about Islam is that "if we must speak of love here, God would be the beloved and man the lover."[167] Such a situation reverses Rosenzweig's notion of Revelation, "which goes from God to man." Rosenzweig declares this reversal as a sort of arrogance on the part of man, or as he puts it, "In Islam, it is actually man who in the end forces Revelation."[168] God is not the agent; instead human beings follow a code of duty seeking to actualize God. Again, this description could easily apply to the moral strain of German Idealism in Kant and Cohen. For Rosenzweig, such a view is unacceptable and pagan, because God is not a living presence that one experiences, but instead is distant, like an ideal.

If "God's ways" are unknowable, proceed in mystery, and without a discernible plan, "Islam has before its eyes such an exact, positive image which tells us how the world must be transformed by walking the way of Allah; precisely here its work in the world is proved to be pure obedience to a law imposed once and for all upon the will." That is, rather than God understood as an agent, revealing himself and making his love manifest, Islam and Idealism pursue God through reason. "The way of Allah is not elevated above the way of man inasmuch as the heavens are above the earth; on the contrary, the way of Allah means directly the way of his faithful."[169] For Rosenzweig, this is an intolerable violation of God's independence.

The distinction between Islam and the religions of faith (Judaism and Christianity), between obedience and neighbor love, manifests itself clearly in regard to religious war.[170] However, it is important to recognize that Rosenzweig also notes the humane side of Islam, that "Mohammed's prescriptions, as well as the right of war and of conquest formed on the basis of these precepts, go far beyond the contemporary practice of war, including the Christian in certain respects, Islam demanded and practiced 'tolerance' long before Christian Europe discovered this concept."[171] The difference between Islam and Christianity (Judaism is depicted as apolitical because it has no pagan element) is not the content, but the mode in which politics and war are carried out. Islam is more ethical, especially because it is seriously committed to something very close to the ethics of Idealism.[172] Rosenzweig's amoral view of neighbor love is rather chilling. Rosenzweig writes, "Love of the neighbor could lead to consequences that were not degenerations, but legitimate developments and which yet at first sight do not at all enter into the framework of this love, like the religious war and the Inquisition."[173] Rosenzweig's critique of holy war is not that it uses violence; instead his ire is directed toward its all too human source: God's Revelation does not drive it, but rather agency lies squarely with the Human Being.[174]

If Hermann Cohen sought to demonstrate the ways in which Kant's thought was harmonious with the prophets and is thus Jewish, Rosenzweig casts Kant and his thought as Muslim. Again using very Kantian language, Rosenzweig insists that Islam's notion of law is absolute, "once and for all" and that it proceeds to reach its conclusions with "reason" in contrast to the "totally free and unpredictable love" of Judaism and Christianity.[175] The act of submission to God and God's law is a perpetual one. Indeed, it is not individuals who are to be recognized but God and God's will:

> In Islam, there are no accounts of the saints; their memory is honored, but this memory is without content, it is only the memory of piety in general. This piety that simply obeys is based on free self-denial, laboriously re-conquered at every moment: it is noteworthy that it finds it exact counterpart in worldly piety which freely inserts itself into the general law, as in modern times, the ethics of Kant and his followers, for example.[176]

Indeed, as Schwartz and Palmer highlight, Rosenzweig uses here the Christian critique of legalism usually directed against Jews, but shifts it against Islam instead. However, where Judaism is faulted for reducing love to legalism, Rosenzweig seeks here to charge Islam with rendering love "exclusively as ethicism."[177] For Rosenzweig, Islam lacks God's presence, God's call. Indeed, Islam is precisely the ethical, that which has measure and proceeds from reason to the world. Its fault lies precisely in its lack of a teleological suspension of the ethical, its lack of zealotry. It is too Kantian.

Similarly, the genuine religions of Revelation for Rosenzweig experience eternity, the future, as always possible at any moment, its in-break as a genuine possibility. In contrast, Islam appears quite close to—and probably modeled on—Cohen's notion of the future as an eternal process that is never fulfilled, an ideal one strives for but never reaches. Islam's notion of the future, like Idealism's, is the counter-image of genuine Revelation.[178] In Islam "the times represent an infinite series, but infinite does not mean eternal, infinite only means 'always.'" In other words, all people face the same duty, the same relationship to God. For Rosenzweig, there is an endless succession of time, an infinite sequence that "more closely resembles a past than a future."[179]

> So nothing runs more counter for this authentic idea of progress than the possibility that the "ideal goal" could and must be realized perhaps from the moment that is coming, and even at this moment. This is almost the shibboleth by which one can tell the believer in the Kingdom (who uses the word "progress" only so to speak the language of the times and in reality means the Kingdom) from the true worshiper of progress.[180]

Cohen, whose thought is often linked to the notion of progress and who certainly employs the notion of the ideal goal, is clearly a—if not *the*—target of this critique ostensibly directed towards Islam.

Islam is, then, all too human. By prizing rationality rather than Revelation it is heretical, trying to force God's hand rather than letting God reveal God's self.[181] Rosenzweig's account of Islam is a slightly veiled depiction of rational religion, particularly liberal Judaism as expounded by Hermann Cohen. In Rosenzweig's Occident, Judaism and Christianity—the religions of Revelation, are bound together by God's love, which is irreducible to reason.

Yet has Rosenzweig really undercut Islam? Has Rosenzweig really described Islam at all? Although critics are uncomfortable with the pejorative and frankly Orientalist language Rosenzweig uses to describe Islam and for his banishing it from the Abrahamic religions, his account of Islam is—beneath all of the insults and trumped-up charges—nothing other than an account of religious liberalism. Indeed, if one is to read his claims abstractly, to take a step back from his rather declamatory style[182] and the authority that is granted to his voice in the academy, and simply analyze his arguments as presented, he offers no reasons why Islam or, to be more accurate, religious liberalism of any sort deserves less respect other than the emphasis on Revelation that he advocates. By no means does Rosenzweig convincingly establish that his system is to be preferred to Kant's or Cohen's: he merely asserts it. Its power, I contend, lies not in the argument itself, but in the manner in which Rosenzweig—and his generation of German Jews—shifted the focus from religious liberalism, from rationality, to the irrational, to conceiving of Revelation as an irruption of the divine, as something beyond the ken of reason.

* * *

Rosenzweig offers a system that radically separates the Jews from the nations of the world and, indeed, from history itself. Thus, if Cohen emphasizes the philosophical dimensions of Judaism at the expense of the corporeal and lived, Rosenzweig's "factuality" imbues the Jews with a unique significance for the West by nothing less than theological fiat. To be sure, Rosenzweig's *The Star of Redemption* claims that Revelation (more specifically Jewish and Christian Revelation) is part of the human experience and thus needs to be incorporated into philosophical discourse, because philosophy must speak to life. By turning to Revelation as defined in this idiosyncratic manner, Rosenzweig indeed creates a new language, a new idiom, through which he hopes to transcend the world religions discourse and the scholarship and institutions seeking to legitimate it. But such a strategy consists in the construction of philosophical/theological structures that are, at best, tendentious and, at worst, arbitrary in order to avoid history and to introduce the content of theology into philosophy. It is nothing less than an attempt to (re)constitute the Occident, to demonstrate that Judaism and Christianity, in their antagonism and their complementarity, constitute the "genuine" Occident. They are the recipients of God's Revelation. His strategy saves Judaism by placing it in a dialectical relationship with Christian *Heilgeschichte*, and it renders all other religions as obstacles of redemption.

4 Redeeming This World: Buber's Judaism and the Sanctity of Immanence

In the previous chapters I discussed the respective ways in which the world religions discourse affects and is reflected in the works of Hermann Cohen and Franz Rosenzweig. Hermann Cohen, as discussed in chapter 1, posits a rationalized notion of *Deutschtum* or Germanism. As the exemplar of the religion of reason, Judaism is correlated with Germanism by Cohen both in his wartime writings and in his methodological discussions of the concept of religion. However, as we saw already starting in chapter 1 and more explicitly in chapter 2, if read with sufficient care—particularly with regard to the manner in which he incorporates the figure of Jesus into Judaism in *Religion of Reason out of the Sources of Judaism* and select other writings—Cohen makes the case that Judaism should be the foundational source for Germany and Europe more generally. That is, he attempts nothing less than to offer a Judaic foundation for Christianity and the West.

In chapter 3, I explored the work of Franz Rosenzweig. Where Cohen argues that antisemitism is a sign of the need for rational/Jewish foundations, for the purification of culture through reason and science, Rosenzweig sees it as evidence of the inner tension—expressed as the inner connection—between Judaism and Christianity. That is, in his theological-cum-philosophical method, Rosenzweig thinks that Revelation, as understood in a quasi-phenomenological manner, demonstrates not only the inextricable bond between Judaism and Christianity but also their mutual antagonism—at least until the end of history when Redemption will occur. Christianity, which Rosenzweig envisions as the West in its political form, is charged with conquering the rest of the world (i.e., the Orient), while Judaism, being nonpolitical but religiously fulfilled, spurs on Christianity. Antisemitism serves as a theological tension driving the Occident ever outward against pagan within and non-Christian without. Rosenzweig's thought rejects Cohen's Idealism, emphasizing instead the power of a theologically imbued actuality.

If Rosenzweig follows Cohen—however significant their differences—in attempting to embed Judaism in the spiritual core of the Occident, the work of Martin Buber more closely resembles Cohen's interventions in the field of comparative religions. Of course, Buber has very different sensibilities than does Cohen, not philosophically but also with regard to the world religions discourse in general. *Ich und Du* [I and Thou] (1923),[1] unlike Cohen's *Religion of Reason out of the Sources of Judaism* or Rosenzweig's *The Star of Redemption*, does not emphasize Judaism's uniqueness; indeed, Judaism remains tacitly in the background,[2] while Buber employs figures from traditions prominent in the world religions discourse, including Greek and Indian. Where Cohen's *Der Begriff der Religion im System der Religion* seeks to intervene in methodological disputes in regard to the study of comparative religion—indeed, he wants nothing less than to question the validity of the field as a whole when it is not grounded in a philosophically rigorous foundation—as numerous scholars have pointed out, *I and Thou* is a bona fide foray into *Religionswissenschaft.*[3] Indeed, as Guy Stroumsa notes, "Buber conceived of *I and Thou* as a general introduction to a major interpretive effort on the phenomenology of religion,"[4] a core tool of the field of *Religionswissenschaft.*[5]

There are two consequences of approaching Buber as a *Religionswissenschaftler* that this chapter seeks to show are inextricably tied—at least in Buber's own mind. First, Buber's work is designed ultimately to counteract what he perceives to be the theological and philosophical foundations of what Paul Mendes-Flohr, following Ernst Bloch, calls "metaphysical anti-Semitism," namely, "the tendency to repudiate Judaism as a spiritually and culturally jejune religion 'essentially' alien to the Christian and European sensibility."[6] As we have seen, what Mendes-Flohr and Bloch term metaphysical antisemitism is bound up with the world religions discourse. Given our previous discussions of this discourse, it is clear that its methodological foundations were by no means neutral or disinterested. Thus, the fact that Buber is a Jew and nevertheless is taking part in the general study of religion, and not just speaking on behalf of Judaism, is itself subversive and political. To understand Buber within the context of this larger discourse, then, is to understand him as challenging and reinterpreting the prominent theological and philosophical assumptions of his non-Jewish German contemporaries.[7] In this vein, not only did Buber use, as Stroumsa points out, "the tools developed by scholars of comparative religion"[8] but he also did so in a manner that, in the words of Michael Zank, diminished any sense of "the difference between paganism and a religion of revelation."[9] That is, in *I and Thou* Buber boldly embraces the paradigm of the world religions discourse, although he seeks to provide a new philosophical foundation that is denuded of its antisemitism.

Second, Buber is writing in a time of great cultural pessimism.[10] Buber's studies in religion, as Zank points out, seek to demonstrate that the conditions of faith "attested to in the Bible" could be revived and were "a still-relevant possibility of human behavior and experience."[11] Central to Buber's work as a *Religionswissenschaftler* and philosopher, I argue, is his contestation of the resurgence of

Marcionism, in various configurations, among his Christian contemporaries. During the Weimar era, the figure of the first-century Christian heretic, Marcion of Sinope, played a pivotal role in the relationship between Jews and Christians and moreover served as a lightning rod within Christian thought itself.[12] As mentioned in the last chapter, in 1920 a major work by Adolf von Harnack, *Marcion: Das Evangelium vom fremden Gott* [Marcion: The Gospel of the Alien God],[13] brought fresh attention to this figure who sought to sever not merely the God of Creation from the God of Redemption but also the Old Testament from the New. Buber sees the resurgence of Marcionism as a result of alienation, of the great cultural pessimism of his age.

However, Buber does not simply offer a rival notion of God to that presented by Marcion. He offers a *Heilsgeschichte* [salvation history] of sorts, one that accounts for the illness of the present age. Indeed, it is not much of a stretch to find in this diagnosis an account of the roots of the resurgent Marcionism. Where Hermann Cohen finds the crisis of modernity to lie in threats to reason such as vulgar nationalism, xenophobia, and irrational forms of religiosity, Buber sees the problem of modernity to be spiritlessness in the West, with the "cultivation [*Ausbildung*] of experiencing and the capacity to use" at the expense of the "man's power to enter into relation [*Beziehungskraft des Menschen*]—the power in virtue of which alone man can live the life of the spirit" [*der Mensch im Geist leben kann*].[14] According to Buber, the present age is saturated with a feeling of overwhelming pessimism, where feelings of stifling predestination and powerlessness in the face of cosmic and social forces leave its inhabitants hopeless. It is against such a dismal horizon that the idea that redemption can only come from outside the world, from a radically transcendent God, might seem attractive and plausible. However, for Buber, to reject transcendence in favor of immanence is to profoundly misunderstand not only the human predicament but also the metaphysical structure of reality. To grasp the manner in which Buber seeks to counteract Marcionism we must explore the philosophical vision and its concomitant *Heilsgeschichte* as elucidated in *I and Thou*.

The chapter proceeds as follows. It begins with a discussion of Harnack's account of Marcion. It then offers a careful reading of *I and Thou*, highlighting the manner in which Buber's phenomenology of religion offers a profoundly worldly and therefore anti-Marcionite account of holiness and redemption. This reading shows that Buber departs from Cohen and Rosenzweig, who see Jews as relatively powerless witnesses to higher orders of reality, whether reason or redemption respectively. Buber instead links Judaism to the Orient, to "primitives," and to worldly vitality. Indeed, Judaism, which for Buber celebrates this world and its endless potential for the manifestation of the divine, is the antidote to the Marcionism then capitalizing on the enervated spiritual energies of the modern West. Buber's emphasis on sanctifying the world, on divine immanence, is a clear rebuff to the spiritual core of Marcionism, rooted as it is in alienation from the world.[15] Yet it is not enough to counter its political expressions, because they are but symptoms of a deeper underlying spiritual illness. Using a notion of decisionism, tied to his distinction between Fate [*Verhältnis*] and Destiny [*Schiksal*], Buber offers a new basis in which to understand religion. By offering a notion of God inextricable from, but not reducible to, the world, Buber, in contrast to Marcion, emphasizes the unity of God of Creation and Redemption and the relationship of this God with human beings.

Marcion

Although fascination about the Gnostics surged dramatically in Weimar Germany among Jewish and Christian scholars and theologians,[16] Buber's attitude toward Gnosticism remains almost uniformly negative. In contrast to nuanced studies among Jewish philosophers such as Hans Jonas and Jacob Taubes regarding the differences and subtleties of various gnostic movements, Buber tends to conflate these movements with Marcionism.[17] Indeed, it is difficult to overestimate the centrality of the figure of Marcion of Sinope (d. 160) and the central tenets of Marcionism to Buber's understanding of "authentic" religiosity. Buber steadfastly contests the resurgence of Marcionism in its various configurations, particularly its emphasis on the otherworldly and transcendent as the site of holiness.

In 1920, Adolf von Harnack's *Marcion: The Gospel of the Alien God* brought fresh attention to the figure of Marcion of Sinope. Marcion claimed that there existed a thoroughgoing distinction between the God of Creation on the one hand and the God of Redemption; as a result, the Old Testament, tied to the God of Creation, is profoundly at odds with the New Testament, which is bound to the God of Redemption. During the Weimar era, Marcionism played a pivotal role in the relationship between Jews and Christians and galvanized Christian thought.[18] An oft-quoted passage from Harnack's book states, "*The rejection of the Old Testament in the second century was a mistake which the great church rightly avoided; to maintain it in the sixteenth century was a fate from which the Reformation was not yet able to escape; but still to preserve it in Protestantism as a canonical document since the nineteenth century is the consequence of a religious and ecclesiastical crippling.*"[19]

Harnack's widely read study—like his lectures on *What is Christianity?*—loomed large in the mind of his Jewish contemporaries.[20] As mentioned in chapter 1, Harnack, a preeminent Protestant historian of religion, shared the desire of many of his peers to separate Christianity and Germanism from Judaism. In any event, Marcionism as a theological worldview, the desire to separate the Old Testament from the New, and German *Religionswissenschaft* were, if not identical, a constellation of interrelated and overlapping projects and concerns.

It should not be surprising then that, in fin-de-siècle Germany, Marcion enjoyed a surge of interest among German intellectuals and theologians, at least in part because advances in philology and archaeology, as well as the *Orientalistik* vogue, made the great heretic's desire to separate the Old Testament from the New seem tenable on philological or historical grounds. Buber attributes the increasing hostility to Judaism and the Old Testament in German Christianity to the resurgence of Marcionism and its devaluation of this world, which place salvation and holiness in a radical transcendence.[21] In "Die Schrift und Ihre Verdeutschung," [Scripture and its Germanization] Buber acknowledges that his and Rosenzweig's concerns about resurgent Marcionism motivated their effort to translate the Hebrew Bible into German. Specifically, Buber cites a letter from July 1925 in which Rosenzweig expresses his "fear . . . the Marcionites will seek to expel the [Hebrew] Bible from German culture."[22] Rosenzweig's worries were not unfounded, but prophetic. Far from an abstraction, the heresy of Marcionism was tied to efforts to de-Judaize Christianity and Germany itself. Indeed, as Buber says in his 1939 speech, "The Spirit of Israel and the World Today,"

> Three years after the death of Harnack in 1930, his idea, the idea of Marcion, was put into action; not however by spiritual means but by means of violence and terror. The state of which Harnack was a citizen placed before the Church one of two alternatives: either to exclude Judaism and the spirit of Israel entirely from its midst, and thereby to renounce any influence over the affairs of this world, the affairs of the state and society; or else to be overthrown together with Judaism.[23]

As Susannah Heschel chronicled in *The Aryan Jesus*, the Institute for the Study of the Eradication of Jewish Influence on German Life was formally established in 1939 under the German Protestant theologian Walter Grundmann.[24]

Buber sees Marcion's radical separation of justice and love in the "vulgarizing of a spiritual process" [*Vulgariesierung eines geistigen Prozesses*] whereby "'German Christians' and the ongoing 'German faith-movement'" seek to create a fissure in the notion of God itself, depicting the God of Creation as a God of justice but not love. This rupture in the Christian notion of God is inextricably bound, in Buber's eyes—and historically in the teachings of Marcion—with the attempt to sever the Old Testament from the New.[25] This attempt, which also severs God from the world, leads to the stripping away of divine significance from the actual world. Buber's emphasis on sanctifying the world, on divine immanence, is a clear rebuff to the spiritual core of Marcionism. It allows for quietism, a forfeiture of the political to the powers of the world. In Buber's estimation, Marcionism is a religiosity that exacerbates the travails of modernity. It is not enough to counter its political expressions, because they are but symptoms of a deeper underlying spiritual illness.

One cannot help noticing that Harnack's depiction of Marcion has much in common with the methods of his fellow Protestant theologians who had long sought to undermine the Jewish elements of the Bible. Marcion, who made no pretense to divine revelation, sought to free himself of later interpretations that he considered corrupt and too Jewish, relying instead on reasons internal to the text "only with the means of philology"[26] as support. Indeed, when speaking about Marcion's attempt to get behind the text, to retrieve Paul's genuine thoughts, Harnack explicitly compares him with Ferdinand Christian Baur, founder of the Tübingen school of higher criticism: "The parallels with the work of the Tübingen school are here everywhere so striking that they do not require any singling out."[27] However, where *Religionswissenschaft* studied the history of Judaism to explain and shore up Christian foundations,[28] Marcion sought to excavate an Ur-text from beneath the accretions of the "'psuedoapostoli et Judaici evangelizatores'" [false apostles and Jewish evangelists].[29] For members of the Tübingen school and for Marcion, that which is Jewish serves as an otherness against which to define and illuminate the New Testament.[30]

However, as I mentioned earlier, it would be a mistake to simply conflate Harnack, or *Religionswissenschaft* more generally, with Marcion's exegetical project. Where *Religionswissenschaft* was driven by some combination of linguistics, Assyriology, and racial theory, Marcion was guided by a philology oriented to a specific theological vision. Yet, Marcion's theology seemed quite compatible with the new scholarly technologies developed by the *Religionswissenschaftlers,*[31] whose methodologies accorded quite well with his de-Judaizing agenda. To best understand Buber's thought, it is helpful to think of Marcionism or, at least its resurgence in modernity, as having a core philosophical/theological level that can be viewed apart from scholarly methodologies which might foster it. Indeed, *I and Thou* targets this theological/philosophical core of Marcionism.

What is the philosophical/theological core of Marcionism?[32] Harnack treats Marcion as one who "*developed with utmost consistency the religion of inwardness,*" as the culmination of a "five-hundred-year development in the internalizing of religion."[33] That is, for Harnack, Marcion recognizes in the newness of Paul's message a radical change in the nature of God; indeed, the change is so radical that we must speak of two Gods: the World-Creator God of the Old Testament and the alien God who brings redemption from grace alone. Paul relegated all value to this unknown, alien God, and thus the "world became a hell, something without meaning, an idle fantasy, indeed a Nothing."[34] That is, he established a radical dichotomy between the alien God and humanity, making impossible mutuality of any sort between human beings and God.[35] This radical asymmetry— the radical nature of which exceeded the disparity inherent in the covenant between the Creator God and his chosen people—is bound up with Marcion's negation of the world, which stems from the alien God's sheer foreignness.

The God of redemption neither created nor governs this world[36] and is altogether other than it. Rather, this God comes to save people from this world out of grace—undeserved love. Thus, if grace, unwarranted and from beyond this world, is to be granted sovereignty, then justice—the assessment of actions in this world— must be devalued completely. Indeed, not just actions but also this world as a whole must be negated.[37]

Not justice but love redeems. Yet love, that which redeems, is other than this world and comes from without; it is alien. Thus emerges the split between the evil Creator God of the Old Testament and the good Redeemer God of the New. Marcion speaks of an alien God, unknown to the "World Creator" God who is obsessed with a notion of justice, and thus sin and failure. Harnack emphasizes that for Marcion, God is both "'just' and malevolent."[38] Indeed, Marcion casts righteousness as "the *essential* characteristic of the Creator-God."[39] The problem with the notions of righteousness and justice, and why, paradoxically, these notions are evil and malicious, is that the Creator God made "man weak, helpless, and mortal and allowed him to be tempted: and it is also shown in the fact that he even tolerates sin, death, and the devil . . . .as well as every kind of evil."[40] Justice then does not evoke perfection, but reveals weakness. The Creator God is not a wise sovereign whose creation he seeks to perfect, but rather is a "a *despot* who proceeds on the principle that 'the will of the king is the supreme law,' who seeks above all his own honor, who treasures as the highest virtues in his subjects their submissiveness and obedience and who declares his adversaries, as impious folk to be without rights."[41] Righteousness and justice, then, are misnomers because they, like the world, are about the honor of the Creator God—a God that is imperfect, even wicked. Justice then is not really justice because it is earthly and thus imperfect, just as holiness is not really holy when it is bound to the Creator God who is petty and tyrannical.

The rupture between the Creator God and the Redeemer God is mirrored in the fissure between the Jews and the true followers of Christ. Marcion, who is at great pains to link Jesus—indeed, to equate Jesus modally—with the alien God, severs the link between the New Testament and the Old Testament, thus rejecting the allegorical exegesis central to Christian efforts to tie the two testaments together. Rather, the alien God, separate from the Creator, only redeems, offering "a universal redemption" rather than showing any "partiality for one people." However, this redemption is ultimately from "the world and its creator" and, perhaps most importantly, from "the *law*" of this despotic God. Indeed, for Marcion, the alien God redeems not merely from "the law" but also from "the lawgiver, for the two belong together." There are then two Gods. In contrast to the faulty, even evil World Creator God stands the good, alien God, who "*came in order to dissolve the law and the prophets,* not to fulfill them. He does this by means of the gospel, in order to redeem souls."[42]

Harnack rejects the Creator God of the Old Testament, partly because this God is denuded of his numinous mystery. He writes, "The creator of the world is 'known' absolutely and therefore also can be given a name: nature can be read off fully and without remainder from his creation and revelation. This profane re-vealedness which leaves no mystery shows him to be an inferior God."[43] As God is denuded of mystery and holiness, so too is the world. Actions in the world, works, and law are rendered useless or worse. Genuine holiness pertains only to the inner part of the human—the soul—and not the flesh,[44] and those following the law—the standards of righteousness—are lost to the alien redeemer, caught as they are in this world; they thus belong to the Creator. The Creator God offers a path of righteousness in the Law, but "[t]his righteousness itself is most pro-foundly immoral, and that precisely where it appears the purest and has more or less brought what is natural under control, for it is devoid of love, it places every-thing under constraint, precisely thereby it lures one to sin, and *it does not provide a way out of the world.*"[45] Love, not a righteousness that, in this logic, is tanta-mount to worldliness and thus sin, is what leads to redemption. The world, the worldly, is sinful and corrupt, and redemption is removed from this world, from action; it is purely a passive receiving from beyond.

The Primordiality of the Thou

Whereas Marcion seeks to sever God—or at least the redeeming God—from the world, thereby bifurcating human beings into either the saved or the drowned, Buber's *I and Thou* emphasizes the profound unity of creation and redemption, which are joined in revelation, or the center, as aspects of the one God. That is, God is both Creator and Redeemer, as disclosed through God qua Revealer. Buber accomplishes this unity by rejecting Marcion's emphasis on radical tran-scendence, championing instead a notion of God that is both immanent and tran-scendent: In fact, the transcendence of Buber's God is rooted in his immanence.[46] Ultimately, the world is the site of encounter with God; thus any otherworldly theology such as Marcionism is profoundly erroneous, even idolatrous. For Buber, "to look away from the world, or to stare at it, does not help a man to reach God; but he who sees the world in Him stands in his presence."[47] Buber offers a notion of God that is bound to the world, rather than a God alien from the world;[48] this world is the site of the holy, of redemption.

In *I and Thou* Buber famously offers a strong ontological foundation for his philosophy of religion. There are two "primal words" [*Grundworte*]: the I-Thou [*Ich-Du*] and I-It [*Ich-Es*]. These primal words are two related, yet distinct modal-ities of existence in the world. Whereas "I-Thou establishes the world of relation" [*Das Grundwort Ich-Du stiftet die Welt der Beziehung*],[49] the root word "I-It" takes place in the separation of subject and object. Buber plays on the root *gegen* to help elucidate this distinction. In the I-Thou mode the *Gegenwart*—presence—is primary, and the distinction between subject and object does not arise or it ceases to apply. More precisely, there are no objects and no subject in the sense of something that takes an object. In the I-It modality, however, the key term is the *Gegenstand*, the object. The It-world is understood as experience [*Erfahrung*], and a subject, in the world of space and time, experiences "things bounded by other things and events, measured by them, comparable to them."[50] It is not a world of relation [*Beziehung*]. When one is present, one does not have an object, but rather one encounters [*begegnen*] a Thou with which one exists in relation. When one experiences, one is oriented in such a manner that one does not encounter; one does not exist alongside, but rather grasps, knows, and orders.[51] In short, one has objects.

Buber's ontology and metaphysical anthropology not only repudiate Harnack's Marcionism but also counteract its lure by explaining the roots of the enervation of Western culture, which fails to appreciate or even recognize the presence of the actual [*wirklich*]. It is in this context that we must grasp Buber's twofold account of reality, I-It and I-Thou, and his emphasis on the ontological priority of the latter. Buber seeks to demonstrate the ontological primordiality of the Thou by presenting two different but overlapping genealogies, one rooted in "primitive" human beings and the other in children. Before the I of either the I-It or I-Thou modality of being in the world is the *Between*—an ontological structure that grounds the possibility for the I-Thou relation and is the source of spirit. Indeed, Buber's critique of Western thought—in this case, the Critical Idealism of Kant and Cohen—is precisely that it is derivative of the It mode of being and thus does not emerge from the most ontologically fundamental structures of existence.

Where Cohen makes reason the core of his philosophy of religion, Buber roots his account of religion in the Thou relation. Although both use the term *Geist*, for Cohen it is an expression of the telos and highest aspirations of a community, whereas Buber understands spirit as the "answer of man to his Thou."[52] Whereas Cohen defines *Geist* in terms of the unfolding rationality of sources of culture, primarily literary, and thus emphasizes its temporal character, Buber characterizes it primarily in spatial terms.[53] More specifically, for Buber, "Spirit [*Geist*] is not in the I, but between I and Thou. It is not like the blood that circulates in you, but like the air in which you breathe."[54] For there to be spirit for Buber, there must be distance between the I and the Thou.[55] Cohen depicts Judaism as an exemplary instance of rationality, which he uses to secure Judaism's place in Germanism and in the foundations of European identity. In contrast, Buber uses the language of philosophical anthropology, an anthropology where reason is not the primary characteristic of the human. He casts exemplarity in terms of spirit, which is by no means limited to Europe. Indeed, he often characterizes

Oriental and so-called primitive religions as more spiritual and more vital than the enervated religions of the modern West.[56]

The notion of the primitive plays an essential role in *I and Thou*. As mentioned earlier, Buber offers two genetic accounts of the human being, or two philosophical anthropologies from which the I emerges: One is grounded in the primitive and the other in the child.[57] These accounts enable Buber to elucidate the relationship between the two ground words, I-It and I-Thou, in such a way that grants decisive ontological priority to the latter.[58]

In contrast to Cohen, Buber uses, rather than decries, the methods of *Religionswissenschaft*, such as philology and linguistics, in his effort to lay the foundation of his philosophical anthropology. The language of primitives [*Primitiven*], like the early developmental stages of children, testifies, so Buber maintains, that, at its most primordial level, human existence consists in a "true original unity, the lived relation" [*die wahre ursprüngliche Einheit, die gelebte Beziehung*].[59] Or as Buber famously puts it, "In the beginning is the relation."[60] Buber is not merely positing the priority of the I-Thou modality to the I-It but is also maintaining that the relationship, the I-Thou, is prior to the emergence of a distinct I, which he refers to as "still only in relief and without finished independence."[61] In other words, Buber maintains that relationships and events are ontologically prior to the self, the I.

With his insistence that the relationship between the I and the Thou—indeed the realm of the Between [das *Zwischen*]—is more primordial than any distinct I (or Thou), Buber overturns atomistic notions of identity. Scholars such as Michael Theunissen, Paul Mendes-Flohr, and Robert E. Wood have noted the "ontological significance" of the Between.[62] As Mendes-Flohr puts it, "The Between—das Zwischen—is the extramental, supersensible realm in which dialogue peculiarly takes place."[63] Similarly, Wood points out that the Between is "beyond subjectivism and objectivism—indeed, it is always implicit as their sustaining ground."[64] Theunissen goes so far as to characterize Buber's thought as "an ontology of the Between."[65] Buber's notion of the Between accounts for the ontological structures informing human (but not just human) existence. Of course, as Wood notes, the Between "is always in danger of being forgotten."[66] This loss of awareness, which seems inevitable in Buber's conception of history, predominates in ages where the It-world overshadows the Thou-world.

By universalizing the I-Thou and the Between, Buber breaks with the strategies of Cohen and Rosenzweig and embraces the world religions discourse while simultaneously rejecting its emphasis on philology. Buber emphasizes the role of the Thou as underlying the experiences of so-called primitives, the "nature peoples" [*Naturvölker*].[67] Indeed, the notion of magic, Buber claims, "is but an abstraction," based on profound Thou encounters with the sun, moon, memories of the dead, and so on. Magic is an abstraction of an encounter "probably more primitive than [the concept of] number [in general], but not any more supernatural than it."[68] Buber rejects common philosophical attempts to derive identity from the notion of self-preservation [*Erhaltungstrieb*] as the basis of identity as well as the cognosco ergo sum.[69] Ultimately the notion of the "I" emerges from the "originary experience [*Urerlebnisse*] of the vital primal words I-affecting-Thou and Thou-affecting-I, only after they have been split asunder and the participle has been hypostasized and substantialized as a subject" [*nach der Substantivierung, Hypostasierung des Partizip, elementhafthervor*].[70] Thus the I only emerges after the immediacy of the I-Thou encounter has broken. The I-Thou relationship, the Between, is prior and more primordial than the I of either the I-It or I-Thou.

Only after the I of the I-Thou modality or root word is severed from the Thou can the I-It modality of being emerge. Thus, whereas the I of the I-Thou is inherently bound up with the entire relation and does not exist apart from it, the I-It only emerges after that relation has been dissolved. Buber attributes this dissolution to a natural or corporeal differentiation from one's environment: "The body comes to know and to differentiate itself in its peculiarities." However, this differentiation of the body from its environment does not yet enable the epistemological juxtaposition of a knowing I to its world, because the I as a noun has not yet formed or coalesced. However, this separation and juxtaposition of the body are the requisite conditions for a notion of a self, an I that is distinct from its environment. Yet, even when the I does emerge and understands itself as the bearer of perceptions and experiences, this cognition does not yet take place on a conscious level.[71] Indeed, one must assume that the emergence of the I happens prior to consciousness.[72] Thus, the shift to I-It is inevitable and natural, and yet, in regard to primitive cultures it is much less pronounced than more "civilized" cultures.[73]

Buber also provides the derivation of the I from the child—indeed, he claims this derivation offers a better glimpse than that from the primitive into the primacy of the I-Thou.[74] Buber casts the child, like the primitive, as living between sleep and sleep without yet having a fixed identity. Buber, waxing metaphysical, claims that all children express a yearning [*Sehnsucht*] that "aims for its worldly association [*welthaften Verbundheit des zum Geiste*] to spirit, of the being that has burst into spirit with its true Thou."[75] Buber speaks of "the womb of the great mother, the undivided primal world that precedes form" from which one must break to "enter personal life."[76]

What emerges with this account of the child's development that is not present in Buber's description of primitive religions is the notion of creation [*Schöpfung*]:[77] The child "has stepped out of the glowing darkness of chaos into the cool light of creation." However, consistent with Buber's message later in the text, creation is not simply givenness, but rather results from the encounter between the

I and Thou. Or as Buber puts it, "But he does not possess it [creation] yet; he must first draw it truly out, he must make it into a reality for himself [*sich zur Wirklichkeit machen*], he must find for himself his own world by seeing and hearing and touching and shaping it." Indeed, the I plays an active role in creation, actualizing and hallowing it in the manner requisite to render that which is as creation. The world is not simply given, but must be actively created by the self. "Creation reveals, in meeting, its essential nature as form. It does not spill itself into expectant senses, but rises up to meet the grasping senses." That is, there is not yet a given object, but what will become an object is first a Thou, an occasion for the "flash and counter-flash of meeting" [*Blitz und Wiederblitz der Begegnung*].[78]

It would be a mistake to overlook the philosophical complexity of Buber's account of creation. Much can be gleaned by juxtaposing Buber's discussion of creation with Cohen's neo-Kantian critique of givenness.[79] The first element to acknowledge in such a juxtaposition is that Buber's account of creation critiques the central tenet of all Idealism—that it is the mind that imposes form on reality. Buber does not reject this tenet outright, but he argues that the mind is not ontologically primordial. Rather, the attempt to grasp reality as filtered through the mind cannot access true actuality (*Wirklichkeit*) or is at least removed from it, because the account of actuality that it gives is one derived from an It-modality of being, whereas the originary form of being with things is encounter, relation, creation. Indeed, Buber uses Cohenian language, particularly evident in the German, to drive home this point: "*Die Ursprünglichkeit des Beziehungstrebens zeigt sich schon auf der frühesten, dumpfsten Stufe.*"[80] Gregor Smith translates the line as "[t]he primal nature of the effort to establish relation is already to be seen in the earliest and most confined stage,"[81] but this language loses the reference to origin and striving, words that resonate with Cohen. As with Cohen, for Buber the object is increasingly determined in a process—although for Cohen it is one of knowing and for Buber it is one ultimately characterized by relating—and both emphasize the role of striving in this process. However, Cohen's thought elucidates the emergence or determination of objects proceeding from a system rooted in a logic of origins, and this striving is directed toward an unrealizable ideal. In contrast, Buber's system originates with the striving for relation with a Thou. For Buber there is an actual metaphysical relationship between the I and Thou that, even when the I-Thou relation is latent, nevertheless permeates the object.

The relationship [*Beziehung*], rooted as it is in the Between, is metaphysical. As Buber puts it,

> It is simply not the case that the child first perceives an object, then, as it were, puts himself in relation with it. But the effort to establish relation comes first— the hand of the child arched out so that what is over against him may nestle

under it; second is the actual relation, a saying of Thou without words, in the state preceding the word-form; the thing, like the I, is produced late, arising after the original experiences have been split asunder and the connected partners separated.[82]

The constitution of objects as understood by Critical Idealism—whether Kantian or Cohenian—is secondary to an original Thou state prior to individuation. In his discussion of the child, Buber reiterates his claim made in regard to the primitive nature religions—that "in the beginning is the relation." However, now he adds a notion of "the apriori of relation, the inborn Thou" [*das Apriori der Beziehung, das eingeborene Du*].[83] Buber uses explicitly Kantian terminology here to talk about the category of the Thou, claiming that it is an inherent aspect of the human condition. One might characterize this use of Kantian terms as a bit of methodological crudeness, because the category of the Thou is not like the categories of understanding in the *Critique of Pure Reason*—indeed, it is incommensurable with Kant's table of categories and, in fact, would undercut it. However, one can also read his use of Kantian terms as a signal that Buber is critiquing Kantianism (and Cohen's neo-Kantianism) for making the notion of relation ontologically prior to the act of understanding, where the manifold is submitted to the table of categories and synthesized (Kant) or the object is generated by the logic of origin and increasingly refined through successive stages of judgment (Cohen). That is, it is a stance that seeks to place the I-Thou relation, a relation that defies all categories (including Kant's table of categories), back behind the axiomatic beginnings of Idealism. I prefer the latter interpretation.[84]

Whereas Cohen sought to maintain a distinctly non-metaphysical account of knowing, Buber emphasizes that genuine understanding requires that creation be understood as having a "cosmic or metacosmic origin."[85] For Buber, creation involves a relationship, an actual meeting, which implies an event of metaphysical significance taking place. In what is clearly a reference to Kant and Cohen, Buber explains, "But the instinct to originate [*Urhebertrieb*], which is established later (that is, the instinct to set up things in a synthetic, or, if that is impossible, in an analytic way[86]—through pulling to pieces or tearing up), is also determined by this inborn Thou, so that a 'personfication' of what is made, and a 'conversation' takes place."[87] In this peculiar passage Buber emphasizes that in contrast with Cohen, the epistemic—indeed, ontological—priority is on presence [*Gegenwart*], rather than the knowledge (i.e., determination, categorization, and ordering) of an object [*Gegenstand*]; the I-Thou is prior to and preeminent over the I-It. The constitution of reality via the mind in the Kantian sense of the manifold, or the Cohenian sense of *Ursprüngslogik*, is secondary to the more primordial longing for relationship. Thus, the notion of abstraction and the hypostatized self only emerges "from the longing for a Thou" and the various experiments of the child and the earnestness of his or her perplexity. But all attempts to reduce the role of encounter, and one's innate yearning for it, to "more confined spheres" of epistemology and other forms of categorization invariably do damage to its true metacosmic (read metaphysical) nature.[88] Creation then—the ordering of the world—is a response to a Thou; the idealistic configuration of reality, that which gives shape to the It-world, is derivative of this more primordial encounter—which itself is rooted in the metaphysical yearning for encounter as part of the anthropological constitution of the self.

In this vein, Buber makes clear metaphysical assumptions about a real world external to cognition, casually dismissing the " 'world of ideas' " as a flight from "real man, of you and me, of our life and of our world." Idealism, Buber suggests, emerges from a deracinated I of an I-It pairing.[89] Buber, playing on words, maintains that "the ordered world is not the world order."[90] That is, rationality, which is essentially a construct of the It-understanding, fails to grasp the true essence of life. This is not to say that Buber glorifies the irrational or the absurd, but rather that he claims that there are limits to reason, which by nature deals with the ordering and categorization of concepts and objects—with Its. Reason is bounded by the suprarational mystery of the world of the Thou. As Zachary Braiterman emphasizes, "The presence of God becomes manifest through nothing more than ordinary, unsubstanted light."[91] The I-Thou encounter is a form of *"transcendence within the immanent"*[92]—it is not a projection beyond what is. Cohen gives priority to the ideal, rather than actuality, thus transcending the world. In contrast, in attempting to go beyond the actual, Buber maintains that one, in fact, falls short, because one ignores the very site of the manifestation of the divine. Cohenian Idealism maintains a notion of transcendence that goes beyond the immanent, harboring a transcendent horizon of the future against which to measure and critique the present. As such, it is a form of It-thinking, one that fails to accord to what is actual.

The Return

Buber offers a history of the It and Thou worlds, a history that is universal even as it is manifested and iterated differently in particular communities. According to Buber, the history of the human race can be understood as the progressive expansion of the world of It. In the It-world, the ability to experience, grasp the world, and further the ends of human life evolves and becomes more developed. However, Buber emphasizes that the development in technology and knowledge of the natural world [*Naturerkenntnis*] is not a refinement in spirit.

Buber finds that each specific culture, as does each human individual, develops along a parallel path in "that they indicate a progressive augmentation of the world of It."[93] All cultures, Buber claims, begin with a "small world of objects," but before a culture reaches its "great age" [*Zeitalter der Höhe*],[94] it first takes over the It-worlds of other "pre-existing cultures."[95] Indeed, it is no coincidence that Buber emphasizes the manner in which "Greece accepted the Egyptian world," and "western Christianity accepted the Greek world." Buber is clearly rejecting notions of innate genius, not uncommon in the world religions discourse, as well as the increasing celebration of autochthony, claiming, "These cultures, then, enlarge their world of It not merely through their own experience, but also through the absorption of foreign experience. Only then does a culture, thus grown, fulfill itself in decisive, discovering expansion."[96] Thus, even as Buber accepts and uses the parameters of the world religions discourse, he challenges many of the methodological assumptions which emphasize purity by excluding the role of external influence.

There is an inherent tension in the development of human life on earth. As human mastery and knowledge increase—that is, as the human relation to the It-world expands—human beings' relationship with and access to the Thou dimension recede. Like Cohen, Buber thinks that the era in which he is living is in grave danger. However, where Cohen finds the crisis of modernity to be in threats to reason that lead to irrationalism, racism, bigotry, and xenophobia, Buber sees the problem as the decreased access to the Thou dimension, the world of relation. As I mentioned earlier, Buber's notion of spirit is derivative of the I-Thou encounter. However, not only do all I-Thou encounters end up being objectified, rendered into Its, but also, as the It-world expands, the ability to relate becomes more and more ossified. Indeed, these two tendencies go hand in hand for Buber.[97] For example, religious traditions are generally rooted in a profound encounter, but as the generations pass, these rituals tend to become frozen, such that what was once a Thou, a living presence, becomes increasingly mediated, walled into the edifice of tradition, and rigidified.

However, although all Thous are fated to become Its, and presence becomes increasingly mediated, that does not mean the world is becoming increasingly lifeless. The It-world and the Thou-world are not as incompatible and inimical to one another as one might think, and the Thou-latent-within-the-It can be retrieved and recovered. "Every response binds up the Thou in the world of It. That is the melancholy of man, and his greatness."[98] One can reverse this process and retrieve the Thou—doing so is redemption, the spirit within the It-world. "But that which has been so changed into It, hardened into a thing among things, has had the nature and disposition put into it to change back again and again . . . again and again that which has the status of the object must blaze up into presentness and enter the elemental state from which it came, to be looked on and lived in the present by men."[99] Religious movements and upheavals can renew that which has become frozen, rigid. Buber often uses the word *Umkehr,* or return, as the equivalent to the Hebrew word *teshuva.*[100] As Wood points out, "Here

Buber is . . . translating a Jewish conception into a universal notion: turning" [*Umkehr, teshuva*] such that it "stands at the center of *I and Thou*, for, with the announcement of turning, attention shifts to the individual who awakens to the emptiness and despair involved in the separate IT-world and thus stands at the beginning of redemption."[101] That is, the Jewish notion of *teshuva* [*Umkehr*] functions as a central pivot between the It-world and the Thou-world in Buber's "universal" theory of religion, and it renders the former open to the influence of the latter. If the world of human beings or, more specifically, the relation between human beings and God inevitably ossifies into an It-relation, there is nevertheless the possibility of a return to the Thou-relation. Buber is emphatic that "in the return [*Umkehr*] the word is born on earth," and "in a new return it [religion] is reborn with new wings."[102] Revelation, the relationship with God, is never fixed; there is no single image, but it renews itself again and again in new iterations.[103]

The Thou is more primordial and primary than the It; as a result, the It-world is derivative from the Thou, and much of our civilization and the material of daily life, experienced as so many Its, can, under the right circumstances, become Thous once more. Indeed, for Buber, the history of religion, East and West, is a history of encounter, distance and objectification, and then renewal. Presumably this pattern is universal, because all communities share a similar structure. That is, they all begin with profound acts of Thou-saying that allow the "cosmos, an apprehended world" to become a "home" for human beings.[104] Although the details of these homes may differ, the basic pattern, grounded in the polar nature of human beings, is parallel.

The Present Age: Fate and Freedom

If *teshuva* [*Umkehr*] serves as a mode of connectivity between the It-world and the Thou-world, Buber also accounts for a more common intersection: the gradual ossification and objectification of the Thou-world into the It-world. A key determinant of this process is the different character of causality in different epochs. In colorful language, Buber explains the oscillation between ages, when "smooth causality, which before had no power to disturb the spiritual conception of the cosmos, rises up till it is an oppressive, stifling fate" [*Verhältnis*].[105] Buber opposes fate to destiny, which is the cosmic horizon of the free man: "Wise and masterful destiny [*Schiksal*], that reigned in harmony with the wealth and meaning of the cosmos over causality, has been changed into a demonic spirit adverse to meaning, and has fallen into the power of causality."[106] Within religio-cultural traditions, fate and freedom collide and undercut one another. Indeed, this collision is itself bound up with a tension between the It- and Thou-worlds. What was once living and vital now obstructs. Buber maintains, "Every great culture that comprehends nations rests on an original relational event, on an answer to a Thou made at its source, on the essential act [*Wesensakt*] of spirit."[107] Each culture and religion develop their own sense of the cosmos, their own way of making the universe a home for the human being and the divine. In such contexts human beings are free. Buber sets the free human being, the human being who "believes in actuality . . . in the real bond between the duality of I and Thou"[108] in opposition to the arbitrary human being [*willkürliche Mensch*], who lives without encounter. A culture is living and those who dwell in it free as long as the connection with that profound, initial relation remains vital.

However, cultures inevitably harden and diverge from those processes that renew this relation; as a result, the It-world becomes not only increasingly severed from the Thou-world, from the originary relationship at the core of the community, but it also becomes increasingly threatening as it looms more and more over the horizon. Destiny becomes fate, causally deterministic in such a manner that freedom is lost. It is surely no coincidence—given their prominence in the world religions discourse—that Buber draws his examples of such transformations from Indic and Greek religions, namely, karma and Dike, respectively.[109] "The very karma that appeared to the forefathers as a charitable dispensation— for what we do in this life raises us up for a future life in higher spheres—is now recognized as tyranny: for the karma of an earlier life of which we are unconscious has shut us up in a prison we cannot break in this life."[110] Similarly, Dike, which offered "the heavenly 'way,' which also means our way, in order to dwell with a free heart in the universal bounds of fate," has been transformed such that it now "ladens [us] with the whole burden of the dead weight of the world, with a fate that does not know spirit" [*geistfremde Heimarmane*].[111] In both cases, what began as freedom, as a belief in the capacities of what one might accomplish in this life, of what one can experience and live through encounter, has been stifled by the baggage of that which came before, and cosmic forces that once promised to liberate now become so much accumulated detritus. One can no longer engage the present or presence because impersonal forces overwhelm and undermine one's ability to encounter a Thou unencumbered.

The present age, Buber argues, is sick in precisely such a way, yet it is sicker than any other has been. "The quasi-biological and quasi-historical thought of today, however different the aims of each, have worked together to establish a more tenacious and oppressive belief in fate than has ever before existed."[112] New forms of predestining laws, often in uneasy conjunction with one another— psychologism, sociologism, vitalism, racialism, and so on—loom over the horizon. Wood speaks of this crisis in regard to the death of God, emphasizing that in "the modern world, ... The suprasensible world has disappeared . . . and God has died. The atheism inherent in the world of It has worked itself out of its logical conclusion. We have reached the age of the eclipse of God."[113] The world no longer serves as a home for human beings but a prison. The danger, as Buber sees it, is not only the stultifying nature of the It-world clouding out the influence of Thous but also the emergence of conditions where human beings feel world weary and without access to spirit. As I mentioned earlier, it is precisely under such conditions that the Marcionite heresy and its promise of an otherworldly God utterly foreign to this world, offering an alien grace taking one away from the world, become a terrible lure. This heresy is particularly tempting when human beings no longer feel at home in the world and seek an exit from it. Yet, as with other moments in the history of religion, the possibility of renewal remains vital. Alluding to a famous passage by Friedrich Hölderlin, Buber writes, "But where there is danger what saves grows, too" [*Wo aber Gefahr ist, wächst das Rettende auch.*][114] The alternative of escape, of taking flight from the world, is the renewal of the world, which I argue is the main argument of *I and Thou*.[115]

Renewal and the Unity of God

I and Thou is marked by what seems to be a series of interrelated binaries: It and Thou, present and past, fate and destiny, presence and object. Even the most fundamental of these binaries, that between It and Thou, is not without overlap; the It-world has been and can be again permeated by the spirit of the Thou. That the influence of the Thou world can saturate the It world is what makes renewal possible. Buber characterizes such a process in terms of renewal and return.

To understand the notion of return, we must grasp the antinomy between fate and freedom, which Buber casts as between fate/doom [*Verhängnis*] and the self-willed person [*willkürliche Mensch*], on the one hand, and destiny [*Schicksal*] and the free individual, on the other. By *Verhängnis*, Buber denotes a state of living-in-the-world where the past, understood not just temporally but also as the play of forces and powers beyond one's control or even ability to confront, dominates one's life and undermines one's ability to encounter, to live in the present. The notion of fate is false or insufficient insofar as it understands being in It-terms, where the I-It primal word is taken as alone being real; thus it renders the "presence of the Thou . . . inaccessible."[116] *Verhängtnis*, fate, is the result of a distorted relationship with the ground words such that the It-world not only dominates the Thou world but also presents an obstacle to any encounter with the Thou. In such a world, a world that cannot be a genuine home for human beings, lives the "self-willed man" who cannot encounter a Thou, who cannot say Thou, who does not know "the solidarity of connection" [*Verbundenheit*] but only the "feverish world outside and his feverish desire to use it."[117] Or as Buber puts it elsewhere in *I and Thou*, "Without sacrifice and without grace [*Gnade*], without encounter [*Begegnung*] and without presence [*Gegenwart*], he has as his world a mediated world cluttered with purposes. His world cannot be anything else and its name is fate. And so he is in his sovereignty [*Selbstherrlichkeit*] inextricably entangled in the unreal" [*Unwirklichkeit*].[118]

The existence of the human being of fate, the self-willed person is ultimately arbitrary. Buber explains, "The only thing that can become fate for man is the belief in fate; for this suppresses the movement of turning" [*er halt die Bewegung der Umkehr nieder*].[119] Without the capacity to return to the Thou, one becomes bound up with causality, with impersonal forces, such that one may seek to define oneself for oneself, to express a certain form of mastery, but one that is ultimately arbitrary given that it is cut off from the Thou, which alone provides genuine meaning.[120]

Buber opposes fate to destiny. According to Buber, the free man "believes in destiny [*Schicksal*], and believes that it stands in need of him. It does not keep him in leading strings, it awaits him, he must go to it, yet does not know where it is to be found. But he knows he must go out with his whole being. The matter will not turn out according to his decision; but what is to come will only come when he decides on what he is able to will."[121] If the self-willed person, bound up in the world of fate, experiences the world in terms of mastery, knowledge, and objects, it is because this person cannot believe in freedom, in decision, but only in the play of forces that have conditioned her world of possibilities, that have predestined what she may be and do. It is not that the free person [*der Freie*] is unhampered by a horizon of possibilities and limits; instead, she experiences the world in a fundamentally different way from knowing, using, and mastery, the characteristic attitudes of the world of the self-willed human being, the denizen of the It-world. Buber uses the language of an unconditioned decisionism to get at the play between freedom and arbitrariness, between destiny and fate. Perhaps it should not be surprising, given their close historical and professional association, that Buber, like Rosenzweig, makes use of decisionism. In both cases, there is a crossroads: between paganism and true religion for Rosenzweig and an orientation guided by Thou or an orientation guided by It for Buber.

Buber defines freedom in opposition to the autarkic, arbitrary individual, the individual of fate. "The free man is he who wills without arbitrary self-will."[122] He "believes in" and dwells in "actuality" [*Wirklichkeit*].[123] The free man directly encounters the Thou, which is engaged in relation with the I, "without mediation" [*unmittelbar*], whether said mediation is understood in terms of a priori categories, fantasies one might project, goals, or forms of anticipation. In Buber's insistence on immediacy, we see echoes of the earlier critique of Kantian and Cohenian Critical Idealism. That is, because the I-Thou disposition is more primordial than the I-It disposition, we are to conclude that forms of mediation are not inherent, a priori facets of the human mind, but rather accretions of the culture in which one finds oneself. All such forms of mediation must be undermined for the event of encounter to take place.[124] Or, as Buber puts it, "What is essential is lived in the present, objects in the past."[125]

To make sense of Buber's use of this antinomy between destiny and freedom, which although posed in book II is only solved in book III, we must turn to his account of the eternal Thou [ewiges Du]. Buber augments his phenomenological methodology with a positively metaphysical notion of God, namely, the Eternal Thou.[126] Underlying the Thou-world, giving it presence and normativity, is the Eternal Thou. The Eternal Thou undergirds all particular Thous: "Every particular Thou is a glimpse to the eternal Thou."[127] If mediation is what is characteristic of the I-It world, then the Eternal Thou offers a form of mediation in a qualitatively different sense. That is, it facilitates and preserves, even imbues, with presence; it does not reduce or contextualize. "Through this mediation of the Thou of all beings fulfillment, and non-fulfilment, of relations comes to them" [Aus diesem Mittlertum des Du aller Wesen kommt der Erfülltheit der Beziehungen zu ihnen, und die Unerfülltheit].[128] The Eternal Thou is unlike anything else; it cannot become an It. Where other Thous are bounded or limited, the Eternal Thou is not delimited by any other because it offers a relation "that gathers up and includes all others" [zu dem er in einer Beziehung steht, die alle andern einschliesst.][129] That is, rather than a contextualization as a chain of objects, it presents the metaphysical or ontological grounds that enable the Thou relation to exist.

The Eternal Thou is the precondition for Buber's notion of return [Umkehr, teshuva]. As Wood points out, "Through turning back to meeting [with the Eternal Thou], new meaning is born upon the earth."[130] Religion and holiness, God's very domain, are inextricably bound up with this world. God is utterly worldly even as God's transcendence cannot be reduced to simple immanence. The notion of return, even when brought about by a direct encounter with the Eternal Thou, can only be verified or manifested in this world; there is no transcendence beyond this world because transcendence is bound up with immanence.[131] As we mentioned, Wood notes that with the idea of return "Buber is . . . translating a Jewish conception into a universal notion."[132] Buber would no doubt approve of Wood's association of Jewishness with a process that gives meaning to the this-worldly. However, we must also bear in mind that the emphasis on this world is not arrived at by a disinterested, abstract study of the Jewish sources. Instead, it is formulated—implicitly in I and Thou and explicitly elsewhere[133]—against the otherworldly transcendence of Marcionism, particularly its modern iteration. Buber's notion of God is the antithesis of Marcion's otherworldly, alien God.

The rootedness of revelation, of the religious event, in the Between, in the world—that world that Marcion casts as evil—is evident in Buber's use of spatial imagery to understand religious phenomena. In contrast to interpretations of religious phenomena that emphasize intuition or an experience internal to the subject, such as those proffered by Rudolf Otto and Friedrich Schleiermacher, Buber emphasizes the duality between the individual and God: The encounter can only exist between the self and God, not within the self or within God. It precludes both the subsumption of God to the human being and the human being to God. Buber explains, "In [the] pure relation you have felt yourself to be simply dependent" [*schlechthin abhängig gefühlt*]. However, the relationship between God and human being does not stop with "feeling dependent"[134]—clearly, a reference to Schleiermacher's famous phrase. Rather, according to Buber, with the awareness of one's dependence on and need for God comes a correlative awareness that "God needs you—in the fullness of His eternity needs you."[135] The encounter goes beyond the limits of the self. Presumably, Buber would argue that this going beyond is experienced and based on the encounter itself, but he posits it as metaphysical and thus offering content that transcends the encounter.

In the section on childhood in part I of *I and Thou*, Buber describes creation [*Schöpfung*] as the meeting between the self and the world—emphasizing the active nature of the self on the manifold of the world. In part III, however, he characterizes the self as being more passive in this process: "Creation happens to us, burns itself into us, recasts us in burning—we tremble and are faint, we submit." However, human beings are not entirely passive because "we take part in creation, meet the Creator, reach out to Him, helpers and companions."[136] Thus, we are passive in the sense that in an encounter something happens *to* us, but we are active in that this event calls us to respond to God's presence, and to do so in *this* world.[137] Creation, then, is not merely the manner in which the self encounters the world, but rather it is also the call to actualize the It-world, to permeate it with the residual presence of the eternal Thou.

Yet a distance between God and the human being is preserved even in the moment of direct encounter with the divine, what Buber terms "revelation." From revelation, "from the moment of the highest encounter,"[138] the human being steps forth, somehow changed. Again, revelation is not an experience [*Erlebnis*] within the self, but rather a meeting. Indeed, it is an event, an encounter from which the human being "emerges" such that he "has now in his being something more that has grown in him, of which he did not know before and whose origin he is not rightly able to indicate."[139] The human being does not receive a " 'content' [*Inhalt*] but a Presence, a Presence as power" [*eine Gegenwart als Kraft.*][140] This presence, although contentless, nevertheless serves as "a confirmation of meaning"—indeed, the meaning of this life.[141] Elliot Wolfson elucidates the correlative nature of the relationship between God and the human being: "Revelation does not obscure but rather highlights the distance which stands between God and man; it is only through this distance that man receives his task to unify the world, i.e., to prepare the world for the dialogical relationship."[142] There is no unity with God in revelation, nor does revelation disclose content. Rather, it reorients the self away from God to the world. The world, which is a third term between God and the human being, is the locus of the manifestation of the divine-human relationship, and it preserves the distinction between God and human beings necessary for the very possibility of the dialogical relationship.

Indeed, it is precisely in this presence as confirmation of meaning that we see most clearly Buber's response to Marcionism. Recall that Marcion claimed that the redeeming God is radically distinct from the world such that, in Harnack's reconstruction "the world came to be so utterly devoid of value . . . [that the] world became a prison, a hell, something without meaning, an idle fantasty, indeed a Nothing."[143] Buber asserts, in contrast, that it is as a result of the encounter with God, who is both Redeemer and Creator, that "meaning is assured. Nothing can any longer be meaningless." However, because Buber insists that the confirmation of meaning takes the form of a presence [*Gegenwart*] that is not a content [*Inhalt*] because that would possess a clear object [*Gegenstand*], the response to Marcionism lies in a sensibility or, rather, a reawakening of one's capacity to experience the Thou, which entails a return [*Umkehr*]. There is no set doctrine nor any guidelines for behavior, only a transformation in the manner in which one lives-in-the-world.

Unlike Marcionism, the meaning of which Buber speaks—which does not possess a content—"is not that of 'another life,' but that of this life of ours, not one of a world 'yonder' but that of this world of ours [*an dieser Welt von uns*], and it desires confirmation in this life and in relation with this world."[144] Buber claims, "The question about the meaning of life is no longer there. But were it there, it would not have to be answered." Instead, the meaning conferred is an imperative of sorts to transform the world, "to be born by me into the world."[145] This reorientation of the self to the world, the demand to transform the world, cannot be equated with ethics because there is no express content or set of principles.

The very manner in which Buber expresses revelation shows that it cannot be subsumed into the ethical. Buber writes that revelation

> cannot be transmitted by an ought; it is not prescribed, it is not specified on any tablet above all men's heads. The meaning that has been received can be proved true by each man only in the singleness of his life. As no prescription can lead us to the meeting, so none leads from it. As only acceptance of the Presence is necessary for the approach to the meeting, so in a new sense is it so when we emerge from it.[146]

Where Marcion claims that genuine revelation leads to a rejection of this world, to a recognition that the world is the antithesis of holiness, Buber holds that such a position, clearly rooted in It ways of thinking, fails to do justice to the primal experience of the eternal Thou. Worse, it demonstrates a profound alienation and estrangement from that Eternal Thou. There is no content, no single doctrine, but rather a presence resistant to any final instantiation in form, but only expressed in endless iterations and images that testify to the wholeness, the integrity, the sanctity of this world.[147] Marcionism is a doctrine that denudes this world of value. In contrast, Buber presents a God whose transcendence is inextricable from immanence and whose interaction with the world is constant, such that world is perpetually a site of encounter—and therefore a site of inexhaustible meaning.

However, before delving further into how Buber's notion of the Eternal Thou relates to his response to Marcion, it is helpful first to understand his critique of Cohen. Buber addresses the often discussed distinction between religious and moral individuals. The moral man—and one suspects Buber has Cohen in mind, given that his language echoes *Ethik des reinen Willens*—"is still burdened with responsibility for the action of those who act," because he remains "in tension between being and 'ought to be,' and in grotesque and hopeless sacrificial courage casts his heart piece by piece into the insatiable gulf that lies between them" [*weil er nämlich ganz bestimmt sei von der Spannung zwischen Sein und Seinsollen, und in die unausfüllbare Kluft zwischen beiden werfe er in grotesk aussichtslosen Operfermut Stück im Stück seines Herzens.*][148] Notice that what Buber calls "moral" accounts for Cohen's moral and religious notion of the human being. Yet, from Buber's point of view, such a notion of selfhood is sacrificial, even monstrous, in that it rejects actuality [*Wirklichkeit*] and thus is engaged in nothing but a constant process of tearing itself asunder in the chasm between the ideal and the actual. It fails to grasp the world in its pursuit of the ideal; in its pursuit of radical transcendence it fails to grasp the genuine transcendence that is to be found in immanence.[149] Indeed, like Rosenzweig, Buber thinks that revelation is profoundly bound up with morality, and yet it transcends what we commonly mean by this term. In contrast to Cohen, Buber, like Rosenzweig, offers a teleological suspension of the ethical that overflows the rigid categories of ethics into an ethos grounded in affirming the worldly in its totality.

In the genuinely "religious" individual, Buber insists that the cognitive, judgmental aspect of ethics is removed, because such a person acts in harmony with destiny and is thus harkening to the transcendence within immanence. Or as Buber puts it, "The 'religious' man, on the other hand, has emerged from that tension into that between the world and God." Only by exiting It modes of being/thinking, which, presumably, to Buber's mind includes Cohen's ethical philosophy of religion, can one genuinely encounter and engage the divine, or better, bind the divine and the world together in one's actions. Indeed, in the individual who has experienced revelation, the tension between is and ought, the role of judgment, fades. Rather, "there is no willing of one's own, but only being joined into what is ordained." According to Buber, the teleological suspension of the ethical is supererogatory; it is more ethical than ethics. Buber uses the trope of stranger [*Fremden*] and confidant [*Vertrauten*], or formality and informality, to explain how ethics is transcended in/after the religious encounter. "Duty and obligation are rendered only to the stranger; we are drawn to and full of love for the intimate person." "He who approaches the Face"—Buber is here speaking about God, the eternal Thou—is guided by intimacy not ethics, love not duty. As such, the religious individual "has indeed surpassed duty and obligation." In surpassing duty and obligation, the religious individual, in contrast to the mystic, has not fled the world, but rather "he has truly drawn closer to it. The world, lit by eternity, becomes fully present [*die Welt ganz gegenwärtig*] to him who approaches the Face, and to the Being of beings, he can in a single response say Thou. Then there is no more tension between the world and God, but only one reality."[150] For one who has undergone/engaged in revelation, not only does the tension between God and the world, the tension that Marcion could not abide, cease to exist but also the It-world becomes permeated with religious significance, with the Thou.[151]

From Buber's vantage point, Cohen's thought is insufficiently this-worldly to counter Marcionism.[152] For Buber, the encounter with God is bound up with actuality—not an ideal but the world—and it is an event within the world [*Welteinbezogensein*], not a cognitive process about the world. Thus, although Cohen's notion of ethics and religion is bound up with a responsibility for the world and with ethics, it remains too cognitive and thus bound to the It-world; in addition, to the degree that it offers an account of redemption, it remains predicated on a transcendence that is divorced from immanence. To be sure, Cohen's Idealism is a far cry from Marcion's desire to depart from the world, but we might conclude that for Buber it is insufficiently radical, insufficiently worldly—insofar as it is rooted in a non-immanent transcendence—to counter the lure of Marcion. Holiness transcends the cognitive dimension and the ideal and embraces the many forms of actuality and acting without doing. Buber explains, "The man is not freed from responsibility; he has exchanged the torment of the finite, pursuit of effects, for the motive power of the infinite, he has got the mighty responsibility of love for the whole untraceable world-event, for the profound belonging to the world before the Face of God."[153] In contrast to Cohen's notion of God as the ultimate exemplar or archetype of morality, Buber rejects morality as a sufficient medium of holiness, insisting that although morality is tied to holiness, holiness surpasses the strictures and limits of morality: "He has, to be sure, abolished moral judgments [*sittliche Urteilen*] forever; the 'evil' man is simply one who is commended to him for greater responsibility, one more needy of love; but he will have to practice, till death itself, decision in the depths of spontaneity, unruffled decision, made ever anew, to right action."[154] The religious individual is beyond good and evil, not because there is no good and evil but because of a supererogatory relation to all of existence. Nothing is beyond redemption, and redemption is what the religious individual is called on to facilitate. Where Marcion sees Hell, a vile world utterly worthy of condemnation, Buber emphasizes the supererogatory responsibility for redeeming this world, and that redemption is inextricable from this world.

Buber and the Jewish Jesus

Buber illuminates this teleological suspension of the ethical through the figure of Jesus. In contrast to traditional Christian theology, Buber humanizes Jesus. Thus, Buber reverses the Marcionite position elaborated by Harnack, that Jesus "had nothing about him that was earthly and thus no flesh and no physical body: he cannot have been born and cannot have had relatives."[155] For Buber, there is nothing metaphysically distinctive about Jesus. His exemplarity lies in the manner in which he says I to the Thou of God, understood as a father: "For it is the I of unconditional relation in which the man calls his Thou Father in such a way that he himself is simply Son, and nothing else but Son."[156] Jesus exemplifies the relation between an individual and God—that "every man can say Thou and is then I, every man can say Father and is then Son" [*jederkann Du sprechen und ist dann Ich, jeder kann Vater sprechen und ist dann Sohn*].[157] There is nothing supernatural in Jesus or in his relation to God, only the heightened actuality of spirit, of his saying I to the eternal Thou. Buber thus explicitly breaks with the Johannine gospel, particularly where the author presents Jesus as claiming, "I and the Father are one."[158] Buber completely rejects all attempts to establish an undifferentiated unity between the human individual and the divine.[159]

For Buber, Jesus exemplifies love, the superogatory nature of the one who has undergone revelation.[160] He claims that love cannot be reduced to feelings, because even if feelings "accompany the metaphysical and metapsychial fact of love . . . they do not constitute it." Or as Buber rather poetically expresses it, "Feelings dwell in man; but man dwells in his love."[161] "Love does not cling to the I in such a way to as to have the Thou only for its 'content,' its object; but love is between I and Thou."[162] Love is a positive, "worldly force" [*ein welthaftes Wirken*].[163] Thus, love, as exemplified by Jesus, explodes the binaries between "good people and evil people, wise people and foolish people, beautiful people and ugly people." Love breaks down the categories in which people become ensconced; it wrenches one loose to emerge in one's individuality, to be confronted as a Thou.[164]

If Buber's Jewish Jesus exemplifies the teleological suspension of the ethical as present in *I and Thou*, the Jews exemplify, as witnesses, God's profound unity. In "The Faith of Judaism,"[165] (1928), an essay published five years after *I and Thou*, Buber ruminates on Christianity and Marcionism. Buber opposes Judaism to Iranian dualism that "reaches its Western completion" in Marcion where "the duality of man, estranged from his natural, vitally trustful faith, finds its theological sanction. No longer does redemption crown the work of creation; redemption vanquishes creation. The world *as such* can no longer become the Kingdom of God."[166] Buber insists that the Marcionite desire to sever the Old from the New Testament, tacitly driving so much scholarship in the world religions discourse, is inextricably bound to a worldview that posits an ontological division in the heart of existence, a division "religiously beyond [the] possibility of redress into a 'world' of matter and moral law, and an overworld of spirit and love."[167]

In "The Faith of Judaism," Buber casts the dualism inherent in Marcionism as a response to the imperfect nature of the world around us, to its unredeemed state, and the consistent failures of human beings. In contrast to Christianity, Judaism was inoculated against Marcionism. As Buber puts it,

> What saved Judaism is not, as the Marcionites imagined, the fact that it failed to experience "the tragedy," the contradiction in the world's process, deeply enough; but rather that it experienced that "tragedy" in the dialogical situation, which means that it experienced the contradiction as theophany. This very world, this very contradiction, unabridged, unmitigated, unsmoothed, unsimplified, unreduced, this world shall be—not overcome—but consummated.[168]

Redemption and holiness for Buber do not lie in the rejection of the world, but rather with the unification of the divine with the world. Evil is not a positive force that exists independently. Rather, " 'inertia' is the root of all evil."[169] Evil is the failure to redeem the world, to fail to embrace destiny and thus remain rooted in fate. Christianity is caught, Buber suggests, on the need for grace, on waiting for God. It forfeits the dialogical relationship with God and thus the possibility of return. Evil must be overcome and redeemed, and this by human beings ascending to meet the divine, not by a divine descent.

Marcionism is a religion of division, and Buber, like Harnack, finds its seeds in Paul and thus very deeply planted in Christianity. Buber claims that Jews—and Jesus of the Synoptic Gospels belongs in this company—maintain that

> the fundamental attitude . . . is characterized by the idea of yihud [unity] . . . . Again and again this recognition, acknowledgment, and reacknowledgment of the divine unity is brought about through human perception and verification [Bewährung] in the face of the monstrous contradictions of life, and especially in the face of that primal contradiction which shows itself in multitudinous ways, and which we call the duality of good and evil.[170]

Buber's philosophy of dialogue contends that human beings are God's partner in the redemption of the world. Redemption happens between God and the human being; it does not descend from God.

It is Judaism and not Christianity—which, particularly under Marcion's sway, dissolves the human pole of the dialogue—that exemplifies this dialogical relation. Buber asserts this not through recourse to rationality (Cohen) or theology (Rosenzweig), but from a claim to history. That is, Buber resorts to

Religionswissenschaft, to a phenomenology of religion—although one not without metaphysical commitments—to establish Jewish exemplarity in this regard. He writes, "I am far from wishing to contend that the conception and experience of the dialogical situation are confined to Judaism. But I am certain that no other community of human beings has entered with such strength and fervor into this experience as have the Jews."[171] Although such a claim is dubious on methodological grounds, Buber is clearly embracing the comparative framework of the history of religions to render Judaism exemplary. If Harnack turns to what he perceives to be the essence of Christianity, where the connection between Jesus and Judaism is dissolved, Buber claims that Jesus can only save, can only be exemplary, if he is understood as a Jew. In this age of the eclipse of God, when the It-world threatens to blot out all traces of the Thou, Judaism and its teaching of return are bulwarks against the Marcionite heresy.

5   Prophets, Prophecy, and Divine Wrath: Heschel and the God of Pathos

Heschel and the Worlds Religions Discourse

Before we turn to the work of Heschel, it is important to summarize the course of thought—and the thinkers—we have already covered. Hermann Cohen's work uses—indeed, it combines—two strategies to defend the place of Judaism in German culture: placing Judaism in the center of the metanarrative of Western/ universal history and critiquing the methodology of comparative religion. To implement the first strategy Cohen offers an overarching philosophy of the West, a metanarrative as it were, that places Germany at the intellectual and spiritual forefront of the West, as its educator. However, Cohen's metanarrative is one in which Germany—or better, Germanism—is inconceivable without Judaism. Cohen also casts Jesus as a Jew in order to both undercut Christianity's theological foundations as well as to render Christianity into the myth-bound and irrational foil against which he illuminates and elaborates his concept of Judaism. By "rationalizing" the figure of Jesus, Cohen does not merely attempt to bring about transformations within Protestantism—to guide it toward rationality, to make it more Jewish, as it were—but he also increasingly displaces Greece as the arbiter of rationality. His wartime writings and his Jewish writings sufficiently disentangle culture, religion, and race such that the ideational cores of Judaism and Germanism are not only inextricable but also the two together perform a function of exemplarity. That is, all peoples and cultures can participate in the universality represented by and exemplified in Germanism and Judaism.

Second, in response to the antisemitic implications of comparative religion, Cohen does more than offer a fundamental critique of the methodological foundations of the world religions discourse; he also seeks to establish the primacy of Judaism by using a new, philosophically oriented method. Cohen's critiques of comparative religion are always bound up with his larger philosophy of Western culture; indeed, he seeks to bring the might of the spirit of the West to bear on what he sees as the perversion of reason taking place in the work of these scholars of religion.

Subsequent thinkers have taken up these two strategies used by Cohen. However, where Cohen seeks to maintain both simultaneously such that they are of one piece, later thinkers—with the exception of Soloveitchik—privilege one over the other.

Although Rosenzweig rejects Cohen's rationalism he takes up Cohen's strategy of offering an overarching philosophical metanarrative of the West in which Judaism holds central significance. Yet in doing so Rosenzweig also decidedly rejects Cohen's nationalism, instead emphasizing the unity of the West in theological terms. It is not reason or culture that binds Jew and Christian together, but a suprarational revelation, albeit one filtered through a philosophical system rooted existentially in phenomenology, history, and, above all, lived actuality. Revelation—the process by which God approaches human beings—joins Judaism and Christianity and radically separates them from the religions of the Orient: those of China, India, and Islam.

Buber, unlike Rosenzweig, follows Cohen's attempts to intervene in the academic study of religion. However, in contrast to both Cohen and Rosenzweig, Buber embraces the world religions discourse, breaking down barriers between Judaism and non-Western religions rather than emphasizing Judaism's uniqueness. Where Cohen sought to undermine the empirical foundations of the academic study of religion using Critical Idealism Buber, with *I and Thou*, offers an attempt to philosophically ground this field of discourse. However, like Cohen and Rosenzweig, a key element of Buber's work is its opposition to the pronounced de-Judaizing tendency reigning in German culture at the time of its publication. And although Buber operates with a very different philosophical idiom from Cohen, like his forebear he challenges the Hellenistic elements of Christianity by presenting Jesus as fundamentally a Jew.

Like Buber, Abraham Joshua Heschel follows Cohen's second strategy— that of engaging and critiquing *Religionswissenschaft*. He wrote his dissertation, "Das prophetische Bewusstsein," between 1930–1932, and it was published as *Die Prophetie* in 1936.[1] Published by a Polish press very near in time to the Shoah, *Die Prophetie* has been fairly marginal in Heschel's celebrated oeuvre; it was made accessible to an English-speaking readership in 1962 in a widely celebrated translation and expansion, *The Prophets*.[2] My focus in this chapter is primarily on *Die Prophetie*, although I at times reference *The Prophets*, which is largely continuous with the earlier work.

Where Buber intended *I and Thou* to serve as a phenomenological grounding, a prolegomenon, to *Religionswissenschaft* in general, Heschel's *Die Prophetie* is an actual exercise in this field. Heschel's investigation into prophetic consciousness raises philosophical and methodological challenges to dominant norms in the study of comparative religions [*vergleichenden Religionsgeschichte*].[3] Indeed, even though Heschel uses the format and terminology of *Religionswissenschaft*, he is at the same time challenging its foundations, highlighting what he sees as its fundamental deficiencies. To elucidate the figure of the prophet, Heschel must expose the disparity between the modern Western mindset and that of the biblical.

Thus, although itself a work of *Religionswissenschaft, Die Prophetie* highlights the limits of the scope and nature of this field of inquiry. Ostensibly, what Heschel finds so troubling in comparative religion—at least as it was practiced at the turn of the twentieth century in the German-speaking world—is its claim to find "equivalence [*Gleichartigkeit*] among the religious phenomena" that it examines.[4] According to Heschel, comparative religion makes the mistake of overemphasizing superficial similarities and underemphasizing what is unique and particular to each religion. As a result, he concludes that these historians conflate the "particular singularity" [*eigentümlichen Besonderheit*][5] of the prophetic with "the rapture of the Indian Fakir, with the frenzy of the Greek orgy and Bacchanals, with the intoxication of the Arab dervish, and with the exuberance of the Syrian priest."[6] In his account, comparative religion equates distinct phenomena, claiming thereby to gain greater clarity. However, in fact, this process distorts and obscures, rather than illuminates. As we see, for Heschel, these assumptions of comparative religion also reflect those of modernity about religion as such. They are derivations of Greek modes of thinking about God and thus wholly inappropriate for properly understanding the biblical God and biblical religiosity in its own terms.

Die Prophetie, then, can be seen as the attempt to utilize then contemporary philosophical and methodological terminology from the study of religion in order to translate the biblical into the Greek modes of thinking.[7] That is, Heschel seeks to use the language of modern philosophy and religious studies to explain that which escapes and defies not only their categories but also their implicit—and unexamined—philosophical and theological foundations. In this work, he challenges not only the Christian and naturalist assumptions of the leading figures of the field of comparative religions and the history of religions but also the philosophical presumptions of the German-Jewish critics of the world religions discourse whom we have been reading, thinkers whom Heschel would regard as being in their own way "prisoners of a German-Greek way of thinking."[8] He goes to great lengths to distinguish Judaism from Near Eastern, Greek, and Asian religious traditions—common reference points in the world religions discourse—maintaining that Judaism is fundamentally a unique phenomenon and thus irreducible to other traditions, religiosities, and philosophies. According to Heschel, the failure to recognize this uniqueness is a tragic error, rooted in the mistaken belief that the biblical and the Greek ways of thinking are commensurable and leading to the Hellenization of Judaism.

Die Prophetie and the Possibility of Prophecy

Die Prophetie explores the contours of the classical prophets, the *Schriftpropheten*, in their uniqueness. In doing so Heschel departs from comparative religion and biblicism, with their emphasis on naturalism, historical influences, and psychopathology.[9] To capture the "wholeness of the prophetic personality as unity from *inspiration* and *experience*" [*die Ganzheit der prophetischen Persönlichkeit als* Einheit *von* Eingebung *und* Erlebnis],[10] Heschel instead turns to phenomenology (Edmund Husserl and Max Scheler) and philosophical hermeneutics (Wilhelm Dilthey), thereby generating a richer range of categories through which to elucidate the nature of prophecy. Indeed, *Die Prophetie* (and its later iteration *The Prophets*) often is read as a work of phenomenology or as a work of phenomenology in the service of theology.[11] Although its phenomenological element is undeniable, this should not obscure a fundamental problem that engages Heschel's attention throughout the work. He is not merely providing a phenomenological description of prophecy but is also seeking to secure the very possibility of prophecy. Heschel's *Die Prophetie,* although academic in nature, is at its most profound level nothing less than a meditation on and challenge to the manner in which God and revelation have been understood in Western thinking—in regard to the modes of thought employed not only in comparative religions or the world religions discourse but also in philosophy and theology.

To understand Heschel's attempt to elaborate the uniqueness of the prophets, a process that entails disentangling Judaism from its ancient Near Eastern context, it is helpful to briefly explore the critique of Heschel's methodology offered by the biblicist Jon Levenson in his essay "Religious Affirmation and Historical Criticism in Heschel's Biblical Interpretation."[12] Although Heschel's work has often been criticized for rejecting the position of the disinterested observer, for employing an implicit shift from the descriptive to the prescriptive,[13] Levenson's critique is particularly useful for our purposes because it faults Heschel for his relationship to the disciplines of history of religions and comparative religions, thus bringing questions of Heschel's methodology to the fore.

According to Levenson, Heschel is attempting to "build a bridge between the ancient 'teachings' and those modern persons committed to them in faith and through a 'personal stance in the present.'"[14] However, as Levenson notes, Heschel's *The Prophets* (and, one could add, his *Die Prophetie*) virtually ignores "the meat and potatoes of biblical scholarship" such as the "compositional history of books," source variations, comparison with other ancient Near Eastern sources, and so on.[15] Nevertheless, Heschel is no traditionalist unconcerned with historical criticism. As Levenson correctly points out, modern biblical scholarship provides much of the background assumptions of *The Prophets* and, though he does not mention it, of *Die Prophetie* as well.[16]

Levenson's critique of Heschel's engagement with extant biblical criticism is not unproblematic. Levenson plays down Heschel's critique of prominent critics (Hermann Gunkel, Gustav Hölscher, Bernard Duhm, and Hans Schmidt) who study the prophets primarily in terms of psychopathology, particularly their manifestation of epilepsy and ecstatic fits.[17] Indeed, Heschel's uses phenomenology precisely to serve as a corrective to the psychologistic reductionism of the reigning German Protestant biblical criticism of his time, which focused solely on the "*facts of consciousness [Bewusstseinstatsachen]*" of the prophet,[18] thereby reducing prophecy to mere feelings with no objective correlate.[19] Such a methodology, Heschel charges, fails to do justice to the prophetic personality in its structural entirety [*Ganzheit*]. And yet, Levenson characterizes Heschel's use of the phenomenological method as an attempt to "skirt . . . major theoretical issues in the historical application of psychology."[20]

The fundamental question behind Levenson's critique of Heschel, a question he presumably thinks cannot or at least has not yet been answered, is this: "How can a literature so variegated and contradictory speak with a normative voice today?"[21] According to Levenson, Heschel does not take the prophets seriously because he fails to acknowledge that tradition is "not monolithic and static but diverse, in flux, and not lacking in inner contradiction and conflict."[22] This failure to appreciate the inner complexity of tradition can be seen, so Levenson avers, in Heschel's very distinction between prophecy, on the one hand, and ecstasy and psychopathology, on the other. Indeed Levenson, like the first reviewers of *The Prophets*, points out that Heschel never discusses Ezekiel, "the prophet most often diagnosed as abnormal."[23] It would seem that, for Levenson, taking seriously the inner complexity of the biblical canon and recognizing its multiplicity of voices are at odds with articulating a normative account of the tradition.

Levenson's critique is illuminating precisely because it fails to consider Heschel's study on its own terms. It is based on the assumption that methodological rigor is at odds with normativity. It presupposes that modern scholarship requires mediation; that if one takes the many extant complexities of any phenomenon into account, then a gap between the descriptive and the normative must persist. Presumably, it is because Levenson does not recognize the methodological legitimacy of phenomenology—or at least phenomenology in the manner it is employed here—that he neglects to mention that in *The Prophets* Heschel explicitly states that, to understand the prophet, one must recognize that this figure cannot be an indifferent object of inquiry, that "impartiality is but a pretense."[24] To demand impartiality, often seen as the starting point of scholarly inquiry, is already to have ruled out the ability to understand the prophet.[25] That is, "the mind must shed certain habits of inquiry," "traps and decoys of conventional patterns are to be avoided," and we must reject the "preconceived certainty of being able to explain him."[26]

For many critics, the rejection of impartiality amounts to mere question-begging obscurantism. Yet for Heschel, the shift from the descriptive to the normative is the key characteristic of the religious experience he seeks to describe, an experience where "man's knowledge of God is transcended in God's knowledge of man." In that experience a profound shift takes place such that "the subject—man—becomes object, and the object—God—becomes the subject."[27] Indeed, for Heschel, this de-centering by the divine—this shift from being subject and knower to object and known—is central to biblical religiosity. It is precisely that which distinguishes biblical from Greek thinking. In *Die Prophetie* Heschel attempts to reconstruct the consciousness of the prophets and to offer a conceptual genealogy explaining how the events disclosed in the works of the prophets were diluted and compromised in subsequent Western thought—an approach justified through argumentation in his later works. Heschel proffers an account of Judaism that seeks to recover it from Hellenistic admixtures and dilutions. In striking contrast to the Christian theologians attempting to denude the Christian tradition of its Jewish roots, Heschel is trying to purify the Hebrew Bible of Greek accretions.

But who is the prophet for Heschel? Levenson is certainly correct in noting that Heschel does not prioritize the polyvocality and complexity of the biblical tradition. However, Levenson is guilty of his own failure to attend to history here—in this case, ignoring the larger intellectual milieu in which Heschel's work appeared. Unlike contemporary scholarship that is interested in contesting boundaries and showing their complexity and fuzziness, at the time Heschel was writing, the emphasis was on sharpening and hardening distinctions. For example, Heschel's notion of the prophet must be thought along the lines of Max Weber's notion of the "ideal type" and Eduard Spranger's notion of "life totalities." Weber's ideal type

> is formed by the one-sided accentuation of one or more points of view and by the synthesis of a great many diffuse, discrete and more or less present and occasionally absent concrete individual phenomena, which are arranged according to those one-sidedly emphasized viewpoints into a unified analytical construct (*Gedankenbild*). In its conceptual purity, this mental construct cannot be found empirically anywhere.[28]

Weber's ideal type is a heuristic device, not designed to describe the messy panoply of reality or acknowledge the plurality of its voices, but rather to provide a standard against which to measure and find order.

Similarly, Eduard Spranger, in *Types of Men: The Psychology and Ethics of Personality*,[29] lays out the manner in which archetypes, or "life totalities," are distilled. He explains his methodology as follows:

> (1) First we isolate a psychic value-tendency from the totality of the soul. (2) Then we think of this value-tendency in its pure form; that is, we *idealize* it. In this way we construct ideal types which we use as regular though artificial outlines. This abstraction is counteracted by our third step. (3) The relation of the one-sided type to the whole (the method of *totalization*). (4) The fourth step also counterbalances the initial artificiality of our method by the process of

individualization which emphasizes special historical, geographical, and wholly personal circumstances. Thus we develop a scientific method similar to Galileo's. First, we think of the abstract, pure case and then we add more and more concrete conditions.[30]

One such typology, or life totality, that Spranger introduces is the religious individual. According to Spranger, "we can now define *religiosity* as the condition, instinctive or rational, in which a single experience is either positively or negatively related to the total value of life."[31] For Spranger, "[a] religious man is he whose whole mental structure is permanently directed to the creation of the highest and absolutely satisfying value experience."[32] Indeed, if Weber's ideal type is a heuristic designed to bring clarity to the messy nature of political reality, Spranger's typologies are, or claim to reflect at least on some level, actual existence. Regardless, both methods distort the details pertaining to a given person or phenomenon with the intent of providing, at least for thought, a more fully realized, that is, a more abstract and general, view of it.

In *Die Prophetie*, Heschel is not seeking to offer an encyclopedic account of the prophets and their influences (*pace* Levenson), but rather to provide a typology of them. Indeed, Heschel's language is unmistakably clear in this regard. In *Die Prophetie* he explains that the prophet is "the man of sympathy" [*Sympathetiker*], which "is a religious type sui generis."[33] Heschel finds the characteristics of this ideal in the figures of Amos, Hosea, Isaiah, and Jeremiah. (Micah and Habakkuk are included as well in *The Prophets*.) In his description of a prophet, Heschel uses the typology of the "man of sympathy" as the counter-type [*Gegentypus*] to the ecstatic. He draws the distinction between "the Stoic sage who is a homo apathetikos" and "the prophet" who "may be characterized as a homo sympathetikos."[34] This typological form of thinking blurs the boundaries between the descriptive and the normative.[35] Not insignificantly, both Spranger's typology and Max Scheler's notion of exemplary individuals, when applied to the religious type, conflate the mystical attitude with the prophetic. It is against this dominant tendency to conflate the mystical and the prophetic that Heschel devotes so much energy, as we see, to the task of distinguishing between mysticism and prophecy or between theotropism and anthropotropism.

Levenson's critique, in fact, pays no attention to typology or exemplarity, strategies employed in scholarship prominent particularly in theory-laden forms of inquiry in Germany at the turn of the century. It also pays no attention to the manner in which scholarship and theory were urgently tied to questions of life and identity.[36] To be sure, Levenson's observation is correct that Heschel leaves Ezekiel out of his considerations. Given Heschel's concern in recovering the prophets as living voices, in combating a reductionism that conceived of them as mentally ill or as ascetics, his avoidance of Ezekiel may have been in response to the venerable tradition of scholars diagnosing that prophet with mental disorders.[37] Yet Levenson's reading refuses to recognize the philosophical dimensions of Heschel's engagement with biblical criticism, reducing it, rather tendentiously, to an evasion of historicism. Yet it is precisely the historicist assumptions and the hermeneutical implications for biblical criticism that Heschel seeks to problematize.

What Levenson cannot tolerate, it seems, is that *Die Prophetie* and its later iteration in *The Prophets* are simultaneously descriptive and normative endeavors. It is not merely that one cannot study the prophets in a disinterested manner but also that they—like the pious person in other works by Heschel—are exemplars for others to emulate. Prophetic sympathy—a core phenomenon that Heschel elaborates in *Die Prophetie*—like piety, its modern correlate, operates in Heschel's thought as "both a substantive theological concept as well as a spiritual ideal."[38] That is, prophetic sympathy and piety are to be understood in both a descriptive and a prescriptive manner. Like prophetic sympathy, which Heschel correlates to divine pathos, "piety is . . . not only a sense for the reality of the transcendent, but the taking of an adequate attitude toward it, not only a vision, a way to belief, but adjustment, the answer to a call, a mode of life."[39] The pious individual, like the prophet, represents a model to be emulated; he or she is a person who holds attitudes and sensibilities that we, modern readers, must seek to embody in our daily lives. Thus, offering a descriptive account of the pious individual is also offering an imperative, albeit a tacit one, for the reader. And in arguing on behalf of the uniqueness of the prophets, Heschel reclaims the great originary exemplars of piety, seeking to free them to speak anew to the world and to articulate an account of Judaism no longer bound to the Greek legacy of the modern West.

A brief discussion of an autobiographical reflection toward the end of *Man's Quest for God* (1954), in which Heschel discusses his time studying philosophy at the University of Berlin, will help further illuminate his methodology.[40] In his telling, Heschel worked with "erudite and profound scholars" in courses ranging from "logic, epistemology, esthetics, ethics and metaphysics." These scholars opened the world of Western philosophy to him and taught him "the austere discipline of unremitting inquiry and self-criticism."[41] However, despite the integrity and intellectual fortitude he recognized in his professors, Heschel writes of becoming "increasingly aware of the gulf that separated my views from those held at the university."[42] He charges his "teachers" with being "prisoners of a Greek-German way of thinking" and thus bound to categories and metaphysical assumptions that were incompatible with his own: "The questions I was moved by could not even be adequately phrased in categories of their thinking."[43] Where God was an overriding reality for Heschel, to his teachers, "God was an idea, a postulate of reason. They granted Him the status of being a logical possibility. But to assume that He had existence would have been a crime against epistemology."[44] Heschel recognized that he and his teachers maintained significantly different orientations toward the relationship between philosophy and Judaism.

As Heschel tells it, he became convinced that "there is much that philosophy could learn from Jewish life." Although he does not say this explicitly, Heschel implies that, at least in regard to the order of thinking, for his professors—those bound to German and Greek categories—Judaism was at best ancillary to philosophy. Or more specifically, where they found the ultimate question to be "how to be good," for Heschel it is "how to be holy." For "Judaism the idea of the good is pen-ultimate. It cannot exist without the holy. The good is the base, the holy is the summit. Man cannot be good unless he strives to be holy."[45] What, then, are we to make of this distinction between the good and the holy? It would appear that it is between an abstract notion and the living God, the God of the Jewish tradition, the God of the Bible. "To have an idea of the good is not the same as living by the insight, *Blessed is the man who does not forget Thee*."[46] Abstract notions of the good are insufficient; they must be rooted in the living God.

No less than Rosenzweig and Buber, Heschel faults the neo-Kantian notion of the religion of reason—dominant at the time of his studies in Berlin[47]—for being arid and lifeless. As he puts it in *God in Search of Man* (1955), one does not grasp God or, more importantly "the realness of God" in "insipid concepts." Rather, "consciousness of God is a response, and God is a challenge rather than a notion. We do not think Him, we are stirred by Him. . . . We may address ourselves to Him; we cannot comprehend Him."[48] Like Rosenzweig and Buber, Heschel insists on the priority of contact, of encounter, to conceptual knowledge. Indeed, both Heschel and Rosenzweig insist that an active God is the initiator of contact and subsequent knowledge on the part of human beings.[49]

Heschel shares Rosenzweig's and Buber's frustration with Cohen's austere rationalism. He asks, "Must speculation and existence remain like two infinite parallel lines that never meet?"[50] He then suggests, "Or perhaps this impossibility of juncture is the result of the fact that our speculation suffers from what is called in astronomy a parallax, from the apparent displacement of the object, caused by the change of our point of observation."[51] One must begin with God, not the human being and reason. However, rather than the innovations and reinventions of tradition that Buber and Rosenzweig offer, Heschel thinks that only the tradition, or a reappropriation of the tradition, can articulate the proper response. Or, as he puts it in *God in Search of Man*, "In thinking about the living God we must look to the prophets for guidance."[52] Heschel is writing figuratively in this later work, which is devoted not to the prophets but to Jewish piety in general, and by looking to the prophets he means tradition, prayers, and the piety of the great figures of Judaism.

The Eclipse of (the Biblical) God

In *Die Prophetie*, Heschel begins with the assumption that the God of the Bible, the "God of the Old Testament"[53] in particular, has been not only fundamentally distorted and misrepresented but also "entirely driven out" [*ganz verdrängt*][54] of the West. Heschel provides a narrative of sorts for this elimination of the God of the Hebrew Bible, attributing it to a collision between Greek philosophical theology and the Christian controversy around Marcion of Sinope.[55]

Heschel's history of the Greek philosophical account of God distinctly recalls Hermann Cohen's chapter on "Creation" in *Religion of Reason out of the Sources of Judaism*. Both Heschel and Cohen attempt, using philosophical language, to account for the conceptual incommensurability between the biblical and the Greek accounts of God. This demonstration is essential for Heschel's subsequent genealogical delineation of Christian theology, which he charges with reverting to Greek rather than biblical ways of accounting for God. In *Religion of Reason*, Cohen traces the notion of God as it evolved in Greek philosophy beginning with the pre-Socratics to contrast it with his notion of creation or, more pointedly to show that Being [*Sein*] is distinct from actuality [*Wirklichkeit*]. In a strikingly similar manner, Heschel recounts Greek notions of God in regard to Being and motion [*Bewegung*] to demonstrate its aversion to pathos, and thus its incommensurability with the biblical God.

If Cohen's primary concern, in his review of Greek thought, was pantheism, the identity between God and the world, Heschel is troubled by the immutability of the divine. Beginning with Parmenides, Heschel emphasizes that for Greek philosophy "the conception of Being" [*Seinsauffassung*] was such that "the true being is *immutable*" [*das wahrhafte Seiende sei* unverärderlich].[56] Indeed, "this ontological insight was utilized in the determination of the concept of God" such that it becomes the "main theological feature [*theologischen Hauptmerkmal*] of Greek philosophy." Heschel traces the manner in which "the idea of God as true being" comes to entail the exclusion of mutability, a course of thought developed and carried forward in the philosophies of Anaxagoras, Plato, and Aristotle.[57]

As a sign of how fluid the notions of "Greek" and "biblical" are in these works, Cohen critiques Christianity for being too Greek in the sense that human beings and the world are too similar to God (see chapter 2). Heschel, however, criticizes Christianity for the exact opposite reason. It errs in following the Greeks in making God impassible, incapable of suffering or feeling pain, and thus too different from human beings. Of course, at stake in both Cohen's and Heschel's respective notions of God is the issue of personhood; God's personhood is anathema to Cohen's religion of reason, but is central to Heschel's philosophical theology. Indeed, this difference is reflected in their respective methodologies: Cohen uses a hermeneutic rooted in ethical, humanistic culture to rationalize and de-mythologize Scripture, whereas Heschel attempts to recover the consciousness of the prophet, who has been overcome by sympathy for the living God.

For Heschel, the notion of an immutable God, central to Greek thought, en-tails a rejection of affects understood as "psychical motions" [*seelischer Bewegun-gen*].[58] Thus, it would appear that "the irreconcilability of [the affects] with the essence of the divine [is made manifest] from ontological reasons."[59] Pathos is a type of movement, a being moved. To be sure, this movement is spiritual or emo-tional in nature, but is movement nonetheless. As such, it cannot apply to true being (i.e., God). Therefore, God is conceived as beyond pathos, as apathetic in the etymological sense. This notion subsequently influenced the monotheistic traditions that came to use Greek philosophical concepts to elaborate their theol-ogies. This notion of the immutable God extends beyond the thought world of ancient Greece to the Stoics and to Christian thinkers such as Augustine. In-deed, it remains prevalent in Jewish rationalists like Cohen.[60] While Heschel emphasizes the dichotomy of Biblical and Greek thought in a manner foreign to Buber[61] and Rosenzweig,[62] all three share a rejection of the ideal, impassive no-tion of God. That is, one ought to read his work, despite its significant depar-tures, as taking place in the wake of the existentialist, or the dialogical, critique of Cohen's idealist notion of religion.

Heschel illuminates the discrepancies regarding the view of the emotions in Greek and biblical thought. Pointing to Plato's distinction between the ra-tional and nonrational parts of the soul, Heschel insists that "this value dual-ism [*Wertdualismus*] is utterly foreign to Biblical thinking."[63] Indeed, Heschel claims that nowhere is this divergence between Greek and biblical thought starker than in the question of whether it is appropriate to apply emotional lan-guage to God. In biblical thinking the emotions are bound up with spiritual knowledge, and thus they are not irrational. In Greek thinking, in contrast, pa-thos "is a condition of passivity. In regard to the affects, one is impressed upon and determined by another being [*Wesen*]."[64] For the Greeks, reason ought to dictate action, and *sophrosyne*, the virtue of moderation, was paramount. The ideal, as introduced by Zeno, was "*apatheia*," which is a moral ideal of the "total extirpation of the affects, the total overcoming of suffering."[65] In this matter, Heschel finds a surprising ally in Cohen, who rejects the passivity of affects, par-ticularly in the case of pity. Knowledge and emotions are, for Cohen, integrated into ethics, particularly in regard to the transformation of the other [*Gegen-mensch*] to one's fellow human being [*Mitmensch*].[66] Nevertheless the difference between Cohen and Heschel remains significant. For Cohen, the affects are an essential part of the human being becoming an ethical agent, but they never ap-ply to God; for Heschel pathos is a notion that is directly applicable to God, or at least God-in-relation-to-human-beings.

Heschel examines the Greek philosophers who take offense at and offer critiques of the anthropomorphic accounts of the gods in Homer and folk poetry. He notes how the critiques of Xenophanes, Plato, and Aristotle—aimed at "the capriciousness and corruptibility of the gods" and the manner in which they are swayed by sacrifices—are later applied, rather uncritically, to the God of the Bible.[67] However, Heschel claims that the two accounts of God are not comparable, and thus the appropriation of Greek critiques of "demythologization" is problematic.

In *Die Prophetie* Heschel challenges the application of Greek philosophical categories to Jewish thought, and in doing so he goes against the dominant tendency of the Jewish philosophical tradition from Philo to Cohen. When discussing the Greek philosophical critique of anthropomorphism, Heschel asks, "Why, in Palestine, where the primordial sentiment [*urtümliche Empfindung*] for the purity of the representation of God was so at home, did no one raise an objection against making similar [*Verähnlichung*] which is employed so often in Scripture?"[68] The reason, Heschel claims, is that philosophers such as Xenophanes found objectionable the "humanization" [*Vermenschlichung*] of the gods, of the divine. They decried the depiction of divine beings as licentious and driven by base instincts; the Greek philosophers objected to the process of reducing the divinity to the level of human beings, of characterizing gods by human traits and thereby debasing the sense of the divine. However, the Bible does not humanize God even when it offers "expressions of affect" [*Affektäusserungen*] that indicate some sense of similarity with human beings.[69]

According to Heschel, there is a fundamental distinction between the depiction of the divine in Greek folk poetry—to which the philosophers objected—and the depiction of God in the Bible. Even if both use anthropomorphic language they do so to different effects.[70] What is the source of this difference? For Heschel, what separates the biblical God's "jealousy" and "wrath" from the "lust" of Zeus are two very different notions of the significance of the human being. For the Bible, the human condition is exemplary or, at least can be, of holiness, whereas for the Greek philosophers the basic human condition—as opposed to the rational part of the soul—is that which is worthless, to be shed. What links the all-too-human Greek gods to the utterly transcendent and utterly apathetic God of Aristotle is the lack of concern for the intrinsic value of human life. In contrast, the sublime and ethical God of the Bible "does not simply command and expect obedience; he is also moved and affected by what happens in the world and he reacts accordingly." In the biblical view, deeds of human beings "move Him, affect Him, grieve Him, and on the other hand, gladden and please Him . . . events and actions in the world bring him joy or pain, pleasure or displeasure." [71] If God is concerned with history, if God is pathos laden, then there is some level of commonality, shared concern, and resemblance between God and human beings. According to Heschel, the site of this commonality is the correlation between divine pathos and sympathy.

To be sure, in every depiction of God in the Bible it is understood that God is fundamentally distinct from human beings. Even when emotions are ascribed to God in the Bible, according to Heschel, God is conceived as being radically different than humans such that "'objective' processes are 'subjective' for him." God's radical difference, God's sublimity, is always front and center in any recourse to anthropomorphic language so that it "would not be blasphemy."[72] The biblical use of anthropomorphic language, of "expressions of affect," is "always sublime, always ethically conditioned and ethically necessary."[73] God's pathos is inherently ethical. The very emotional charge characterizing God's relationship with the world—including anger—does not oppose, so much as offer "an enrichment of the structure the ethical" in biblical thinking.[74] That is, "an ethos is immanent in pathos."[75]

Heschel's not uncontroversial support of divine pathos comes to a head in his elaborations of the prophets' relationship to divine anger. Eliezer Berkovits compares Heschel's rehabilitation of divine anger and divine pathos unfavorably to Maimonides' rejection of anthropomorphism and the general Hellenization of Jewish thought.[76] Berkovits finds the very notion of divine anger unacceptable because anger means "an uncontrolled outburst," in which case "even in man, anger . . . is not too laudable a quality."[77] In addition, Berkovits thinks that the term "anger" when applied to God is not used in the normal way, since "God controls His anger, He is its master."[78] If this is the case, then Heschel is really not talking about emotions, but "an educational gimmick."[79] Berkovits's argument, then, is that Heschel does not, despite his claims, escape Maimonides' rejection of affect. However, whether Berkovits's argument has merit or Heschel is able to ethicize anger, what is imperative is to recognize the context in which Heschel deliberately uses this term, with all of its theological baggage. As Shai Held points out, "Hovering in the background [of Heschel's account of divine anger] is the spirit of Marcion, the anathematized second-century Christian who insisted upon the 'radical disparity and absolute discontinuity' between the Old Testament and the New, and who thus taught that 'Christianity has no relation to the Judaism from which it sprang.'"[80] At stake in Heschel's argument is not the nature of God-talk in general, which is Berkovits's primary concern, but the very ontological distinction between the respective notions of God in Greek and biblical thought. Although Berkovits recognizes that Heschel's notion of pathos is a form of drawing a distinction between the God of Abraham, Isaac, and Jacob, on the one hand, and the God of the philosophers, on the other,[81] he seems to completely miss the larger philosophical and cultural implication for Heschel of this distinction, which is one of the main threads tying *Die Prophetie* and *The Prophets* together.

The centrality—and moral integrity—of divine pathos in the God of the Hebrew Bible is one of, if not, the, central topics of *Die Prophetie* and is a major element in subsequent works by Heschel. Although Heschel's account of pathos denotes God's emotional life and the correlation between God's subjectivity and objectivity, it is imperative to recognize that pathos is not something inherent in God's essence or is what God is in God's self [*God als sein Ansichsein*].[82] That is, pathos is a relational characteristic; indeed, Heschel argues that it is a theological category sui generis, characterizing the "dynamic relationship between God and human beings."[83] Pathos is not ontologically fundamental or primordial, but rather is "an induced condition,"[84] a "reaction to human history."[85]

Yet, according to Heschel, the biblical notion of divine pathos has been forgotten and lost. Instead, in Christianity the notion of God's anger, or *ira dei*, becomes the subject of a prolonged and impassioned controversy. Heschel emphasizes the influence of Gnosis, which rejected the notion of pathos and which reached its high point in Marcion. Marcion, himself influenced by Paul's distinction between grace and works, rejects the "God of the Old Testament," the God of justice, whose "inferiority and imperfection" [*Unvollkommenheit*] are manifested most clearly in "anger" [*Zorn*].[86] According to Heschel, this rejection spurred on a controversy that caused the question of God's affects and thus pathos to become central in the church; it led in turn to the tension between the Greek philosophical critique of anthropomorphism and an erroneous—according to Heschel—understanding of biblical pathos. Although Marcion's theology was rejected as a heresy, his critique of divine anger in the Old Testament ultimately succeeded in undercutting and fundamentally distorting the notion of biblical pathos.

As Heschel understands it, the attempts of the Church Fathers such as Tertullian and Origen to defend divine anger from Marcion's critique only further estranges Christian doctrine from pathos in the biblical sense. Tertullian insists that divine anger is necessary to judge human activity properly. Yet God remains beyond affect, beyond pathos, although the Logos retains anger, which for Tertullian, is necessary for theological judgment. Origen rejects the literal notion of God's anger. Following Philo of Alexandria's allegorical reading of the Old Testament, Origen holds that notions such as anger, wrath, and jealousy are to be interpreted ultimately in a process meant to educate human beings. Doing so preserves the Old Testament alongside the "Marcionite account of God."[87] In either case, pathos is no longer seen as appropriate to apply to God. Indeed, according to Heschel, Marcion's criticism merged with the Greek philosophical critique of anthropomorphism in subsequent Jewish and Christian polemics against pagan gods, which often focused on their affects. Heschel views as "an all but tragic chapter of theological thinking" the manner in which the Abrahamic monotheisms come to reject pathos as " 'notorious' anthropomorphism."[88] Heschel, like Buber and Rosenzweig, is intensely worried about the Marcionite heresy and its resurgence, which undergirds a great deal of theoretical and cultural antisemitism. It also, Heschel thinks, has led Jews to misunderstand their own theology.

Clearing the Ground

If Heschel is to recover the God of the Hebrew Bible, to undo the Marcionite distortion, it is incumbent on him to offer a notion of prophecy that exposes the problematic assumptions of two of the most prevalent notions of prophecy in his day: the ecstatic and the Kantian models. Although the former was favored by scholars of comparative religion and the latter by Jewish rationalists, Heschel finds both to be too Greek, albeit in different ways.

The basis of Heschel's repudiation of both prevailing notions of prophecy is a distinction fundamental to the entire study. According to Heschel, at the heart of the religious phenomenon is a relationship between the immanent, that which is within the realm of human experience, and the transcendent, that which is beyond it. In religious phenomenon, there is a genuine occurrence, a "*breach* [*Durchbruch*] in the inevitable," which sets in motion an "event" [*Ereignis*].[89] However, a great deal is at stake in the particular manner in which the immanent and the transcendent relate in this "event": There is "either the turn [*Wendung*] of the transcendent in the direction [*Richtung*] of the human being or the turn of human beings in the direction of the transcendent." The former Heschel names anthropotropic and the latter theotropic.[90]

In the anthropotropic turn, the breach with the everyday is such that a turning [*Wendung*] takes place on the part of the divine and is directed toward [*Richtung*] a particular human being: "The turn [of God to the human being] is an event [initated on the side] of God [*Ereignis Gottes*]. . . . The inspiration as event, as the turn, is not conditioned through history, but rather [it is conditioned] through the character of God."[91] Whereas prophecy is uniquely anthropotropic for Heschel,[92] theotropism, or the human turning to God, is not unique to the Israelites; nor is it foreign to the Hebrew Bible. The Psalms, rooted in the cultic and priestly context, Heschel argues, are the repository of the theotropic dimension in the Hebrew Bible.[93] As we see later, it is not merely anthropotropism nor its combination with theotropism per se that makes the religion of Israel unique, but the distinct nature of God's pathos as manifested in anthropotropism.

The occlusion of and the discomfort with anthropotropism can be seen in the manner in which the study of comparative religion has failed to grasp the difference between prophecy and ecstasy. The academic study of religion would rather conflate the anthropotropic and the theotropic than keep them distinct. Yet the blurring of the distinction between the two is not due solely to comparative religion and its inability to recognize prophecy; rather, the operating assumptions of comparative religion are merely one more instance of the theotropic being elevated over the anthropotropic and, indeed, being used to obscure it altogether from view. In *Die Prophetie*, Heschel traces the long history of thought in which ecstasy and prophecy are treated as equivalent. To challenge that conception, Heschel offers a clear typological and phenomenological distinction between the basic structures of the ecstatic-mantic religious experience and that of the prophetic. The prophet's experience is fundamentally anthropotropic in nature, whereas that of the ecstatic is theotropic. That is, God comes to the prophet, while the ecstatic seeks out God. Prophecy is characterized by theophany, God's active manifestation, whereas ecstasy is characterized by the use of "narcotic means, asceticism, breathing exercises," and other means to attempt to distance oneself from one's consciousness to gain "visionary knowledge"[94] and to approach the divine.

The conflation of prophecy and ecstasy was no doubt bound up with the larger, long-term effort to rule out the uniqueness of the Israelites. *Die Prophetie* emphasizes the widespread nature of ecstatic religion in the ancient Near East. Interestingly, both the Greeks and the Israelites lived in an environment rife with ecstatics: "The motherland of ecstasy was Asia-Minor and Syria."[95] The cult of Dionysus penetrated Greece from Thrace, and "[b]etween the sixth and eighth centuries BC there can be seen in Greece a series of seers and prophets referred to as sibyls and Bacchanals."[96] The term "ecstasy" was coined in Greece and means "a condition of rapture [*Entrücktheit*] . . . in which the soul has fled the body and united with the divine" [*Gottheit*]."[97] Plato talks about holy madness and neo-Platonists elaborate on this notion. Although Heschel acknowledges that ecstatic religion has infiltrated the monotheisms, particularly in the mysticisms that developed in postbiblical times, he draws a sharp distinction between the prophetic experience and the mantic, which he insists are associated with the Canaanite religions.

Heschel claims that the distortion of prophecy taking place in the work of nineteenth- and twentieth-century scholars of comparative religion has its roots in the occlusion of the distinction between anthropotropism and theotropism. Indeed, one might say that what is characteristic of or defines the biblical perspective is the anthropotropic, whereas for the Greek it is the theotropic. Thus, even though the ecstatic religions of Greece stand at odds with the rigorous rationalism of the philosophers, both presuppose theotropism. As distinct as Aristotle's notion of *Theoria* is from the mystery religions, in both views the human being ascends to God, and God remains indifferent.[98]

Heschel posits a fundamental opposition between prophecy and ecstasy. He secures this distinction by grounding prophecy in theophany, which he insists is autochthonous to Israel; it was not something the Israelites borrowed from neighboring communities: "Theophany is already detectable in the oldest biblical sources: it is already in opposition to ecstasy in a serious and national fundamental representation in Israel *"echte und ursprüngliche volkstümliche Grundvorstellung in Israel]*."[99] In theophany, God possesses agency and indeed becomes manifest, yet God's transcendence is not compromised; there is a concealing simultaneous with revealing such that one never perceives God directly. Rather, "the Lord appears in fire, storm, earthquake and thunder."[100] According to Heschel, the contrast between prophecy and ecstasy was sufficient to imbue the Israelites with an ethnic/religious national identity. Indeed, it would not be too much of a stretch to claim that, for Heschel, Judaism—and indeed the integrity of the biblical tradition—stands or falls on the notion of an active God that can be manifested in the consciousness of human beings in some manner or another.

This same anthropotropic foundation of Judaism leads Heschel to reject another prominent interpretation of the prophets in his day. With Cohen likely in mind, Heschel emphasizes that "monotheism in its universal and ethical form is not the particular achievement of the classical prophets."[101] That is, Heschel takes aim at the Kantian interpretation of the prophets common among many Jewish thinkers in early twentieth-century Germany; he maintains instead that the notion of divine pathos, particularly the manner that the "personality" of the divine infuses ethics, is the core of the prophetic message. With clear reference to Kantian moral terminology, Heschel rejects attempts to "appoint . . . the prophetic God to the first citizen in the moral kingdom" because it fails to recognize the "divine subjectivity of prophetic Pathos" and thus "contradicts the prophetic understanding of God."[102] That is, it is not hermeneutically plausible to maintain that the prophets, anticipating Kant, posited the idea of God as a moral postulate to ensure the coherence of the right and the good and thus secure the rational coherence of "the moral order." Heschel charges that "grace, repentance and forgiveness, 'the freedom to return'" [*Umkehr*]—staples of prophetic literature (not to mention modern Jewish thought)—would be incomprehensible "from the point of view of a God subordinated to a moral principle."[103] This reading stands in stark contrast—indeed, it evinces a willful disregard and therefore an outright rejection—of Cohen's account of repentance grounded on a non–pathos- laden notion of God.

Although Heschel insists that the relationship between God and human beings is moral in nature, as we have seen he rejects the formal structure of the Kantian framework. God's relationship with human beings is not mediated by abstract ideas of the good or of the essence of the human being. Rather, Heschel claims that the relationship between God and human beings "is not completely reducible to the value of morality. The pathos-laden construction of the good results from the unlimited sovereignty of God."[104] Indeed, the unlimited sovereignty of God rooted in pathos—what Heschel refers to as the "subjectivizing of ethical thought, the pathetic modification of morality"—is an "irreducible presupposition for prophetic religion."[105] Although he does not mention Cohen explicitly, much less that thinker's celebrated account of ethics,[106] Heschel's critique of Kant functions equally well as a critique of Cohen in regard to the notion of God's pathos and the lack of a direct relationship between God and the human being.[107] In this respect, Kant and Cohen are Greek rather than biblical.

Knowing God

If Heschel rejects Kantian interpretations of the prophets as well as those of comparative religion, he offers an alternative account of the prophet's experience of inspiration [*Eingebung*] by means of a phenomenological and hermeneutical inquiry into the prophetic consciousness. For the prophet, Heschel insists, inspiration can only be understood as "an objective transcendent event." If one reduces the prophetic event to pathology or to spiritual exercises or claims that it is merely ethical and philosophical teachings dressed up in symbolic and visionary garb, then one distorts it beyond all recognition. What is intrinsic and fundamental about this experience is precisely the sense that the impetus for the event takes place on the side of transcendence, "as a time-bound [zeitlich] shining forth [*Erscheinung*]: as a moment, not as something eternally enduring or perpetually encountered."[108]

Undergirding or grounding inspiration is divine pathos. However, pathos is no simple substance, but is itself an act and relation. Or, as Heschel puts it, "Pathos constitutes a binding [*Verknüpfung*] between God and the human being. It is not the indifferent will of God, but rather the definiteness of pathos, is the place where the theological and the anthropological encounter one another."[109] It is pathos, God's active engagement with the world, that is primordial and the precondition for prophetic sympathy, its correlate.

According to Heschel, philosophy fails to recognize the sublime nature of God even if, like medieval scholasticism, it speaks in superlatives, declaring God to be *ens realisimum,* the highest of all beings that exist, characterized by omnipotence, omniscience, omnibenevolence, and omnipresence. Philosophical attempts to grasp God, even those that seek to do so in the superlative, fail because they objectify. Indeed, in a deliberate play on Protagoras's famous dictum, God, not the human being, "is the measure of all things."[110] It is the priority of the divine subject over the human that in Heschel's view gives the lie to the Kantian position that seeks to prioritize reason and that only grants God the form of a postulate. Rather, for Heschel, it is experience—at least the experience (as interpreted by the consciousness) of the prophet and later of the pious individual—that reveals God's priority to the human subject, that it is God that knows human beings, not human beings who know God. By referring to God as the measure of all things in this passage, Heschel is speaking in a phenomenological sense of disorienting and de-centering the subject. To be sure the phenomenological sense is complementary with traditional theological notions of God as the creator of the universe, and thus that which bestows meaning.

Radical priority must be granted to God to properly grasp the prophet's experience of revelation.[111] For the prophet, God "is always seen as sentient, grasped as a thinker, never as an object."[112] Like Buber, Heschel uses the language of encounter; like both Buber and Rosenzweig he uses the language of actuality to describe the interaction between God and the prophet. He writes, "In the prophetic act an encounter [*Begegnung*] takes place, a dialogical, concrete interchange. God as a personality stands over against the human personality, both in the fullness of their actuality[*Wirklichkeit*]: God in the manifestation of his Pathos and the prophet with his humanity intact [unüberwundenen Menschlichkeit].[113] Like Buber and Rosenzweig, Heschel maintains that the prophetic act has "a subject-subject structure," such that "the self-conscious, active I of the prophet encounters the actuality of the Subject who is the Inspirer" [*der Subjektwirklichkeit des Einge-benden*].[114] Yet, although it can be said that Buber and Rosenzweig maintain an active notion of God, that notion is inextricable from larger metaphysical structures. Heschel goes further than Buber and Rosenzweig in denuding this encounter of such structures through recourse to Max Scheler's notion of sympathy.

Indeed, Heschel's use of sympathy as a means of understanding the prophet is one of the most widely celebrated elements of *Die Prophetie* and *The Prophets*. For Heschel, prophetic "knowledge" is not metaphysical and does not reach God's essence, but rather, in a Schelerian vein, offers "an understanding" [*Einfühlung*] or a "feeling the same" [*Gleichgefühl*] with God's pathos.[115] For Heschel, what distinguishes the prophet from others is not superior theoretical knowledge or even ethical teachings per se, but that he or she possesses a singular "*understanding for God*" which culminates in a shared understanding with God [Einverständnis].[116] Heschel insists that there is a correlation between "prophetic sympathy" and "divine pathos." "There is no naïve, naturally given feeling, but rather the sympathy with God is the ground of motion, which determines affinity and animosity in the prophet."[117] That is, the prophet always speaks from the position of God's "manifestion, from God's turning" [*Wendung*]. Such a disclosure is always "relational," whether in regard to "Israel or to the world."[118]

Appropriating Scheler's notion of sympathy enables Heschel to break with intellectualist conceptions of prophecy. Scheler, in describing the concept of "fellow feeling" [*Mitgefühl*], which is synonymous with sympathy, explains that it is distinct from theoretical knowledge. According to Scheler we do not learn about one another's feelings through reasoning by analogy or projection. We do not reproduce the other person's emotion within ourselves to understand what she is feeling. Rather, sympathy connotes that, as part of our intersubjective nature, we possess the capacity for "feeling the other's feeling, not just knowing of it, nor judging that the other has it."[119] However, where Scheler uses this notion to explain how we know and experience other human beings, Heschel employs it in regard to how the prophet knows and experiences God or, more specifically divine pathos.

Scheler's notion of sympathy offers a hermeneutical tool for disclosing the interaction between the divine and human. Heschel is quite explicit that by using the term "sympathy" he intends "to eliminate the old, traditional notion of God-knowledge" [*Gotteserkenntnis*]. However, his purpose is "not only to show the inadequacy of the latter, but above all through the fruitfulness of the former."[120] When the prophet has a dialogical encounter, is called forth, he discovers that "[God] is not the object of religious discovery but rather the sovereign subject of a revelation" [*das souveräne Subjekt einer Offenbarung*].[121] The notion of sympathy enables Heschel to depart from the intellectualist understanding of prophecy dominant in Jewish rationalism and continuing through Cohen, which configures prophecy as a form of knowledge. Heschel insists instead that "in terms of content, prophetic revelation does not reveal the divine essence."[122] Heschel is quite critical of theological terms that evoke a theoretical grasp of the essence of God as atemporal and ahistorical, thus resembling the Greek conceptions of the divine. Rather, the prophet, bound by sympathy to this divine "sovereign," cedes the center of gravity of his or her outlook to the divine, such that "God is the point of view [*Angelpunkt*] of his thinking. The peculiarity [*Eigenart*] of the prophetic valuation of the world [*Gefühlswelt*] is conditioned through this disposition" [*Haltung*].[123]

The prophet, as the receiver of revelation, participates in a dialogical encounter with the divine. "Revelation is an interchange, it is experienced as dynamic, as a *giving* [Geben] not only as a given" [*Gegebenes*].[124] That is, as opposed to Cohen, who actively rationalizes a given source of tradition, Heschel describes the prophet as one who experiences a revelatory event: "Transcendence is grasped in the giving of words [*Wortgaben*], is the generating of movement [*Bewegungserzeugnis*], as becoming word [*wortwerdende*] or as having becoming word."[125] In this sense, revelation is ongoing, but it is driven by events, by responses to "historical actuality" [*Aktualität*],[126] rather than by a fixed, eternal process. Where Cohen rationalizes the tradition, finds the sources of tradition, and reads them in light of critical idealism, Heschel reinterprets the tradition in light of the consciousness of prophetic sympathy or of the pious individual.

Although Heschel's account has a certain metaphysical dimension, he insists that metaphysics as an activity remains remote and irrelevant to the prophet. What emerges is the immediate, emotional intertwining of God and the prophet through sympathy, which takes place in the revelatory event. For Heschel, the prophet never encounters God in Godself, God as apart from the world. Rather, the consistent element in the prophetic writings on which Heschel grounds his phenomenologically based hermeneutics is God's pathos. Divine pathos is always relational, whether in regard to the dialogical relationship with the prophet, the collective relationship with the Israelites, or a more universal relationship with the peoples of the world—indeed, it is often the case that some combination of all three is in play. Pathos itself is liminal, where opposites overlap or come together. It is "the nexus [*Verknüpfung*] between God and human being" and the "unity of the temporal [*Unewigem*] and eternal [*Ewigem*], the rational and the irrational, the metaphysical and historical and it is therefore the essential ground [*Realgrund*] and epitome of all relationships between God and human beings."[127]

Pathos, Heschel avers, is neither God's essence nor even the foundation of God's engagement with the world. Heschel reasons, "Pathos itself cannot be the ultimate given [*das letzt Gegebene gewesen sein*], because it is always a special case, a mode, a variable, not something absolute, immutable."[128] Regardless of its mode (mercy, jealousy, anger), pathos is always directional. And what is directed through pathos, what underlies it and gives it substance, is "transcendent *concern*" [transzendente *Aufmerksamkeit*].[129] Indeed, methodologically speaking, transcendent concern is as far as Heschel is willing to proceed with his phenomenological-hermeneutical method; it is the "limit concept [Grenzbegriff] for the prophetic understanding" [*prophetische Verstehen*].[130]

The prophet, bound by sympathy to God, is called by a "prophetic appointment" [*Prophetischen Berufung*][131] to serve as an intermediary between God and the people. The inspiration of the prophet, although he or she is the locus of revelation, is not its goal. The prophet, who experiences and sympathizes with "God's private and intimate participation in the life and fate of the people,"[132] is directed by God to the world out of concern. Indeed, the figure of the prophet reveals divine concern with the Israelites and the world more generally. The Greek notion of God as an object of knowledge fosters a desire to obtain knowledge so one can adapt oneself to better fit the world and can cultivate that which is highest in oneself, thereby resembling the universe most closely. In contrast, in the prophetic system, God does not stand above, beyond, and indifferent to the universe, to be sought out by humans who theotropically detach themselves from lived reality. Rather, the prophet teaches the importance of this world, of the present, of history. When God speaks to the prophet and sends him forth, it is not for his enlightenment so that he may better comport himself to the true nature of reality. God's "utterances, commands and requirements" do not "only have meaning for human beings, but rather in the deepest sense, are a matter of deepest meaning, of divine concern, whose fulfillment or neglect possesses personal importance for God."[133] Even if God is the measure both phenomenologically and metaphysically, the figure of the prophet and the phenomenon of sympathy for divine pathos reveal that the universe is not cold and indifferent to human concerns, even if it is a "nightmare."[134]

This bestowal of meaning upon the universe is not merely abstract; it is more than an inexpressible confirmation of meaning (*pace* Buber). Rather, pathos entails the paradoxical notion that this sovereign God is nevertheless profoundly concerned with and interested in the world, "in human history," such "that [God] is affected by all events. This insight into the immediate referredness and directedness of the divine is essential to understand the *worldiness* [*Weltzugewandtheit*] of God."[135]

Heschel and German-Jewish Thought

In *The Earth Is the Lord's* (1950),[136] his eulogy for Eastern European Judaism, Heschel draws a striking contrast between Ashkenazic and Sephardic Jews. It is instructive to consider Heschel's juxtaposition in light of the tendency of German-Jewish historians to idealize the (Sephardic) Jews of Muslim Spain at the expense of the (Ashkenazic) Jews of Eastern Europe, as models for modern liberal Judaism.[137] Heschel explicitly states, "Ashkenazic" Judaism reaches its spiritual "climax . . . in Eastern Europe, particularly with the spread of the Hasidic movement."[138] Heschel claims that where the Judaism of Eastern Europe existed largely "in isolation," and thus "grew out of its own ancient roots and developed in an indigenous environment, independent of the trends and conventions of the surrounding environment,"[139] the Sephardic Jews were "distinguished not only by monumental scientific achievements, but also by a universality of spirit."[140] Although Heschel charges the Sephardic Jews with emphasizing "the elements Judaism had in common with classical philosophy" in their desire for "a synthesis of Jewish tradition and Moslem civilization,"[141] it is not far-fetched for a contemporary reader to suspect that he is obliquely criticizing German Jews for their failure to recognize and preserve their own cultural and religious uniqueness in their quest for a symbiosis between their Judaism and German culture.

If we recall, Rosenzweig breaks with Cohen's notion of a correlation between Judaism and Germanism, in which Judaism serves as a primary conceptual source driving Germanism to greater spiritual purity. For Rosenzweig, Jews and Christians are inextricably bound—the Jews as the adumbration of eternity within history but devoid of political might, whereas the Christians, possessing political power, yet unredeemed, are driven by jealousy of the Jew to conquer the world and in the process conquer themselves of their paganism. Whereas Cohen focuses on the ideal nature of Jewish and Christian (and German) identity, Rosenzweig focuses on the actual (i.e., as opposed to the ideal). However, for both the relationship is symbiotic.

Like Rosenzweig, Heschel is known as a thinker of both Judaism and Christianity. His efforts in bringing about reforms in the Catholic Church and working with Christian leaders in the civil rights and other activist movements is well documented. However, Heschel's thought is less beholden to Christianity than is that of either Cohen or Rosenzweig.

In "No Religion Is an Island" (1966),[142] Heschel's famous piece on Jewish-Christian dialogue, one can perceive echoes of Cohen and Rosenzweig, as well as a significant distance from them. Given that Cohen and Rosenzweig seek to account for a partnership or interconnection between Judaism and Christianity in their respective accounts of the co-constitution of the West, it may appear at first glance that Heschel follows suit when he says as a Jew he realizes "that it was Christianity that implanted attachment to the God of Abraham and involvement with the Hebrew Bible in the hearts of Western man."[143] However, unlike Cohen and Rosenzweig, Heschel is explicitly following theological precedents set by Maimonides and others.[144]

Heschel's stance toward Christianity is also more critical than is often acknowledged. Written after the Shoah and with attention to the world religions discourse and its Marcionite roots, Heschel's "No Religion Is an Island" addresses the legacy of Christian antisemitism:

> Nazism in its very roots was a rebellion against the Bible, against the God of Abraham. Realizing that it was Christianity that implanted attachment to the God of Abraham and involvement with the Hebrew Bible in the hearts of Western man, Nazism resolved that it must both exterminate the Jews and eliminate Christianity, and bring about instead a revival of Teutonic paganism.[145]

The insinuated affinity between Judaism and Christianity may appear overly generous, given overwhelming Christian capitulation and cooperation with the Nazi project,[146] yet things are not as they first appear. Heschel claims that the true heart of the Bible is the God of Abraham or, as he states elsewhere, the God of the prophets or the biblical (not the philosophical or Greek) God. Christianity in this account is merely the messenger, charged with implanting the "Hebrew Bible in the hearts of Western man." One notices a Rosenzweigian echo, in that Judaism represents the core and Christianity an extension of it.[147] Heschel states, "Jews and Christians are called upon to work together" when it comes to preserving the "radiance of the Hebrew Bible."[148] Indeed, Heschel insists that antisemitism and anti-Christianity are inherently linked. However, what is striking is that the anti-Christian movements to which Heschel refers are fascism and communism, movements taking place in formerly Christian countries and that, although they are inimical to Jews and Christians alike, represent more of an immediate, existential threat to Jews.

For Heschel, Jews, as practitioners of the more primordial religion, have a right to be concerned with the developments in the later, derived faith. Or as he puts it, "Judaism is the mother of the Christian faith. It has a stake in the destiny of Christianity. Should a mother ignore her child, even a wayward, rebellious one?" Heschel insists in turn that the church must not only acknowledge the Jewish tradition and the claims it possesses toward Jews but also that Jews "have a stake in its faith, have a stake in its faith, recognize our vocation to preserve and to teach the legacy of Hebrew Scripture, accept our aid in fighting Marcionite trends as an act of love."[149] In short, because anti-Christian trends can affect Christianity by seeking to de-Judaize or paganize it, and that which is true and holy about Christianity is the connection to the God of the prophets, the God of the Hebrew Bible, Jews are charged with preserving the integrity of Christianity.

Heschel's later books were written in the pluralistic United States, a quite different environment from the often overtly antisemitic, Christian Germany. Thus, it is not surprising that the tone of his later writings differs significantly from that of Cohen, Rosenzweig, and Buber. Heschel, who was known for possessing great tact, was able to work with Christian theologians without being patronizing. And to be sure, given his emphasis on biblical faith, which enabled him to critique extant forms of Judaism and Christianity alike, it does not go against the grain of his thought to find this spirituality in non-Jewish traditions such as the black church. Indeed, he considered Martin Luther King Jr. a veritable modern-day prophet. Yet it is important to recognize that Christian theologians who have been so eager to appropriate Heschel's thought, as well as Jewish theologians so eager to celebrate this hero of the civil rights era, have not adequately attended to the differences he maintains between Judaism and other traditions, including Christianity.

Although Heschel acknowledges deep connections between Judaism and Christianity—at least when the latter is properly grounded in the spirit of the Hebrew Bible rather than the Marcionite heresy—unlike Rosenzweig and Cohen, he finds no essential connection between Judaism and Europe. Or as Heschel puts it in a striking manner in *God in Search of Man* (1954),

> Geographically and historically, Jerusalem and Athens, the age of the prophets and the age of Pericles, are not too far removed from each other. Spiritually they are worlds apart. On the other hand, had Jerusalem been located at the foot of the Himalayas, monotheistic philosophy would have been modified by the tradition of Oriental thinkers. Thus, our intellectual position situated as it is between Athens and Jerusalem is not an ultimate one.[150]

Thus, in a manner not altogether different from Buber, Heschel sees Judaism as at once distinct and yet also the answer to the spiritual travails of the West. On the one hand, Heschel's notion of Judaism is spiritually unique and self-contained. On the other hand, it remains part of European civilization to the degree that the Hebrew Bible does.

6 Cultivating Objectivity: Soloveitchik, the Marburg School, and Religious Pluralism

As WE HAVE seen, although subsequent thinkers roundly broke with his Critical Idealism and his valorization of science and rationality, Hermann Cohen very much laid the ground on which later thinkers would tread. That is, his writings on Germanism made a powerful case that Jews were central to German and thus Western identity, thereby challenging those tendencies then reigning in German thought that were eager to free German culture of Jewish influences. His works on Judaism and the study of religion not only sought to displace Greece as the arbiter of rationality when it came to religion; they were a formidable challenge by a Jewish thinker to the contemporary methodologies being used to actively displace Jews and Judaism from Germany and Germanic visions of the Occident.

To be sure, even though Rosenzweig, Buber, and Heschel follow in Cohen's wake, this does not mean they are slavish followers or even good or devoted pupils of the Marburg philosopher (as Rosenzweig indeed seeks to position himself). Rosenzweig turns to a philosophy enmeshed in theology—or, rather, a philosophy that takes the experience of revelation seriously—to upend the sensibilities of the world religions discourse. Using revelation rather than philology or history, Rosenzweig posits a dialectical unity between Christianity and Judaism over against the religions of the Orient, namely, Islam and the religions of India and China.

Buber and Heschel are less eager to proceed according to Cohen's metanarratives about the West. Rather, they follow the trail he blazed in regard to the critical engagement with *Religionswissenschaft*, particularly as it undergirded the world religions discourse. However, where Cohen used his philosophical methodology to rein in or domesticate the scholarly disciplines and their technologies being used to actively de-Judaize Germany, Buber and Heschel seek to colonize them. With *I and Thou* Buber offers a philosophical foundation for comparative religion, and Heschel's *Die Prophetie,* although cast as an exercise in comparative religion, calls into question the underlying assumptions of the field. Both *I and Thou* and *Die Prophetie* proffer ontological frameworks that are deeply complementary, if not indebted outright, to sensibilities found in Jewish theological traditions, and as a result, both works challenge the Eurocentric, Christocentric, positivistic, and Romantic assumptions undergirding the study of religion at the core of the world religions discourse.

In regard to the basic structures or strategic positioning of Cohen's thought—at least as reflected in the works investigated here—Joseph Soloveitchik (1903–1993), of the four subsequent thinkers examined in depth in this study, is the one who most resembles Cohen. Soloveitchik is the only one of the four to take up both prongs of Cohen's strategy, offering a metanarrative of the West and an engagement with *Religionswissenschaft*. Indeed, like Cohen, he ties his account of the metanarrative of the West, or the history of reason, directly to the manner in which religion ought to be conceived and, by so doing, to secure the autonomy of Judaism (and indeed, Orthodox Judaism). One might say that the project of *The Halakhic Mind* (1986)[1] is not so much in opposition to Cohen as it is post-Cohenian. In this respect, Soloveitchik resembles Rosenzweig. However, rather than turn to lived experience and theology, he situates his account of religion within a historical narrative about the sciences from the vantage point of the collapse of the unity between the "scientific" and the "philosophical."[2] And yet, Soloveitchik's investigation into *homo religiosus*, which allows him to offer a normative account of religiosity, shows his engagement with the other path of the post-Cohenian trajectory that is followed by Buber and Heschel. In the foundering of traditional neo-Kantianism, Soloveitchik tries to reconstruct the other prong of Cohen's twofold approach so that it can become more conducive to championing an Orthodox—rather than liberal—religiosity.

This chapter focuses on *The Halakhic Mind*, written in the 1940s but not published until 1986. This book differs from Soloveitchik's other philosophical works. Rather than illuminating the inner life of the *ish ha-halakha* (halakhic man) as do other works of Solovietchik that date to the 1940s, such as *Halakhic Man* and *From There You Shall Seek*, *The Halakhic Mind* is a technical treatise on the philosophical repercussions of the upheavals in the sciences in the twentieth century. Indeed, one of its primary goals is to legitimate the autonomy of religious cognition by demonstrating that recent developments in science have undermined the dream of a single, comprehensive theory or system for accounting for the whole of reality. Lawrence Kaplan refers to it as "the most 'non-Jewish,' the most abstractly philosophical of Rabbi Soloveitchik's essays."[3] Similarly, Jonathan Sacks, the former Chief Rabbi of Great Britain, notes that *The Halakhic Mind* is "different in kind from [Soloveitchik's] other writings,"[4] that it "disclos[es] a tone of voice we had not heard before, the Dr. Soloveitchik of Berlin rather than the Rav of Yeshiva University."[5]

The Halakhic Mind not only explicitly engages Marburg neo-Kantianism but it also does so precisely at the intersection of science and the world religions discourse. Indeed, it is its sustained engagement with the themes of Marburg neo-Kantianism, in general, and the philosophy of Hermann Cohen, in particular, that accounts for its different tone from that of his other works. This engagement not only makes this work particularly relevant to our ongoing exploration of works by Cohen, Rosenzweig, Buber, and Heschel; it also supports Sacks's trenchant observation that there is a significant link between *The Halakhic Mind* and Soloveitchik's later essay on Jewish-Christian relations, "Confrontation" (1964),[6] although Sacks pays little attention to the role of Cohen in this connection.[7]

Given the longstanding disagreements among scholars over whether Soloveitchik's corpus should be read as eclectic or complementary in nature,[8] and given the political disputes about his legacy,[9] it should not be surprising that there are disagreements over Soloveitchik's relationship to the Marburg School in general and to Cohen in particular. For instance, in an systematic study of Soloveitchik's work, Reinier Munk emphasizes that Soloveitchik's (or Solowiejczyk's) dissertation on Cohen, *Das reine Denken und die Seinskonstituierung bei Hermann Cohen* [Pure Thinking and the Constitution of Being According to Hermann Cohen][10] (1932)—which I explore later in depth—"exemplifies a fundamental and unbridgeable difference of opinion with Cohen" on epistemological and ontological matters.[11] On the penultimate page of his study, Munk writes, "It is . . . , legitimate to conclude that epistemologically speaking, although not only in that sense, Cohen's thought is of little importance to Soloveitchik's thought."[12] In striking contrast, Kaplan describes a conversation he had with famed scholar and father of Jewish political theology Jacob Taubes in which Taubes laments Soloveitchik's emphasis on mathematics and physics. Kaplan recounts Taubes as saying, "Unfortunately, R. Soloveitchik when he studied at Berlin went 'barking up the wrong tree.' He came under the dominant influence of Hermann Cohen when he should have followed the path of Heidegger and later on of Gadamer and Riceour."[13] It is hard to say how much other scholars writing on Soloveitchik, in particular his *The Halakhic Mind*, follow Munk's position and reject Taubes's regarding the significance of Cohen's influence on Solovietchik. It is quite possible, indeed likely, that silence about this issue is due to a lack of familiarity among scholars with the requisite works by Cohen, infamous for their difficulty and long out of fashion in the academy.[14]

I argue that Soloveitchik, much like Buber, Rosenzweig, and Heschel, is dissatisfied with the conceptual austerity and quantitative emphasis of Cohen's philosophy. Like them, he emphasizes the priority of actuality over Cohen's abstract, generative mathematical logic. In this, Soloveitchik, like the other post-Cohenian thinkers discussed here, also takes part in the generational shift that saw a marked departure from rationalism and Idealism to existentialism and lived experience. Yet, Soloveitchik not only offers a more sustained engagement with Cohen's thought than the other thinkers—even Rosenzweig—but is also less eager to jettison Cohen's rationalism than they are. Instead, he seeks to marry it with certain existential and pluralistic commitments.

And yet, although Soloveitchik breaks with Cohen on such issues as the sui generis notion of religion and the notion of epistemological pluralism, Soloveitchik's *The Halakhic Mind*, if more than a family quarrel with Cohen and the Marburg School, is by no means a thoroughgoing repudiation. This chapter, which traces his appropriation and transformation of the Marburg School, elucidates the manner in which Soloveitchik arrives at a pluralistic position. Although Soloveitchik rarely invokes the world religions discourse directly, his work nevertheless participates in our ongoing discussion by breaking with the foundations of this discourse: emphasizing the importance of the lived, religious, and metaphysical element of religious difference and thereby downplaying the linguistic and philological study of traditions as a source for spiritual and racial affinity. Instead, Soloveitchik emphasizes the dimension of practice and radical divergences in the inner lives of members of different religious communities. As a result, he casts Judaism as metaphysically distinct from Christianity and offers a political solution for situating the Jewish community in the West, rather than claiming that Judaism is somehow already part of Christianity in the manner of the other thinkers explored in this book.

I begin by situating Soloveitchik in relation to Cohen and contemporary discussions about the sui generis concept of religion. Next, I turn to a reading of Soloveitchik's dissertation to explore his sustained engagement with Cohen. I then analyze his appropriation and reformulation of the methods and commitments of the Marburg School of neo-Kantianism in *The Halakhic Mind*. I conclude with an exploration of his notion of Jewish distinctiveness as developed in "Confrontation."

Cognitive Pluralism and the Rational Foundations of Culture, or Why Soloveitchik Is Not an Orthodox Cohenian

The Halakhic Mind argues at length for the legitimacy of the sui generis method of knowing that is unique to religion.[15] In this regard, this work clearly breaks with Cohen's emphasis on a singular religion of reason that takes its bearings from culture (meant in an ideal rather than an empirical sense). And yet, as we see, *The Halakhic Mind* retains many elements that resonate with Cohen and his Marburg colleague Paul Natorp. Soloveitchik's choice of invoking the sui generis account of religion is itself interesting because it seems rather counterintuitive given his professed sensibilities. As Wayne Proudfoot has famously argued, Christian theorists such as Friedrich Schleiermacher, Rudolf Otto, and Mircea Eliade have invoked and sought to elaborate the notion of religion as an autonomous sphere of cognition employed as a "protective strategy adopted for apologetic purposes."[16] The appeal to the unique domain of immediate experience, or the irreducible nature of religious cognition, was a strategy used to evade developments of post-Kantian epistemological sensibilities and modern science thought to be incommensurable with traditional religious beliefs.

In the wake of the Enlightenment and its efforts to domesticate religion through reason, scholars and theologians turned to affects and "unmediated" experience to carve out an autonomous and pure domain of the religious. As Russell McCutcheon, perhaps the most outspoken critic of the sui generis concept of religion, points out, "That the discourse on sui generis religion is implicitly involved in a political and intellectual clash with the descendants of the Enlightenment should be more than obvious."[17] Although McCutcheon's claim about the discourse of sui generis religion and its most famous propagators—namely, Schleiermacher, Otto, and Eliade—is accurate, it is less clear that it straightforwardly applies to Soloveitchik, who steeps himself in neo-Kantian terminology and methods. Indeed, in *The Halakhic Mind*, Soloveitchik, an explicitly Jewish theorist of "religion," seeks to marry the sui generis method with the last bastion of Enlightenment thought in pre–World War II German philosophy.

If, as is generally accepted, the sui generis notion of religion arose as a protective strategy—turning to private, unverifiable experiences to ward off the objectifying claims of the sciences—Soloveitchik is unusual in adopting the sui generis notion of religion because of developments in the sciences themselves. That is, at least in its rhetorical staging, *The Halakhic Mind* prefers scientific methodologies to humanistic ones,[18] claiming that the sui generis notion of religion is warranted not as a protection from the sciences, but because the sciences themselves now leave a legitimate opening for it. Soloveitchik writes,

> It would be difficult to distinguish any epoch in the history of philosophy more amenable to the meditating of *homo religiosus* than that of today. The reason for this is the discrepancy that exists at present between the mathematico-scientific and philosophical methodologies. A schism of enormous magnitude has developed between the scientist and the philosopher, between the regional viewpoint of the empiricist and the universal vision of the metaphysician. The scientific method, which exalts the microscopic idea and integrates reality out of the simplest elements, has collided with the metaphysical world-view which strives towards boundless ontological totality. As a result of this conflict, new vistas now beckon to the *homo religiosus*.[19]

This paragraph, as well as much of *The Halakhic Mind*, argues that the loss of a universal perspective of the whole is a result not of newly recognized limits of the human mind, but rather of the fracturing of science that was once thought to be unified.[20] That is, recent developments in science—one should bear in mind that this work was written in the 1940s—demand that the multiplicity inherent in the nature of reality itself be acknowledged.[21] According to the narrative Soloveitchik offers in *The Halakhic Mind*, philosophy—which has a noticeable neo-Kantian ring in this work—has long sought to encompass the whole by means of accounting for the transcendental conditions of science. If we recall, the Marburg School of neo-Kantians acknowledged science to be the supreme authority when accounting for reality.

According to Soloveitchik, however, science is no longer in harmony with itself; methods of particular scientific disciplines conflict in principle with one another, revealing a plurality of ontic dimensions. Soloveitchik terms this fracturing in the nature of reality itself "epistemological pluralism." As Soloveitchik explains, "Epistemological pluralism does not deny the absolute character of Being. . . . Pluralism asserts only that the object reveals itself in manifold ways to the subject, and that a certain *telos* corresponds to each of these ontical manifestations."[22] In other words, there are many faces of reality, and there is no one way that we as finite beings might grasp the whole. This opens the door to an exploration of the manner in which *homo religiosus* accesses this manifold reality.

To understand the lengthy passage cited above beyond its plain sense, let us turn to Hermann Cohen's conception of the relationship between science and culture and to his *Einleitung mit kritischen Nachtrag zur F. A. Langes, Geschichte des Materialismus* [Introduction with Critical Supplement to F. A. Langes's "History of Materialism"] (1914), which offers an overview of Cohen's system and its relationship to culture.[23] Cohen argues that all dimensions of culture, which includes ethics and aesthetics—not to mention religion—have "logic as their foundation" [*Grundlage*].[24] Cohen's notion of *Logik,* which is closer to what we today term "epistemology," is inextricably bound up with science and is derived from the reconstruction of the mathematical foundations of the natural sciences: "Critical Philosophy is that which is not merely united with just any science, but only those natural sciences which have mathematics in their foundations, and through mathematics [philosophy] has its hand in natural sciences."[25] The mathematical natural sciences [*mathematische Naturwissenschaften*] are not only the foundations of knowledge but secure the interface between reason and culture.

It is important to understand the ethical and cultural motivations underlying Cohen's emphasis on the transcendental foundations of the mathematical natural sciences. As Ursula Renz puts it, "Cohen attempts . . . to recover [the] Enlightenment concern with the critique of prejudice as a matter of principle. In his view, one can only be free of prejudices if the sensory given is denied any epistemological function and legitimacy is refused on principle to any appeal to the given."[26] That is, by emphasizing the constructed nature of being, especially in regard to such matters as race and culture, Cohen articulates the grounds enabling the rejection of prevalent naturalistic theories of the human being.[27] As Michael Zank explains, Cohen's logic is not merely concerned with offering a new foundation for "mathematics and physics but [it] also aspires to demonstrate its fertility for the foundation of the humanities, i.e., for morality (*Sittlichkeit*) and ethics."[28] Science, for Cohen, is part and parcel of culture and of the world of culture encompassing ethics, politics, and, indeed, religion.[29]

What Soloveitchik seems to be saying at the beginning of *The Halakhic Mind*—written more than two decades after the death of Cohen—is that, in light of recent scientific developments, Cohen's use of the transcendental foundations of the natural sciences to offer a critical idealist account of culture is no longer tenable. As Soloveitchik puts it, "At the turn of the century, the harmony between the philosopher and scientist was disturbed. The dissonance arose out of the discovery that scientific data presented by biology and psychology clash with the forms set by the mathematical sciences which had been adopted by philosophy as the model of knowledge."[30] In other words, philosophy, which sought its unity, security, and purity by reconstructing the transcendental conditions of science through mathematics, founders once the sciences begin to use methodologies and theorems that are no longer compatible with or are even antagonistic to classical mathematics and physics.[31] Cohen's philosophy of culture, so Soloveitchik implies, is undone by modern developments in science. Thus, Munk is correct to read "Soloveitchik's plea for cognitive pluralism in *The Halakhic Mind* . . . as a response to Cohen's epistemology."[32] However, one might take it further and see it as a challenge to Cohen's philosophy of culture, which is grounded in his unitary notion of science.

Contra Cohen: From the Dissertation to *The Halakhic Mind*

It is not too big of an interpretive leap to conclude that, despite the metanarrative at the heart of *The Halakhic Mind*, Soloveitchik never really thought that Cohen's Critical Idealism was actually tenable; that is, he never believed that Cohen's vision foundered only because of recent scientific developments. Munk is not far off the mark when he suggests that the two thinkers had incompatible sensibilities regarding epistemology and, indeed, even ontology. In his dissertation Soloveitchik's chief critique of Cohen is the closed nature of his system, its lack of access to a world beyond "pure" knowing; that is, its lack of transcendence.[33] Soloveitchik takes it as axiomatic that the object—indeed the world—exists beyond or outside the process of knowing. He believes that Cohen's failure to grasp the importance of the actual world-in-itself stems from a prior refusal to adequately recognize the individual (the psychological self) and his or her perceptions. In *The Halakhic Mind* these concerns manifest in Solovietchik's emphasis on epistemological plurality, a stance that explodes the closed nature of Cohen's system. In what follows I summarize aspects of the critique of Cohen's logic in Soloveitchik's disertation. My focus is on how Soloveitchik understands Cohen, rather than on evaluating the validity of this assessment.[34]

According to Soloveitchik, Cohen maintains a peculiar and remarkably rigorous form of Idealism. That is, "while other idealistic theories assume certain absolute, metaphysical quantities, Cohen rejects any absolute principle that serves as a constant."[35] Indeed, although many idealists embrace metaphysics grounded in the absolutization of consciousness or subjectivity, Cohen not only rejects metaphysical speculation en toto but also denudes consciousness and subjectivity of any "psychic-metaphysical dimension." In the place of "a [purely] epistemological (*erkenntnistheoretisches*) [and thus] non-actual (*wirklichkeitsfreies*) subject," Cohen's inserts "'pure' generative thinking,'" which takes place "without a subject."[36] "Pure thought" is not rooted in subjectivity, but rather "is identical with the mathematical and natural sciences."[37] There is no interior life, no psychic constitution of objects, but instead the spontaneous process of creation by pure thinking, which proceeds by the laws of the mathematical natural sciences, the mathematico-scientific approach.[38] Soloveitchik argues that Cohen presents an idealism whose grounds emerge from the side not of the subject, but of the object.[39]

Soloveitchik charges that Cohen's notion of pure thinking [*reine Denken*] is an entirely self-constituting endeavor that "excludes both sensations . . . [and] inborn ideas of rationalism."[40] That is, "thinking unfolds itself in an infinite process,"[41] before, beyond, or outside of which nothing registers. Cohen begins with a reality that is already filtered through the reflection of the sciences, such that its very grounds are quantified and lawful. Thus, he grounds his logic in a postulated "methodological infinity, which knowledge posits as its ground."[42]

Soloveitchik charges that, for Cohen, basic experience is not that of the individual but of the mathematico-scientific methods, primarily physics. Cohen's conception of basic reality is inextricably bound up with the infinitesimal method, in which primacy is given not to the sensations, but rather to the "infinite[ly] small foundation of experience," to which "concrete thinking is dependent . . . [and] which one can designate as a *regressus in infinitum*."[43] Soloveitchik highlights that for Cohen "the transition from thinking to the objectified object [*objektivierten Gegenstand*] is an infinite process."[44] The process of thinking is always developing, always in flux, and thus never complete; it never culminates in access to transcendence, in that which lies beyond the system. That is, the process of thinking never culminates in the generation of actual concrete objects. Rather, the process of knowing or generating [*erzeugen*] objects remains mired in the principle of the infinitesimal.

The infinitesimal, so central to Cohen's *Logik*, is a target of Soloveitchik's critique. Soloveitchik explains, "The infinitely small is Being, such that becoming is made into an element of knowing."[45] This process of Cohen's *Logik* transforms the qualitative dimension of things and experience—indeed, even the act of perceiving [*Empfindung*]—into quantitative data. By incorporating perception into the "spontaneous process of thinking," by making it "a logical element," sensation becomes constituted by, rather than that which constitutes, pure thought. Cohen denudes perception of access to any sort of givenness or quality.[46] Perceptions are an "'otherness'" awaiting "objectivization."[47] As a result, the contents of sensation are actually already contents of consciousness and are generated by thinking.[48]

Cohen accomplishes this quantification of the qualitative by giving primacy to "rigorous results and the lawful procedural process" of the mathematical natural scientific modes of knowing.[49] Or as Soloveitchik puts it, for Cohen, "true thinking, that which constitutes being, is the mathematico-scientific."[50] According to Soloveitchik's reading, the mathematico-scientific process, which for Cohen is oriented around the infinitesimal method, secures the basis of being and thus closes off the system, excluding any given that is not already filtered through its own process of purification and generated by pure thinking. Cohen's insistence on purity and his emphasis on the elimination of the given, of that which is transcendent, are part and parcel of the same strategy: "Nothing can precede thinking, nothing is given."[51]

One key implication of Cohen's strategy, as Soloveitchik perceives it, is that there is no distinction between "the spheres of thinking and that of being"[52]: There is only the "mathematico-scientific" sphere. The external world, the thing-in-itself is lost, and all that exists is the thing-as-it-exists-for-judgment. Thus "for pure thinking, there is no mental [*seelisch*] reality, no inner world."[53] There is only the process of knowing, which lacks any finality and from which actual, concrete things are forever excluded. The result is that Cohen has undermined the distinction between thinking and being.

Cohen's failure to do justice to perception and the qualitative dimensions of knowing is rooted in the manner in which he orders his system. For him, perception lies beyond the pale of the process of knowing; it "is a foreigner [*Fremdling*] in the process of knowing" and cannot be grasped by logic.[54] Perception has this status because it dwells in the realm of psychology or, more specifically, the transcendental psychology of the individual.[55] But because "Cohen has banished any notion of the subject from logic,"[56] he is unable to do justice to perception and its modes of knowing; they become derivative of the background process in which quantitative processes generate knowledge.

Soloveitchik's dissertation, despite its technical and abstract tone, is marked by a yearning for transcendence from the strictures of Cohen's system, a yearning for access to the given, to the "actual" world beyond the immanence of generative thought. Soloveitchik is quite troubled by the subsuming of the qualitative into the quantitative, which he sees as the conflation of thinking and being. Indeed, because Cohen has banished the qualitative and has grounded everything in the quantitative, Soloveitchik concludes that "the infinitesimal," the process of knowing itself, is rendered "absolute."[57] Thus, the concrete particular can never be fully determined and reached. Cohen's thought always hovers between the general lawfulness of thinking and the world of the individual, which can never be fully distinguished.[58] By dissolving the synthetic structure of the "naïve thinker" so that everything can proceed analytically, Soloveitchik claims that Cohen has severed all ties to actuality: "Cohen, with this method, fails to achieve individual, concrete things."[59]

At this juncture, Munk's conclusion that Soloveitchik "exemplifies a fundamental and unbridgeable difference of opinion with Cohen regarding the character and methodology of thought and the correlation of thought and actuality" seems warranted.[60] Soloveitchik is clearly dissatisfied with Cohen's emphasis on the purity of thought, insisting instead that there is a given world transcending the grasp of the capacities of knowing in scientific idealism, a world out there beyond that is open to nonscientific methods of knowing. Munk writes, "According to Soloveitchik, there is a transcendent component in being that is not generated by thought, whereas thought is considered to be an act of intentionality, instead of an ongoing process of generating itself from its origins."[61] Indeed, Soloveitchik embraces the (at least potentially) inherently meaningful nature of such "impure" modes of cognition as perceptions, emotions, and intuitions. There is a striking parallel here with the respective attempts of Buber, Rosenzweig, and Heschel to critique philosophical abstraction and retrievals of actuality. However, the methodology employed in *The Halakhic Mind*, where Soloveitchik likewise attempts to retrieve actuality, differs markedly from their approaches.

Soloveitchik as a Marburg Neo-Kantian?

In *The Halakhic Mind*, Soloveitchik insists that nonscientific modes of accessing reality can be just as meaningful and valid, if not more so, than scientific ones. Indeed, much like Protestant theorists of religion from Friedrich Schleiermacher to Rudolf Otto, Soloveitchik offers an account of the religious human being or *homo religiosus*, whose relationship to reality is not, and cannot be, circumscribed by the purely quantitative and mechanistic forms of science that Cohen champions. Soloveitchik seeks to account for the "autonomous method" as the only way for an individual to properly understand religion and the qualitative dimensions of religious experience in relationship to the paradigms of science.[62]

How, we may ask, does this foundering of neo-Kantianism help the *homo religiosus*? To answer this question, we must first recognize that the very notion of *homo religiosus* or maintaining the sui generis notion of religion brings Soloveitchik into disagreement with Cohen. In *Der Begriff der Religion im System der Philosophie* and *Religion of Reason out of the Sources of Judaism*, Cohen emphatically contests the autonomy of religion. He repeatedly insists that religion is and must remain an *Eigenart* [particularity] of the system of philosophy; it is not *selbstandig* or sui generis because it is ultimately grounded on logic and must complementarily coexist with other elements of the system of philosophy. Cohen's argument in regard to religion has significant political and cultural overtones. Indeed, he is often quite explicit about how the other elements of the system of philosophy and the "purity" that rigorous philosophy brings are key to containing the confessional biases that contribute not only to the Protestant degradation of Judaism (both theoretically and politically) but also to dangerous forms of exclusionary nationalism.[63] For example, Cohen sees as dangerous anything, including the autonomy of religion, that can impede the purity of reason. In the case of religion, he sees the current intellectual and political climate in which he lives as corrupted by the intermixing of religion and nationalism.

Despite their different views regarding the status of religion vis-à-vis other branches of culture, Soloveitchik shares Cohen's concerns about irrationalism. However, he proposes an alternative response. Soloveitchik considers Cohen's attempt to stave off antisemitism and violent nationalism through the appeal to a pure and unified reason to be grounded on a univocal notion of Being that has been exploded by developments in the sciences that have taken place since Cohen's death. Soloveitchik is also dissatisfied with Cohen's approach, which privileges the realization of Judaism and religion in general through ethics.[64] Perhaps this is why a jubilant tone occasionally creeps into Soloveitchik's somber prose when it comes to the collapse of the union of science and philosophy despite the numerous dangers that he, in a manner not altogether different from Cohen, sees cropping up as a result.

Soloveitchik's philosophy of religion proffered in *The Halakhic Mind* maintains an ambivalent relationship to Cohen's philosophy. On the one hand, Soloveitchik's concept of the *homo religiosus,* which makes religion an autonomous sphere, can be seen as a clear departure from Cohen and a step toward Protestant theorists of religion such as Schleiermacher and Otto and philosophers like Scheler (who was, at least for a period, Catholic). On the other hand, he insists that *homo religiosus* "is a cognitive type, desiring both to understand and interpret."[65] Thus he rejects these theorists' conception of the decidedly subjectivist, noncognitive, irrational nature of the numinous. Although Soloveitchik suffers neither Cohen nor the subjectivists, as we see, he ends up being closer to the former.

To be sure critics like Wayne Proudfoot charge that the turn to the sui generis understanding of religion is, or has functioned as, an attempt to evade not simply the perceived reductionism associated with the sciences but also the authority of the sciences themselves. Soloveitchik, however, sees the autonomy of the religious as a logical outcome of the development of the sciences and even a further extension of it. Indeed, it is only at this historical juncture, when what Soloveitchik terms "epistemological pluralism" has disrupted the harmonious relationship between philosopher and scientist, that the cognitive existence of *homo religiosus* can be explored.

To understand how Soloveitchik reconciles his commitment to science with the autonomy of religion, it is important to elucidate his notion of epistemological pluralism. Looking to the "history of philosophy," Soloveitchik asserts that "great philosophical systems are never produced in a scientific vacuum, but usually follow the formation and completion of a scientific world-perspective."[66] Where the Aristotelian scientific worldview dominated the metaphysics of the ancient and medieval world, modern philosophy was rooted in the mechanistic view of the universe expressed in the physics of Galileo and Newton. In both cases, the ancient and the modern, philosophers "adopted a scientifically purified world as the subject matter for their studies. The only realm of reality to which the philosopher had access was, for them, the scientifically charted universe."[67]

Although philosophers may look to the sciences for their notions of the universe, important extra-scientific methodological disputes still arise. To address them, the scientist uses the "explanatory method" whose concerns are "interrelations and interdependencies of successive phases in the objective order." She eliminates all contingency in nature to arrive at rational necessity. In and of itself, existence does not require a causal interpretation, and therefore the scientist rationally postulates this order of interpretation out of necessity; it is an order where causality reigns. Such causality, it is to be noted, can only apply to the objective order; "it cannot be applied to the qualitative universe."[68] However, at this point a controversy has long plagued epistemology. It centers on "the emergence of knowledge, or the 'movement of the logos.' How does knowledge proceed? Does the 'logos' move from sense experience to a postulated world or conversely? In other words, is subjectivity to be construed in terms of objectivity or vice versa?"[69] For Kant, whose thought marks a watershed moment in this discourse, knowledge is constituted by both receptivity and spontaneity, with the receptive element as logically prior to the spontaneous act. However, the neo-Kantians reverse this order. Helmut Holzhey explains:

> With Cohen's *Logik der reine Erkenntnis,* the transcendental theory of knowing [*transcendental Wissenschaftheorie*] of the Marburg School bring[s] the conditions of validity of scientific thinking entirely into the sphere of pure thinking. The presuppositions of a given manifold [*Mannigfaltigkeit*] and the general duality of intuition [*Anschauung*] and thinking in its Kantian application are discarded.[70]

Thus, for the neo-Kantians the objective sphere is primary. In fact, it is the objective sphere that serves as the condition for the manifestation of the subjective. As Soloveitchik explains, for the neo-Kantians "it is the objective sphere that makes it possible for subjective 'data' to spring into being. . . . Any sensational apprehension is conditioned by its antecedent, the act of creative objectification." The subjective background can be accessed only by means of the objective order.[71] At stake in this debate is, as Soloveitchik points out, "the method to which the philosopher needs recourse in his attempt to reconstruct the process of noetical experience." Must the philosopher begin with the objective world, with the ordered world of things, or can the philosopher begin with his or her subjectivity and emotions? At first glance, this may seem like a minor methodological question, but Soloveitchik insists that a great deal is at stake in its answer.[72]

According to Soloveitchik, modern philosophy, as a "satellite of science," insisted that priority be given to the objective order of things. That is, by prioritizing science, it emphasized the quantifiable and neglected the qualitative, the inward, as being beyond its concern:[73]

> Modern philosophical criticism, (Kantian, Neo-Kantian schools alike) and positivism also looked askance upon the qualitative world. Thus, the world comprising the sum total of our consciousness, the world of the senses with which our very being is integrated, was rejected by these philosophical systems, as relativistic, subjective and ephemeral.[74]

Both the philosopher and the scientist turned to a mathematical world, a postulated universe of the quantitative, thereby neglecting the private world of the interior, the world of the consciousness and psyche. It is important to bear in mind that Soloveitchik has some sympathy with this approach. A postulated universe constituted by numbers and "relational constructs" is "immune to any metamorphosis of metaphysical strain." There is no "susceptibility to an ever modulating 'private world.'"[75] Indeed, the firm bounds of the postulated universe, although not without limits, are also a powerful force for keeping the chaotic and often dark world of the interior in check; when those bounds are abandoned, philosophical catastrophe follows.

Of course, one of the basic premises on which *The Halakhic Mind* is grounded is that recent developments in the sciences have rent asunder this unity between philosophy and science. Much to the chagrin of the philosophers, scientists bringing forth conflicting methodologies with incompatible assumptions have revealed, so Soloveitchik asserts, that "every system of cognition strives to attain a distinct objective." In short,

> Systematic knowledge means the understanding and grasping of the universe in consonance with a definite telos. It is interested primarily that reality reveal itself in a fashion which is suited to a final noetic goal; the telos is the determining factor in the methodological construction employed by the scientist

and philosopher. Teleological heterogeneity, however, does not invalidate the cognitive act, for, in the final analysis, pluralism is founded on reality itself.[76]

The gist of this dense passage is that reality remains telic, but instead of there being one single overarching telos for the whole, there are a plurality of divergent tēle. Thus, one can study the "objective" side of reality and discover that Being itself is diffuse, that it shows multiple faces, each of which has its own end. To be sure, Soloveitchik rejects Cohen's attempt to ground culture in the mathematical and natural sciences. However, Soloveitchik never accepts anything like irrationalism. The recent developments in science of which Soloveitchik speaks only fissure the notion of the unity of knowledge—and thus the very "modern" notion of a unified world in the quantitative relata postulated by the scientist and philosopher.

In light of this fissure, it is no longer warranted to privilege "science"—taken to mean the objective or public—over the private or interior world of the emotions and psyche. In short, one can no longer privilege only those aspects of reality that can be mapped onto the mathematical grid of the scientifically charted universe, because there is no longer unity in the sciences themselves, which was the source from which philosophers postulated such a grid in the first place. Thus, one can no longer claim that the private world of the psyche is merely evanescent and irrelevant, because there is no longer a single standard by which to judge validity.

However, if this frees the *homo religiosus* to pursue his or her own cognitive approach to reality, it also frees the humanist to reject science in the exploration of the private world of the qualitative. The humanistic disciplines have wasted little time in rejecting "all the categories and principles of theoretical philosophy formed under the hegemony of the modern mathematical sciences."[77] They have enumerated their own approaches to the spirit. Indeed, in their haste to abandon the external, objective order of the sciences, philosophers plunged into the dimension of subjectivity: "Modern anti-intellectualistic epistemology and metaphysics as conceived by Rousseau (feeling), Schopenhauer (will), and Schelling (intuition), and developed by Royce, Krueger, Volkelt, Maier and Scheler, seized upon Pascal's *Logique du Coeur*."[78] If Soloveitchik is critical both of Cohen and the logical positivists who try to hold onto objectivity at the cost of subjectivity, it is clear that his greatest concern lies with the philosophers who take up the opposite tendency—who lay claim to the subjective, particularly the religious experience:

> As a matter of fact, many enthusiastic philosophers and students of religion have but recently started out on this adventuresome road. Following the footsteps of phenomenological zealots, they have attempted to apprehend the religious experience through a hypersensible act of intuition which is tantamount

to a frank admission of defeat for reason. It indicates that the "public" critical reason has been renounced for the sake of a "private" distorted subjective experience.[79]

Soloveitchik charges many philosophers with seeking to grasp the religious experience through purely subjective means, a move Soloveitchik links to mysticism, obscurantism, and the forfeiture of reason. Such explorations of the interior, subjective realm that eschew objectivity have grave consequences, not the least of which is a "de-intellectualized philosophy."[80] "Phenomenological emotionalism and the so-called humanist hermeneutics, and the modern existential philosophy" have significantly contributed to the "confusion that pervaded European thought." Soloveitchik also sees a significant connection between the abandonment of reason and "moral corruption." Indeed, although expressing sympathy for Husserl, the mathematician and founder of phenomenology, Soloveitchik is more wary of Husserl's students: "It is no mere coincidence that the most celebrated philosophers of the Third Reich were disciples of Husserl." Soloveitchik charges Husserl's students with rejecting his commitment to mathematical rigor and using his methods for "emotional approaches to reality." It is difficult to imagine any worse philosophical abdication for Soloveitchik: "When reason surrenders its supremacy to dark, equivocal emotions, no dam is able to stem the rising tide of the affective stream."[81]

The subjective/objective binary leads to a dead end either way: One either has Cohen's idealism without a subject, without an interior, or the dark forces of the psyche ride roughshod over reason—in a subjectivity without any objectivity to measure and check it. For Soloveitchik it is no coincidence that the latter position reached the height of its popularity and influence with the rise of the Third Reich. If the quantitative, objective approach that neglects the qualitative and subjective is bad, the alternative that prioritizes the immediacy of the subjective affects is worse.

Epistemological pluralism offers a way out of this binary. Even though the attempts of thinkers like Cohen, who undercut or convert the private, qualitative realm into something quantitative and thus suitable for the public realm, have been rendered untenable by developments in the sciences, it is nevertheless urgent to reject the tendency of some philosophers to tap into "some recondite, subjective current."[82] The newly emergent epistemological pluralism opens the door for the *homo religiosus* to investigate reality through its own autonomous lens. Soloveitchik is quite clear that grave dangers for philosophy and culture have already emerged as a result of the uncoupling of science and philosophy, and thus he concludes, "It is of greater urgency for religion to cultivate objectivity than perhaps any branch of human culture."[83] Thus, although it embraces the sui generis approach to religion, Soloveitchik's method seems at odds with the manner in which that approach is generally understood, as subverting claims to testing and validity.

For contemporary critics of the sui generis discourse such as Wayne Proudfoot and Russell McCutcheon, cultivating "objectivity" in regard to the study of religion—as much as it is possible—is done through offering genealogies of the field and thereby uncovering the hidden cultural and historical assumptions and ideologies that inform and constitute the supposedly sui generis concept of religion. For example, although McCutcheon would bristle at the term "objectivity," his work emphasizes that relying "on interior, private experiences" is a pretext to "exclude a discourse from critical scrutiny."[84] For McCutcheon, objectivity or, perhaps better, making discourse public and transparent involves the explicit opposition to the autonomy of religion as a sphere of human experience. In the preface to *Manufacturing Religion*, McCutcheon writes, "Although the sui generis claim makes possible an autonomous discourse, complete with the benefits and authority of practitioners—complete with the privilege of their sociopolitical claims—it does so in noncriticizable, non-public, nontestable fashion, thereby ensuring that the standards of evidence and falsification that operate in much of the university have little bearing on the study of religion."[85] The study of religion, McCutcheon avers, should be like all other topics of inquiry: verifiable, testable, and transparent.[86] There can be no special "religious" claims, no recourse to religious experience. The "cultivation of objectivity," to use Soloveitchik's term, would, for McCutcheon, mean breaking down the protective barriers around religious discourse and revealing its historical, cultural, and ideological entanglements.

As we see, breaking down those barriers is clearly not what Soloveitchik means when he talks about the "urgency for religion to cultivate objectivity."[87] Solovietchik demands precisely what McCutcheon rejects: the autonomous realm of the religious. For Soloveitchik, objectivity is neither bound up with rendering the sociopolitical dimension of religious authority (and the study thereof) transparent, which McCutcheon seeks, nor the genealogical/historical investigations of Jonathan Z. Smith or Tomoko Mazusawa,[88] but rather with epistemology and the hard sciences. Keeping with Cohen and the neo-Kantians, Soloveitchik asserts, "Epistemological pluralism has not abandoned the realm of logic." That is, in contrast to the philosophers who have embraced the subjective tout court, who have used Husserl's notion of intuition to proceed unchecked into the dark affective stream of the interior, Soloveitchik insists instead that "the student of religion . . . would act wisely in taking his cue from the scientist rather than the philosopher."[89] However, Soloveitchik's terminology becomes a bit murky here. Presumably, the "philosopher" he refers to is one of those who have sought independence from science by turning to the subjective realm, indeed to religious experience in particular, and in the process, their work has not only become dangerous and "prone to abstruseness" but also "arbitrary."[90] Thus, Soloveitchik wants to embrace the sui generis model, but in a fundamentally different way from Schleiermacher, Otto, and Scheler.

Soloveitchik claims that we gain "access to religious knowledge of reality with its unique structural aspects in a two-fold way: First, by coordinating two series in the religious sphere, the subjective and the objective; and second, by reconstructing the former out of the latter."[91] He explicitly acknowledges that this methodology is that of Cohen's colleague and fellow Marburg neo-Kantian, Paul Natorp. Natorp offers Soloveitchik the method by which to transcend the subjective/objective binary left by the respective approaches of Cohen and Husserl and his disciples. Thus, Soloveitchik, in spite of his critique of the Marburg School, clearly takes up a strand of Marburg neo-Kantianism in opposition to the "disciples of Husserl," the "most celebrated philosophers of the Third Reich" who plunged recklessly and headlong into the subjective.[92]

In *Allgemeine Psychologie nach kritischer Methode* [Universal Psychology according to Critical Method] (1912), Natorp, breaking with Cohen, seeks access to access *Erlebnis*, the flowing current of the emotions that remains recalcitrant to the objectifying, abstracting gaze—what we have been referring to as subjectivity.[93] Although Natorp's seeking access to subjectivity is a clear difference from Cohen's devaluation of psychology in the process of knowing, Natorp also shuns philosophical realism and emotionalism, stressing that *Erlebnis* cannot be accessed directly. Or as Natorp explains, "The immediacy [*Unmittelbare*] of consciousness cannot be grasped and observed immediately [*unmittelbar*]. With good reason therefore is 'reflection' [*Reflexion*] that is equally a mirroring [*Spiegelung*]—the designation for the way which can alone bring the subjective [side] of consciousness to consciousness" [*Bewusstsein*]. Of course, Natorp reiterates, "As reflected in the 'self-observation' [*Selbst-beobachtung*], the immediate [*Unmittelbare*] is no longer the immediate."[94] The subjective level of existence, prior to any objectivization, is all flux, all potency [*potenz*]. There is no way to grasp this fluid, pulsating, ever-changing flux other than by freezing it through abstraction.

Because one cannot approach this primordial level of subjectivity directly, one can only reconstruct it based on events in the objective sphere and the manner in which these fluctuating impulses and drives manifest themselves in actuality. One works backward from these manifestations. Or as Natorp puts it, in reconstruction "one can see a complete reversal of the procedures and criteria of objective knowledge [*Erkenntnis*], scientific as well as prescientific forms."[95] One thus works backward from an event where the subjective potentialities realized themselves in some actuality or objectivity, carefully reconstructing the moments in order to freeze this flux, thereby abstracting a momentary picture of the subjective realm for inspection by the consciousness.

It is difficult to overestimate the influence of the methodology laid out in Natorp's *Allgemeine Psychologie* on *The Halakhic Mind*. Soloveitchik emphasizes that science acknowledges distinct orders of being. In classical mechanics, there was the world of the "subjective qualitative" world of "sense experience" as opposed to the "objective quantitative" realm "postulated by scientific methodology." However, reconstruction—the method of (transcendental) psychology according to Natorp—has as its object the primeval subjective order that lies "beyond the pale of science." There can be no verification or logical legitimation of this subjective order.[96] For the natural sciences, since their methodologies can establish no correlation between the primal, subjective order and the objective order the former is of no interest.[97] The scientist eschews the qualitative and only explores the quantitative. It is only with recent developments in physics, and the disruptions they bring to a monolithic vision of Being, so Soloveitchik claims, that there emerges a "third order, the subjective structural which is reconstructed out of the summative object."[98]

Soloveitchik uses Natorp's methodology to break the impasse between what he perceives as Cohen's one-sided emphasis on objectivity and phenomenology's one-sided emphasis on subjectivity: Natorp's method allows for the objectification of the subjective. That is, if objectivity is prior to subjectivity (at least in terms of access), and if subjectivity and objectivity cannot be separated, then one can use the tools of "science" to reconstruct the qualitative world of the interior. Soloveitchik continues, "The process of objectification is not limited to that reality enveloped by space and time, but extends to the one embraced by time and consciousness. Whenever we speak of spiritual phenomena, we already have in mind objectified phenomena."[99] Although spiritual phenomena may not be as "complete and ideal" as phenomena in nature, they are nevertheless accessible. Thus, the "elusive subjective stream" becomes objective in works of art, in moral creeds, and so forth. Whereas Natorp is equally interested in gaining access to ethical, aesthetic, and religious dimensions of culture through his transcendental psychology, Soloveitchik not only focuses on the religious but also privileges it. He asserts, "Religion, which is perhaps more deeply rooted in subjectivity than any other manifestation of the spirit, is also reflected in externalized phenomena which are evolved in the objectification process of the religious consciousness."[100] Where religion is only one sphere of culture for Natorp and for which its underlying subjectivity can be rigorously traced, for Soloveitchik it is the preeminent sphere. Indeed, he writes, "The aggregate of religious objective constructs is comprised of ethico-religious norms, ritual, dogmas, theoretical postulates, etc."[101] It is not one sphere among many, but a sphere that contains manifold others. And as we see, Soloveitchik does not leave the religious sphere vague or numinous, but prioritizes its legalistic, ritual, and cultic aspects.

Soloveitchik, the Sui Generis, and Objectivity, or the Methodological Primacy of Religious Orthodoxy

The manner in which Soloveitchik describes the religious sphere is significant and by no means neutral; it is very much an authorizing discourse. Not only is his approach a protective strategy, warding off reductionist critiques that presume to fully fathom the subjective realm, but it also attacks liberal approaches to religion (whether theological, philosophical, or scholarly) that privilege the subjective. As we see, Soloveitchik, using Natorp's *Allgemeine Psychology* as his philosophical foundation, finds the error of religious liberalism in the priority it grants to subjectivism in its process of inquiry. For Soloveitchik following Natorp, there is no direct access to primordial subjectivity, and thus one cannot directly trace the influence of the subjective realm on the objective. And yet, one cannot merely remain with the objective:

> Any objective series in the field of religion can neither be understood nor explained on its own merit. The subjective track must be explored, for sometimes identical objective constructs may represent antipodal subjective aspects. The historian of religion, engaged in comparative studies, is powerless to interpret his data unless he traces a positive set of beliefs, dogmas, norms and customs to the subjective sphere. Any comparison of objectified norms, without the perspective of subjectivity, is totally misfounded [*sic*].[102]

To merely study texts, textual criticism, or even the details of liturgy and history is insufficient for a philosophy of religion, because that study fails to grasp the subjective level of *homo religiosus*. The "correct" understanding of religion lies in the proper ordering of data and perspectives. Although Solovietchik appropriates Natorp's methodology fairly closely, his normative and essentializing agenda for Judaism (and beyond this, religion) is clear—and transcends Natorp's own tightly circumscribed limits in the *Allgemeine Psychologie*.

The scholar of religion cannot simply take up the methodologies of the scientist. Scientists of old—before the revolution in the sciences with which Soloveitchik begins the book—were able to firmly establish a causal nexus between quantitative phenomena, and this is all that they sought. Yet it is important to bear in mind that "a causal nexus between quantitative phenomena does not imply a parallel relation between their qualitative counterparts. The latter escape the scientists' measuring rods."[103] If the sciences construct an ideal, quantitative world to access the objective, public face of reality, the study of religion scrutinizes the private, qualitative interior. Instead of quantitative construction, the "philosophy of religion performs an act of reconstruction."[104] (Of course, those scholars advocating the social scientific study of religion would reject that the study of religion entails only the study of the private, qualitative interior). A reconstruction of the murky depths of the spirit cannot proceed according to causality, at least not in the same sense of causality as in the objective realm. That is because there is not the same direct correspondence of stimulus and event. Thus, in "reconstruction, the principle of causality assumes new and modified significance."[105] That is, unlike the quantitative objective world postulated by the physicists of old, filled with intersecting causal nexuses, when it comes to religion,

> it is impossible to construct a causal bond in objectified spiritual reality without recourse to its subjective correlate. When we speak, for instance, of a causality in the realm of religion, we cannot say that A (a certain religious norm) is the cause of B, since there is no direct contact between A and B. A and B are not autonomous phenomena but rather the end-products of a long process of objectification.[106]

Soloveitchik emphasizes the ineffectiveness of relying on the purely "objective" product to access the particular logic of the religious sphere. Again parroting Natorp, he states, "What we call subjectivity is only a surface reproduction which still needs exploration. An infinite regression takes place along the stationary track left behind [by] the objectifying 'logos.'"[107] He continues, "It is therefore impossible to discover final causation in the spiritual realm. Any subjective stage to which we may point with satisfaction can never be considered ultimate. We may always proceed further and discover yet a deeper stratum of subjectivity."[108] For example, if one were somehow given access to the mysterious inner world of Plato, one would not be able to predict how the currents and fluctuations of his subjectivity would manifest objectively, much less could one predict the specific nature of his corpus. However, if one studies Plato's works, one can get an idea about the subjectivity that produced it. Indeed, and here we see Soloveitchik's Natorpian grounding, "the starting point in any analysis of subjectivity must be the objective order. It is impossible to gain any insight into the subjective stream unless we have previously acquired objective manifestations."[109]

Despite its unusual turn to Enlightenment rather than Romantic philosophical foundations, Soloveitchik's approach may seem to be merely a modification of the sui generis theory of religion and thus a defense against secular reductions of religion—and surely it does function as such. But Soloveitchik's argument is more than this. Indeed, although the manner in which one ought to study religion is a source of debate in contemporary scholarship in religious studies, it would be a mistake to attribute our own concerns to Soloveitchik. That being said, Soloveitchik's argument has implications for the academic study of religion. To understand these implications it is helpful to turn to McCutcheon, a key critic of the sui generis approach to religion. Regarding the study of religion in America, particularly the work of Mircea Eliade and his disciples, McCutcheon comments,

It is all the more ironic, then, when one considers that the emphasis on the ir-reducible element of religious experience, understood here as a potent means for excluding significant aspects of historical existence, has often been pre-sented by some scholars as an attempt to protect what they understand as an essentially human characteristic from a mechanistic reduction at the hand of the antihuman social sciences . . . However, such talk of abstract sameness can effectively overlook the differences that most often define actual lived experience.[110]

Soloveitchik, who studied philosophy in Berlin and whose work is peppered with references to Schleiermacher and Otto, is keenly aware of the Protestant tendency to essentialize the idea of religion in terms that resonate with (liberal) Protestant sensibilities. He is also aware of how this essentializing of religion—often a central component of the world religions discourse—worked to margin-alize Judaism (academically and politically) as part of the process of shoring up the power and authority of liberal Protestantism. However, whereas McCutcheon is writing about the North American academy and the methods it uses to study religion, Soloveitchik is more concerned with establishing a philosophy for eluci-dating Judaism. Thus, where McCutcheon seeks to highlight liberal Protestant biases, Soloveitchik offers an alternative notion of religion—one that is perhaps even more eager to dispense with the bias in modern Jewish thought toward lib-eral Judaism than with the unspoken biases of liberal Protestantism. That is, rather than highlight reigning ideologies and thus deconstruct the field (an agenda that itself is not free of biases or politics),[111] Soloveitchik seeks to rewrite the study of religion. Rather than deconstruct the essentialized notion of "reli-gion," Soloveitchik offers—using a particular reading of Natorp's *Allgemeine Psy-chologie* as his foundation—an essence that is hostile to liberal Protestantism and liberal Judaism alike. Soloveitchik's method in *The Halakhic Mind* is perhaps best read as a philosophical justification for traditionalism and Orthodoxy.

Solovietchik, the Orthodox Jew cum theorist of religion, offers a very differ-ent model of and justification for the sui generis approach than his predecessors. Schleiermacher, the liberal Protestant theologian and father of the sui generis approach, claims, "Religion's essence is neither thinking nor acting, but intuition and feeling."[112] For Schleiermacher, the sphere of religion ends with intuition, with the interior life, such that "should [these feelings] cause actual actions and incite you to deeds, then you find yourselves in an alien realm [from religion]."[113] If Schleiermacher and Otto privilege the unique quality of religious feelings as opposed to deeds, Soloveitchik prioritizes ritual and cult as the core of religion. However, Soloveitchik, building on his Natorpian foundation, asserts that al-though "the ethos and the cult" are two methods of objectification that pertain to religion, "it is the latter that is more typical of the unique religious experience." Clearly, Soloveitchik is critiquing not only Christian (and Buberian) antinomianism here but also Hermann Cohen's *Religion of Reason,* which prioritizes ethical monotheism. Soloveitchik argues that ethics is not unique to the religious sphere, but also pertains to secular domains. In contrast, "when religious subjectivity is crystallized into forms of ritual, the subjective and objective lie within the framework of the religious consciousness."[114] Soloveitchik claims that the cult, because it includes the unity of subjectivity and objectivity, is complete and distinctly religious and thus the most proper object of focus for the philosopher.

Soloveitchik goes beyond Natorp's cautious exploration of the fluctuating realm of originary subjectivity, offering an explicitly metaphysical statement regarding human beings. He states, "There is a definite trend towards self-transcendence on the part of the spirit. It strives to escape its private inwardness and infiltrate the concrete world encompassed by space and pervaded by corporeal forms. The morphological process of self-realization from the inward to the outward is typical of the spiritual act."[115] Thus, the study of religion is not about the internal; it is not about feelings, which as any good Natorpian would tell you, remain an indeterminate flux, pure chaos, until they are crystallized and objectified. One can only reconstruct this dimension after it has been fixed in the objective realm through action. The inward, or what Soloveitchik terms the spirit, is objectified only through concrete action: "This concrete physical order, enveloped by time and space, is coordinated with its correlate in the internal world. The internal subjective correlate is, in turn, the objectified expression of some more primitive subjectivity." Only by studying the "objectified expression" can we go beyond the quantitative to gain access to the qualitative dimension of "religious subjectivity," which "strives towards the mysterious junction *psyche* and *physis.*"[116]

Against liberal religiosities, both Jewish and Christian, Soloveitchik emphasizes the preeminence of cult, of praxis over ethos. Contra Cohen, one ought not to look for a philosophy of religion to come from the sources of Judaism, but rather Jewish philosophy must proceed "out of the sources of Halakhah," which objectifies Jewish subjectivity most perfectly.[117] It is from Jewish law, the halakha, not the literary sources of Judaism, that gains philosophical access to the tradition. However, Soloveitchik's break from Cohen has social and political consequences, and not merely an interdenominational impact.

From *The Halakhic Mind* to "Confrontation"

Like Cohen, Soloveitchik is concerned about the political and social relationship between Judaism and Christianity. However, where Cohen pursues a strategy of inclusivity, Soloveitchik emphasizes pluralism and the importance of emphasizing distinctions between communities. That is, Cohen attempts to secure Judaism's place in the West by means of elucidating (an idealized) Germany's rational and cultural predominance and then demonstrating Judaism's foundational role in Germanism. In contrast, where Cohen sought to demonstrate that Judaism is an inextricable part of German—and thus Christian—identity or vice versa, Soloveitchik takes pains to insist that Judaism and Christianity are, in their respective theological cores, radically incommensurable, such that their only legitimate means of relationship can be political. That is, for Soloveitchik, the liberal democracy of the United States provides the conditions for mutual respect because it ensures and protects communal difference.

The occasion for "Confrontation" (1964) was Vatican II, in which the Catholic Church—in consultation with a variety of leaders in the Jewish community—contemplated, and ultimately enacted, reforms pertaining to its theological judgments concerning the Jews and Judaism.[118] "Confrontation" is not a halakhic tract, but rather a theological and philosophical statement about the chasms between religious communities.[119] Soloveitchik emphasizes the incommensurability between experiences and understanding in various faith traditions, a difference that "reflects the numinous character and the strangeness of the act of faith of a particular community which is totally incomprehensible to the man of a different faith community."[120] According to this logic, the language of theology cannot bring together two different faith traditions. On these grounds and as we see, political ones as well, Soloveitchik rejects Jewish involvement in the Vatican II process.

Critics have speculated that Soloveitchik opposes interfaith dialogue in "Confrontation" for reasons ranging from the political[121] to the psychological.[122] I follow Daniel Rynhold's argument that Soloveitchik does not rule out interfaith dialogue tout court, but instead limits its scope. If we acknowledge "the incommunicable nature of faith experiences particular to each community," dialogue cannot cover theological matters directly, but rather only indirectly—by focusing on the shared world of the public.[123] As Soloveitchik writes, "The confrontation [between members of different faith communities] should occur not at a theological, but at a mundane human level. There, all of us speak the universal language of modern man. As a matter of fact, our common interests lie not in the realm of faith, but in that of the secular orders."[124] This helps explain the paradoxical nature of the "Addendum to the Original Edition of 'Confrontation,'"[125] in which Soloveitchik reiterates the impossibility of "mutual understanding" between Jews and Christians on theological topics such as the nature of God or messianism, which pertain to the private world of faith, but nevertheless insists that in the "public world of humanitarian and cultural endeavors" such dialogue between faith communities is desirable.[126] Indeed, interfaith dialogue should not take place between "Jewish rabbis and Christian clergymen" in their nonreligious roles, but rather when they act explicitly as "men of God," which differs from how a "secularist" would act.[127]

It is important to understand how Soloveitchik reaches his theological, philosophical, and political conclusions in "Confrontation," which as I mentioned previously, stem from his critical engagement with the Marburg School. The essay begins with a meditation on the two creation accounts in Genesis, from which he derives three different levels of human existence.[128] These levels pertain to different aspects of development undergone by all human beings, who are inextricably caught in existential oscillation and struggle.[129] The first level is that of a "non-confronted being," whose existence is simple, whose place in the cosmos is not problematic. Soloveitchik stresses that this level is by no means limited to some sort of "primitive" human being, but rather indicates the state in which a human being is not aware of the genuine otherness of either the world or other human beings. Instead a person at this level experiences "existence [as] unbounded, merging harmoniously with the general order of things and events."[130]

The second level emerges from the first when the human being encounters the natural world as other and as something that "defies and challenges" her. It is this "awesome and mysterious domain of things and events," recalcitrant and resistant to her powers, that makes the human being aware of herself as an individual. It is at this moment that Soloveitchik brings in the notion of the divine norm, which defines the human being as such and gives her the "singularly human" task to master nature.[131] Mastery, for Soloveitchik, is bound up with cognition, where the "subject-knower . . . gain[s] supremacy over the objective order." That is, "the intellectual performance is an act of conquest."[132] However, Soloveitchik thinks that gaining control is a perpetual task and that the human being will never fully "succeed in his bold attempt to unravel the *mysterium magnum* of being able to control nature as a whole."[133] Thus, the confrontation with nature is perpetual.

Finally, there is the third level of existence, where a different sort of confrontation takes place. It is "not the confrontation of a subject who gazes, with a sense of superiority, at the object beneath him, but of two equal subjects." Now, Soloveitchik notes that both I's are "lonely in their otherness and uniqueness, both opposed and rejected by an objective order," and both are "craving for companionship."[134] However, despite our status as social beings, we are inherently lonely, and the relationship with the Other must attend to both our singular identities and our yearning to be part of communities. To the degree that one has not fully experienced the confrontation on the second level of existence (i.e., encountering the otherness of the world), one cannot fully appreciate the confrontation on the third level of existence.

Soloveitchik finds the roots for the totalitarian tendencies of "modern man" in the failure to fully come to terms with the challenges of the second level of existence.[135] As a result, Soloveitchik thinks that modern human beings privilege the "subject-object" relationship of knowing qua mastery, which is itself bound up with the tendency to "dominate and subordinate" appropriate to nature, and they apply it to the human realm. Although he specifically critiques modern individuals for failing to treat their fellow as an equal with intrinsic dignity, he also levels essentially the same charge at Christians for how they have historically related to Jews. Indeed, this failure to treat the Jew as an equal is at play in the very discussions in Vatican II, where Christians debate about whether or not there are reasons to change their theological conceptions of Jews or to continue to charge them with deicide—and this in the wake of the unprecedented mass murder of Jews by Christians.

Soloveitchik ties his discussion of the relations between Christians and Jews to the typology or levels of the human being. Jews can relate to those of different religions—in this case, Christians—in matters pertaining to the second level of human existence, namely "the cosmic confrontation" where human beings toil with nature to sustain life. Thus, Soloveitchik maintains that Jews are "committed to the welfare and progress of mankind," "are interested in combating disease, in alleviating human suffering,"[136] as well as "joining the cultural enterprise of all men."[137] Culture and the well-being of the general community then are tied to this second level of human existence, to the cosmic confrontation, which is a point where faith communities can intersect or meet on common ground without effacing the deep and substantive "metaphysical" otherness dividing them.

This brings us to the manner in which Soloveitchik uses language that is directly relevant to the larger world religions discourse that orients this study of modern Jewish philosophy. He mentions that Judaism and Christianity have an ambivalent relationship. On the one hand, "Judaism as a culture has influenced, indeed molded the ethico-philosophical Christian world-formula. The basic categories and premises of the latter were evolved in the cultural Judaic orbit." In addition, "our Western heritage was shaped by a combination of three factors, the classical, Judaic, and Christian, and we could readily speak of a Judeo-Hellenistic-Christian tradition within the framework of our Western civilization." However, in the same paragraph, he emphasizes that, when it comes to faith rather than culture, the religious traditions are radically incommensurable and make use of "different frames of reference": To speak of a Judeo-Christian tradition is "utterly absurd."[138] Thus, only on a cultural level is there continuity. On a structural level, however, the traditions, and those subjectivities produced by their respective practices and liturgies, are radically distinct.

It would be a mistake, however, to think of this cultural common ground as devoid of religious significance. Although Soloveitchik rejects interfaith dialogue, he promotes interfaith cooperation (i.e., "coordination of interests"). In cooperation, the link is temporary; it "does not spell an existential union." Whereas interfaith dialogue attempts to somehow translate and render commensurable the radically distinct cores of different traditions, interfaith cooperation uses the secular as a bridge, a common space, where both can meet, without any tradition

forfeiting its metaphysical individuality: "We frequently engage in common enterprise and we prudently pursue common goals, travelling temporarily along
parallel roads, yet our destinations are not the same."[139]

Soloveitchik's notion of pluralism is foreshadowed in *The Halakhic Mind*,
with its claim that objective practices shape one's subjectivity, and is developed
further in "Confrontation." In the later work, he avers that the "individuality of a
faith community expresses itself in a threefold way." First, "the divine imperatives
and commandments to which a faith community is unreservedly committed
must not be equated with the ritual and ethos of another community."[140] There
are no common denominators, no universal principles through which different
religions can find common ground or be reduced and equated. Second, each community maintains an exclusive "axiological awareness" of its ultimacy, such that
each faith community believes that its values and doctrines are most suitable for
attaining the "ultimate good." Indeed, Soloveitchik insists that "this belief is indispensable to the survival of the community."[141] Finally, "each faith community
is unyielding in its eschatological expectations." This element is crucial, and
because Soloveitchik's writing is a bit terse and opaque I quote it at length. With
its apocalyptic expectations, the faith community

> perceives the events at the end of time with exultant certainty, and expects
> man, by surrender of selfish pettiness and by consecration to the great destiny
> of life, to embrace the faith that this community has been preaching through-
> out the millennia. Standardization of practices, equalization of dogmatic cer-
> titudes, and the waiving of eschatological claims spell the end of the vibrant
> and great faith experience of any religious community. It is as unique and enig-
> matic as the individual himself.[142]

Soloveitchik is ostensibly making a metaphysical claim here that only at the end
of time will there be any sort of consensus in regard to religious views. However,
the significance of this claim is that any attempt to achieve a unity of faiths pre-
emptively will be bad for everyone involved, in that it will dilute the particularity
and uniqueness of every tradition. Here, it would seem that Soloveitchik can only
allow this plurality to be resolved in an apocalyptic event (i.e., the *eschaton*). Until
then, each community should—or, perhaps better, has no justifiable reason not
to—maintain its uniqueness. This metaphysical claim then has a clear social and
political function.

A striking feature of "Confrontation" is that the terminology of liberal democracy not only exists side by side with theological concepts like revelation and
eschatology but also often takes precedence. Soloveitchik insists that a genuine
"confrontation of two faith communities is possible only if it is accompanied by
a clear assurance that both parties will enjoy equal rights and full religious freedom." He continues,

A democratic confrontation certainly does not demand that we submit to an attitude of self-righteousness taken by the community of the many [i.e., Christianity] which, while debating whether or not to "absolve" the community of the few [i.e., Judaism] of some mythical guilt, completely ignores its own historical responsibility for the suffering and martyrdom so frequently recorded in the annals of the history of the few, the weak, and the persecuted.[143]

Here, Soloveitchik is obliquely referencing Vatican II. The very idea that Jews participate in a process whereby Christians contemplate changing their theological stance (i.e., that Jews bear guilt for the rejection and death of Christ) is unacceptable for Soloveitchik.[144] Although Soloveitchik finds galling discussions about Jewish guilt in the wake of the long history of Christian oppression and especially Christian complicity in the Holocaust, what is perhaps more troubling for him about Vatican II is that the participation of Jews in this process creates an asymmetry between the two communities. Soloveitchik thinks that this asymmetry reduces Jews, the minority community, to becoming "an object of observation, judgment, and evaluation" of the Christians, the majority community.[145] Instead, he insists that the Jews are "a totally independent faith community" and thus do not "revolve as a satellite in any orbit" around the Christian community.[146]

The promise of democratic liberalism is the promise of symmetrical relations between communities, even if one community is larger than the other. A "democratic confrontation" between two faith communities implies that each community possesses intrinsic worth; it is demeaning and unjust to subjugate the narrative of one community to fit the doctrine of another just because it is larger and therefore more politically powerful. Instead, Soloveitchik contends that the integrity of Judaism entails its absolute distinction from Christianity. He refutes any supersessionist implication in the conjunction of "Judeo-Christian"—that the "Christian" is somehow a furthering and completion of the "Judeo"—by maintaining that religious communities, "endowed with intrinsic dignity and metaphysical worth," are absolutely unique and utterly incommensurable with one another.[147] He does not use doctrinal or other theological forms of argument to critique Christianity, because this would imply that the two communities share a language in common when it comes to their faith. Rather, he takes recourse to the language of democratic liberalism to maintain the "metaphysical" distinctiveness of the two communities.

Indeed, Soloveitchik criticizes the "emancipated modern Jew" for attempting to abandon her dual status as a human being and as a Jew.[148] Authentic Jews, for Soloveitchik, are bound up in a dialectic state, "a double confrontation," in that they are part of both "the universal human and the exclusive covenantal confrontation." According to Soloveitchik, "modern" emancipated Jews seek to escape this dialectical existence by wholly embracing the universally human dimension and jettisoning their covenantal community. Soloveitchik frowns on such a shirking of one's duty, indeed of one's existential nature, and explains that, as Jews

> our approach to and relationship with the outside world has always been of an ambivalent character, intrinsically antithetic, bordering at times on the para-doxical. We relate ourselves to and at the same time withdraw from . . . the world. . . . We cooperate with the members of other faith communities in all fields of constructive human endeavor, but, simultaneously, with our integra-tion into the general social framework, we engage in a movement of recoil and retrace our steps.[149]

The authentic Jew, then, is both a member of the larger society and indepen-dent of it and a member of a unique community. Similarly, Judaism is situated in and related to the West, but it is essential to recognize that this relationship does not compromise the absolute, metaphysical uniqueness of the Jewish community.

* * *

In this chapter, we followed a trajectory from Soloveitchik's dissertation, *Das reine Denken und die Seinskonstitutierung bei Hermann Cohen*, through *The Halakhic Mind* and culminating in "Confrontation." In doing so we see that Soloveitchik, more than any other thinker we have discussed, follows Cohen in attempting to weave together a philosophical metanarrative with *Religionswis-senschaft*. And yet, if Soloveitchik resembles Cohen in the structure or form of his philosophizing, in terms of content, he is quite different. Like Buber, Rosenzweig, and Heschel, he rejects Cohen's Idealism in favor of a more existentially inflected phenomenological grounding. His methodology, which affirms a religious plu-ralism, is perhaps the most modest of all the thinkers explored in this study in terms of Judaism's world-historic significance. Although he argues for Judaism's radical uniqueness from other religious communities, its truth cannot be veri-fied, if at all, until the apocalyptic eschaton. And yet, if he is modest in regard to Judaism's place vis-à-vis other traditions, more than any other thinker we have discussed, including Rosenzweig, he is the most Orthodox and unyielding when it comes to what forms Judaism may legitimately take. Indeed, it is safe to say that his insistence on the primacy of law is in many ways a tacit critique of his German-Jewish forebears—Buber, Rosenzweig, and even Cohen.

Conclusion

In this book, I examined the thought of five philosophers in the German-Jewish tradition over a span of roughly fifty years. By foregrounding the world religions discourse in my reading of the major works of these canonical thinkers, I emphasized the importance of the historical, cultural, and discursive situatedness of modern Jewish philosophy. Where the project of modern Jewish philosophy is often thought of in apolitical terms, as reconciling traditional Jewish beliefs with modern sensibilities, I highlighted its polemical nature.

In doing so, I recovered a dimension of modern Jewish philosophy: its critical, even bellicose, relationship with Europe and European Christianity, which is too often minimized. By focusing on works from (although not strictly limited to) five decades in the early to mid-twentieth century and reading them in light of the then-dominant world religions discourse, this book attended to the distance and difference that separate the contemporary study of Jewish philosophy from those earlier canonical works. It emphasized the manner in which the project of modern Jewish philosophy has been—and still is, albeit differently—bound up with the nature of "Europe" and the Jew's place therein. Modern Jewish philosophy took up the world religions discourse, a discourse that fostered the exclusion of Jews from Europe, and used it not only to contest Christian triumphalism but also to inscribe—at the expense of Christianity—Judaism in the heart of European identity.

If this book challenges the tendency to emphasize continuity over difference in our reading of major works of the tradition, its goal is by no means to reduce the works of the canon of modern Jewish philosophy to mere historical interest. Rather, it is to call us to reconsider our relationship to thinkers and works in the canon of modern Jewish philosophy. The situation of those of us working in Jewish philosophy today is quite different from that of the canonical thinkers examined in this study. They lived and worked in a time when the field of Jewish Studies was largely excluded from the academy; today it flourishes in the United States, Europe,[1] and Israel. Where their works bear the traces of the horrors of the early and mid-twentieth century, including the Holocaust, we live in a time where—despite rising antisemitism in Europe—Jews are no longer a disenfranchised minority.

The differences between our predecessors and us matter because they both affect and reflect the manner in which the very task of Jewish philosophy is envisioned. The works of our predecessors are remarkable, filled with brilliance, desperation, and no small amount of audacity. We must not only keep the precarious positions of our predecessors in mind, but also the role of the world religions discourse in shaping the very contours of their work. In such a context, their use of the logic of exemplarity and their attempts to inscribe Judaism into the heart of Europe at the expense of other traditions were cogent strategies for illuminating the meaning and value of Judaism. Yet, our situation is quite different, and we can no longer simply take these ways of conceptualizing Judaism and its significance for granted. This is by no means to say that the canon of modern Jewish philosophy is incomprehensible or an esoteric affair today or that it has nothing to offer us. Rather, those of us who continue to study and practice Jewish philosophy should acknowledge that different problems and concerns animate our reflections. We not only face different problems—conceptual, as well as theological and sociopolitical—but we also articulate our responses in an institutional framework that is quite alien to the work of our predecessors.

As a result of these differences, we must carefully consider how we relate to and derive meaning from the canon of modern Jewish philosophy. The world religions discourse—the idiom and framework our predecessors both used and inverted—is an antiquated one today.[2] Indeed, it would seem that we are at something of a crossroads, at which two alternatives, two different ways forward, present themselves to us. On the one hand, we can emphasize continuity (at the expense of distance or difference) with the canonical figures of modern Jewish philosophy. That is, rather than situating their arguments within the intellectual horizons of their historical and cultural moment, we can appropriate and critique their arguments and strategies in relation to our own contemporary sensibilities and judgments. On the other hand, we can emphasize difference in our relationship to these thinkers.

If we choose the first alternative, we will treat our predecessors as something like contemporaries with whom we argue on philosophical grounds. This approach emphasizes continuity with the past, such that even if we acknowledge, in a by-the-way manner, differences in social and intellectual context, we engage the arguments of our predecessors on philosophical or theological grounds. We can do so by examining the arguments of a particular thinker to test their internal coherence or by positing a conflicting argument, often about the "true" nature or essence of Judaism, the "Jewish way of thinking," or "what the Torah teaches" (i.e., through the use of conflicting essentialisms).

Indeed, just as the thinkers studied in this book posited normative notions of Judaism so too do many prominent contemporary Jewish philosophers. For example, David Novak (born in 1941) challenges Hermann Cohen's account of Judaism by rejecting his emphasis on reason over revelation. According to Novak, the authentic understanding of Judaism prioritizes revelation, the Torah, over human reason and to philosophy. [3] Novak has written numerous studies and constructive works that engage modern Jewish philosophy as well as classical theological texts, elucidating what he considers to be the proper version of Judaism.

The other alternative, here rooted in religious studies methodology, is at odds with the first. This way forward, which emphasizes difference rather than continuity, explicitly rejects reified, essentialist accounts of religious traditions. [4] At first glance such a strategy might seem to put the student of Jewish philosophy in a peculiar position because, at least historically, the philosophy of religion (of which Jewish philosophy is rightly counted as a subset) has often proceeded on the basis of essentialist premises. Indeed, in *The Sacred Is the Profane* (2013), [5] William Arnal and Russell McCutcheon note with some approval that there has been a "widespread turn from practicing our field as if it was a branch of the history of ideas toward studying what is now known as 'religion on the ground' or 'material religion.'" This shift "estranges former close relationships with our cousins in philosophy and, instead, forges affinities with our new friends, the social anthropologists and culture studies." [6] Although it would be premature to rule out the philosophy of religion (and thus Jewish philosophy) in toto—which is not necessarily what Arnal and McCutcheon are saying here—it is certainly true that recent methodological shifts in the study of religion entail a change in sensibility. In terms of Jewish philosophy, the critiques of essentialism championed by scholars like Arnal and McCutcheon undermine such anti-historical and essentialist talk of a "Jewish way of thinking" or of "what the Torah teaches." Such phrases, they argue, position one as a theologian, a spokesperson, a caretaker, and thus obscures the porosity and plurality of voices within the Jewish tradition. [7]

In *Rethinking Jewish Philosophy* (2014), Aaron W. Hughes highlights and critiques the normative dimensions that permeate the activity of Jewish philosophy. Actively rejecting any semblance of an essence to Judaism, Hughes conceives of Jewish philosophy or, as he more appropriately puts it, "something amorphously and monolithically referred to as Jewish philosophy" [8] as continually renarrating and redefining its subject matter to make it appear stable and fixed. For Hughes, the aim of Jewish philosophy, or what he calls Jewish metaphilosophy, is to expose the socially constructed nature of different iterations of Judaism.

In conjunction with Hughes's demystifying Jewish metaphilosophy, there is another sense in which modern Jewish philosophy and religious studies theory might be profitably studied in conjunction with one another. As I mentioned in the introduction, within religious studies there is a significant body of scholarship on the history, nature, and theoretical underpinnings of the modern category of religion. Often such studies emphasize the European legacy of this term and how it has shaped the West's encounter with its others. However, the study of the category of religion must also account for the ways in which this category and the discourse around it have been incorporated into non-Christian and non-European traditions. Masuzawa points out that there is a "process of mutually interactive development" between "European representations of non-Christian religions and, on the other hand, the native appropriation, reaction, or resistance to such representations."[9] Non-European (and Jewish) philosophers and intellectuals adapted European paradigms, methodologies, and assumptions without accepting—and often, actively resisting—their Eurocentric conclusions. Indeed, these thinkers often appropriated European ideas and philosophical idioms, incorporating them into their own accounts of their "native" traditions.

To be sure, the story of modern Hinduism is not that of modern Judaism or modern Buddhism. However, all of these traditions have been shaped, and not merely negatively, by their engagement with Europe. I do not mean this solely or even primarily in a political sense, but rather the new language and set of social, theological, and philosophical, categories that emerge in the relationship with Europe have been taken up and employed, in new ways to be sure, by philosophers, theologians, and other intellectuals in non-Christian and non-European traditions. The world religions discourse has affected and shaped the traditions with which it has come into contact. The category of religion binds together various traditions, and Western philosophy has played a major role not only in the way in which these traditions were interpreted within Europe but also in how non-Christian philosophers, theologians, and other intellectuals articulated their respective traditions to their peers as well as to Europeans. The category of religion and its theological and philosophical underpinnings ceased to be simply Christian or European as other traditions appropriated and internalized them.

Although many scholars of religion such as McCutcheon seek to demystify arguments that trade on essentializing a tradition or traditions, there is no denying that such "caretaking" constituted (and in many places still constitutes) one of the central responses to and is itself a legacy of the world religions discourse. Studying how non-European—and Jewish—religious traditions adapted themselves to modernity and appropriated and engaged European discourses, including those related to the study of religion, is not merely ideological or to engage in advocacy. This study is necessary to grasp how different religious traditions have assumed, each in its own polyvocal, fragmented manner, the shapes they now take.

The intersection of the history of philosophy with the category of religion or, more particularly, with how Western philosophy was used, albeit quite differently, by different parties in the world religions discourse needs further study. Two related descriptive tasks are necessary. First, further elucidation is needed regarding the ways in which Jewish philosophers employed reigning theories and methods in the study of religion. For example, twentieth-century philosophers used such staples of the modern study of religion as the sui generis conception of religion and the phenomenology of religion to interpret Jewish theology and "religious experience" in a philosophical idiom. However, they did so in ways that were different from their Christian contemporaries. Further inquiry can shed more light into the dense intersection of form and content, method and use, when it comes to religious difference and the terminology used to articulate and translate the insights and beliefs at the core of distinct religious traditions.

Second, greater exploration is needed of the overlapping and contradictory ways in which different non-European traditions encountered, engaged, and used European intellectual traditions. This means both exploring how different religious and cultural traditions were perceived and represented in different European cultural contexts and elucidating how theologians, philosophers, and other intellectuals in these traditions employed the discourse around the category of religion and European philosophy in general in articulating accounts of their own respective traditions. Significant comparative work on the world religions discourse, its many vectors, and its tense interchange between cultures is required to grasp how non-Christian traditions simultaneously internalized and appropriated traditions of European thought.

* * *

Let me close by suggesting that I may have framed the opposition between the two alternatives now facing us—either continuing to engage in Jewish philosophy in an essentializing manner like our forebears or shifting to a more deconstructive and historicizing approach to Judaism—in too stark a manner. Indeed, the two alternatives are inextricably tied to each other. First, the historicizing and deconstructive approach is itself bound up with normative presuppositions.[10] Second, its consequences generate the need for constructive philosophy, albeit in a form that is sensitive to the constructed nature of Judaism and the historicity of the various voices in the canon of modern Jewish philosophy. Another way to think of it is that, as anyone with even the most basic familiarity with hermeneutics understands, we cannot help but approach texts from the past from within the horizons of concern of our present. That being said, this analysis can be done with more or less nuance.

This book has made explicit the manner in which so much of the canon of modern Jewish thought is bound up with the world religions discourse. Once we recognize the connection of the world religions discourse to modern Jewish philosophy, it is incumbent on us to acknowledge that today, when this discourse no longer holds sway (or no longer holds sway in the same manner), our understanding of the task of Jewish philosophy must change. We have seen how the essentialist accounts of Judaism put forward by thinkers in the canon of modern

Jewish philosophy utilized the category of religion. Similarly, the precarious position of Judaism in the world religions discourse fostered arguments employing the "logic" of exemplarity and the use of grand metanarratives, strategies that went hand in hand with such essentialism. Today, in our pluralist, multicultural world, where Jewish Studies is no longer excluded from the academy and Jews are no longer a disenfranchised minority, such strategies are no longer appropriate either methodologically or rhetorically.

However, the value of studying the canon of modern Jewish philosophy is not merely negative (i.e., to glean what strategies Jewish philosophy can no longer employ in good conscience). Constructive Jewish philosophy is still needed, perhaps even more than ever, as essentialist notions of Judaism are abandoned. Thus, for instance, we desperately need careful reflection on the implications on the proliferation of the diverse and conflicting voices speaking from within, and ostensibly for, the Jewish tradition. Additionally, there is an urgent need to conceptually clarify the relationship between Diasporic Jewish existence to the state of Israel, given that Israel proclaims to speak on behalf of Jews everywhere and is often seen to do as much by non-Jews. These are only two of the numerous issues that call for further reflection.

However, there is another, perhaps deeper level in which the works of Cohen, Rosenzweig, Buber, Heschel, and Soloveitchik can continue to inspire. Even if we resist certain strategies they employed, or feel the need to make their thought address questions they never asked, their works offer outstanding examples of how a philosophical idiom can be used to revitalize and reenergize a tradition. Even if we acknowledge the plurality of voices within Judaism and all religious traditions, this does not mean that one cannot offer creative reconstructions of "Judaism" that prioritize one particular strand or thread of the tradition. The works of the canonical thinkers studied here present profound reimaginings or rearticulations of different themes from various texts and motifs within the Jewish tradition. Thus, they demonstrate the manner that different threads in a much larger tapestry of a tradition broadly construed can be mobilized and reinvigorated when combined with modern philosophical idioms to address contemporary existential and philosophical problems. Even if we do not share all the sensibilities of our predecessors, they remain important sources to think with and through.

Like the figures studied here, we too face a period of profound change and uncertainty. Where they confronted a discourse that was systematically devaluing Judaism and Jewish sources, declaring them (and the Jews) alien to Europe, today we face the challenge of making the sources of Judaism (however configured) relevant in an increasingly pluralist world where community and authority within Judaism are extremely fragmented. At the same time, we are confronted by the fact that Judaism (in its many iterations) is only one tradition among many others. That is, we face the challenge of pluralism. Not only must Jewish philosophy address the challenge of an proliferation of voices within but it must also come to grips with the challenges posed by an increased awareness of the radical plurality of religious and nonreligious traditions without.

Often philosophical accounts of pluralism, whether from social and political philosophers like Jürgen Habermas or from philosophers of religion, emphasize that a—indeed the primary—solution to the challenge of pluralism lies in cultivating an epistemic humility. However, such stances tend to treat religious traditions like closed-off monads. Such a solution clearly fails to grapple with the fact that traditions (or iterations of traditions)[11] interact, influence, and enter into conflict with one another in history. Here too modern Jewish philosophy can continue to inspire us today. Modern Jewish philosophy was a form of critical pluralism insofar as it actively worked to deconstruct and subvert the hegemony of the world religions discourse, as well as the Germanic, Aryanized Christianity that went hand in hand with it.

Today, the example of this critical pluralism can serve as a model of critiques in contemporary religious and national discourse. In different ways, the tradition of thinkers extending from Cohen to Soloveitchik can lend inspiration and resources for challenging forms of Judaism that prioritize "Jewish interests" in the Middle East to the point of failing to recognizing the suffering, indeed the humanity, of the Palestinians. It can help us challenge militant orthodoxies that not only perpetuate homophobic and sexist behavior but also refuse to respect other religious modes of existence. Similarly, just as it can help us critique aspects of contemporary Jewish life we deem to be problematic, so too it can help provide a religio-philosophical basis, a language as it were, for critiquing and resisting rising economic and political inequality in many democracies around the world; it can also provide resources for recognizing and resisting newly emergent forms of antisemitism without falling into nationalist jingoism. Thus, even if their answers will not be ours, their incorporation of philosophy into their reflections which challengeed and rethought dogmas, will continue to exert formative influence on our own endeavors.

Notes

Introduction

1. I use the term "canon" somewhat loosely. When I refer to a canonical text in Jewish philosophy I am referring to a work that has set the terms according to which scholarly discussion and debate have proceeded and continue to proceed. I may refer to a thinker, usually the author of one or several canonical texts, as canonical if his or her concerns, methodologies, and arguments—as they manifest in his or her works—have significantly shaped the landscape of the field. On a more prosaic note, the term "canonical" can be used in the sense that one can reasonably expect to find either the author or one of his or her texts represented on most syllabi devoted to modern Jewish philosophy or modern Judaism.

2. It should be noted that historians, who do not have as much at stake in emphasizing the preponderance of continuity over difference, acknowledge this dimension of Jewish thought much more readily than do students of Jewish philosophy. A prime example can be found in the work of Susannah Heschel. In a striking passage, when speaking about German Jewish Studies in general, which would include modern Jewish philosophy, Heschel writes, "The first practitioners of Jewish studies saw the study of Judaism as not simply an addition to the general curriculum but as a revision of that curriculum, an effort to resist and even overthrow the standard portrayal of Western history. In this version, at the heart of the West would stand the Hebrew Bible and rabbinic literature, not classical Greek civilization or the New Testament, and the history of Christian thought would be presented as a derivatory offshoot of Jewish ideas." Susannah Heschel, "Jewish Studies as Counterhistory," in *Insider and Outsider: American Jews and Multiculturalism*, ed. David Biale, Michael Galchinsky, and Susannah Heschel (Berkeley: University of California Press, 1998), 102–103, cf. 101–116. See also Susannah Heschel, *Abraham Geiger and the Jewish Jesus* (Chicago: University of Chicago Press, 1998) and Jonathan M. Hess, *Germans, Jews and the Claims of Modernity* (New Haven, CT: Yale University Press, 2002).

3. Michael Zank has written trenchantly about the transformation in the task and character of modern Jewish philosophy as it has migrated from Europe to the United States. See Michael Zank, "Jüdische Religionsphilosophie als Apologie des Mosaismus," *Archivio di Filosofia* LXXI, nos. 1–3 (2003): 173–182; idem, "Zwischen Den Stühlen? On the Taxonomic Anxieties of Modern Jewish Philosophy," *EJJS* 1, no. 1 (2007) 105–134; and, idem, "The Heteronomy of Modern Jewish Philosophy," *Journal of Jewish Thought and Philosophy*, 20, no. 1 (2012): 99–134.

4. It is perhaps the largely unacknowledged chasm between our predecessors and us that contributes to the numerous conflicting notions of what precisely Jewish philosophy is. For a list of recent work regarding the contested nature of Jewish philosophy see Steven Schwarzschild, "Modern Jewish Philosophy," in *The Pursuit of the Ideal: Jewish Writings of Steven Schwarzschild*, ed. Menachem Kellner (Albany: State University of New York Press, 1990); David Novak, *The Election of Israel: The Idea of the Chosen People* (Cambridge: Cambridge University Press, 1995); Norbert Samuelson, "Is Jewish Philosophy Either Philosphy or Jewish?" in *La Storia Della Filosofia Ebraica*, ed. Irene Kajon (Milani: Casa Editrice Dott. 1993), 463–485; Michael Zank, "Jüdischen Religionsphilosophie als Apologie des Mosaismus," "Zwischen Den Stühlen?" and

"The Heteronomy of Modern Jewish Philosophy"; Michael L. Morgan and Peter Eli Gordon, "Introduction: Modern Jewish Philosophy, Modern Philosophy, and Modern Judaism," in *The Cambridge Companion to Modern Jewish Philosophy* (Cambridge: Cambridge University Press, 2007), 1–13; Aaron W. Hughes and Elliot R. Wolfson, "Introduction: Charting an Alternative Course for the Study of Jewish Philosophy," in *New Directions in Jewish Philosophy* (Bloomington: Indiana University Press, 2010), 1–18; Leora Batnitzky, *How Judaism Became a Religion: An Introduction to Modern Jewish Thought* (Princeton, NJ: Princeton University Press, 2011); Martin Kavka, "Introduction," in *The Cambridge History of Jewish Philosophy.* Vol. 2, *The Modern Era* (Cambridge: Cambridge University Press, 2012), 1–31;Willi Goetschel, *The Discipline of Philosophy and the Invention of Modern Jewish Thought* (New York: Fordham University Press, 2013); and Aaron Hughes, *Rethinking Jewish Philosophy: Beyond Particularism and Universalism* (Oxford: Oxford University Press, 2014).

5. Tomoko Masuzawa, *The Invention of World Religions: Or How European Universalism Was Preserved in the Language of Pluralism* (Chicago: University of Chicago Press, 2005). Although Masuzawa's magisterial study works within a broadly European context and focuses on the emergence of the so-called science of religion, in particular the discipline of philology, my own interests are more specifically related to the Germanic context. And, given the thinkers I study, I include more phenomenologically oriented theories of religion than does Masuzawa. None of this diminishes the manner in which the world religions discourse, which Masuzawa illuminates, has brought about profound transformations in European identity, ones that particularly affect the status of Jews and Judaism.

6. Although the primary focus of this study is on the German-speaking world or on the German-speaking parts of Europe, when I do use the terms "Europe" or "European civilization" I also include North America (the United States and Canada).

7. On the difficulties of situating the study of modern Jewish philosophy in the academy, see the thoughtful reflections of Aaron W. Hughes and Elliot R. Wolfson in "Introduction: Charting an Alternative Course for the Study of Jewish Philosophy," 1–2.

8. Not all inquiries about the emergence of the category of religion are equally useful. For example, Timothy Fitzgerald's *The Ideology of Religious Studies* (New York: Oxford University Press, 2000) offers a critique of the ways in which the local concept of the Western notion of religion is used in a universal sense, and thus distorts the manner in which scholars interpret Asian cultures. The manner in which Fitzgerald executes his critique however, is such that his work is not particularly helpful and indeed may be harmful for our purposes. Fitzgerald is not wrong, of course, to maintain that religion is in fact an "ideological category" that emerges in the modern West, "with a specific location in history, including the nineteenth century period of European colonization" (4–5). Again, his contention that the concept of religion is itself bound up with a "liberal ecumenical theology" is also correct (5). However, given the careful studies of the shifting role of Judaism and the Semitic in general, his charge that the concept of religion as created by scholars such as Max Mueller and Friedrich Schleiermacher is grounded in the "Judaeo-Christian idea" of a transcendent God that is consequently "smuggled into cross cultural research" (7) is problematic. Fitzgerald decries the tacit "Judaeo-Christian" assumptions underlying the notion of religion used by Western scholars when studying Eastern cultures. Yet, the term "Judaeo-Christian" is one that only emerges as part of the world religions discourse, which itself is very much a theological construct. On the history of the "Judeo-Christian" construct, see Masuzawa, *The Invention of World Religions*, 301–303. Fitzgerald inadvertently accepts the terms of the very theological discourse he sets out to critique.

9. Masuzawa notes that of great concern to Europeans, and thus tacitly or explicitly at stake in the study of religion in the nineteenth century, was "the historical (or possible con-

genital) relation between Christianity and Judaism, and the question of whether Jews and Judaism had a role in the future of Europe." *The Invention of World Religions*, 18.

10. On the role of crisis and dislocations in philosophy, particularly Jewish philosophy, see Morgan and Gordon, "Introduction: Modern Jewish Philosophy, Modern Philosophy, and Modern Judaism," 1–2.

11. I am paraphrasing Masuzawa, *The Invention of World Religions*, xii.

12. For an incisive account not only of the relationship of German theology and race but also of the nadir of the world religions discourse in Germany, see Susannah Heschel, *The Aryan Jesus: Christian Theologians and the Bible in Nazi Germany* (Princeton, NJ: Princeton University Press, 2008), 1–66.

13. Masuzawa, *The Invention of World Religions*, 149; Suzanne Marchand, *German Orientalism in the Age of Empire: Religion, Race, and Scholarship* (Cambridge: Cambridge University Press, 2009), 254.

14. See S. Heschel, *Abraham Geiger and the Jewish Jesus*, 106–161; idem, *The Aryan Jesus*, 59; Masuzawa, *The Invention of World Religions*, 18–19; and Marchand, *German Orientalism*, 255.

15. In *German Orientalism*, 230, Marchand notes, "Scholars really did believe that finding a *Volk's* roots would offer insight into its destiny. The Germans were by no means the only group seeking their ancestral origins or their racial identity, but perhaps the swiftness of the new state's rise in the international firmament, coupled with the continuing anxieties about what 'Germanness' meant, resulted in peculiarly deep cultural investment in these quests."

16. Masuzawa, *The Invention of World Religions*, 282.

17. In *The Sacred Is the Profane: The Political Nature of "Religion"* (Oxford: Oxford University Press, 2013), William E. Arnal and Russell T. McCutcheon note the irony of Indian scholars publishing works on postcolonialism that criticize European scholars for trivializing their religion in English. Such critiques, Arnal and McCutcheon note, use thoroughly Western notions of religion—and indeed language and publishers—to critique Western imperialism. Arnal and McCutcheon lament that Indian scholars do not "try to change the scholarly game altogether" by using a local, Indian religious concept, such as Dharma, to examine other religions (9). This lament highlights—which is their point—the fact that the European category of religion comes to be absorbed and internalized by non-European traditions.

18. Although McCutcheon has discussed this distinction, or similar ones, in many different locations, it is most acutely attended to in Russell T. McCutcheon, *Critics Not Caretakers: Redescribing the Public Study of Religion* (Albany: State University of New York, 2001).

19. Ibid., 22.

20. Ibid., 25.

21. Perhaps no one has called attention to and problematized the predominance of the caretaker tendency in Jewish Studies more than Aaron W. Hughes. See for example, Hughes, *The Study of Judaism: Authenticity, Identity, Scholarship* (Albany: State University of New York Press, 2013). He continues this trend in *Rethinking Jewish Philosophy*. For an interesting exchange on the role of authenticity and identity in Jewish Studies, see Aaron Hughes, "Jewish Studies Is Too Jewish," *Chronicle of Higher Education* (last accessed 6/11/14) http://chronicle.com/article/Jewish-Studies-Is-Too-Jewish/145395/ and the response by Zachary Braiterman (last accessed 6/11/14), http://jewishphilosophyplace.wordpress.com /2014/05/08 /too-jewish-studies-response-to-aaron-hughes/, and Sarah Imhoff, "Reflections on Jewish Studies" (last accessed 6/18/2014), http://www.equinoxpub.com/blog/2014/05/reflections-on -jewish-studies/.

22. McCutcheon, *Critics Not Caretakers*, 116.

1. Exemplarity and the German-Jewish Symbiosis

1. Leo Strauss, "Introductory Essay," in Hermann Cohen, *Religion of Reason out of the Sources of Judaism,* trans. Simon Kaplan (Atlanta: Scholars Press, 1995), xxiii.

2. Hermann Cohen was the leading member of the so-called Marburg School of Neo-Kantianism. As Rudolf Makkreel and Sebastian Luft write, "Neo-Kantianism in Germany could be viewed as a typical phenomenon of the Bismarckian era or of the last manifestations of the German Kaiserreich. Indeed, at the end of the First World War, Neo-Kantianism itself seems to have come to an end in Germany: The end of a political era thus coincided with that of a philosophical era." "Introduction," in *Neo-Kantianism in Contemporary Philosophy,* ed. Rudolf A. Makkreel and Sebastian Luft (Bloomington: Indiana University Press, 2010), 2.

3. Scholars have noted that particularly Martin Heidegger but also Hans-Georg Gadamer actively sought to eliminate Cohen's legacy after his death. See Steven Schwarzschild, in "Authority and Reason contra Gadamer," in *Studies in Jewish Philosophy: Collected Essays of the Academy for Jewish Philosophy, 1980–1985,* ed. Norbert M. Samuelson (Providence: Brown University Press, 1987), 161–190; see also Peter E. Gordon, *Continental Divide: Heidegger, Cassirer, Davos* (Cambridge, MA: Harvard University Press, 2012), 136–143.

4. For a reading of Cohen's thought as part of the prewar generation, the generation that would give birth to the crisis of historicism, see Georg G. Iggers, *The German Conception of History: The National Tradition of Historical Thought from Herder to the Present* (Middletown, CT: Wesleyan University Press, 1968), 124–173; On the divide between Cohen and the next generation, see Steven Wasserstrom, "A Rustling in the Woods," in *Religion after Religion: Gershom Scholem, Mircea Eliade, Henry Corbin at Eranos* (Princeton, NJ: Princeton University Press, 1998), 112–124, and Paul Mendes Flohr, *German Jews: A Dual Identity* (New Haven, CT: Yale University Press, 1999). See, also, Michael Brenner, *The Renaissance of Jewish Culture in Weimar Germany* (New Haven, CT: Yale University Press, 1996).

5. Franz Rosenzweig reflects the changing sentiments of the next generation when he writes, "Judaism and Germanism are not on the same level. One can compare Germanism and Britainism, Germanism and Ottomanism, not Germanism and Judaism." Rosenzweig, "Deutschtum und Judentum," in *Zweistromland: Kleinere Schriften zu Glauben und Denken,* ed. Reinhold Mayer and Annemarie Mayer (Dordrecht: Martinus Nijhoff Publishers, 1984), 173. See Mendes-Flohr, *German Jews,* 66–88.

6. In regard to the standard of authenticity used by thinkers in the next generation who found Cohen wanting, see Michael Brenner, *The Renaissance of Jewish Culture in Weimar Germany.* Despite its pretensions, Brenner writes, "Jewish culture in Weimar Germany was characterized neither by a radical break with the past nor a return to it. Indeed, it used distinct forms of Jewish traditions, marked them as authentic, and presented them according to the demands of contemporary taste and modern cultural forms of expression. What might have appeared as authenticity was in fact a modern innovation" (5).

7. Hermann Cohen, "Deutschtum und Judentum mit grundlegenden Betrachtungen über Staat und Internationalismus," in *Hermann Cohens Jüdische Schriften* II (Berlin: C. A. Schwetschke & Sohn, 1924), 237–290. There was an immediate controversy on the publication of "Deutschtum und Judentum." In the hopes of explaining himself further, Cohen wrote "Eine Kritische Nachwort als Vorwort" [A Critical Afterwords as Forward] (1916) and a second version of the essay titled simply "Deutschtum und Judentum" (1916). See Hermann Cohen, "Ein kritisches Nachwort als Vorwort," in *Hermann Cohens Jüdische Schriften* II (Berlin: C. A. Schwetschke & Sohn, 1924), 291–301, and the second version of "Deutschtum und Judentum"

from 1916 in *Hermann Cohens Jüdische Schriften* II (Berlin: C. A. Schwetschke & Sohn, 1924), 301–318. In this chapter I only reference the first edition of this text, which I henceforth refer to as "Deutschtum und Judentum," unless otherwise noted.

8. The term "German-Jewish Symbiosis" is not without problems, as there are many, such as Scholem, who argued there never was any genuine mutuality much less complementarity in the relationship. Indeed, in *The Jews and Germany: From "Judeo-German Symbiosis" to the Memory of Auschwitz*, trans. Daniel Weissbrot (Lincoln, NA: University of Nebraska Press, 1995), 4–5, Enzo Traverso points out that German Jews often used the biological term "symbiosis" to describe what they argued was a complementary relationship with the larger German culture. Traverso suggests this was, at least in part, to counter the biological language of antisemites, who characterized the Jewish presence in German culture as one of parasitism. I will nevertheless continue to use this term in relation to Cohen's project, which in many ways is the apotheosis of the effort to emphasize the complementarity of the relationship between German Jews and German Christians.

9. For a helpful account of the response to Cohen's "Deutschtum und Judentum," see Hartwig Wiedebach, *The National Element in Hermann Cohen's Philosophy of Religion*, trans. William Templer (Leiden: Brill, 2012), 15–19. On pp. 1–50, Wiedebach explains in some detail the history of Cohen's concept of nationality, developed in relation to Judaism, and discusses in depth his confrontations with Zionists.

10. It is important to bear in mind the ambivalence of the term "assimilation." As Uriel Tal explains, "German Jewry understood emancipation in a sense contrary to that in which the Christians understood it, namely, not as the removal of barriers that had hitherto prevented Jews from completely assimilating to their environment, but rather as an incentive to continue to cultivate their Jewish uniqueness." *Christians and Jews in Germany: Religion, Politics, and Ideology in the Second Reich, 1870-1914* (Ithaca: Cornell University Press, 1975), 58.

11. Mark Lilla, *The Stillborn God: Religion, Politics, and the Modern West* (New York: Alfred A. Knopf, 2007), 239.

12. David Myers, "Hermann Cohen and the Quest for Protestant Judaism," *Leo Baeck Yearbook* (2001): 211.

13. Micha Brumlik, "1915: In *Deutschtum und Judentum* Hermann Cohen Applies Neo-Kantian Philosophy to the Jewish Question," in *The Yale Companion to Jewish Writing and Thought in German Culture, 1096-1996*, ed. Sander L. Gilman and Jack Zipes (New Haven, CT: Yale University Press, 1997), 347.

14. Gershom Sholem, "Against the Myth of German-Jewish Dialogue," in *On Jews and Judaism in Crisis: Selected Essays*, ed. Werner Danhauser (New York: Schocken Books) 62. Indeed, Myers explicitly references this essay by Scholem in "Hermann Cohen and the Quest for Protestant Judaism,"197.

15. Wendell Dietrich, "The Function of the Idea of Messianic Mankind in Hermann Cohen's Later Thought," *Journal for the American Academy of Religion* 48, no. 2 (June 1980): 256 n.6.

16. In this vein, perhaps the most devastating critique of Cohen's account of Germany comes from one of his most sensitive readers, Hartwig Wiedebach. In his exhaustive and penetrating study, *The National Element*. Wiedebach charges, and demonstrates, Cohen's mystification of German identity. However, it should be noted that Wiedebach acknowledges the self-critical manner in which Cohen employs the concept of Germanism (104, 246).

17. Hermann Cohen, "Über das Eigentümliche des deutschen Geistes," in *Schriften zur Philosophie und Zeitgeschichte*, V. I (Berlin: Akademie-Verlag, 1928), 527–570.

18. Hermann Cohen, *Der Begriffe der Religion im System der Philosophie* (Giessen: Töpelmann, 1915).

19. Hermann Cohen, *Religion der Vernunft aus den Quellen des Judentums*, Zweite Auflage (Cologne: J. Melzer Verlag, 1959) 1–40; *Religion of Reason out of the Sources of Judaism*, 1–34.

20. Although it may seem odd or idiosyncratic to look at these works together, there are some very good reasons to do so. First, these works were all written in Cohen's late period, between 1914 and 1918, when his arguments about the role of the Jews in Germany are at their most radical. (*Religion of Reason* was first published in 1919, a year after his Cohen's death.) Second, and as I emphasize shortly, a similar logic—what I call exemplarity, borrowing from Jacques Derrida—links both texts. See Derrida, "Onto-Theology of National Humanism (Prologomena to a Hypothesis)," *Oxford Literary Review* 14, nos. 1–2 (1992): 3–24 and Dana Hollander, *Exemplarity and Chosenness: Rosenzweig and Derrida on the Nation of Philosophy* (Stanford, CA: Stanford University Press, 2008).

21. The two most sustained discussions of this work, Wiedebach, *The National Element*, and Steven Schwarzwschild "'Germanism and Judaism'—Hermann Cohen's Normative Paradigm of German-Jewish Symbiosis," in *Jews and Germans from 1860 to 1933: The Problematic Symbiosis*, ed. David Bronsen (Heidelberg: Winter, 1979), 129–172, both acknowledge, albeit in different ways, the esoteric strategies employed by this text.

22. Cohen frequently inveighs at great length against the German idealist tradition that broke with Kant (i.e., Fichte, Schelling, and particularly Hegel). In "Über das Eigentümliche des deutschen Geistes," Cohen states, "Es ist für die Fortführung der deutschen Philosophie eine Frage nicht nur der geistigen Gesundheit, sondern schlechthin die Lebensfrage des deutschen Geistes für seine Wahrhaftigkeit: *ob Kant oder Hegel* ... Der deutsche Idealismus ist der Idealismus *Kants*." (546) "For the continuation of German philosophy it is a question not only of spiritual [geistigen] health, but rather the very life question par excellence for of the German spirit regarding its own truthfulness: whether Kant or Hegel ... *German Idealism is the Idealism of Kant*."

23. However, race is not entirely absent from Cohen's thought. In the second edition of "Deutschtum und Judentum," Cohen rejects the notion of a cultural divide between Jews and Christians and defiantly asks, "Where else in Germany is an opposition between Christians and Jews found if we fitly ignore the question of race?" *Hermann Cohens Judische Schriften* II, 308. For a fascinating discussion of the role of race in Cohen's thought, see Wiedebach, *The National Element*, 33–34, 81–85.

24. Steven Schwarzschild, "'Germanism and Judaism,'" 138.

25. Michael Zank, *The Idea of Atonement in the Philosophy of Hermann Cohen* (Providence: Brown Judaic Studies, 2000), 266.

26. As Schwarzschild puts it,

> In Critical philosophy [Cohen's method] "idealization" not only does not mean what it generally means in our current English ordinary usage—glorification, enveloping grimy reality with a nimbus of ideality, etc.—but, in fact, it means exactly the opposite: "idealization" is the rational, conceptual construction, the postulation of a morally desirable condition (A), for the purpose of measuring against it any actually given condition (B), so as necessarily to reveal that (B) falls short of (A)[(B) = (A) − x], and entailing the categorical challenge that the most strenuous efforts must be made to narrow this gap urgently and increasingly [so that (B) = (A) − (x − a)]. "Idealization" is then a critical and meliorist tool. ("'Germanism and Judaism,'" 142).

27. Although Schwarzschild's account of idealization is correct, it does necessarily justify the specific instances in which Cohen employs this method. Schwarzschild, "'Germanism and Judaism," 153. According to Schwarzschild, sentences like "Germany is the spirit of Kant and

Beethoven" need to be decoded. Although they appear to be descriptive (and highly problematic descriptions at that), the discerning reader realizes that they are, in actuality, normative. Schwarzschild emphasizes that Cohen is not saying that Germany possesses the spiritual depth of Kant and Beethoven by dint of their German heritage. Rather, Germany as a culture, to truly embody the German *Geist* rather than merely represent Germany on an empirical level, must seek to live up to the ideals that Kant and Beethoven represent. The sentence is a moral and cultural imperative. Wiedebach, however, highlights the problem with Cohen's method and its spirited defense by Schwarzschild. Schwarzschild's example, namely, "Germany is the spirit of Kant and Beethoven," is really an instance of "mystification" because it "is a declaration of existence on the one hand and a declaration of what ought to be on the other." Wiedebach, *The National Element*, 120 n.50. Wiedebach trenchantly highlights that Cohen wants it both ways. Germany ought to embody the ideals represented by Kant and Beethoven. And yet, at the same time, Germany is somehow uniquely situated to do so. The mystification for Wiedebach lies in Cohen's ascription of a unique access to universal ideals, a unique sort of universality to Germany. Although Schwarzschild acknowledges that Cohen does at moments succumb to "the seductions of patriotism" (157) he emphasizes that Cohen's argument does not need to grant any such special status to Germany. Schwarzschild rejects any unique significance, any exemplarity to Germany. He writes,

> In all of these historic cultures (Greek, English, French etc.) their past and present chauvinistic and immoral features are, as it were, locked away from future historical effectiveness—be this the pantheistic danger in Judaism and German Romanticism no less than the empiricistic (sic) one in England, feudalism in Russia, etc. It would not be very hard to show how Cohen, had he been, say, a Frenchman and immersed in French historical culture as he in fact was in German sources, would doubtless have written about "Frankism and Judaism" in which he would have said in principle precisely what he said in *Deutschtum und Judentum*. Let us use the best resources put at our disposal by the historical cultures and political structures into which history has placed us in order therewith to create a decent cosmopolitan human society. ("'Germanism and Judaism,'" 145–146).

However, in making this claim, Schwarzschild ignores Cohen's often—to my eyes, at least—unseemly critiques of other nations and their cultural and philosophical productions. As we see, at stake in Cohen's discusson of Germanism is the notion of exemplarity that Cohen embraces (with his argument of the *Eigentümlich* nature of Germanism), a notion that Jacques Derrida will later problematize in numerous writings.

28. Cohen is actually quite critical of Mendelssohn's famous book *Jerusalem, or on Religious Power and Judaism*, claiming that its "theoretical expression is the weakest point [*die Schwächste Seite*] of this great epoch in the history of Judaism". "Deutschtum und Judentum," 257.

29. Ibid., 260; Clearly, Cohen sees Yiddish as a deficient form of German, which he seems to associate with the isolation brought on by the persecution of the Jews in the past. But he also sees it as evidence of the Germanic influence on international Judaism, even if he prefers proper German (255).

30. Ibid., 268.

31. Ibid., 237.

32. Ibid., 238.

33. Cohen explicitly mentions "Über das Eigentümliche des deutschen Geistes" in *Schriften zur Philosophie und Zeitgeschichte*, V. I (Berlin, Akademie-Verlag, 1928) 527–570, and its role in the formulation of "Deutschtum und Judentum," in Cohen, "Ein kritisches Nachwort als Vorwort," 292.

34. These last three sentences are indebted to Michael Zank's formulation of the universal/particular paradox in regard to Greek philosophy in his essay "The Heteronomy of Jewish Philosophy," 100. This is precisely what Cohen is getting at, although Zank applies it to both Greece and Germany without specifically mentioning Cohen.

35. Cohen, "Über das Eigentümliche des deutschen Geistes," 528. It is important to recognize the cultural context of Cohen's liberalism. He is clearly emphasizing the key role of Greece as opposed to the ancient Near East. As Suzanne Marchand in *German Orientalism* has pointed out, the struggle between classics and *Orientalistik* had major philosophical, theological, and political implications. Although liberals contemporary with Cohen were embracing the Greeks, they often did so at the expense of the Israelites. However, as we see, Cohen insists that Judaism, Greekism, and Germanism have profound spiritual affinities, and he is thus placing himself at odds with the Orientalists whom he—not wrongly—saw as trying to de-Judaize Germany.

36. See chapter 5, "The Furor Orientalis," in Suzanne Marchand, *German Orientalism*, 212–251. As Marchand explains, the German scholars of this generation were interested in "seizing humanistic and theological territory from liberal-era theologians and old-fashioned classical philologists. It was not simply a battle over the East; it was also a battle over the West" (216). Indeed, as Marchand demonstrates throughout her book, Orientalists frequently emphasized the notion of cultural diffusion and influence, which privileged older traditions, as a way to emphasize the priority of the East over Greece and Israel. Cohen is clearly repudiating such attempts to de-center Greece and Israel by the younger generation. It is not age or diffusion of ideas that matter but purity of reason, and in this regard Greekism, Judaism, and Germanism are exemplary.

37. As we see in chapter 2, in *Religion of Reason out of the Sources of Judaism*, Cohen replaces—or, perhaps better, displaces—the unique status of ancient Greece with ancient Israel in regard to religious/practical reason.

38. Derrida, "Interpretations at War," in *Jacques Derrida: Acts of Religion*, ed. Gil Anidjar (New York: Routledge, 2002), 152.

39. This is not to claim that Derrida is uncritical of Heidegger. For a prolonged and insightful reflection on the relationship between Greece and Germany in Heidegger's thought, see Derrida, *Of Spirit: Heidegger and the Question*, trans. Geoffrey Bennington and Rachel Bowlby (Chicago: University of Chicago Press, 1991). Derrida also probes the thorny issue of the relationship between Heidegger's philosophy and his Nazism at length in this work.

40. Cited in Peter Eli Gordon, *Rosenzweig and Heidegger: Between Judaism and German Philosophy* (Berkeley, University of California Press, 2005), 296 n.28; cf. Schwarzschild, "'Germanism and Judaism,'" 136. According to Schwarzschild there is some dispute about who said this. Nachum Goldmann argues that it was Heinrich Rickert, whereas Jakob Klatzkin claims it was Kuno Fischer. In the footnotes, Schwarzschild thinks it is more likely that Klatzkin was correct in attributing it to Fischer (163, n.33); Ernst Troeltsch wrote a scathing rebuke of Cohen's "Über des Eigentümliche des deutschen Geistes," in which in a pun on Cohen's title he questions Cohen's Germanness. Troeltsch writes, "Es ist der reine Rationalismus. Ich vermag darin, ebenso wie in Cohens Sprache, nicht viel eigentümlich deutsches zu erblicken. . . . Höchstens das Schulmeisterliche könnte man daran 'eigentümlich deutsch' finden" (Rezension von "Hermann Cohen Über des Eigentümliche des deutschen Geistes, Berlin 1914," in *Theologische Literaturzeitung* 41 (1916), 90, cited in Ulrich Sieg, *Aufstieg und Niedergang des Marburger Neukantianismus* (Würzburg: Königshausen & Neumann, 1994), 394. "It is pure rationalism. I am unable to catch a glimpse of anything particularly [eigentümlich] German in Cohen's speech . . . At most in the schoolmasterly tone can one find the particularly [eigentümlich] German."

41. Cohen, "Über das Eigentümliche des deutschen Geistes," 529. Italics in the original.

42. Ibid., 545.

43. Ibid., 545.

44. See Derrida's remarkable essay, "Onto-Theology of National-Humanism," 12–13, which argues that the philosophical definition of German identity—as opposed to the ethnic/racial—goes back at least as far as Fichte. Derrida explicitly discusses Cohen's Fichtean connection in "Interpretations at War," 174–176.

45. As we see, religion occupies a unique place in the system because it is not one of the core fields.

46. For the most programmatic discussion of the relationship between Cohen's method, his larger philosophical system, and the ethical improvement of culture, see Hermann Cohen, *Einleitung mit kritischen Nachtrag zur F. A. Langes,'Geschichte des Materialismus.'* This text went through several editions. It offers a general overview of Cohen's system and its relationship to culture. I use the 1914 version, which has been included in the critical editions of Cohen's *Werke*; see also Gregory Moynahan, "Hermann Cohen's Das Prinzip der Infinitesimalmethode, Ernst Cassirer, and the Politics of Science in Wilhelmine Germany," *Perspectives on Science* 11, no. 1 (Spring 2003): 35–75, on the optimism in science for culture at this time. See also Ursula Renz, "Critical Idealism and the Concept of Culture: Philosophy of Culture in Hermann Cohen and Ernst Cassirer," in *Hermann Cohen's Critical Idealism*, ed. Reinier Munk (Dordrecht: Springer, 2005), 336, and Zank, *The Idea of Atonement*, 242, for the ethical implications of his system for culture.

47. Cohen referred to the specific Idealism of Kant and the Marburg School as Critical Idealism. This designate drew a sharp distinction from the Idealisms of Hegel, Fichte, and Schelling, which he referred to as Romantic.

48. Cohen has different theoretical meanings for *Humanität* and *Menschheit*. I translate the term 'Menschheit' here to mean "humanity."

49. Cohen, "Über das Eigentümliche des deutschen Geistes," 553

50. For a nice account of the complex and convoluted relationship between the Jews and the legacy of Luther in English, see Alan Mittelman's introduction to his translation of Cohen's "The Jew in the Christian World," in *Modern Judaism* 23, no. 1 (2003), 51–73; Hermann Cohen, "Der Jude in der christlichen Kultur," in *Hermann Cohens Jüdische Schriften*, Bande 2, (Berlin 1924: C. A. Schwetscheke & Sohn/ Verlagsbuchhandlung); Derrida, "Interpretations at War," 153; and for the most rigorous and in-depth account of the role of Germany and the Reformation in Cohen's thought, see Wiedebach, *The National Element*, 87–166. For a careful and nuanced critique of Cohen's use and abuse of Luther throughout his writings, see Robert R. Geis, "Hermann Cohen und die deutsche Reformation," *Gottes Minorität: Beiträge z. jüdische Theologie u.z. Geschichte der Juden in Deutschland* (Munich: Kösel Verlag, 1971) 136–151. In the concluding pages of the study, Geis traces Cohen's reading to the influence of Albrecht Ritschl's school of theology, which sought to modernize Lutheranism. Included in this school was Cohen's colleague and interlocutor, Wilhelm Hermann (149–150).

51. Cohen, "Deutschtum und Judentum," 242.

52. Ibid., 242. Emphasis in the Original; Readers familiar with Cohen's *Ethik des reinen Willens* (1904/1907) and his *Religion of Reason out of the Sources of Reason* will recognize that truthfulness [*Wahrhaftigkeit*] is an essential term in Cohen's philosophical vocabulary. For an account of the development of the virtue of *Wahrhaftigkeit* in *Ethik des reinen Willens* compared to that in *Religion of Reason out of the Sources of Judaism*, see Robert Erlewine, "Hermann Cohen, Maimonides, and the Jewish Virtue of Humility," *Journal of Jewish Thought and Philosophy* 18, no. 1 (2010): 27–47.

53. Cohen, "Deutschtum und Judentum," 242. Emphasis in the original.

54. Ibid., 243–244; See Derrida, "Interpretations at War," 153–156, for a trenchant account of Cohen's reading of Protestantism and conscience.

55. Although Derrida's notion of "exemplarity" is certainly apt in regard to Cohen, he fails to acknowledge its rhetorical power for a Jew in Wilhelmine Germany. He almost solely focuses on its negative connotations. Perhaps, this is because Derrida has his eye on his own contemporaries in his reading of Cohen. Sarah Hammerschlag suggests that Derrida's critique of Cohen's "Deutschtum und Judentum" in "Interpretations at War" is an implicit critique of Emmanuel Levinas, *The Figural Jews: Politics and Identity in Postwar French Thought* (Chicago: University of Chicago Press, 2010), 232.

56. Cohen, "Deutschtum und Judentum," 268–269.

57. As we see later, those in the next generation, namely Martin Buber and Franz Rosenzweig, will vehemently reject Cohen's diminution of the importance of race. Indeed, as many scholars have indicated, there was a profound generational shift in sensibilities within German notions of culture. Brenner, in *The Renaissance of Jewish Culture*, 1–36, has shown that Buber's and Rosenzweig's rejection of Cohen's rationalism is indicative of a larger generational shift within German notions of culture as a whole (not just German Jewish communities). See also Mendes-Flohr, *German-Jews* and Peter Gay, *Weimar Culture: The Outsider as Insider* (New York: W. W. Norton, 1968).

58. Cohen, "Deutschtum und Judentum," 238.

59. Cohen, "Kritische Nachwort," 296.

60. This increasing emphasis on Germany's reliance upon Judaism and on Judaism's surpassing of Greece in terms of religious rationality is further developed in Cohen's late writings. I discuss this at length in the next chapter.

61. Cohen, "Deutschtum und Judentum," 256.

62. Cohen's recourse to Greece is a rejection of the furor orientalis and the search for lost origins. Heidegger's, on the other hand, is very much part of a quest for that which has been lost. Indeed, where Cohen sees the Germans as taking a step beyond Greece in their rationality, Heidegger sees German philosophy as working through the forgetfulness of Being that began in Greece with the very "rationality" Cohen celebrates. Heidegger is appealing to Greece in a very different way than does Cohen. For a still relevant discussion of Heidegger's reactionary politics, see Gay, *Weimar Culture*.

63. Ibid., 263. Emphasis in the original.

64. Ibid., 263. Emphasis in the original.

65. Ibid.

66. Ibid.

67. Ibid.

68. Ibid. When lauding German culture, Cohen acknowledges problematic figures such as Nietzsche, Schopenhauer, and Wagner. He recognizes that the culture still needs refinement; it is not yet the ideal. Yet, he then proceeds, two paragraphs later, to refer to the "*Dostojewski*" whose work possesses "the entire danger of Byzantinian Christian and the fanaticism of an Oriental Mystic" (284). Indeed, ameliorating the plight of the Russian Jews was one of Cohen's justifications for World War I, and his critique of Dostoevsky seems to reflect what he sees as "Russian Imperialism." But the entire section of Cohen's "Deutschtum und Judentum" is quite chilling, because he talks about the need to expel troubling foreign literature, such as Doestoevsky, and of the need to purify German literature (285).

69. The full passage from Derrida reads,

The logic here is more extraordinary than ever: there will be no understanding and no peace among nations unless our example is followed. But let us follow the progression, which is also a redundant tautology, between the a priori synthesis and the analytic explication: our example (Beispiel) must be followed as an example (Vorbild) in order to acknowledge of our Vormacht, German hegemony or preeminence. The progression from Beispiel to Vorbild to Vormacht is tautologous, since an example is not an indifferent case in a series. It is exemplary, a premodel, a preformatory model. To acknowledge it as such is to acknowledge German hegemony (Vormacht.) Acknowledgement cannot remain merely theoretical. It doesn't go without political subjection, in the spiritual and psychic domain, of course, where all this teleological discourse belongs, while nevertheless proliferating purifying remarks vis-à-vis foreigners and aliens." ("Interpretations at War," 183–184).

For a stinging critique of Derrida's reading in "Interpretations at War," see Gillian Rose, "Of Derrida's Spirit," in *Judaism and Modernity: Philosophical Essays* (Oxford: Blackwell, 1993), 65–88.

70. This latter sentiment finds its highest expression in Schwarzschild's "'Germanism and Judaism."

71. Cohen emphasizes this point in his 1917 essay, "Der Jude in der christlichen Kultur," in *Hermann Cohens Jüdische Schriften*, Bande 2, (Berlin 1924: C. A. Schwetscheke & Sohn/ Verlagsbuchhandlung), 193–209 / trans. Alan Mittleman, "'The Jew in Christian Culture' by Hermann Cohen: An Introduction and Translation," *Modern Judaism* 23, no. 1 (2003): 51–73. Indeed, Cohen would go even further in undercutting this divide. He writes: "Just as 'Jew or German' is offensive, so must it be recognized as offensive to make 'Jew or Christian' into a slogan. The ghost that haunts the Jew, making him think that he is a stranger in the Christian, indeed, in the German Protestant culture must disappear" ("Der Jude," 209 / "The Jew," 72).

72. Cohen, "Deutschtum und Judentum," 263.

73. Ibid.

74. Ibid., I have relied in large part on the translation of this passage provided in Ritchie Robertson, *The "Jewish Question" in German Literature 1749–1939: Emancipation and its Discontents* (Oxford: Oxford University Press, 1999).

75. Derrida, "Interpretations at War," 181; see See Wiedebach, *The National Element*, which discusses Cohen's mystification of Germany throughout; *pace* Schwarzschild, "Germanism and Judaism," 145–146.

76. Cohen, "Deutschtum und Judentum," 264; Schwarzschild does not address this dimension of Cohen's wartime literature.

77. See Wiedebach, *The National Element,* ad passim, for a nuanced discussion on the tense intersection between the historical and the ideal in Cohen's notion of Germanness.

78. Of course, Cohen would insist that Germany is an elect nation only to the degree that it embodies the spirit of Germanness. However, at what point does Cohen's idealization turn into problematic chauvinism? As Wiedebach has pointed out, Cohen provides no grounds to justify why he is idealizing Germany and not England, Russia, or any other nation. As a result, it is hard to conclude that this is not simple mystification. See n. 27 for a more thorough discussion of this issue.

79. S. Heschel, *The Aryan Jesus,* 59; see, also, Tomoko Masuzawa, *The Invention of World Religions,* 18–19.

80. Marchand, *German Orientalism,* 263. In the larger environment of Wilhelmine Germany, in which Cohen discusses the German-Jewish symbiosis, the separation of church and state was a core postulate of liberalism. However, cultural Protestantism exerted increasing

influence during this era, especially in regard to the search for identity that was so central to Germany at this time. Friedrich Wilhelm Graf explains that rather than trying to subjugate the state to "churchly heteronomy," cultural Protestant theologians sought to facilitate "the penetration of all of the cultural spheres by the moral spirit" such that "Protestant Christianity could create the unity of national culture." Graf, "Kulturprotestantismus. Zur Begriffsgeschichte einer theologiepolitische Chiffrem" in *Archiv für Begriffsgeschichte* 28 (1984): 220. Cultural Protestants emphasized a brand of religion that reconciled Christianity with modern culture; cf. Wilhlelm Pauk, *Harnack and Troeltsch: Two Historical Theologians* (New York: Oxford University Press, 1968), 18–21.

81. Harnack, *Reden und Aufsätzen*, 4:7, cited in Claude Welch, *Protestant Thought in the Nineteenth Century*, Vol. 2: *1870–1914* (Eugene, OR: Wipf & Stock Publishers), 177.

82. Harnack, *What is Christianity?*, trans. Thomas Bailey Saunders, introduction by Rudolf Bultmann (Philadelphia: Fortress Press, 1957), 129.

83. Ibid., 48.

84. Ibid., 16.

85. Susannah Heschel writes, "Harnack's attempt to salvage Jesus's originality [from the critiques of Jewish scholars who claimed his teachings were not unique] comes by constructing a negative context within Judaism for the teachings shared by Jesus and the rabbis. Judaism is excessive, dark and dirty; Christianity is vigorous, pure, and pristine," "Theological Bulimia: Christianity and its Dejudaization," in *After the Passion is Gone: American Religious Consequences*, ed. J. Shawn Landres and Michael Berenbaum, (Walnut Creek, CA: Altmira Press, 2004), 183. Christian Wiese points out that in these lectures, Harnack's "remarks about Pharisaic Judaism had a purely instrumental function and aimed at distinguishing the timeless, abstract and ideally pure image of Jesus' outstanding personality and teachings from the Jewish tradition," *Challenging Colonial Discourse: Jewish Studies and Protestant Theology in Wilhemine Germany* (Leiden: Brill, 2004), 164–165.

86. Wiese, *Challenging Colonial Discourse*, 214.

87. Cohen, *Einleitung mit kritischen Nachtrag*, 103.

88. Ibid., 102; In this work Cohen reveals a profound concern with the historical critical study of religion taking place among his Christian theologian contemporaries. The so-called scientific theology of his contemporaries, Cohen charges, fails to overcome "sectarian narrowness" or achieve genuine scientific rigor (101–102). Picking up a refrain from Abraham Geiger's famous critique a generation earlier, Cohen claims that without knowledge of the "contemporary Talmudic literature" these scholar/theologians in search of the historical Jesus cannot possibly adequately understand the "Hellenistic sources" from which they derive their theology (103).

89. Scholars frequently associated with this school are Adolf von Harnack, Ernst Troeltsch, and Wilhelm Bousset.

90. In *Abraham Geiger and the Jewish Jesus*, 19, Susannah Heschel describes the power dynamics between Christians and Jews regarding Biblical scholarship in a very helpful manner:

> Christian scholarly investigation of Jewish history established a radical dichotomy between Christianity and Judaism, which was required to maintain Christian theological order. Presenting the historical relationships between the two religions was simultaneously a construction of contemporary social relations and relations of power within the realm of scholarship. The Christian made himself the transcendent subject of theological *Wissenschaft*, necessitating a radical dichotomy with an "Other" in order to maintain order. The gaze of historical theology was Christian; the ordering of history, the questions raised, the evidence examined, all revolved around the central

issue, explaining the rise of Christianity. Other religions, other peoples' histories, other texts, were viewed from the Christian perspective, weighed and evaluated with reference to the Christian standard of measurement.

91. On this tendency in the world religions discourse, see Masuzawa, *The Invention of World Religions*, 24–25, and Marchand, *German Orientalism*, ad passim.

92. Cohen, "Religion und Sittlichkeit," in *Herman Cohens Jüdische Schriften*, Vol. III, p. 151; on this point and its relationship to both "Religion und Sittlichkeit" and *Ethik des reinen Willens*, see Andrea Poma, *The Critical Philosophy of Hermann Cohen*, trans. John Denton (Albany: State University of New York Press, 1997), 307, n.19.

93. Cohen, *Der Begriff*, 9.

94. Andrea Poma helpfully points out the continuity of Cohen's notion of religion (and culture, from his systematic work on aesthetics) with the epistemological/ontological foundations of Cohen's *Logik der reinen Erkenntnis*, by explaining that for Cohen notion of "'Culture' [is] not [to be seen] as an empirical given, justified by its mere factuality, but as a product of the spirit, i.e. of thought, whose 'facts' are not immediate data, but results of a productive spiritual process." Poma, *Yearning for Form* (Dordrecht: Springer, 2006), 171.

95. As Poma notes, too often religion is thought of as an *Eigenart* only for ethics, as developing and refining it further in regard to the single individual. However, he insists that religion must also apply to the other elements of the system (i.e., logic and aesthetics. *Yearning for Form*, 176–177); cf. Alexander Altmann, "Hermann Cohens Begriff der Korrelation," in *Zwei Welten: Festschrift für Siegfried Moses*, ed. Hans Tramer (Tel Aviv: Bitaon, 1962), 377–399. Here, I am at odds with Wiedebach, who reads the religious works as outside of the system, but tied to ethnicity, *The National Element*, 167–236.

96. Cohen, *Der Begriff*, 8.

97. See Poma, *Yearning for Form*, 172.

98. Cohen, *Der Begriff*, 5.

99. Herman Cohen, *System der Philosophie. 2. Teil. Ethik des reinen Willens*. Band 7, Werke Herausgegeben vom Hermann-Cohen-Archiv am Philsophischen Seminar der Universität Zürich unter der Leitung von Helmut Holzhey, (Zürich: Georg Olms Verlag, 2012). This discussion about the relationship between ethics and sociology is on pp. 40–43.

100. Ibid., 5.

101. Ibid. Poma points out that the transcendental method operative in Cohen's system of philosophy is in play here. There are "three indispensable stages in Cohen's transcendental method: 1) a[n empirical/historical] fact as a departure point: 2) the identification of the rational conditions of the fact: 3) the determination of the fact on the basis of those a priori conditions." Poma, *Critical Philosophy of Hermann Cohen*, 160.

102. See Cohen, *Einleitung mit kritischen Nachtrag*, 101; Indeed, the major critique of religious studies by figures such as Jonathan Z. Smith, Tomoko Masuzawa, Russell McCutcheon, and others for being normative has, in a manner adumbrated by Cohen, been a calling out of the tacit nature of the biases of so-called historians of religion. However, while Cohen would agree with the above-mentioned figures in identifying the prevalence of the Protestant bias in religious studies, he rejects that one should attempt to eschew all normative motivations. Clearly, Cohen's conclusions and his own very activist engagement with the study of religion would not be viewed as viable by figures like Smith, Masuzawa, or McCutcheon. Of course, perhaps because it is so upfront about its agenda, Cohen's work so readily lends itself to the analytic lenses of these figures, particularly Masuzawa and McCutcheon.

103. Cohen, *Religion der Vernunft aus den Quellen des Judentums*, 3 / *Religion of Reason*, 2–3. Italics in Original.

104. Cohen, *Begriff,* 21.

105. Ibid., 32.

106. Cohen, *Religion der Vernunft aus den Quellen des Judentums,* 4–5 / *Religion of Reason,* 4.

107. Harnack, *Reden und Aufsaetzen,* 4:7, cited in Welch, *Protestant Thought in the Nineteenth Century,* Vol. 2, 177.

108. Cohen, *Religion der Vernunft aus den Quellen des Judentums,* 6 / *Religion of Reason,* 5–6. "What is most important is that the historical fact of religion, from which and for which critical philosophy produces the concept of religion, cannot be considered either a fact of faith, as revelation, or an institutional system, as a church . . . it must be understood as a fact of culture, and thus only in its "literary sources," investigated by an objective historical method, since only thus, as an analogue of science, is the fact of religion methodologically homogeneous with the philosophy that must investigate it, and besides, is the bearer of universal meaning." Poma, *Yearning and Form,* 120.

109. For a nice account of this point in Cohen's thought and of his dispute with his colleague and friend Wilhelm Hermann over whether or not religion is *selbstandig,* see William Kluback, "Friendship without Understanding: Wilhelm Hermann and Hermann Cohen," *Leo Baeck Yearbook* 31 (1986), 317–338. Also, see Wilhelm Hermann's stinging critique of *Der Begriff der Religion im System der Philosophie* in his "Der Begriff der Religion nach Hermann Cohen," in *Schriften zur Grundlegung der Theologie* (Munich: Ch. Kaiser, 1966–1967), 318–323.

110. For an argument concerning the potential relevance of his project in our pluralistic world, see Robert Erlewine, *Monotheism and Tolerance: Recovering a Religion of Reason* (Bloomington: Indiana University Press, 2010).

111. Cohen, *Religion der Vernunft aus den Quellen des Judentums,* 3 / *Religion of Reason,* 3.

112. Cohen, *Religion der Vernunft aus den Quellen des Judentums,* 9 / *Religion of Reason,* 7–8.

113. Cohen, *Religion der Vernunft aus den Quellen des Judentums,* 1 / *Religion of Reason,* 1.

114. Cohen, *Religion der Vernunft aus den Quellen des Judentums,* 2 / *Religion of Reason,* 2.

115. Cohen, *Religion der Vernunft aus den Quellen des Judentums,* 2 / *Religion of Reason,* 2.

116. Harnack, "Die Aufgabe der theologische Fakultäten und die allgemeine Religionsgeschichte," *Reden und Aufsätze* (Giessen, 1904), Bieden 2, S. 172. Italics added for emphasis.

117. Harnack is generally included among the history of religions school, but he primarily looked to Greece rather than the surrounding Near East for his account of Christian origins.

118. Of course, less than two decades later Harnack, in *Marcion: Das Evangelium vom Fremden Gott,* trans. John E. Steely and Lyle D. Bierma, (Leipzig, 1924) [*Marcion: The Gospel of the Alien God* (Eugene, OR: Wipf & Stock, 2007], would famously embrace the Marcionite heresy, and call for the separation of the Old Testament from the New. Philhellinists were not necessarily more likely to be philosemitic than the Orientalists. Indeed, as we see later, Cohen, like many of his fellow German Jews, was not entirely without antagonism to the Greeks. This antagonism is noted by Marchand: "Interestingly, one of the normative strains of thought mid-century [nineteenth] Jewish scholars believed they needed to challenge, at least in part, was philhellenism. If the Greeks had bequeathed modern Europeans so many of their secular arts—philosophy, the sciences, the fine arts—it must not be forgotten, the argument went, that monotheism was a Jewish invention." *German Orientalism,* 116. That is, as Marchand points out, Jewish thinkers attempted to demonstrate that if Greece brought science, the Israelites brought morality and spirituality. Again, Derrida completely misses this dimension of Cohen's work, which is present even in his nationalist writings.

119. Cohen, *Religion der Vernunft aus den Quellen des Judentums,* 8 / *Religion of Reason,* 7.

120. Cohen, *Religion der Vernunft aus den Quellen des Judentums,* 8–9 / *Religion of Reason,* 7–8.

121. Cohen, *Religion der Vernunft aus den Quellen des Judentums*, 9 / *Religion of Reason*, 8. Steven Schwarzschild emphasizes that the title of Cohen's posthumously published opus is not "*The* Religion of Reason of Reason out of the Sources of Judaism," but rather *Religion of Reason out of the Sources of Judaism* precisely because "Cohen held that there can be only one rational religion, which would have to be as universal and necessary as pure reason itself, and that consequently all human beings, at least regulatively speaking, would subscribe to it." "The Title of Hermann Cohen's 'Religion of Reason out of the Sources of Judaism,'" in *Religion of Reason out of the Sources of Judaism*, trans. Simon Kaplan, 2nd ed., 8. He recounts the error made by the publisher in the first edition of the text of including 'The' in the title, but it was corrected in subsequent editions (7). Schwarzschild is not wrong, yet his explanation here, as in his account of "Deutschtum und Judentum," downplays the role of exemplarity, which is essential for our reading, because it tacitly invokes the Orient/Occident dichotomy.

122. Cohen, *Religion der Vernunft aus den Quellen des Judentums*, 9–10 / *Religion of Reason*, 8. Emphasis in original.

123. Cohen, *Religion der Vernunft aus den Quellen des Judentums*, 10 / *Religion of Reason*, 8.

124. Steven Schwarzschild, "The Title of Hermann Cohen's "Religion of Reason out of the Sources of Judaism," 10–11.

125. Andrea Poma astutely notes,

> It is difficult to accept the fact that, though only recognising the originative, not sole, source in Judaism, [Cohen] never referred to other sources and other religious faiths. In fact, the only faith he did not ignore, apart from Judaism, in his research, i.e. Christianity, not only did not constitute a positive point of reference for the concept of religion, but was criticised and denied legitimacy as a source of the religion of reason, inasmuch as it was accused of pantheism. So, from this point of view, it would appear that Cohen not only saw Judaism as the originative, but also the only source for the religion of reason. (Poma, *Yearning for Form*, 124–125).

126. I argued against such a claim in *Monotheism and Tolerance*, 150–176.

127. See "Deutschtum und Judentum" for the confluence of the Bible, Germanism, and Idealism, 241–246.

128. Ernst Troeltsch, "Glaube und Ethos der hebraeischen Propheten,"which was written in 1916. It is included in *Aufsätze zur Geistesgeschichte und Religionsoziologie, Gesammelte Schriften*, Band 4. Ed. Hans Baron (Tübeingen: J. C. B. Mohr), 34–64.

129. Cohen, "Der Prophetismus und die Soziologie," in *Hermann Cohens Judische Schriften*, II, 398–402. For good accounts of the Troeltsch-Cohen dispute with an emphasis on rival methodologies at work in the differing neo-Kantianisms of Cohen and Troeltsch, see Alisha Pomazon, "Hermann Cohen and the Prophetic *Eigenart*," *Journal of Jewish Thought and Philosophy* 23, no. 1 (2015): 1–26, and Wendell S. Dietrich, *Cohen and Troeltsch: Ethical Monotheistic Religion and Theory of Culture* (Atlanta: Scholars Press, 1986). See also Robert S. Schine, *Jewish Thought Adrift: Max Wiener (1882–1950)* (Atlanta: Scholars Press, 1992), 54–70, for the repercussions of this dispute between Cohen's disciples and his Zionist opposition.

130. Troeltsch, "Glaube und Ethos," 52.

131. Ibid., 53.

132. Troeltsch describes Cohen's idealizing method on p. 35 and names Cohen explicitly on p. 39. Additionally, the final sentence of the essay on p. 65 questions the fruitfulness of this method.

133. See Robert Erlewine, "Reclaiming the Prophets: Cohen, Heschel, and Crossing the Theocentric/Neo-Humanist Divide," *Journal of Jewish Thought and Philosophy* 17, no. 2 (2009): 177–206.

134. Cohen, "Der Prophetismus und die Soziologie," 400–401.

135. Ibid., 401.

136. Ibid., 399; in the final paragraph of this essay, Cohen writes, "Echte Wissenschaft, echte methodische Philosophie kann immer nur zum Echten und Wahrhaften der Religion hinführen. Die Wahrheit unserer Religion besteht in unser Weltreligion. Weltreligion kann aber nur die Religion der reinen Sittlichkeit sein" (401); "Serious science, serious methodological philosophy can always only drive serious and truthful aspects of religion. The truth of our religion is found in our world religion. A world religion can however only be the religion of pure morality."; see Dietrich, *Cohen and Troeltsch*, 29–44.

137. See Troeltsch, "Glaube und Ethos," esp. 40–42.

138. For Cohen's account of the ethical philosophy of the prophets, see Erlewine, "Reclaiming the Prophets," 182–183 and Pomazon, "The Prophetic *Eigenart*," 17–26.

139. In *The Stillborn God: Religion, Politics, and the Modern West*, Mark Lilla remarks, "Reading the German liberal theologians [in whose company he includes Cohen; my addition] is not easy. It is astonishing to see how easily they were lulled to sleep by their faith in the natural goodness of man and the benevolence of the historical process that had issued in their bourgeois world. The great exception was Ernst Troeltsch, who had genuine insight into the subtle workings, and not so subtle contradictions, of modern life" (249). Like so many interpreters of Cohen, Lilla fails to take into account the context of Cohen's work, the antisemitism that he battled, and that his struggles for a German-Jewish synthesis were highly subversive. Lilla, who derives much of his account of Cohen from "Deutschtum und Judentum," falls into the trap that Steven Schwarzschild points out. Schwarzschild writes, "The standard procedure in the last few decades has been to identify Hermann Cohen with the motto and ideology of 'Germanism and Judaism'—to take it for granted that by the term 'Germanism' he meant to refer to empirical Germany, or at least to actual, historical German culture—and then to refute his thesis of an identity or symbiosis by simply pointing to the blatant discordancy between the two entities. But this presupposes that Cohen was blind and insensitive to the historical realities that surrounded and even impinged so painfully on his own life. He would have had to be stupid for this claim to be valid. The facts overwhelmingly refute it" ("Germanism and Judaism," 138).

2. Symbol Not Sacrifice

1. This chapter was published, in a slightly modified form, as "Hermann Cohen and the Jewish Jesus," *Modern Judaism* 34, no. 2 (May 2014): 210–232.

2. Susannah Heschel, "Jesus as a Theological Transvestite," in *Judaism since Gender*, ed. Miriam Peskowitz and Laura Levitt (New York: Routledge, 1997), 189.

3. Christian Wiese is not wrong in his claim that "Cohen was, of course, completely aware of the deep differences between Judaism and Christianity . . . he sincerely hoped for a gradual rapprochement of modern cultural Protestantism with the principles of Jewish 'ethical monotheism,' which seemed to him the embodiment of the superior religiosity and morality." Wiese, "'The Best Antidote against Anti-Semitism?' Judaism, Biblical Criticism and Anti-Semitism prior to the Holocaust," in *Modern Judaism and Historical Consciousness: Identities–Encounters–Perspectives*, ed. Christian Wiese and Andreas Gotzmann (Leiden: Brill, 2007), 147. However, Wiese's claim does not go far enough. Although Wiese recognizes that Cohen maintains that Judaism "possess[es] superior religiosity and morality," as we see, the rapprochement he envisions entails that Christianity make itself more Jewish.

4. Heschel, "Jesus as Theological Transvestite," 189.

5. Cohen does acknowledge, if indirectly, the claims of Geiger, when he writes, "Who does not know that at that time, many men emerged in Judea, and similar doctrines emerged, as were associated with Jesus." Cohen, *Der Begriff der Religion im System der Philosophie*, 93. But for Cohen, prioritizing biography and literary contexts interferes with the process of rationalization. With such a claim, he is not critiquing Geiger as much as rejecting the larger Protestant fixation on the search for the historical Jesus. Where Geiger engages historians on the question of Jesus's uniqueness, locating his teachings within Jewish sources, Cohen engages the soteriological elements of the crucifixion, arguing that Jesus's martyrdom is of profound continuity with Judaism rather than a break from it.

6. Cohen, *Religion der Vernunft aus den Quellen des Judentums*, 508 / *Religion of Reason*, 440.

7. The passage Cohen refers to is Sanhedrin 7a.

8. Cohen, *Religion der Vernunft aus den Quellen des Judentums*, 506–507 / *Religion of Reason*, 438.

9. Cohen, *Religion der Vernunft aus den Quellen des Judentums*, 508 / *Religion of Reason*, 439–440.

10. Cohen, *Religion der Vernunft aus den Quellen des Judentums*, 272 / *Religion of Reason*, 233.

11. Cohen's rationalist foundation of the concept of religion on ethical monotheism should be understood in the context of the prominent tendency among scholars and theologians to find non-Semitic foundations, which as we saw in the introduction, was a central element of the world religions discourse. On this topic, see Masuzawa, *The Invention of World Religions*; Marchand, *German Orientalism*; and S. Heschel, *Abraham Geiger and the Jewish Jesus*, and *The Aryan Jesus*.

12. Masuzawa notes that not only were the ancient Greeks considered Aryans like the Persians and Indians, but they enjoyed a unique privilege in the mythology of Europe. "Ancient Greece was now recognized as the absolute origin of nearly everything that constituted Europe; at the same time, Greek civilization attained a status that was at once suprahistorical and nearly supernatural." *The Invention of World Religion*, 171.

13. Cohen, *System der Philosophie. Erster Teil. Logik der reinen Erkenntnis*, Werke, Band 6, Werke (Hildesheim, Zürich, 2005), Henceforth I refer to this text as "the *Logik*" in the text and abbreviate it in the notes as *LrE*.

14. Cohen, *LrE*, p. 588; "absoluten" was in italics in the original German.

15. Cohen, *Religion der Vernunft aus den Quellen des Judentums*, 185 / *Religion of Reason*,160; Cohen emphasizes the radical distinction of God as possessing *Sein* as opposed to either *Dasein* or *Wirklichkeit*.

16. Cohen, *Religion der Vernunft aus den Quellen des Judentums*, 186 / *Religion of Reason*, 160.

17. Cohen seems to want it both ways. On the one hand, he claims that his systematic critical philosophy is grounded in modern developments in the natural sciences and thus is a corrective to the philosophies of antiquity. On the other hand, his philosophy of Judaism, which he conflates with Judaism itself, is expressed in the idiom of his new critical philosophy. Thus, he reads ancient Jewish texts as modern.

18. Cohen, *Religion der Vernunft aus den Quellen des Judentums*, 52 / *Religion of Reason*, 45. It is worth mentioning that Cohen's theoretical writings valorize Greek philosophy, such that, as mentioned earlier, he even refers to his own Idealism as a form of Eleatism (*LRE* 588). The Eleatic philosophers are important interlocutors throughout the entire *Logik*, and Cohen celebrates Plato as the first and greatest Idealist, the founder of critical Idealism. Cohen

nevertheless breaks sharply from the Greeks in regard to the normative notion of religion. For Cohen, the Eleatics fail to distinguish between theoretical and practical reason, and Plato, an inheritor of this tradition, by way of introducting the Demiurge in his *Timaeus*, paves the way for a divine mediator and eventually to the Logos so central to Christianity. (Cohen, *Religion der Vernunft aus den Quellen des Judentums*, 56 / *Religion of Reason*, 48).

19. In many of his works, Cohen emphasizes that the proper conception of God is essential for preserving the distinction between "is" and "ought" and thus securing the rigor of morality. Again, we see that Cohen cannot abide by pluralism, and for him the very idea of comparative religions is problematic, at least insofar as the focus is on descriptive historiography and worldviews rather than the purification of the God-idea (i.e., the concept of religion), which is firmly bound up with the idealistic foundations of ethics. Cohen writes, "The concept of the unique God is an exact and univocal concept of religious knowledge. Even for the common religious consciousness it is of univocal content, excluding everything related to sensibility" (Cohen, *Religion der Vernunft aus den Quellen des Judentums*, 485 / *Religion of Reason*, 418).

20. Cohen, *Religion der Vernunft aus den Quellen des Judentums*, 56 / *Religion of Reason*, 48. Emphasis in the original.

21. Cohen, *Religion der Vernunft aus den Quellen des Judentums*, 56–57 / *Religion of Reason*, 49.

22. Cohen, *Religion der Vernunft aus den Quellen des Judentums*, 63 / *Religion of Reason*, 54.

23. Cohen, *Religion der Vernunft aus den Quellen des Judentums*, 484–485 / *Religion of Reason*, 418.

24. Cohen, *LrE*, p. 300, italics in the original.

25. Although posed more in the language of Cohen's *Ethik des reinen Willens* than the *Logik* (which adumbrates it), Helmut Holzhey explains, "Der handelnde Mensch steht bei seiner Orientierung an einem Ideal aber in einer unauflösbaren Spannung zwischen der natürlichen Bedingtheit seiner Triebe und Bedürfnisse und der ideelen Unbedingtheit vernunftbestimmten Sollens. Diese Spannung ist keine bloss faktische, sondern eine dem ethischen Begriff des Menschen eingeschriebene. Das beduetet zunächst, dass Ethik vom Interesse am Unterschied zwischen dem Sein der Natur und dem Sein des Sollens getragen ist." Holzhey, "Ethik als Lehre vom Menschen: Ein Einführung in Hermann Cohens Ethik des reinen Willens," in *Hermann Cohen's Ethics*, ed. Robert Gibbs and Giussepe Veltri (Leiden: Brill, 2006), 29. "The human being of action stands in orientation to an ideal but at the same time in an indissolvable tension between his instincts and needs and the ideal, unconditioned reason-determined ought. This tension is not simply factical but rather one inscribed in the very concept of the human being. This signifies above all, that ethics is measured by the interest in the distinction between the being of nature and the being of the ought."

26. Cohen, *Religion der Vernunft aus den Quellen des Judentums*, 56 / *Religion of Reason*, 48. Italics in the original.

27. That is, there is a shift from *Opfer*, which is presumably a translation of a reference to *olah*, to repentance, *teshuva*, which is inextricable from ethics. I would like to thank Martin Kavka for this insight.

28. I have slightly altered Kaplan's translation. Emphasis in original.

29. Cohen, *Religion der Vernunft aus den Quellen des Judentums*, 199 / *Religion of Reason*, 171.

30. See Zank, *The Idea of Atonement in the Philosophy of Hermann Cohen*, 108–134 and Erlewine, "Reclaiming the Prophets," 177–206.

31. It is in this context that Cohen makes this notorious claim: "Pure love is directed only toward archetypes, toward models upon which pure moral action can be established. And no man is able to represent this archetype. This archetype is only an archetype of morality, and only as such could and should it become a model" (Cohen, *Religion der Vernunft aus den Quellen des Judentums*, 186 / *Religion of Reason*, 160). Martin Buber's famous objection is that experience teaches us that God and God's love are more than an idea, but he misses the polemical edge of Cohen's critique of Christianity here. Buber, *Eclipse of God*, trans. M. S. Friedman (New York: Harper, 1952), 81. Kenneth Seeskin offers a spirited defense of the integrity of Cohen's argument in his chapter, "Revelation," in *Jewish Philosophy in a Secular Age*, 99–118, but he too fails to acknowledge that Cohen's argument functions as a critique of Christianity.

32. Cohen is insistent that we should not see them as equivalent or overlapping, *Religion der Vernunft aus den Quellen des Judentums*, 199–200 / *Religion of Reason*, 171.

33. Cohen, *Religion der Vernunft aus den Quellen des Judentums*, 220 / *Religion of Reason*, 188.

34. Cohen, *Religion der Vernunft aus den Quellen des Judentums*, 400 / *Religion of Reason*, 343.

35. See n. 50 in chapter 1.

36. According to Cohen, Western metaphysics, with the notion of the "absolute Seelensubstanz" (*LrE*), is deeply influenced by Christian theology. Cohen, *System der Philosophie: 2. Teil: Ethik des reinen Willens*. In *Ethik des reinen Willens*, Cohen writes, "Das Selbst ist nicht eine Seele, welche dir angehoren ist; es ist überhaupt keine sache, keine Besiz; . . . Und wenn die Tugend den Wegweiser bedeutet fuer die Stetigkeit der sittlichen Arbeit, so bezeichnet die Wahrhaftigkeit die Richtung auf die Erkenntnis, in deren Vollzug, in deren unaufhörlicher ernster Arbeit das Selbst sich vollzieht; so weit überhaupt es Wirklichkeit werden kann" (501) "the self is not a soul that belongs to you; it is no thing at all, no possession . . . And if virtue represents the signposts for the steadiness of ethical work, so truthfulness designates the path of knowledge, in its implementation, in its unendingly serious work, the self fulfills itself, insofar as the self can ever become [part of] actuality [Wirklichkeit]." In this regard, one should consider Zank's contextualization of Cohen's work, noting that following "German unification under Bismarck" long-standing religious prejudices against the Jews intensified.

> Countering this interminable prejudice, Cohen distinguishes Judaism only as a religion, namely as a religion that is paradigmatic, rational, originative, and consistently anti-mythological and therefore a model to be emulated by Christianity. Accordingly, when Cohen discusses religious aspects of the key terms of will, action, and self-consciousness, Christianity is the decisive representative of the Western religious tradition but as such it is critically examined from an ethical perspective and, more often than not, it is severely criticized. On the other hand, where religion functions as the source and well-spring of ethical ideas, the reference is to the ethical monotheism of the Hebrew prophets." (Zank, *The Idea of Atonement*, 269–270).

37. Cohen, *Religion der Vernunft aus den Quellen des Judentums*, 400 / *Religion of Reason*, 344.

38. Cohen, *Religion der Vernunft aus den Quellen des Judentums*, 251 / *Religion of Reason*, 215.

39. For a summary of Kant and Cohen on the issue of autonomy, although one that sees them more as fellow travelers rather than antagonists (which I am doing here), see Seeskin, *Autonomy in Jewish Philosophy*, 149–181.

40. Cohen, *Religion der Vernunft aus den Quellen des Judentums*, 250 / *Religion of Reason*, 214.

41. The Christian theologian and colleague of Cohen at Marburg, Wilhelm Hermann, complains of Cohen's depiction of Christianity as committed to "a pagan representation of the

persuasion of God through a sacrifice" [*heidnische Vorstellung einer Umstimmung Gottes durch ein Opfer berechtigt wäre*] (Hermann, "Der Begriff der Religion nach Hermann Cohen," in *Schriften zur Grundlegung der Theologie* (Munich: Kaiser, 1966–1967), 320.

42. Cohen, *Der Begriff,* 32.

43. Ibid., 66.

44. Cohen, *Religion der Vernunft aus den Quellen des Judentums,* 487 / *Religion of Reason,* 420.

45. Clearly Cohen does not mean the nation-state in the Middle East. This is not only an anachronism but Cohen was also a vigorous opponent of the then-budding Zionist movement.

46. For a discussion of the role of nationality in Cohen's thought, see my "Isolation and the Law: Germanism and Judaism in Hermann Cohen's Reading of Moses Mendelssohn," in *Moses Mendelssohn: Enlightenment, Religion, Politics, Nationalism,* eds. Michah Gottlieb and Charles Mannekin (forthcoming). The title of the Mendelssohn book will be: *Moses Mendelssohn: Enlightenment, Religion, Politics, Nationalism* (Bethesda, MD: University of Maryland Press, 2016).

47. The precise relationship between Cohen's thought and the empirical Jewish people is complex. Cohen"s position cannot do without the ethnic Jewish people and their sources as they provide the empirical foundation from which the process of idealization takes place. Yet, the process of idealization moves toward a cosmopolitanism that is in tension with the focus on ethnicity as a marker of identity.

48. Cohen, *Religion der Vernunft aus den Quellen des Judentums,* 330 / *Religion of Reason,* 283. Emphasis in original.

49. Cohen, *Religion der Vernunft aus den Quellen des Judentums,* 325 / *Religion of Reason,* 279.

50. See particularly Cohen's scattered critique of original sin and myth, which is certainly aimed at Christianity, throughout *Ethik des reinen Willens.* See also his "Religion und Sittlichkeit," in *Hermann Cohens Jüdische Schriften,* Vol. 3, 98–168. On this topic, see Robert Erlewine, *Monotheism and Tolerance: Recovering a Religion of Reason* (Bloomington: Indiana University Press, 2010), 157–165.

51. Of course, Judaism remains bound up with Germany, which is the homeland for Judaism throughout the world. And Germany itself maintains an exemplarity in regard to other nations. See Wiedebach, *The National Element,* 87–120.

52. Cohen, "Der Jude in der christlichen Kultur"/ " 'The Jew in Christian Culture' by Hermann Cohen," 51–73.

53. For a good account of the debate over Cohen's notion of religion and its relationship to his critical idealist system, see Poma, *The Critical Philosophy of Hermann Cohen,* 171–196.

54. Cohen, *Religion der Vernunft aus den Quellen des Judentums,* 15 / *Religion of Reason,* 13.

55. Cohen, *Ethik des reinen Willens,* 446. Or for a more thorough explanation: "Jetzt ist zwar Gott transcendent, zur Natur, wie zur Sittlichkeit. *Aber diese Transscendenz* [sic] *will nichts Anderes bedeuten, als dass kraft ihrer nunmehr die Nature nicht transcendent bleibt der Sittlichkeit, noch die Sittlichkeit der Natur. Das ist der Gewinn der Transscendenz* [sic] *Gottes, dass die Transscendenz zwischen Natur und Sittlichkeit aufgehoben wird*" (466) "Now God is transcendent to nature as to morality. *However, this transcendence signifies nothing else than that the force of nature does not remain transcendent to morality, nor does morality remain transcendent to nature.* The achievement of God is that the transcendence of nature and morality is sublated."

56. I side with those scholars who find that Rosenzweig reads too much into this shift in his "Einleitung in die Akademieausgabe der Jüdischen Schriften Hermann Cohens," in *Zweistromland,* 177–225, and that his claims that Cohen breaks with Idealism and becomes a forerunner

of dialogical thinking are far-fetched and self-serving. I discuss Rosenzweig's appropriation and tacit critique of Cohen in the following chapter.

57. Cohen, *Religion der Vernunft aus den Quellen des Judentums*, 216 / *Religion of Reason*, 185.

58. Cohen, *Religion der Vernunft aus den Quellen des Judentums*, 234 / *Religion of Reason*, 201.

59. Ibid.

60. Cohen, *Der Begriff*, 116.

61. Ibid.

62. Ibid.

63. Cohen, *Religion der Vernunft aus den Quellen des Judentums*, 234–235 / *Religion of Reason*, 201.

64. On this paradoxical aspect of the Protestant quest for the historical Jesus, see S. Heschel, *Abraham Geiger and the Jewish Jesus*, 226.

65. Again, see n. 50 in chapter 1.

66. Cohen does note that "only the symbolism of human suffering must not reach too far. It must not, that is, penetrate into the essence of the unique God"("Der Jude in christliche Kultur," 199 / "The Jew in Christian Culture," 64).

67. Cohen, "Der Jude in christliche Kultur," 205/ "The Jew in Christian Culture' by Hermann Cohen," 69.

68. Cohen, *Der Begriff*, 67.

69. Ibid., 65.

70. Immanuel Kant, *Religion within the Limits of Reason Alone*, trans. Theodore M. Greene and Hoyte H. Hudson (London: Harper & Row, 1960), 55.

71. Cohen, *Der Begriff*, 93.

72. Cohen, *Religion der Vernunft aus den Quellen des Judentums*, 313 / *Religion of Reason*, 268. Emphasis in text.

73. Cohen, *Religion der Vernunft aus den Quellen des Judentums*, 10–11 / *Religion of Reason*, 9.

74. Cohen, *Religion der Vernunft aus den Quellen des Judentums*, 55 / *Religion of Reason*, 48.

75. Cohen, *Religion der Vernunft aus den Quellen des Judentums*, 10 / *Religion of Reason*, 9.

76. In Cohen's work we see two profound tendencies that are made sharper and more polemical in later Jewish thinkers such as Leo Baeck and Martin Buber. First, the Jewish dispute with Christianity is not with Jesus but with Paul. This is perhaps most explicit in the work of Baeck. Indeed, it is not until very recently that Jewish thinkers such as Daniel Boyarin have begun to reclaim Paul as a Jew. Second, Jewish thinkers made use of the Greek heritage of the New Testament, long a source of pride for Europeans, to question whether their Christian contemporaries had deviated from the beliefs and teachings of the founder of their religion— himself a Jew. Cohen does not merely undermine the German tendency to Hellenize Jesus, but he is instrumental in fostering a tradition in Jewish thought that challenges the very attempt, so enticing to Christians in the nineteenth and twentieth centuries, to de-Judaize Jesus. I would like to thank Martin Kavka for pointing this out to me.

3. Fire, Rays, and the Dark

1. I will capitalize the major terms or elements of Rosenzweig's system: God-World-Man, and Creation, Revelation, and Redemption. When these terms are not being used in the specific terms set by the system, I will not capitalize them.

2. See Alexander Altmann, "Franz Rosenzweig on History," in *Between East and West: Essays Dedicated to the Memory of Bela Horovitz* (London: East and West Library, 1958),

200–203, for the relationship between Jews and Christians in the Johannine age (the present age) of (Christian) history.

3. See my discussion of the eclipse of Cohen's legacy in chapter 1, pages 14–16.

4. Peter Eli Gordon, in "Rosenzweig Redux: The Reception of German-Jewish Thought," *Jewish Social Studies* 8 (2001): 18, suggests that the robust reception of Rosenzweig in America has more to do with the details of Rosenzweig's life and the needs of American Jews than the particular merits of his thought.

5. Franz Rosenzweig, *Der Mensch und Sein Werk: Gesammelte Schriften II: Der Stern Der Erlösung* (Martinus Nijhoff: Haag, 1976) / *The Star of Redemption*, trans. Barbara Galli (Madison: University of Wisconsin Press, 2005).

6. Michael Oppenheim, "Foreword," Franz Rosenzweig, *The Star of Redemption*, xii.

7. For the role of Levinas in Rosenzweig's reception, see Gordon, "Rosenzweig Redux," 30–37.

8. Although Gil Anidjar's reading of Rosenzweig *in The Jew, The Arab: A History of the Enemy* (Stanford, CA: Stanford University Press, 2003), 87–98 is somewhat polemical, it has the virtue of calling attention to certain issues that many specialists would rather ignore or dismiss. To be sure, Rosenzweig scholars openly acknowledge the problematic nature of Rosenzweig's account of Islam and the religions of India and China, but most would prefer to leave it at that (although some like Wayne Cristaudo celebrate his accounts of these traditions or at least of Islam). Anidjar's argument that the notion of Islam is central to Rosenzweig's philosophy, has made it much more difficult for scholars to dismiss it as a mere prejudice.

9. For example, Robert Gibbs critiques Rosenzweig as a historian, that in "*The Star of Redemption* Rosenzweig has not taken history half seriously enough. His accounts of Greece, China, and India in Part I seem barely historical, while his constant use of Islam in Part II reflects an embarrassing prejudice." Gibbs, *Correlation in Rosenzweig and Levinas* (Princeton, NJ: Princeton University Press, 1992), 113. Gibbs's solution is that we must forgive Rosenzweig as a historian and recognize that "the ideas, and not their history is the goal," that is, that history is merely meant to help understand the ideas. If the history is bad, as Gibbs acknowledges it is, then the particular historical judgments can be jettisoned. Indeed, Gibbs's reconstruction of Rosenzweig does precisely this. One finds similar tendency in Michael Oppenheim's "Foreward" to Barbara Galli's new translation of *The Star of Redemption*. Another strategy is taken by Hilary Putnam; he claims that later texts such as *Understanding the Sick and the Healthy* are to be preferred over *The Star* because, in them, Rosenzweig is no longer beholden to the Hegelian principle of the "world-historical," which Putnam believes to be responsible for the "most unfortunate aspects of the *The Star of Redemption*," namely, "its polemical remarks about religions other than these two [Judaism and Christianity]—its scorn for Islam, for Hinduism, and so on." Hilary Putnam, "Introduction," *Understanding the Sick and Healthy* (Cambridge, MA: Harvard University Press, 1999), 18. It is Wayne Cristaudo who, in his problematic defense of Rosenzweig's views of Islam, is perhaps most critical of this tendency among Rosenzweig scholars. See Wayne Cristaudo, "Franz Rosenzweig's Stance towards Islam: The 'Troubling' Matter of the Theo-Politics of The Star of Redemption," *Rosenzweig Jahrbuch* 2 (Freiburg: Karl Alber, 2007), 43–45.

10. Leora Batnitzky, *Idolatry and Representaton: The Philosophy of Rosenzweig Reconsidered* (Princeton, NJ: Princeton University Press, 2000), 72.

11. Our language must be very careful here. For Rosenzweig, the creation of eternity in time is at the same time the dialogical relationship between history and an eternity that can never be subsumed, but instead must always be other than history. As Altmann points out, "Rosenz-

weig realizes that the meaning of history cannot be spun out of its temporal substance. Historical time is incapable of yielding meaning unless it is related to the horizon of eternity. It is through revelation that eternity penetrates time, fulfilling and redeeming it. In a sense, the *eschaton* is in the present, and eschatology points to the future only in so far as it is realized in the present." Altmann, "Franz Rosenzweig on History," 209. In "Facing the Effaced: Mystical Eschatology and the Idealistic Orientation in the Thought of Franz Rosenzweig," *Zeitschrift für neuere Theologiegeschichte* 4 (1997): 39–81, Elliot Wolfson offers a very challenging and nuanced critique of Rosenzweig' ability to sustain such a notion of eternity. As Wolfson puts it, "The eschaton, which Israel anticipates in the present, is not the climax of history but eternity beyond history. Eternal truth belongs only to God who is the Alpha and Omega. . . . Redemption in its absolute sense falls outside of history: the star of eternity casts its light in time only from a distance" (70). The role of history and eternity has central significance in another important piece by Wolfson on Rosenzweig, "Light Does Not Talk but Shine," in *New Directions in Jewish Philosophy*, 87–148, which challenges the long-accepted claim that Rosenzweig succeeds in offering a philosophy that makes room for a dialogical relationship with the traditional notion of the living God of Judaism and Christianity.

12. By the term "non-Western" I mean all religions other than Judaism and Christianity. Or, to be more specific, given the discussions in *The Star of Redemption*, I mean the religious traditions of India and China, as well as Islam—religions that Rosenzweig starkly opposes to Judaism and Christianity. Questions about non-Occidental forms of Judaism and Christianity are not really relevant to Rosenzweig's Euro-centric philosophy of history, and thus there is not room for more nuance when working within the parameters of his thought.

13. This is in contrast to readings by scholars such as Wayne Cristaudo who seek to apply his critiques to the present without recognizing their historical situatedness.

14. It is not my task in this chapter to assess whether or not Rosenzweig's notion of Redemption or his account of the dialogical relationship with God is successful. Again, on this note, see Wolfson's essays "Facing the Effaced," and "Light Does Not Speak but Shine" for important critiques of this aspect of Rosenzweig's project.

15. It is important to recall here what Edward Said highlights in his seminal work, *Orientalism*, that "all of Orientalism stands forth and away from the Orient: that Orientalism makes sense at all depends more on the West than on the Orient, and this sense is directly indebted to various Western techniques of representation that make the Orient visible, clear, 'there' in discourse about it. And these representations rely upon institutions, traditions, conventions, agreed-upon codes of understanding for their effects, not upon a distant and amorphous Orient." Edward Said, *Orientalism* (New York: Vintage Books, 1978), 20–21. Of course, the homogeneous nature of Said's account of the structure of the Orient has been the subject of important critique. See, for example, Daniel Martin Varisco, *Reading Orientalism: Said and the Unsaid* (Seattle: University of Washington Press, 2007). For critiques of Said in regard to the insufficiency of his account of German Orientalism (among other things), see Marchand, *German Orientalism*, and Jeffrey Librett, *German Orientalism and the Figure of the Jew* (New York: Fordham University Press, 2015).

16. On this point, scholars as different as Wayne Cristaudo and Gil Anidjar would agree.

17. For the most expansive work on these two thinkers, at least in English, see Wayne Cristaudo, *Religion, Redemption, and Revolution: The New Speech Thinking of Franz Rosenzweig and Eugen Rosenstock-Huessy* (Toronto: University of Toronto Press, 2012), and Wayne Cristaudo and Frances Huessy, eds., *The Cross and the Star: The Post-Nietzschean Christan and Jewish Thought of Eugen Rosenstock-Huessy and Franz Rosenzweig* (Newcastle upon Tyne: Cambridge

Scholars Publishing, 2009). See also Harold Stahmer, "Introduction," in *Judaism despite Christianity: The "Letters on Christianity and Judaism" between Eugen Rosenstock-Huessy and Franz Rosenzweig*, ed. Eugen Rosenstock-Huessy, trans. Dorothy M. Emmet (New York: Shocken, 1969), 1–25; Alexander Altmann, "Franz Rosenzweig and Eugen Rosenstock-Huessy: An Introduction to Their 'Letters on Judaism and Christianity," in *Judaism despite Christianity*, 26–48; and Dorothy M. Emmet, "The Letters of Franz Rosenzweig and Eugen Rosenstock-Huessy," in *Judaism despite Christianity*, 48–70.

18. Eugen Rosenstock-Huessy, letter November 16, 1916, *Franz Rosenzweig: Briefe und Tagebücher* v. 1 1900–1918, ed. Rachel Rosenzweig and Edith Rosenzweig-Scheinman, and in cooperation with Bernhard Casper (The Hague: Martinus Nijhoof 1979), 298/ *Judaism despite Christianity*, 140 / *Franz Rosenzweig: Briefe und Tagebücher*, 298.

19. Eugen Rosenstock-Huessy, letter November 16, 1916," *Franz Rosenzweig: Briefe und Tagebücher*, 298–299 / *Judaism despite Christianity*, 140.

20. See Marchand, *German Orientalism*, 215, and more generally, 212–251.

21. Eugen Rosenstock-Huessy, letter November 16, 1916, *Franz Rosenzweig: Briefe und Tagebücher*, 298 / *Judaism despite Christianity*, 140.

22. In this rather remarkable letter, Rosenzweig offers some fascinating claims that adumbrate his later position on the peculiar relationship of Jews and Christians in *The Star of Redemption*. Indeed, these very claims help elucidate the significant divergence between Rosenzweig's conception of Judaism and Christianity and that of Cohen.

23. Franz Rosenzweig, letter, November 30, 1916, *Franz Rosenzweig: Briefe und Tagebücher*, 306 /*Judaism despite Christianity*, 161. In "Das Neue Denken" *Zweistromland: Kleinere Schriften zu Glauben und Denken*, ed. Reinhold and Annemarie Mayer (Dordrecht: Martinus Nijhoff Publishers, 1984), 150 / "The New Thinking" (1925), in *Franz Rosenzweig: Philosophical and Theological Writings*, trans. and ed. Paul W. Franks and Michael L. Morgan (Indianapolis: Hackett, 2000), 125, he writes, "And if there were a 'godly ' man—as an enthusiastic German professor under the impact of Ranbindranath Tagore's teaching proclaimed [see n. 28 p. 125]—then this man would actually find himself barred from the path to God, which is open to every human being who is human" (125). Morgan and Franks identify him as Count Hermann Keyserling, who established a School of Wisdom based on Tagore's massively influential ideas. *Franz Rosenzweig: Philosophical and Theological Writings*, 125, n. 28.

24. Rosenzweig, *Franz Rosenzweig: Briefe und Tagebücher*, 306 / *Judaism despite Christianity*, 161.

25. These three figures are quite distinct, but each challenges eternity insofar as they represent claims antithetical to Judaism and Christianity as rooted in Revelation, a meta-historical notion. That is, they reflect the crisis of historicism, the lack of solid foundations, which as Paul Mendes-Flohr has suggested was a strong motivating concern driving *The Star of Redemption*. On the issue of Revelation and the crisis of historicism, see Paul Mendes-Flohr's essay, "Franz Rosenzweig and the Crisis of Historicism," in *Divided Passions: Jewish Intellectuals and the Experience of Modernity* (Detroit: Wayne State University Press, 1991), 311–341, and Altmann, "Franz Rosenzweig on History," 209–210.

26. Note, the translation by Dorothy M. Emmet does not transliterate the Greek.

27. Rosenzweig, *Franz Rosenzweig: Briefe und Tagebücher*, 306/ *Judaism despite Christianity*, 161.

28. Of course, Judaism and Christianity experience history differently. Jews exist outside of history, in the eschaton, whereas Christianity in a sense constitutes history, the struggle of Christianity against paganism. Again, see Mendes-Flohr, "Franz Rosenzweig and the Crisis of

Historicism" and Altmann, "Franz Rosenzweig and History," as well as Wolfson, "Facing the Effaced."

29. This book is discussed in more depth in the next chapter.

30. Franz Rosenzweig, *Der Stern Der Erlösung*, 444/ *The Star of Redemption*, 422; See Benjamin Pollock, "On the Road to Marcionism: Franz Rosenzweig's Early Theology," *Jewish Quarterly Review*, 102, no. 2 (Spring 2012): 224–255.

31. Rosenzweig, *Der Stern der Erlösung*, 461/ *The Star of Redemption*, 437.

32. Rosenzweig, *Der Stern der Erlösung*, 461/ *The Star of Redemption*, 437.

33. Altmann, "Franz Rosenzweig on History," 203.

34. Rosenzweig, "Das neue Denken," 147 / "The New Thinking," 120. Note the similarity in the use of the root word "Geist" as something ethereal, not this-worldly, to describe both the Marcionist heresy and the religions of the Far East.

35. See Christian Wiese, "'The Best Antidote against Anti-Semitism?' Judaism, Biblical Criticism and Anti-Semitism prior to the Holocaust," in *Modern Judaism and Historical Consciousness: Identities–Encounters–Perspectives*, ed. Christian Wiese and Andreas Gotzmann (Leiden: Brill, 2007), 145–193.

36. On Cohen's prominent presence, see Schine, *Jewish Thought Adrift: Max Wiener (1882–1950)*. For the revolt against Cohen and the turn to Schelling among Cohen's disciples after his death and in the wake of World War I, see Steven M. Wasserman, "A Rustling in the Woods: The Turn to Myth in Weimar Jewish Thought."

37. See for instance, Franz Rosenzweig, "Deutschtum und Judentum," in *Zweistromland*, 169–176.

38. Bruce Rosenstock, in *Philosophy and the Jewish Question* (New York: Fordham University Press, 2010), 135, explains Rosenzweig's account of the new, Johannine phase of Christianity well. He writes, "What is the nature of the hope that Johannine Christianity offers? We may first explain it negatively. The task of Johannine Christianity is not to go out into the pagan world with the evangel of love (the task of the Petrine, or Roman Catholic, Church) nor to lift the soul of the converted pagan into the realm of a purely spiritual faith (the task of Pauline, Protestant Christianity). The task of the Johannine Christian—it is an individual's task, and not that of an institutional church—is to make his or her life whole, to create out of life what Rosenzweig calls a 'singularity' (Einzelnes . . .)" (135). Similarly, Altmann, in "Franz Rosenzweig on History," writes, "In this Johannine world, the Christian no longer converts the heathen around him nor the pagan within him. Now the Jew is meant to convert the pagan lurking in the Christian soul. For only in the Jewish blood hope lives eternally, and hope is what the Christian needs today more than anything else. This is why the emancipation of the Jew had to happen precisely in this modern age" (200).

39. Franz Rosenzweig, letter November 30, 1916, *Franz Rosenzweig: Briefe und Tagebücher*, 304 / *Judaism despite Christianity*, 158.

40. Franz Rosenzweig, letter November 30, 1916, *Franz Rosenzweig: Briefe und Tagebücher*, 304 / *Judaism despite Christianity*, 159. Note that Rosenzweig is using the masculine pronoun.

41. Indeed, he thinks that Cohen makes a category mistake in that Judaism is fundamentally incompatible with Germanism. Judaism and Germanism are not on the same level. "One can compare Germanism and Britainism, Germanism and Ottomanism, not Germanism and Judaism." Rosenzweig, "Deutschtum und Judentum," 173.

42. Rosenzweig, *Der Stern der Erlösung*, 461 / *The Star of Redemption*, 438.

43. I take the felicitous term "Messianic Friendship" in the title of this section from Bruce Rosenstock, who in *Philosophy and the Jewish Question*, 124, writes, "If one can speak of

a 'messianic friendship' between Christianity and Judaism as Rosenzweig presents them it is a friendship between partners whose major point of agreement is that they can never allow themselves to agree with each other until the end of time. The beat to which the choreography of each moves must, as it were, remain *off*beat in relation to the other."

44. Rosenzweig, *Der Stern der Erlösung*, 462 / *The Star of Redemption*, 438. For a discussion of Rosenzweig's influence on Christian thought, see Peter Haas and Rosemary Radford Reuther, "Recent Theologies of the Jewish-Christian Relation," *Religious Studies Review*, 16 no. 4 (October 1990): 316–323.

45. Leora Batnitzky, "Dialogue as Judgment, Not Mutual Affirmation: A New Look at Franz Rosenzweig's Dialogical Philosophy," *Journal of Religion* 79, no. 4 (Oct 1999): 523–544; Elliot Wolfson has offered a subtle challenge to Batnitzky's position grounded in the nature of the dialogical itself. In regard to Batnitzky's essay, Wolfson writes, "I would propose, however, that this presentation fails to take seriously that there can be complementarity in the face of irresolvable difference. Indeed, it strikes me that the very heart of dialogical thinking is determined by the indeterminacy that arises from just such a correlativity within diversity." Wolfson, "Apophatic Vision and Overcoming the Dialogical," in *The Cambridge History of Jewish Philosophy. Vol 2, The Modern Era* (Cambridge: Cambridge University Press, 2012), 237 fn 12. Given the ability of Rosenzweig and Rosenstock-Huessy to not just reprimand each other's respective religions but, through critiquing each other, to theorize about—sometimes jointly, but certainly in a complementary, dialogical fashion—Wolfson's point is well taken. On the other hand, what is essential to keep in mind for our purposes is that Rosenzweig's position, unlike Cohen's, incorporates antisemitism into the heart of Christianity, such that it confirms or, at least, ceases to discount the ongoing relationship between Judaism and Christianity.

46. Rosenzweig, *Der Stern der Erlösung*, 462 / *The Star of Redemption*, 438; See Batnitzky, *Idolatry as Representation*, 68–69, 155, 159; Rosenstock, *German Philosophy and the Jewish Question*, 14, 124; and Wolfson, "Facing the Effaced," 60–63, 65–68.

47. Rosenzweig, *Der Stern der Erlösung*, 462 / *The Star of Redemption*, 439.

48. Again, see Wolfson, "Facing the Effaced" and "Light Does Not Talk but Shine," as well as Ben Pollock, *Franz Rosenzweig and the Systematic Task of Philosophy* (New York: Cambridge University Press, 2009).

49. Leora Batnitzky compares Rosenzweig to Gadamer; Peter Eli Gordon compares him to Heidegger. See Pollock for a strikingly rigorous account, in *Franz Rosenzweig and the Systematic Task of Philosophy*, of the idealistic (Schelling in particular) influences on Rosenzweig's philosophy and the manner in which he philosophizes about the whole from within the midst of life.

50. Gibbs, *Correlations between Rosenzweig and Levinas*, 123.

51. Again, see Rosenzweig, "Deutschtum und Judentum," 173.

52. Rosenzweig, "Das neue Denken," 147 / "The New Thinking," 120.

53. Rosenzweig, *Der Stern der Erlösung*, 38 / *The Star of Redemption*, 43.

54. I address this decisionism shortly. But see Ben Pollock, *Franz Rosenzweig and the Systematic Task of Philosophy*, which deals with this issue in some form or another throughout, and Bruce Rosenstock, *Philosophy and the German Question*, 112, 144.

55. Peter Eli Gordon helpfully points out that although Rosenzweig claims and is often understood to be critiquing "philosophy as such," in fact "Rosenzweig had a narrower target in view. Like many of the rebellious thinkers taking off from Weimar *Existenz* philosophy, Rosenzweig was an opponent of cognitivism, the theory that sees our primary relationship to the world as mental rather than care-laden and lived." "Rosenzweig Redux," 8.

56. Rosenzweig, *Der Stern der Erlösung*, 22 / *The Star of Redemption*, 27.

57. Rosenzweig, *Der Stern der Erlösung*, 5 / *The Star of Redemption*, 11.

58. Rosenzweig, *Der Stern der Erlösung*, 24 / *The Star of Redemption*, 29.

59. Rosenzweig, *Der Stern der Erlösung*, 23 / *The Star of Redemption*, 28.

60. Rosenzweig couches his use of Cohen as grasping his importance in a way that perhaps Cohen himself did not: "Hermann Cohen, who was, contrary to what he himself believed, and contrary to the appearance of his works, something other than a simple epigone of that truly completed movement" (i.e., Idealism). Franz Rosenzweig, *Der Stern der Erlösung*, 23 / *The Star of Redemption*, 27. It was Cohen alone, Rosenzweig claims, who "discovered in mathematics the organon of thinking. Precisely because mathematics does not produce its elements out of the empty nothing of the one and universal zero, but out of the nothing of the differential, a definite nothing in each case related to the element it was seeking." Franz Rosenzweig, *Der Stern der Erlösung*, 23 / *The Star of Redemption*, 27–28. As we see later, the differential, as interpreted by Rosenzweig, offers the key for breaking with Idealism. Although Rosenzweig charges Cohen with being more Hegelian than he knew (he makes this charge in *The Star* and also his "Einleitung" in *Hermann Cohens Judische Schriften*, Vol. 1, ed. Bruno Strauss (Berlin: C. A. Schwetschke and Sohn/ Verlagsbuchhandlung, 1924), XVIII), he treats Cohen's logic, with its turn to mathematics, and the differential as non-Hegelian, as evidence that "he broke decisively with the idealist tradition." *Der Stern der Erlösung*, 23 / *The Star of Redemption*, 28. Reiner Wiehl suggests that Rosenzweig knowingly transformed Cohen's logic of origin, extending it to the world of factuality, and thereby offering the foundation of "Rosenzweig's radical critique of rational knowledge" [*Vernunfterkenntnis*]. Weihl, "Logik und Metalogik bei Cohen und Rosenzweig," 631. Wiehl's point about the role of the *Logik* in Rosenzweig's "New Thinking" is quite important because often scholars think Rosenzweig saw Cohen's break with Idealism only in his posthumously published *Religion of Reason out of the Sources of Judaism*. Such a view is not incompatible with Robert Gibbs's claim that "Rosenzweig, however, was suspicious of Cohen's claims to have achieved this correlation of reason and Judaism without recourse to existential experience, and he rejected the theory that reason could generate the plurality of separate and independent entities . . . He portrayed both philosophy and theology as at dead ends: philosophy having lost its sense of purpose, theology its objectivity and historical validity. In the midst of this historicist crisis the two needed each other, and from such a need was born Rosenzweig's New Thinking." Gibbs, *Correlations between Rosenzweig and Levinas*, 19. See Gibbs's helpful account of Cohen's logic on pp. 45–49. Gibbs takes the synoptic view, whereas Wiehl is taking a more biographical view of the relationship, but the two are ultimately compatible in regard to their ends.

61. Rosenzweig, *Der Stern der Erlösung*, 31 / *The Star of Redemption*, 37.

62. Ibid.

63. Rosenzweig, *Der Stern der Erlösung*, 26 / *The Star of Redemption*, 32.

64. Ibid.

65. Rosenzweig, *Der Stern der Erlösung*, 35 / *The Star of Redemption*, 41.

66. See Pollock, *Franz Rosenzweig and the Systematic Task of Philosophy*, 165–169, for a particularly lucid account of the roles of the religions and culture of India, China, and Greece in Rosenzweig's thought. I am indebted to it.

67. Rosenzweig, *Der Stern der Erlösung*, 94 / *Star of Redemption*, 96. As Batnitzky writes, "Rosenzweig's ambivalent attitude toward [Greek] paganism is as significant as his attitude toward Christianity. He argues not only that paganism is true but that paganism is a necessary prerequisite for any dialogical relation, including revelation." *Idolatry and Representation*, 10.

68. For a broad overview of the general intellectual encounter between the West and East, see J. J. Clarke, *Oriental Enlightenment: The Encounter between Asian and Western Thought* (London: Routledge, 1997), 37–92.

69. Rosenstock, *Philosophy and the Jewish Question*, 4.

70. Ibid., 144

71. Rosenzweig, "Das neue Denken," 150 / "New Thinking, "124–125, where Schopenhauer is discussed in relation with the "the godly man"—see n. 24—for whom no contact with God is possible.

72. Rosenzweig, *Der Stern der Erlösung*, 62 / *The Star of Redemption*, 66.

73. Rosenzweig, "Das neue Denken," 154/ "The New Thinking, 130.

74. On the limits of Rosenzweig for religious pluralism, see Robert Erlewine, "The Stubbornness of the Jews: Resources and Limitations of the Jewish-Christian Dialogue of Rosenstock-Huessy and Rosenzweig," in *The Cross and the Star: The Post-Nietzschean Christian and Jewish Thought of Eugen Rosenstock-Huessy and Franz Rosenzweig*, ed. Wayne Cristaudo and Frances Huessy (New Castle upon Tyne, UK: Cambridge Scholars Press, 2009), 191–208.

75. Rosenzweig, "Das neue Denken," 150 / "New Thinking," 125. See n. 23.

76. Rosenzweig, *Der Stern der Erlösung*, 29 / *The Star of Redemption*, 34. See Norbert Samuelson, "The Concept of 'Nichts' in Rosenzweig's *Star of Redemption*," in *Der Philosop Franz Rosenzweig (1886–1929)*, ed. Wolfdietrich Schmied-Kowarzik (Freiburg: Alber, 1998), 648–649; cf. Wolfson, "Light Does Not Talk but Shine," 114.

77. Rosenzweig, *Der Stern der Erlösung*, 31 / *The Star Redemption*, 38.

78. Rosenzweig, *Star of Redemption*, 41 / *Der Stern der Erlösung*, 36.

79. To be sure, the gods "intervene in the world of the living, but they do not reign there—they are living gods, but not gods of the living; because for this they would really have to step outside themselves and that would not suit this 'carefree' life of the Olympians." Rosenzweig, *Der Stern der Erlösung*, 36/ *The Star of Redemption*, 42.

80. Rosenzweig, *Der Stern der Erlösung*, 38 / *The Star of Redemption*, 43.

81. Rosenzweig, *Der Stern der Erlösung*, 39 / *The Star of Redemption*, 43–44.

82. Rosenzweig, *Der Stern der Erlösung*, 38 / *The Star of Redemption*, 43.

83. Ibid.

84. Rosenzweig, *Der Stern der Erlösung*, 40 / *The Star of Redemption*, 45.

85. Rosenzweig, *Der Stern der Erlösung*, 43 / *The Star of Redemption*, 47.

86. Rosenzaweig, *Der Stern der Erlösung*, 40 / *The Star of Redemption*, 45.

87. Rosenzweig, *Der Stern der Erlösung*, 47 / *The Star of Redemption*, 52.

88. Ibid.

89. Rosenzweig writes, "The system of determination of thought is a system not because of its uniform origin, but rather because of the unity of its point of application, the unity of its domain of validity, the world." Thought applies to the world, and that is from where it derives its unity and tenability. Such applied thought, clearly a reference to Idealism, fails to genuinely think, presumably because it is limited to the world in its isolation as opposed to factuality, the world of revelation, which Rosenzweig discusses in part II. Rather, this form of "thinking must console itself with the unity of its point of application inside the hermetic walls of the world." Rosenzweig, *Der Stern der Erlösung*, 46–47 / *The Star of Redemption*, 51.

90. Rosenzweig, *Der Stern der Erlösung*, 48 / *The Star of Redemption*, 52–53. "The sun is no less a miracle than the sunniness of the eye that catches sight of it." Rosenzweig, *Der Stern der Erlösung*, 48 / *The Star of Redemption*, 53. That is, there is the fact of being prior to, and regardless of, its encapsulation in thought.

91. Rosenzweig, *Der Stern der Erlösung*, 50 / *The Star of Redemption*, 55.

92. Rosenzweig, *Der Stern der Erlösung*, 50 / *The Star of Redemption*, 54

93. Rosenzweig, *Der Stern der Erlösung*, 47 / *The Star of Redemption*, 51.

94. Rosenzweig, *Der Stern der Erlösung*, 62 / *The Star of Redemption*, 66. In Rosenzweig's depiction, Hinduism understands things in terms of broad essences, which deprives all existents of their particularity. Buddhism, according to Rosenzweig, goes a step further and "reaches back beyond this objective world of concepts and designates, as essence of these essences, the concept of knowledge." Through knowledge it rejects the I and the world as nothing, but it still remains on the border of nothing and something because "knowledge . . . denies the nothing and thus affirms itself infinitely." Rosenzweig, *Der Stern der Erlösung*, 63 / *The Star of Redemption*, 67.

95. Rosenzweig, *Der Stern der Erlösung*, 64 / *The Star Redemption*, 67, Rosenzweig juxtaposes Confucius and Lao-tse. In Rosenzweig's reading Confucius is entirely concerned with the world, with governing, whereas Lao-tse, while ostensibly moving in a different direction, brings Confucianism to its logical conclusion. Lao-tse, in the face of "a world too visible, too active, too busy, too governed," seeks to go behind it "to the root and source of all this distracted agitation might be." *Der Stern der Erlösung*, 64 / *The Star of Redemption*, 68. Lao-tse's great discovery is that the secret to ruling is precisely "not to rule, not to dominate, not to prescribe nor proscribe in overly busy calculation, but to be oneself, like the root of things, 'without doing and without not doing.'" Rosenzweig, *Der Stern der Erlösung*, 65 / *The Star of Redemption*, 68; Rosenzweig offers a rather simplistic and schematic reading of the relationship between Hinduism and Buddhism that is parallel to his reading of Confucianism and Taoism. In both cases, the latter supposedly takes the logic of the former to its logical conclusion.

96. Rosenzweig, *Der Stern der Erloesung*, 65/ *Star of Redemption*, 68.

97. Rosenzweig, *Der Stern der Erlösung*, 65 / *The Star of Redemption*, 68.

98. Rosenzweig, *Der Stern der Erlösung*, 68 / *The Star of Redemption*, 72.

99. Rosenzweig, *Der Stern der Erlösung*, 69 / *The Star of Redemption*, 73.

100. Rosenzweig, *Der Stern der Erlösung*, 71–72 / *The Redemption*, 75.

101. Rosenzweig, *Der Stern der Erlösung*, 74 / *The Star of Redemption*, 77. Its way of being-in-the-world is "defiance," which characterizes the unconditional nature of freedom even as the Self is bound to a world filled with conditionality. "I is as Self, truly it is not as personality, that man is created in the image of God." *Der Stern der Erlösung*, 75 / *The Star of Redemption*, 78. Indeed, much like Heidegger, it is the awareness of death that first brings man into awareness of the Self, as opposed to the personality, which is bound up with the world, with the species of mankind.

102. Rosenzweig, *Der Stern der Erlösung*, 79 / *The Star of Redemption*, 82.

103. It is worth noting that prior to the Greeks, we see this in the ancient Near East: In "the tragic defiance of Samson and Saul, the most ancient Near East invented the prototype of the tragic hero in that figure bordering between divine and the human, in Gilgamesh." Rosenzweig, *Der Stern der Erlösung*, 83 / *The Star of Redemption*, 85.

104. Rosenzweig, *Der Stern der Erlösung*, 84/ *The Star of Redemption*, 86.

105. Ibid.

106. Rosenzweig, *Der Stern der Erlösung*, 80 / *The Star of Redemption*, 82.

107. Ibid. Rosenzweig is operating with an obvious (and Eurocentric) teleology here.

108. Rosenzweig, *Der Stern der Erlösung*, 82 / *The Star of Redemption*, 84.

109. Indeed, "the highest duty is that man obey this law of his particularity." Rosenzweig, *Der Stern der Erlösung*, 80 / *The Star of Redemption*, 82. Even the ideal of the saint is not open

to anyone, but is merely one more particularity among others, as one must first have established a family. Again, Rosenzweig depicts the Buddha as taking this to its logical extension, rejecting all particularity and everything except "his own perfection." *Der Stern der Erlösung*, 80 / *The Star of Redemption*, 83. However, this is still character, and he is still distinguished from those who are "not-liberated." Ibid. Thus, the Buddha fails to reach the nothing because of this distinction—that individuality and character remain.

110. Rosenzweig, *Der Stern der Erlösung*, 81/ *The Star of Redemption*, 83. In a particularly unsavory remark, Rosenzweig writes, "Confucius, strays from all possible particularity of character: this is really the man without character, that is to say the ordinary man. It must be said to the honor of mankind that really nowhere else except in China could such a boring man as was Confucius have become the classical model of the human." Ibid.

111. As grotesque as these accounts are to our sensibilities, we must recall that the history of Western philosophy is littered with such overly simplistic, Eurocentric accounts of non-European cultures. If we seek to understand Rosenzweig's work, we must understand it in this larger context.

112. Peter Gordon writes as follows in regard to Rosenzweig's *The Star of Redemption*:

> the appearance of systematicity is not altogether convincing. Some readers may indeed find the star configuration almost too clever; there is a touch of wizardry about it, a Kabbalistic symbol-mongering that a philosopher of greater prudence, though perhaps less imagination, might have thought best to avoid. But this is largely a question of standards. One can decide only with deference to the codes of professional philosophy what kind of order should be tolerated and what should be dismissed as mere idiosyncrasy. Intended or not, Rosenzweig's claims to systematicity lapse occasionally into self-parody—at times, one suspects that he is out to explode the idea of a self-grounding philosophical structure from within. (*Rosenzweig and Heidegger: Between Judaism and Philosophy*, 123).

113. For a critique of Rosenzweig's problematic ahistorical notion of Judaism and Jewish experience, see Altmann, "Franz Rosenzweig on History," 204–205. It bears repeating Brenner's point: "Jewish culture in Weimar Germany was characterized neither by a radical break with the past nor a return to them. Indeed, it used distinct forms of Jewish traditions, marked them as authentic, and presented it according to the demands of contemporary taste and modern cultural forms of expression. What might have appeared as authenticity was in fact a modern innovation." *The Rennaissance of Jewish Culture in Weimar Germany*, 5.

114. Ben Pollock, *Franz Rosenzweig and the Systematic Task of Philosophy*, 112. Bruce Rosenstock writes,

> Revelation. does not become audible simply because history has passed on beyond 1800. In fact, each person must return to 1800 and stand before the existential choice posed by Hegel and Goethe in order to hear the word of God once more. What this means, in effect, is that each individual must become aware of his or her radical particularity. In the opening pages of the *Star*, Rosenzweig writes about thinkers like Kierkegaard and Nietzsche who stood before the existential choice named "1800." Rosenzweig's *Star* is written to assist everyone to return to the existential choice of 1800. It seeks to awaken the reader to a crisis of decision, and it assists the reader in recognizing the dangers posed and the hope offered by Hegel and Goethe. (Rosenstock, *Philosophy and the Jewish Question*, 144).

115. Masuzawa, *The Invention of World Religions*, xii.
116. Ibid., xiii; see Heschel, *The Aryan Jesus*.
117. Rosenzweig, *Der Stern der Erlösung*, 365 / *The Star of Redemption*, 348.
118. Cohen, *Einleitung mit kritische Nachtrag*, 103.
119. For in depth scholarly investigations of Rosenzweig's account of Islam in Rosenzweig's thought, see Shlomo Pines, "Der Islam im 'Stern der Erlösung,' Eine Untersuchung zu Tendenzen und Quellen Franz Rosenzweig," *Hebräische Beiträge zur Wissenschaft des Judentums*, deutsch angezeigt (1987–1989), 138–148; Gesine Palmer. "Einleitung," in *Innerlich bleibt die Welt eine: ausgewaehlte Texte Islam*, ed. Gesine Palmer, 9–32; Rosenzweig, Franz, Gesine Palmer, and Yossef Schwartz. 2003. *Innerlich bleibt die Welt eine: ausgewählte Texte zum Islam*. Berlin: Philo and Yossef Schwartz, "Die entfremdete Nähe: Rosenzweigs Blick auf den Islam," in *Innerlich bleibt die Welt eine*, 113–147. For overt criticisms, see Jean Axelrad Cahan, "Rosenzweig's Dialectic of Defiance and Critique of Islam," *Journal of Jewish Thought and Philosophy* 9 (1999): 1–20, and Gil Anidjar, *The Jew, The Arab*. For more positive views see Wayne Cristaude, *Religion, Redemption and Revolution*, 401–416, and "Franz Rosenzweig's Stance towards Islam: The 'Troubling' Matter of the Theo-Politics of The Star of Redemption"; Matthias Lehman, "Franz Rosenzweig's Kritik des Islams im Stern der Erlösung," *Jewish Studies Quarterly* 1, no. 4 (1993–1994): 340–368; and Spengler, "Christian, Muslim, Jew: Franz Rosenzweig and the Abrahamic Religions," *First Things: The Journal of Religion, Culture, and Public Life*, October 2007, issue 176 29–33.
120. Indeed, Gesine Palmer has trenchantly suggested that Rosenzweig's extended critique of Islam is inextricably bound up with his rejection of religious rationalism and liberalism, particularly that of Hermann Cohen. As will become clear, my argument here is indebted to Palmer's work. See Gesine Palmer's "Einleitung," 20–21, and Schwartz, "Die entfremdete Nähe," 143–144. Although Cohen was the leading philosopher of Jewish rationalism in the nineteenth and early twentieth centuries, the leading scholars of the day, including those at the *Hochschule für die Wissenschaft des Judentums*, had rationalist sensibilities. Of course, even if Rosenzweig's critique of Islam extends to Cohen, this does not mean that Rosenzweig did not also, or even primarily, have Islam in mind. As we see later, the particular manner in which Jewish liberal, rationalist scholars depicted Islam at the time may very well have led Rosenzweig to think he was actually talking about Islam.
121. Susannah Heschel, "German-Jewish Scholarship on Islam as a Tool for de-Orientalizing Judaism," *New German Critique* 39, no. 3 (Fall 2012): 101.
122. Hermann Cohen, *Religion der Vernunft aus den Quellen des Judentums*, 107–108 / *Religion of Reason*, 92.
123. Lawrence I. Conrad, "Ignaz Goldziher on Ernest Renan: From Orientalist Philology to the Study of Islam," in *The Jewish Discovery of Islam*, ed. Martin Kramer (Tel Aviv: Moshe Dayan Center for Middle Eastern and African Studies, 1999), 155. Goldziher's account of Islam is heavily mirrored by Rosenzweig to such an extent that Shlomo Pines concludes it can hardly be coincidental. Shlomo Pines, "Der Islam im 'Stern der Erloesung,' " 138–148.
124. Rosenzweig, *Der Stern der Erlösung*, 130 / *The Star of Redemption*, 128.
125. Schwartz, "Die entfremdete Nähe," 144; Similarly, Gesine Palmer sees Rosenzweig's description of Islam in often Cohenian terms; she points out that calling it "the Religion of Reason" is not merely a play on the title of Cohen's posthumous opus, but is a critique of his concept of religion, a critique of the attempt to rationalize it. "Palmer, "Einleitung," 21. Her view builds on other arguments about Rosenzweig's appropriation and creative misreading of

Cohen's thought. Indeed, her argument fills in gaps, because Rosenzweig is both rejecting much of what Cohen argued and claiming to be his genuine heir. This approach allows him, in a disguised form, to reject many elements of Cohen's thought.

126. For an excellent account of the methodological connections between Rosenzweig and Cohen, see Reiner Wiehl, "Logik und Metalogik bei Cohen und Rosenzweig."

127. Rosenzweig, *Der Stern der Erlösung*, 105–106 / *The Star of Redemption*, 105.

128. Technically, there seems to be at least three senses of Revelation in play in *The Star of Redemption*—that which is inherent in Rosenzweig's notion Creation, that which constitutes Revelation proper, and finally that which is encountered in the vision "beyond life." I am only discussing the first two. See Wolfson, "Light Does Not Talk but Shine," and Pollock, *Franz Rosenzweig and the Systematic Task of Philosophy*, 258–311, for in-depth accounts of the third form of Revelation.

129. Rosenzweig, *Der Stern der Erlösung*, 133 / *The Star of Redemption*, 131.

130. Rosenzweig, *Der Stern der Erlösung*, 124 / *The Star of Redemption*, 123.

131. Rosenzweig, *Der Stern der Erlösung*, 133 / *The Star of Redemption*, 131.

132. Rosenzweig, *Der Stern der Erlösung*, 119 / *The Star of Redemption*, 117.

133. Cohen, *Logik der reinen Erkenntnis*, 62. Emphasis in the original.

134. Rosenzweig, *Der Stern der Erlösung*, 179 / *The Star of Redemption*, 174.

135. Rosenzweig, *Der Stern der Erlösung*, 180/ *The Star of Redemption*, 174.

136. Rosenzweig, *Der Stern der Erlösung*, 191/ *The Star of Redemption*, 185.

137. Ibid.

138. In "Light Does Not Talk but Shine" Wolfson argues convincingly that the ultimate primacy that Rosenzweig gives to the God in Redemption threatens to undo the independence of the elements God, World, Man and the relationships Creation, Revelation, Redemption.

139. Rosenzweig, *Der Stern der Erlösung*, 183 / *The Star of Redemption*, 178.

140. Rosenzweig, *Der Stern der Erlösung*, 184 / *The Star of Redemption*, 178.

141. See Martin Kavka, *Jewish Messianism and the History of Philosophy* (Cambridge: Cambridge University Press, 2004), 146.

142. Rosenzweig, *Der Stern der Erlösung*, 243 / *The Star of Redemption*, 234.

143. Ibid.

144. See Kavka, *Jewish Messianism*, 149–154; Wendell S. Dietrich, "Is Rosenzweig an Ethical Monotheist? A Debate with the New Francophone Literature," in *Der Philosoph Franz Rosenzweig*, 891–900; cf., Wayne Cristaudo, "Franz Rosenzweig's Stance towards Islam," 58.

145. Rosenzweig, *Der Stern der Erlösung*, 244 / *The Star of Redemption*, 235.

146. Paul Mendes-Flohr writes, "Rosenzweig presents eternity as the future anticipated in the present. . . . The future—i.e., the future of messianic promise—has thus in a sense ceased, as Alexander Altmann has pointed out, 'to be a historical category . . . Future, the Kingdom, and eternity become synonymous terms in Rosenzweig's eschatological thinking. They are existential terms, not concepts denoting objective reality." "Franz Rosenzweig and the Crisis of Historicism," 328.

147. Rosenzweig, *Der Stern der Erlösung*, 250 / *The Star of Redemption*, 241.

148. Rosenzweig, *Der Stern der Erlösung*, 255 / *The Star of Redemption*, 245.

149. Altmann, "Rosenzweig on History," 209.

150. See Wolfson, "Facing the Effaced," 55–57.

151. Rosenzweig, *Der Stern der Erlösung*, 135 / *The Star of Redemption*, 133.

152. Rosenzweig, *Der Stern der Erlösung*, 130 / *The Star of Redemption*, 128.

153. Rosenzweig, *Der Stern der Erlösung*, 126–127 / *The Star of Redemption*, 125.

154. Rosenzweig, *Der Stern der Erlösung*, 130 / *The Star of Redemption*, 128.

155. Rosenzweig, *Der Stern der Erlösung*, 184 / *The Star of Redemption*, 178.
156. See Palmer, "Einleitung," 21.
157. Rosenzweig, *Der Stern der Erlösung*, 184 / *The Star of Redemption*, 179.
158. Rosenzweig, *Der Stern der Erlösung*, 185 / *The Star of Redemption*, 179.
159. Rosenzweig, *Der Stern der Erlösung*, 185 / *The Star of Redemption*, 180.
160. Ibid.
161. See Erlewine, *Monotheism and Tolerance: Recovering a Religion of Reason*, for a detailed account of the manner in which Kant and Cohen attempt to rationalize the notion of divine election and monotheism generally. Indeed, in this work, Mendelssohn is critiqued for his wavering between a rational God and a God of elective monotheism who loves a particular people. Bruce Rosenstock, in his *Philosophy and the Jewish Question*, trenchantly highlights this link between Mendelssohn and Rosenzweig.
162. Rosenzweig, *Der Stern der Erlösung*, 186 / *The Star of Redemption*, 180.
163. Ibid. Pines reads this as Rosenzweig shifting the Christian polemic against Judaism's emphasis on the Torah toward Islam and the Quran instead. "Der Islam," 143, n 17.
164. See Braiterman, *The Shape of Revelation*, 79–83, for a nice account of the very minimal content of Rosenzweig's notion of Revelation.
165. Rosenzweig, *Der Stern der Erlösung*, 197 / *The Star of Redemption*, 190.
166. It is not too far of a stretch to see this as aimed at Hermann Cohen's method of rationalizing Judaism via literary sources of the tradition, an account of religion that renders any genuine contact between God and human beings impossible except through emulation.
167. Rosenzweig, *Der Stern der Erlösung*, 193 / *The Star of Redemption*, 186–187.
168. Rosenzweig, *Der Stern der Erlösung*, 193 / *The Star of Redemption*, 187.
169. Rosenzweig, *Der Stern der Erlösung*, 240 / *The Star of Redemption*, 232.
170. Although the notion of holy war immediately seems polemical to readers today, for Rosenzweig both Christianity and Islam are political and bound up with war and conquest.
171. Rosenzweig, *Der Stern der Erlösung*, 240–241 / *The Star of Redemption*, 232.
172. With the exception of such sobering arguments in Dietrich, "Is Rosenzweig an Ethical Monotheist"; Kavka's *Jewish Messianism*; Braiterman, *The Shape of Revelation*; and Gordon, "Rosenzweig Redux," which explicitly challenge the conflation of Rosenzweig and Levinas, all too often ethical motives have been purported to Rosenzweig when they are lacking. To be sure, I do not want to ascribe this tendency to all other scholars of Rosenzweig, but certainly much of his celebration in recent years is a result of this conflation.
173. Rosenzweig, *Der Stern der Erlösung*, 241 / *The Star of Redemption*, 232. Interestingly, Wayne Cristaudo, who celebrates Rosenzweig's critique of Islam, explicitly acknowledges the dark side of his notion of love. "Franz Rosenzweig's Stance towards Islam," 58.
174. Gil Anidjar, *The Jew, the Arab*, 97, makes a curious and rather overstated claim that is partially correct and partially incorrect. He states, "No one, has gone as explicitly far as Rosenzweig in extirpating, ultimately eradicating, Islam from the figure of humanity, that is to say, from the theologico-political, from the religious and historical world configuration that is constituted by Judaism and Christianity." While he certainly overestimates Rosenzweig's Islamphobia and polemically overstates the case by equating "the figure of the human" with "the historical world configuration ... constituted by Judaism and Christianity"—especially because he never mentions Rosenzweig's much harsher judgments on the religions of Asia—he does correctly point out that negating certain traditions are essential for Rosenzweig's positive construction of the Occident in which Judaism and Christianity are central. And this Occident is defined against the Orient.
175. Rosenzwenzweig, *Der Stern der Erlösung*, 241 / *The Star of Redemption*, 233.

176. Rosenzweig, *Der Stern der Erlösung*, 242–243 / *The Star of Redemption*, 234.

177. Palmer, "Einleitung," 25.

178. Ibid., 26.

179. Rosenzweig, *Der Stern der Erlösung*, 253 / *The Star of Redemption*, 243.

180. Rosenzweig, *Der Stern der Erlösung*, 253 / *The Star of Redemption*, 244.

181. For Rosenzweig's commitment to *Offenbarungsglaube* as a solution to the crisis of historicism, see Paul Mendes-Flohr, "Rosenzweig and the Crisis of Historicism"; cf. Elliot Wolfson, "Facing the Effaced," 51.

182. "The [Star of Redemption] is mostly written in a declamatory mode—it does not argue, it simply states—and it is written in a grand and self-confident style that does very little to encourage the reader's confidence in Rosenzweig as a philosophical authority." Gordon, *Rosenzweig and Heidegger*, 122.

4. Redeeming This World

1. Martin Buber, "Ich und Du," in Martin Buber, *Werke-Erster Band: Schriften Zur Philosophie* (Munich: Kösel Verlag, 1962), 77–170. I primarily refer to the Ronald Gregor Smith's translation: Martin Buber, *I and Thou*, trans. Ronald Gregor Smith (New York: Scribner Classics, 1958). However, I occasionally make use of Walter Kaufmann's translation of *I and Thou* (New York: Simon & Schuster, 1970) and specifically note when I do so. I also make note of any changes I make to any translation.

2. To be sure, scholars have noted, and not incorrectly, the Jewish sensibilities and assumptions of this work. See Robert Wood, *Martin Buber's Ontology: An Analysis of I and Thou* (Evanston, IL: Northwestern University Press, 1969), 80–81; Walter Kaufmann, "I and You: A Prologue," in Martin Buber, *I and Thou*, trans. Walter Kaufmann, 21, 32–39; and Daniel Breslauer, *The Chrysalis of Religion: A Guide to the Jewishness of Buber's I and Thou* (Nashville: Abingdon, 1980).

3. There is an important, if still underappreciated, strand of scholarship that emphasizes Buber as a historian of religion. See Michael Zank, "Buber and Religionswissenschaft—the Case of His Studies of Biblical Faith," in *New Perspectives on Martin Buber*, ed. Michael Zank (Tübingen: Mohr Siebeck, 2006), 61–84, and Guy G. Stroumsa, "Presence, Not Gnosis: Buber as a Historian of Religion," in *Martin Buber: A Contemporary Perspective*, ed. Paul Mendes-Flohr (Jerusalem: Syracuse University Press, 2002), 25–48. For a detailed account of the situatedness of *I and Thou* in relation to Buber's lectures on *Religionswissenschaft* and his various plans, see Willy Schottroff, "Martin Buber an der Universität Frankfurt am Main (1923)," in *Martin Buber, Erich Foerster, Paul Tillich: EvangelischeTheologie und Religionsphilosophie an der Universitaet Frankfurt a.M. 1914 bis 1933*, ed. Dieter Stoodt (Frankfurt: Lang, 1990), esp. 79–82. For other studies that consider Buber in connection to *Religionswissenschaft*, see R. J. Zwi Werblowsky, "The Reflections of Martin Buber's Two Types of Faith," *Journal of Jewish Studies* 39, no. 1 (1988): 92–101; Maurice Friedman, "Martin Buber and the History of Religion," in *Martin Buber: A Centenary Volume*, ed. Haim Gordon and Jochanon Bloch (New York: KTAV, 1984), 367–384.

4. Stroumsa, "Presence, not Gnosis," 30. Stroumsa describes the written plans detailing Buber's intentions with *I and Thou* that are housed in the Martin Buber Archive in the Jewish National and University Library in Jerusalem. Stroumsa highlights the need for scholars to grasp the centrality of "the comparative study of religious phenomena" in regard to "Buber's

intellectual life, from his early years on" (30). See Zank, "Buber and Religionswissenschaft," 63–64 and Schottroff, "Martin Buber an der Universität Frankfurt am Main."

5. As I mentioned in the Introduction, Russell McCutcheon lists Buber in the company of Schleiermacher, Otto, Tillich, Barth, and Wach in *Critics Not Caretakers*, 115–116. There is both something profoundly correct and yet at the same time problematic about including Buber in these ranks. It is correct insofar as Buber—in a manner not altogether different from figures like Schleiermacher, Otto, and their colleagues—seeks to offer an essence of religion. What is lacking, however, in McCutcheon's grouping is any acknowledgment of the degree to which Buber is offering an opposing narrative or essence of religion that deliberately conflicts with and challenges the all-too-Protestant and Catholic theologians in whose company McCutcheon lumps him. To be sure, McCutcheon would probably find such a difference unimportant, but as a study such as this hopes to divulge, the study of religion—indeed the very categories of the religionists that McCutcheon seeks to challenge—is itself the product of struggles between different religious groups in tumultuous periods of change.

6. Paul Mendes-Flohr, "Martin Buber and the Metaphysicians of Contempt," 207. The full quote reads as follows: "A careful reading of his writings will show that the issue of anti-Semitism loomed large for him. Especially when read palimpsestically, his writings betray a hidden text that constitutes a sustained critique of what the philosopher Ernst Bloch (1885–1977) was to call 'metaphysical anti-Semitism,' namely, the tendency to repudiate Judaism as a spiritually and culturally jejune religion 'essentially' alien to the Christian and European sensibility" (207).

7. See Zank, "Buber and Religionswissenschaft," 66; see more generally, S. Heschel, *Abraham Geiger and the Jewish Jesus* and "Jesus as a Theological Transvestite," 188–200. On the relationship between Jewish Studies and politics in Wilhelmine Germany, see Wiese, *Challenging Colonial Discourse*, 208; Wilhelm Graf, "Kulturprotestantismus. Zur Begriffsgeschichte einer theologiepolitische Chiffre," *Archiv für Begriffsgeschichte* 28, (1984): 214–268; Uriel Tal, *Christians and Jews in Germany* and "Liberal Protestantism and the Jews in the Second Reich," *Jewish Social Studies* 26 (1964): 23–41.

8. Stroumsa, "Presence, not Gnosis," 26. Indeed, Stroumsa points out Buber's commonalities with other historians of religion of his time: "Students of religion in the early twentieth century were sometimes rather careless about the historical context of religious phenomena, and Buber was no exception. His lack of interest in the minutiae of research is indeed remarkable. . . . Buber's deep interest in the religious phenomena of all cultures, and in their study through most of the methods then available, is obvious" (26).

9. Michael Zank, "Buber and Religionswissenschaft," 62. Zank points out that Buber's academic career, which shifted from a position in Jewish Studies to social studies, "was the very opposite of his inner evolution" (66).

10. For an important study of the role of Buber as a social critic of modernity, see Lawrence J. Silberstein. *Martin Buber's Social and Religious Thought: Alienation and the Quest for Meaning* (New York: New York University Press, 1989). Although this book generally follows the more standard interpretation of *I and Thou* as the culmination of Buber's early work—what Zank refers to as "continuity conjecture [the locus classicus of this is Mendes-Flohr, *From Mysticism to Dialogue*] that takes *I and Thou* as the end-point of a development rather than a point of departure" (Zank, "Buber and Religionswissenschaft," 64), its emphasis on the role of Buber's concerns about the alienating effects of modernity is nevertheless quite valuable to this study.

11. Zank, "Buber and Religionswissenschaft," 62.

12. See Benjamin Lazier, *God Interrupted: Heresy and the European Imagination between the World Wars* (Princeton: Princeton University Press, 2008), 31.

13. Adolf von Harnack, *Marcion: Das Evangelium vom Fremden Gott / Marcion: The Gospel of the Alien God*. Trans. John E. Steely and Lyle D. Bierma (Eugene, OR: Wipf & Stock, 2007).

14. Buber, *Ich und Du*, 103 / *I and Thou*, 48.

15. See Rémi Brágue, "How to Be in the World: Gnosis, Religion, Philosophy," in *Martin Buber: A Contemporary Perspective*, ed. Paul Mendes-Flohr (Jerusalem: Syracuse University Press, 2002), 145.

16. On both Jews' and Christians' widespread interest in Gnosticism in the Weimar era, see Lazier, *God Interrupted*, and Yaniv Fellner, "From Aher to Marcion: Martin Buber's Understanding of Gnosis," *Jewish Studies Quarterly* 20 (2013): 374–397.

17. A good example of Buber's feelings toward Gnosticism, which are usually framed in asides in essays, can be found in "Symbolic and Sacramental Existence," in *The Origin and Meaning of Hasidism*, ed. and trans. Maurice Friedman (New York: Horizon Press, 1960), 175. Buber writes, "The origin of all gnosis . . . is the primal question, intensified to despair of the world. How is the contradiction which in every course of life and history is experienced as insuperable, the corroding essence of existence in the world, to be reconciled with the being of God? The intensification of this question is later than the Old Testament; every true gnosis originates in a cultural sphere that has been touched by the Old Testament, almost every one as a directly or indirectly expressed, rebellion against it."

18. Lazier, *God Interrupted*, 31. I am not the first to suggest the significant role of Marcion in Buber's thought: see Mendes-Flohr, "Martin Buber and the Metaphysicians of Contempt," 207–236, and Brague, "How to Be in the World: Gnosis, Religion, Philosophy," in *Martin Buber: A Contemporary Perspective*, ed. Paul Mendes-Flohr (Jerusalem: Syracuse University Press, 2002), 133–147.

19. Harnack, *Marcion*, 134. Emphasis in original.

20. About the prominent role of the Harnack's lectures published in English as What is Christianity in the minds of his Jewish contemporaries, see Uriel Tal, "Theologische Debatte um das "Wesen"des Judentums," in *Jüden im Wilhelminischen Deutschland, 1890–1914.* e. Sammelband (Tübingen, Mohr, 1976), 599–632.

21. The figure of Marcion looms large, sometimes implicitly but often quite explicitly, in Buber's writings. Indeed, I am following Brague's suggestion that Buber's opposition to Gnosis—and, more specifically, Marcionism—is key to understanding his account of religion, of its this-worldliness, where, "the way that leads to the true God . . . must circle round the whole world—conceived as Creation." Brague, "How to Be in the World," 135.

22. Quoted in Buber, "Die Schrift und IhreVerdeutschung" *Werke Bd. 2, Schriften zur Bibel* (Munich: Koesel Verlag: Heidelberg: Schneider, 1964), 1182. See Mendes-Flohr, "Martin Buber and the Metaphysicians of Contempt."

23. Buber, "Der Geist Israels und die Welt von Heute," in *Martin Buber: Der Jude und Seine Judentum: Gesammelte Aufsätze und Reden*, introduction by Robert Weltsch (Cologne: J. Melzer, 1963), 49 / "The Spirit of Israel and the World of Today," in *Israel and the World: Essays in a Time of Crisis* (New York: Schocken Books, 1948), 192.

24. For a thorough and highly insightful account of the Aryanization of Christian theology, in particular the work of the Institute for the Study and Eradication of Jewish influence on Jewish Church Life, see S. Heschel, *The Aryan Jesus*.

25. Buber, "Die Schrift und Ihre Verdeutschung," 1181; As Paul Mendes-Flohr writes,

> Franz Rosenzweig (1886–1929) was quick to detect in Harnack's fascination with Marcion an ominous development. He read Harnack's monograph not simply as a

scholarly treatise but as indicative of a profound crisis in Christianity and an incipient Gnostic mood encouraging not only a rejection of the Old Testament but the God of Creation but also the hatred of the people to whom this God first revealed himself. In a letter of July 29, 1925, to Buber, with whom he was then working on their translation of the Hebrew Scriptures into German, he wrote: . . . "It should be quite clear to you that the situation for which the neo-Marcionites [e.g., Harnack] have striven to achieve on the theoretical plane in actuality has already been obtained. . . . When the Christian speaks of the Bible, he means only the New Testament, perhaps together with the Pslams, which then he mostly believes already belongs to the New Testament. Thus in our new translation of the Hebrew Bible we are becoming missionaries. (Franz Rosenzweig to Buber, July 25, 1925, *Briefe und Tagebuecher*, ed. Rachel Rosenzweig and Edith Rosenzweig-Scheinmann (The Hague, 1979), 2: 1055-56]." ("Martin Buber and the Metaphysicians of Contempt," 221).

26. Harnack, *Marcion*, 30; cf. 27–28, 49.

27. Ibid., 128.

28. On the relationship of the Tübingen School to Judaism and the history of Jesus, see S. Heschel, *Abraham Geiger and the Jewish Jesus*, 106–127.

29. Harnack, *Marcion*, 123

30. Other Protestant theologians such as Karl Barth and Friedrich Gogarten, who were major critics of the liberal Protestantism of Harnack and his ilk, also found prefigurations of themselves in Marcion. See Lazier, *God Interrupted*, 31–32.

31. Suzanne Marchand suggests that the application of the historical-critical study of the Bible as implemented by J. S. Semmler in the 1770s does not merely foreshadow but also sows the seeds of the Marcionite resurgence in the nineteenth and twentieth centuries because of the manner in which he treats the Old and New Testaments as qualitatively different. Marchand suggests that his willingness to historicize the Hebrew Bible but not the New Testament made the allegorical style of reading that linked the Old and New Testament in traditional Christianity no longer tenable: "In effect, [Semmler's] answer to the Enlightenment's challenge to the Bible would be to do away with the Old Testament as inspired scripture, a reversion to the 'Marcionite' heresy that would appeal powerfully to German philosophers and radical religious thinkers from Schleiermacher and Hegel down to Adolf von Harnack." *German Orientalism*, 35–36. Of course, it would be very difficult to trace the appeal of Marcion to a single source. For an overview of current scholarly trends regarding the fraught relationship between liberal Protestantism and the Jews, see Wolfram Kinzig, *Marcion und das Judentum: Nebst einer kommentarien Edition des Briefwechsels Adolf von Harnacks mit Houston Stewart Chamberlain* (Leipzig: EvangelischeVerlagsanstalt, 2004), 18–33.

32. In what follows, I am summarizing Harnack's account of Marcion. Given that it was Harnack's Marcion that had such a tremendous impact on the intellectual landscape, it is beyond the scope of this chapter to investigate how it tracks with current scholarship on this figure.

33. Harnack, *Marcion*, 3.

34. Ibid., 2.

35. Ibid., 82.

36. Ibid., 45.

37. Ibid., 2, 70–72, 82.

38. Ibid., 45.

39. Ibid., 69.

40. Ibid., 69.

41. Ibid., 69. Emphasis in original.

42. Ibid., 82. Emphasis in original.
43. Ibid., 71.
44. Ibid., 89.
45. Ibid., 140. Emphasis in original. Harnack writes,

> Marcion explained the law, that is, certain parts of it (the moral law) as holy, good, and even spiritual, and therefore as an inviolable norm; but he nevertheless did not derive it from the good God, because it belongs to the sinful situation and serves to increase sin. Then, however, the assumption is unavoidable that he made a distinction between "good" and good, "holy" and holy, "spiritual" and spiritual. The "goodness," "holiness," and "spirituality" of the law follows only from its contrast with evil and sin; in comparison with the goodness expressed in mercy and redemption, however, it is neither good nor holy nor spiritual. Marcion's dialectic thus is of a different kind here than from that of the apostle whom he follows, for the apostle knowns no goodness and holiness of a first and a second order. For Marcion, however, only the concept "wicked" is unequivocal; on the other hand, he distinguishes between a moral goodness, which has only an earthly character, and a religious goodness. Paul places the tension of the unequivocally interpreted concepts "righteous" and "good" in the Deity himself, Marcion frees the Deity of this tension, knows, however, a twofold righteousness and a twofold goodness, and divides them between the two Gods. As a rule he does not describe the inferior righteousness (and thus also the creator of of the world) as "good" but only as "just," and he does not call the higher goodness "just" but only "good." (75)

46. A rigorous formulation of transcendence that meshes well with Buber's thought has been recently elaborated by Elliot Wolfson. Wolfson writes, "In my understanding of transcendence, I retain the qualities of elusiveness and exteriority, but reject the possibility of incorporation into a totality. Indeed, transcendence, as I regard it, precludes that possibility. There is nothing beyond nature that is not already part of nature. . . . Thus, we can think of *transcendence within the immanent*, which would preclude circumscribing immanence as *immanent* to a *transcendent*, that is, an 'encompassing' that 'is no more than a reservoir for eruptions of transcendence' [from Deluzze and Guatarri, *What is Philosophy*, 47]. Because we do not accept the positing of ontologically external entitities or relations, what we can assent to, at best, is a *metaphysics, within physics*." Wolfson, *A Dream Interpreted within a Dream: Oneiropoesis and the Prism of Imagination* (Brooklyn, NY: Zone Books, 2011), 25–26.

47. Buber, *Ich und Du*, 130 / *I and Thou*, 80.

48. Paul Mendes-Flohr, in his justly celebrated essay "Martin Buber's Conception of God," emphasizes that "God's immanence is clearly that which concerns Buber" (262). He continues, "In fact, should the term 'transcendence' imply incorrigible remoteness, he observes with apparent allusion to Kierkegaard's and Barth's conception of God, it is a misleading term, and thus best discarded from one's theological lexicon. Alas, he bemoans, transcendence has come to mean 'something which we cannot establish in immediate relation to the present. Therefore I designate nothing as transcendent'" (263). Mendes-Flohr even describes Buber as possessing an "often nigh-single emphasis on God's immanence" (264). Ultimately, I disagree with Mendes-Flohr here on more of a semantic than substantive level. I take issue with his attempt to clearly distinguish transcendence and immanence in Buber. Instead, I prefer to emphasize that, for Buber, transcendence and immanence are—as expressed in Wolfson's quote in n 46—bound up with one another.

49. Buber, *Ich und Du*, 81 / *I and Thou*, 21.

50. Buber, *Ich und Du*, 98 / *I and Thou*, 42.

51. Much has been written on the distinction between It and Thou. This study is particularly influenced by Wood, *Martin Buber's Ontology*, xii, 14–15, 39, 56, 74–75; Paul Mendes-Flohr, "Martin Buber's Conception of God," 245–253; and Elliot R. Wolfson, "The Problem of Unity in the Thought of Martin Buber," *Journal of the History of Philosophy* 27, no .3 (July 1989): 437.

52. Buber, *Ich und Du*, 103 / *I and Thou*, 48.

53. For a discussion of the role in space in Buber's thought, as well as an overview of scholarly discussions, see Dustin Atlas, "Out of the In-Between: Moses Mendelssohn and Martin Buber's German-Jewish Philosophy of Encounter, Singularity, and Aesthetics" (Ph.D. diss., Rice University, 2013), 138–142.

54. Buber, *Ich und Du*, 103 / *I and Thou*, 49.

55. Wolfson, "The Problem of Unity," 440.

56. On the role of Primitivism in the larger context of Weimar and modern art, and in Buber's *I and Thou*, see Zachary Braiterman, *The Shape of Revelation: Aesthetics and Modern Jewish Thought* (Stanford, CA: Stanford University Press, 2007), 147–151. Buber also turns to peoples and cultures of the Orient in this capacity. For example, see Buber, "Der Geist des Orients und das Judentum," in *Martin Buber: Der Jude und Seine Judentum: Gesammelte Aufsätze und Reden*, introduction by Robert Weltsch (Cologne: J. Melzer, 1963), 45–63 / "The Spirit of the Orient and Judaism," in *On Judaism*, ed. Nahum N. Glatzer (New York: Schocken Books, 1967), 56–78, which was delivered as lectures in Prague between 1912–1914. In this piece, Buber explicitly links Jews to the Indians and Chinese, a remark that is particularly interesting given Rosenzweig's disparaging comments about the Chinese and Indian religions and cultures in book 1 of *The Star of Redemption*; the role of the Orient and of Orientalism was ambiguous for Jews in Weimar Germany. As Paul Mendes-Flohr notes, "The new positive image of the Orient nurtured by fin de siècle aestheticism provided an auspicious opportunity to reevaluate the image of the Jew as Oriental. No less importantly it also allowed the Western Jew to develop a new perception of himself, his Oriental origins, and his East European brethren." "Fin de Siècle Orientalism: The Ostjuden, and the Aesthetics of Jewish Self Affirmation," in *Divided Passions*, 83.

57. Compare my reading of the role of the primitives and children in Buber with Wood's comments in *Martin Buber's Ontology*, 56, 83.

58. Braiterman notes the connection of Primitivism with the crisis of historicism. Turning to "primitives," to "past men," provided "faith in new possibilities." Indeed, the goal "was to transform the present on a prehistorical, ahistorical basis, not [to] mimic the historical past." *The Shape of Revelation*, 146.

59. Buber, *Ich und Du*, 90 / *I and Thou*, 31. Notice Buber's term is not nearly as pejorative as Cohen's use of *Wilden* or savage.

60. Ibid.

61. Ibid.

62. Theunissen, Michael, *The Other: Studies in the Social Ontology of Husserl, Heidegger, Sartre, and Buber* (Cambridge, MA: MIT Press, 1984), 272; Mendes-Flohr, "Martin Buber's Concept of God," 250; see also Wood, *Martin Buber's Ontology*, xii.

63. Mendes-Flohr, "Martin Buber's Concept of God," 250.

64. Wood, *Martin Buber's Ontology*, 112.

65. Theunissen, *The Other*, 272. See the discussion of Theunissen in Atlas, "Out of the In-Between," 133–135.

66. Wood, *Martin Buber's Ontology*, 112.

67. Buber, *Ich und Du*, 91 / *I and Thou*,32

68. Buber, *Ich und Du*, 92 / *I and Thou*, 33.

69. Buber, *Ich und Du*, 92 / *I and Thou*, 34.

70. Ibid. Translation altered.

71. Buber, *Ich und Du*, 93 / *I and Thou*, 35.

72. Wood writes, "But what escapes such acts of attentiveness is presence: the original bond between *subject* and *objects* (which indeed is *always* there as the ground of the mutuality involved). Presence is the mutual givenness of the subject and object, the primary togetherness which antedates their separation through reflection. This is why Buber sees . . . children and primitives as clear instances of the life of relation." *Martin Buber's Ontology*, 55–56.

73. Compare my analyses with Wood's, *Martin Buber's Ontology*, 55, 56, 83.

74. Buber, *Ich und Du*, 94 / *I and Thou*, 36.

75. Buber, *Ich und Du*, 95 / *I and Thou* (Kaufmann), 76 with altered translation. Both Kaufmann and Gregor Smith fail to emphasize the worldly nature of the longing in this passage.

76. Buber, *Ich und Du*, 95 / *I and Thou*, 37. Buber's account of the child has recently been critiqued by Mara H. Benjamin, in her essay, "Intersubjectivity Meets Maternity: Buber, Levinas, and the Eclipsed Relation," in *Thinking Jewish Culture in America*, ed. Ken Koltun-Fromm (Lanham, MD: Lexington Books, 2014), 261–284. Benjamin notes that "a feminist critique of this passage [where Buber discusses the genealogy of the I-Thou in the child] practically writes itself" (266). She is correct in pointing out that Buber fails to mention the role of the human mother and that the "perspective of the gestating woman vis-à-vis the fetus" fails to meet either an I-Thou or I-It role (266). Of course, on one level, criticism such as this is fair. However, it is important to note that it ignores the charged context in which Buber is speaking (i.e., his endeavor to create a universal or generic terminology for religion, one not in the thrall of Protestant *Religionwissenschaft*). In other words, it assumes continuity with Buber at the expense of the differences separating Buber's project from our own.

77. On Buber's notion of creation and its distinction from Rosenzweig's account, see Mendes-Flohr, "Martin Buber's Concept of God," 266–267.

78. Buber, *Ich und Du*, 95 / *I and Thou*, 37.

79. For an insightful account of the role of Cohen's *Logic* in *I and Thou*, see Braiterman, *The Shape of Revelation*, 38–39.

80. Buber, *Ich und Du*, 95 / *I and Thou*, 38.

81. *I and Thou*, 38; Kaufmann translates it as "the innateness of the longing for relation is apparent even in the earliest and dimmest stage" (77). Both the Gregor-Smith and Kaufmann translations lose the Cohenian resonance.

82. Buber, *Ich und Du*, 96 / *I and Thou*, 38.

83. Buber, *Ich und Du*, 96 / *I and Thou*, 39.

84. Of course, this does not mean he is successful in his critique. Assessing the viability of his metaphysics is beyond the scope of this chapter. However, I disagree with Steven Katz's positioning of Buber as a sort of neo-Kantian in his important essay, "Martin Buber's Epistemology: A Critical Appraisal," in *Post-Holocaust Dialogues: Critical Studies in Modern Jewish Thought*, ed. Steven Katz and Francis Gladstone (New York: New York University Press, 1983), 1–51.

85. Buber, *Ich und Du*, 97 / *I and Thou*, 39. I find the metaphysical assumptions that accompany Buber's claims about a real world out there to be present in his casual dismissal of the "world of ideas," which he tends to view as a flight from "real man, of you and me, of our life and of our world," and more the construction of a deracinated I of an I-It pairing. *Ich und Du*, 86 / *I and Thou*, 13.

86. This may very well be a reference to Cohen's controversial attempt to purify Kant by rejecting the notion that there is any such thing as a manifold and, thus, that there would be any such thing as a synthetic judgment.

87. Buber, *Ich und Du*, 97 / *I and Thou*, 39. I have slightly altered the translation.

88. Ibid.

89. Buber, *Ich und Du*, 86 / *I and Thou*, 13.

90. Buber, *Ich und Du*, 99 / *I and Thou*, 41. I have slightly altered the translation.

91. Braiterman, *The Shape of Revelation*, 77.

92. Wolfson, *A Dream Interpreted within a Dream*, 25. Emphasis in original. Perhaps not coincidentally, Wolfson has written important scholarly work on Buber, including "The Problem of Unity in the Thought of Martin Buber." In his recent book, *Giving beyond the Gift: Apophasis and Overcoming Theomania* (New York: Fordham University Press, 2014), he offers a rich account of Buber's critique of Cohen on pp. 25–29.

93. Buber, *Ich und Du*, 102 / *I and Thou*, 47.

94. Buber, *Ich und Du*, 102 / *I and Thou* (Kaufmann), 88.

95. Buber, *Ich und Du*, 102 / *I and Thou*, 47 (resume Gregor-Smith).

96. Ibid.

97. Buber, *Ich und Du*, 104 / *I and Thou*, 49.

98. Ibid.

99. Ibid.

100. As discussed in chapter 2, *teshuva* is a notion of central importance in Cohen's philosophy of religion. However, Cohen translates *teshuva* as *Versöhnung*, or reconciliation or repentance.

101. Wood, *Martin Buber's Ontology*, 81–82. See Kaufmann, "I and You: A Prologue," 35–37.

102. Buber, *Ich und Du*, 157 / *I and Thou*, (Kaufmann) 165.

103. On this point see Mendes-Flohr, "Martin Buber's Concept of God," 268–270; Braiterman, *The Shape of Revelation*, 269; and Wolfson, *Giving beyond the Gift*, 28.

104. Buber, *Ich und Du*, 114 / *I and Thou*, 60; I have slightly altered the translation. See Brague, "How to Be in the World."

105. Buber, *Ich und Du*, 114 / *I and Thou*, 61.

106. Ibid.

107. Buber, *Ich und Du*, 114 / *I and Thou*, 60. I have slightly altered the translation.

108. Buber, *Ich und Du*, 118 / *I and Thou*, 64. I have slightly altered the translation.

109. In his explicitly Jewish writings Buber talks about this happening in rabbinic Judaism, and he considers both the followings around Jesus and Hasidism as movements of renewal. It is noteworthy that he is silent about Judaism in *I and Thou* even if critics have correctly described it as offering a "Jewish" ontology, given the preeminence of *teshuva* in it.

110. Buber, *Ich und Du*, 114–115 / *I and Thou*, 61.

111. Buber, *Ich und Du*, 115 / *I and Thou*, 61. It is worth mentioning that in Buber's *Two Types of Faith* (1950), he ties Paul's notion of wrath to the Greek concept of *heimarmene* (140). This is significant, because Harnack traces Marcion's interpretation of Christianity to Paul. Buber reads Jesus as an authentically Jewish figure, but argues that it is Paul's subsequent interpretation that leads to a radical break between Christianity and Judaism.

112. Buber, *Ich und Du*, 115 / *I and Thou*, 62.

113. Wood, *Martin Buber's Ontology*, 109.

114. Buber, *Ich und Du*, 115 / *I and Thou* (Kaufmann), 105.

115. Buber, *Ich und Du*, 115/ *I and Thou*, 62. I have slightly altered the translation. Note that Wood speaks of this in terms of the dialectic between estrangement and turning (*teshuva*) as

well. Indeed, these sentences follow the passage I quoted earlier. "Yet even this is part of the Way, for the alienation, once seen, provides a turning all the more profound. Out of the experience of dividedness, the drive for unity emerges: a drive for that identity-in-difference through which the eternal Presence shines. This is redemption." Wood, *Martin Buber's Ontology*, 109.

116. Buber, *Ich und Du*, 117 / *I and Thou*, 63.

117. Buber, *Ich und Du*, 118 / *I and Thou*, 65.

118. Buber, *Ich und Du*, 119 / *I and Thou*, 65–66. I have slightly altered the translation.

119. Buber, *Ich und Du*, 116–117 / *I and Thou*, 63.

120. Buber, who struggles to maintain this position, is famously challenged by the Holocaust. In "God and the Spirit of Man," in *The Eclipse of God: Studies in the Relation Between Religion and Philosophy* (Amherst, NY: Humanity Books, 1999), 129, Buber writes, "In our age the I-It relation, gigantically swollen, has usurped, practically uncontested, the mastery and the rule. The I of this relation, an I that possesses all, makes all, succeeds with all, this I that is unable to say Thou, unable to meet a being essentially, is the lord of this hour. This selfhood that has become omnipotent, with all the It around it, can naturally acknowledge neither God nor any genuine absolute which manifests itself to men as of non-human origin. It steps in between and shuts off from us the light of heaven." For a discussion of Buber in the context of post-Holocaust thought, see Zachary Braiterman, *(God) after Auschwitz: Tradition and Change in Post-Holocaust Jewish Thought* (Princeton, NJ: Princeton University Press, 1998), 63–67.

121. Buber, *Ich und Du*, 118 / *I and Thou*, 64.

122. Ibid.

123. Ibid.

124. Buber, *Ich und Du*, 85 / *I and Thou*, 26.

125. Buber, *Ich und Du*, 86 / *I and Thou* (Kaufmann), 64. Note that the German is very difficult to translate: "Wesenheiten werden in der Gegenwart gelebt, Gegenständlichkeiten in der Vergangenheit." Gregor Smith translates it as "True beings are lived in the present, the life of objects is in the past." What Buber is getting at is that the true encounter with a being, with its being-ness, its *Wesenheit*, is in the present [*Gegenwart*]. It cannot be mediated.

126. Mendes Flohr, "Martin Buber's Concept of God," 245, 253–255; Elliot Wolfson, "The Problem of Unity in the Thought of Martin Buber," 434; One might describe Buber's method as phenomenological in the sense one describes the method of Rudolf Otto—exploring a phenomenon—not in the sense of following the strict method laid out by Husserl. Maurice Friedman writes, "If Buber is not, in fact, a Husserlian phenomenologist, it is because he is far more radical than Husserl in just this respect: namely, that he leaves room for a uniqueness and otherness that Husserl does not, a uniqueness that can only be known in dialogue and of which we cannot speak as it is 'in itself.'" "Martin Buber and the History of Religion," 369. Friedman is correct, in that there is a metaphysical dimension in Buber's thought that is different from Husserl, yet his comparison is misleading in that Buber's "phenomenology," although novel and insightful, lacks the hard-nosed rigor painstakingly developed by Husserl.

127. Buber, *Ich und Du*, 128 / *I and Thou*, 77.

128. Ibid.

129. Buber, *Ich und Du*, 128 / *I and Thou*, 78.

130. Wood, *Martin Buber's Ontology*, 80.

131. See Wolfson, *A Dream Interpreted within a Dream*, 25–26.

132. Wood, *Martin Buber's Ontology*, 80.

133. See for example, "Der Glaube des Judentums," 142–150, and "Der Geist Israels und die Welt von Heute," in *Martin Buber: Der Jude und Seine Judentum: Gesammelte Aufsätze und*

Reden, 183–196 / "Faith and Judaism," 13–27, and "The Spirit of Israel and the World Today," in *Israel and the World,* 183–196.

134. Buber, *Ich und Du,* 133 / *I and Thou,* 82.

135. Buber, *Ich und Du,* 133 / *I and Thou,* 82–83.

136. Buber, *Ich und Du,* 133 / *I and Thou,* 83.

137. Of course, God can only be present while also absent. That is, one can never encounter God in God's entirety, but rather God's presence takes different forms or images.

138. Buber, *Ich und Du,* 152 / *I and Thou,* 104. I have altered the translation.

139. Ibid.

140. Buber, *Ich und Du,* 152–153 / *I and Thou,* 104.

141. Buber, *Ich und Du,* 153 / *I and Thou,* 105.

142. Wolfson, "The Problem of Unity," 443.

143. Harnack, *Marcion,* 2.

144. Buber, *Ich und Du,* 153 / *I and Thou,* 105. See Michael Fishbane, "Justification through Living: A Third Alternative," in *Martin Buber: A Contemporary Perspective,* ed. Paul Mendes-Flohr (Jerusalem: Syracuse University Press, 2002), 120–132, and Martin Kavka, "Verification (Bewährung) in Martin Buber," *Journal of Jewish Thought and Philosophy* 20, no. 1, Special Issue: "Re-Imagining the Historical In Jewish Philosophy," (2012): 71–98.

145. Buber, *Ich und Du,* 153 / *I and Thou,* 105.

146. Ibid.

147. On the endless pluriformity of the images of the divine in revelation, see Mendes-Flohr, "Martin Buber's Concept of God," 268–270; Braiterman, *The Shape of Revelation,* 269; and Wolfson, *Giving beyond the Gift,* 27–28. Wolfson captures Buber's notion of God nicely: "The image reveals the imageless One insofar as the immediacy of the latter entails that God hides and appears concomitantly; that is, the God that is revealed is the God that is withheld" (28).

148. Buber, *Ich und Du,* 151 / *I and Thou,* 103.

149. To cite again, in greater length, a passage from before, Mendes-Flohr notes,

> In fact, should the term "transcendence" imply incorrigible remoteness, he observes with apparent allusion to Kierkegaard's and Barth's conception of God, it is a misleading term, and thus best discarded from one's theological lexicon. Alas, he bemoans, transcendence has come to mean "something which we cannot establish in immediate relation to the present. Therefore I designate nothing as transcendent." God's immanence or manifest relation to the world is dependent on man, and thus although man needs God—"for the very meaning of his life"—God similarly needs man. Both God and man have "a share" in "realizing" the dialogical relation—braced as it is by the spontaneous and free interplay of divine grace and man's response—by virtue of which the world "becomes God-real"(Gottwirklich). ("Martin Buber's Concept of God," 262–263).

Again, see n. 48 for my semantic disagreement with Mendes-Flohr over the use of immanence and transcendence; cf. Wolfson, *Giving Beyond the Gift,* 14–33.

150. Buber, *Ich und Du,* 151–152 / *I and Thou,* 103. It is worth mentioning that Levinas's famous critiques of Buber, although perhaps generative for his own project, have a rather tin ear in regard to Buber's theological/philosophical sense of ethics. Emmanuel Levinas, "Martin Buber and the Theory of Knowledge," in *The Philosophy of Martin Buber,* eds. Paul Arthur Schilpp and Maurice Friedman (La Salle, IL Open Court, 1967), 133–150, "Dialogue, Self-Consciousness and Proximity of the Neighbor," in *Of God Who Comes to Mind,* trans. Bettina Bergo, (Stanford, CA: Stanford University Press, 1998),137–151. On the relationship between Buber and Levinas, see Robert Bernasconi, "'Failure of Communication' as a Surplus: Dialogue

and Lack of Dialogue between Buber and Livinas in *The Provocation of Levinas: Rethinking the Other*, ed. Robert Bernasconi and David Wood (New York: Routledge, 1988), 100–135, and Gregory Kaplan, "Ethics as First Philosophy and the Other's Ambiguity in the Dialogue of Buber and Levinas," *Philosophy Today* 50, no. 1 (2006): 40–57.

151. In other words, Buber's teleological suspension of the ethical is rooted in the dialogical. Like Rosenzweig, but unlike Kierkegaard to whom this phrase is indebted—and whom Buber referred to as a Marcionite ("Die Frage Nach Einzelnen," in *Martin Buber Werke: Erster Band Schriften zur Philosophie*, 217–265)—revelation binds one to the world rather than separates one from it. If Cohen misses the holiness of the actual in his recourse to an ideal transcendent and thus alien to the world, Buber thinks Kierkegaard's teleological suspension of the ethical removes the self, in its singular relation to the divine, from the world. See also Buber's, "On the Suspension of the Ethical," in *Eclipse of God*, which also maintains this Marcionite interpretation of Kierkegaard. Of course, Buber's famous critique of Kierkegaard, "The Question of the Single One," has been not unjustly critiqued for a lack of nuance in its account of Kierkegaard's perspective.

152. Mendes-Flohr and Elliot Wolfson both find Buber as overcoming Cohen's religion within the limits of reason alone, but they do so in different ways. Compare Mendes-Flohr, "Martin Buber's Concept of God," 255, with Wolfson, *Giving beyond the Gift*, 25–29.

153. Buber, *Ich und Du*, 151 / *I and Thou*, 103.

154. Buber, *Ich und Du*, 152 / *I and Thou*, 104.

155. Harnack, *Marcion*, 45.

156. Buber, *Ich und Du*, 123 / *I and Thou*, 70.

157. Buber, *Ich und Du*, 123 / *I and Thou*, 70–71, translation slightly modified. Indeed, Buber, as if to preempt any invocation of metaphysics—especially modalism, which dissolves the distinction of Jesus and God—bookends the above mentioned quote with two short passages containing two phrases grounded in the verb *bleiben*, to remain. Buber emphasizes, "It remains I and Thou" [*es bleiben Ich und Du*] and "the actuality remains" (123).

158. On the connection between the Apostle John and Marcion, see Harnack, *Marcion*, 126–128.

159. Recasting the mystical undertones expressed in this and certain Hindu texts, Buber claims that the feeling of unity is, at most, the preparation, the unification of one's soul that makes one ready for encounter, *Ich und Du*, 135 / *I and Thou*, 85.

160. Buber's reading of Jesus, which is most fully developed in *Two Types of Faith*, but whose kernel is present in *I and Thou*, is a repudiation of the account of Jesus in Harnack's *Marcion*. In Harnack's reading, Marcion insists that "the son of the good God, Christ, is to be understood modalistically in his relation to the Father." Harnack, *Marcion*, 45. Jesus is the divine with nothing earthly. There is no tension between the divine and human; Jesus is entirely divine and descends to the world as such. In contrast, Buber reads Jesus in line with what he argues is the Jewish messianic tradition—from which Paul and John, both of whom, not surprisingly were major influences on Marcion deviate—where the "Messianic man is here an ascending and not descending one. He steps forth from the crowd of men and is "chosen" by God." Buber, *Two Types of Faith*, 111.

161. Buber, *Ich und Du*, 87 / *I and Thou*, 28–29.

162. Buber, *Ich und Du*, 87 / *I and Thou*, 29.

163. Ibid. I offered my own translation, because, while both Kaufmann and Gregor-Smith gesture towards it, neither adequately capture the manner in which Buber renders love and the world inextricable. Kaufmann's translation comes closer: "Love is a cosmic force" (66). Gregor Smith writes, "Love ranges in its effect through the whole world" (29).

164. Buber, *Ich und Du*, 88 / *I and Thou*, 29.
165. Buber, "Der Glaube des Judentums," 183–195 / "The Faith of Judaism," 13–28.
166. Buber, "Der Glaube des Judentums," 194 / "The Faith of Judaism," 26.
167. Ibid.
168. Ibid.
169. Buber, "Der Glaube des Judentums," 187 / "The Faith of Judaism," 18.
170. Buber, "Der Glaube des Judentums," 184 / "The Faith of Judaism," 15.
171. Buber, "Der Glaube des Judentums," 185–186 / "The Faith of Judaism," 16.

5. Prophets, Prophecy, and Divine Wrath

1. Abraham Heschel, *Die Prophetie* (Kraków: Nakładem Polskiej Akademji Umiejętności, 1936).
2. Abraham J. Heschel, *The Prophets* (New York: Harper and Row, 1962).
3. In this chapter, I translate *vergleichenden Religionsgeschichte* as "comparative religions." Comparative religion, as practiced in the late nineteenth and early twentieth centuries, is largely synonymous with the world religions discourse.
4. Heschel, *Die Prophetie*, 20. Please note that although I have consulted William Wolf's translated excerpt from *Die Prophetie*, "The Divine Pathos: The Basic Category of Prophetic Theology: Part 3 of Chapter 1 of Die Prophetie," trans. William Wolf, *Judaism* 2, no .1 (1953): 61–67; all translations are my own.
5. One should note the different resonance of *eigentümlich* in Heschel's work than in Cohen's. For Cohen's use, see chapter 1.
6. Heschel, *Die Prophetie*, 20.
7. The notion of translating the Bible into Greek has not without warrant earned Heschel comparisons with Levinas. See Joseph Harp Britton, *Abraham Heschel and the Phenomenon of Piety* (London: Bloomsbury T& T Clark, 2013), 231–252, and Alexander Even-Chen and Ephraim Meir, *Between Heschel and Buber: A Comparative Study*, (Brighton, MA: Academic Studies Press, 2012), 121. But it is perhaps more appropriate to consider Heschel's thought in the broader context of Weimar Germany, where there was a general dissatisfaction with rationalism and a pronounced desire for a recovery of tradition and roots. However, in contrast to the path taken by a philosopher like Heidegger, the turn was not to what Peter Gay calls a secret Germany—Hölderlin's attempt to fuse the German and the Greek in a quasi-spiritual quest for wholeness. Gay, *Weimar Culture*, 59–60, 65–69. Heschel seeks to recover the the biblical tradition instead.
8. Abraham Joshua Heschel, *Man's Quest for God: Studies in Prayer and Symbolism* (Santa Fe, NM: 1954), 95. This comes from an autobiographical fragment in which he reflects on his time studying in Germany.
9. For the tendency to treat prophecy using psychological and pathological terms, see Hans-Joachim Kraus, *Geschichte der historisch-kritischen Erforschung des Alten Testaments*, 2nd ed. (Germany: Neuekirchener Verlag, 1956/1969), 322–324.
10. Heschel, *Die Prophetie*, 2. Emphasis in original. See Britton, *Abraham Heschel and the Phenomenon of Piety*, 12–18, 81–104; Lawrence Perlman, *Abraham Heschel's Idea of Revelation* (Atlanta: Scholars Press, 1989); and Nathaniel Rotenstreich, "On Prophetic Consciousness," *Journal of Religion* 54, no. 3 (July 1974): 185–198.
11. For studies of Heschel's commitment to phenomenology, studies that, whatever their merits, tend in my opinion to overestimate the role of Husserl, see Lawrence Perlman, *Abraham*

Heschel's Idea of Revelation; Nathaniel Rotenstreich, "On Prophetic Consciousness"; and Martin Kavka, "The Meaning of This Hour: Prophecy, Phenomenology, and the Public Sphere in the Early Writings of Abraham Joshua Heschel," in *Religion and Violence in a Secular World: Toward a New Political Theology* (Charlottesville: University of Virginia Press, 2006), 108–136.

12. Jon Levenson, "Religious Affirmation and Historical Criticism in Heschel's Biblical Interpretation," *AJS Review* 25, no.1 (2000–2001): 25–44.

13. For a discussion of the common criticism that Heschel's work lacks philosophical rigor, see Robert Erlewine, "Rediscovering Heschel: Theocentrism, Secularism, and Porous Thinking," *Modern Judaism* 32, no. 2 (2012): 175–181.

14. Levenson, "Religious Affirmation," 28.

15. Ibid.

16. Ibid., 41.

17. Heschel, *Die Prophetie*, 4. See Susannah Heschel, introduction to *The Prophets* (New York: HarperCollins, 2001), xv. For a helpful summary of the role of ecstasy in early twentieth-century Biblicism, see Robert R. Wilson, "Prophecy and Ecstasy: A Reexamination," *Journal of Biblical Literature* 98 (September 1979): 321–323.

18. Heschel, *Die Prophetie*, 1. Italics in the original.

19. For a more thorough account of Heschel's relationship to Biblicism, see Robert Erlewine, "Reclaiming the Prophets," 177–206.

20. Levenson, "Religious Affiliation," 30.

21. Ibid., 25.

22. Ibid., 32.

23. Ibid., 31. For the issue of Ezekiel in the book's early reviews, see Brevard Childs' review of *The Prophets*, *Journal of Biblical Literature* 82 (September 1963): 329; Samuel Terrien, "The Divine Pathos," *Interpretation* 17 (1963): 484; and Norman Gottwald,"Book Review of Abraham Joshua Heschel *The Prophets*," *Religious Education* (March–April 1964): 190.

24. Heschel, *The Prophets*, xxv.

25. In *Die Prophetie* the normative dimension is less explicit than in *The Prophets*—although its presence is unmistakable.

26. Heschel, *The Prophets*, xxiii.

27. Heschel, *The Prophets*, 624; On p. 164 of *Die Prophetie*, Heschel writes, "Erkenntnismässig erwirkt die Aufmerksamkeit im Menschen ein Gefühl des Objektseins für das göttliche Subjekt. Es wird einerseits als ein gewaltsames Hineingestelltsein in das Feld des göttlichen Bewusstseins, als ein sich nicht Verbergenkönnen vor der göttlichen Schau, andererseits als Geborgenheit im Bewusstsein Gottes erlebt." "The concern cognitively affects human beings in a feeling of being an object for the divine subject. It is on the one hand, to be placed forcefully into the field of divine consciousness, as one who is not able to mask oneself before the divine inspection, and on the other hand experienced as the feeling of safety in the consciousness of God."

28. Max Weber "'Objectivity' in Social Science," in *The Methodology of the Social Sciences*, trans. and ed. Edward A. Shils and Henry A. Finch (Glencoe, IL: Free Press, 1949), 90.

29. Eduard Spranger, *Types of Men: The Psychology and Ethics of Personality*, trans. Paul J. W. Pigors (Halle: Max Niemeyer Verlag, 1928).

30. Ibid, x. Emphasis in original.

31. Ibid., 210.

32. Ibid., 213. For Spranger, there are three types of religious man, each of whom is one-sided. There is the mystic devoted toward transcendence, the mystic devoted toward immanence, and the intermediary. Max Scheler, in his "Exemplars of Persons and Leaders," in

Person and Self-Value: Three Essays, ed. and trans. M.S. Frings (Dordrecht: Martinus Nijhoff, 1987) [between 1912–1914], explicitly links the mystic and the prophet as the same type on p. 151. Manfred Frings, in *Max Scheler: A Concise Introduction into the World of a Great Thinker* (Pittsburgh: Duquesne University Press, 1965), speaks of different ideal types of exemplars: "They are not abstracted empirical conceptions, but the personal essence of the modalities, which as models exercise a draw or pull on individuals, groups, peoples, nations, towards their own value content" (130).

33. Heschel, *Die Prophetie,* 167.

34. Heschel, *The Prophets,* 395.

35. Typological thinking also figures significantly in Soloveitchik's work, particularly *Halakhic Man* (Philadelphia: Jewish Publication Society, 1983). Not coincidentally, this work also cites Spranger—and engages, as we see Heschel does as well, with the work of Max Scheler. However, our concern with Soloveitchik in this chapter does not deal with *Halakhic Man.*

36. The political and social nature of disciplines such as philosophy and history, no less than art and drama, is a recurring theme in Peter Gay's *Weimar Culture.*

37. In *Introduction to the Hebrew Bible* (Minneapolis: Augsburg Fortress Press, 2004), John J. Collins writes, "More than any other prophet, Ezekiel exhibits phenomena that are associated with unusual psychological conditions, and that seem to call out for psychological analysis" (357).

38. Britton, *Abraham Heschel and the Phenomenon of Piety,* 18.

39. Abraham Joshua Heschel, *Man Is Not Alone: A Philosophy of Religion* (New York: Farrar, Straus and Giroux, 1951), 281. Of course, the prophet is often called against his will, such that the voice of God is often unbearably painful. In later times, piety is attunement to the stillness of the divine voice, its whispering presence.

40. For a general background on Heschel's time in Berlin, see Edward K. Kaplan and Samuel Dresner, *Abraham Joshua Heschel: Prophetic Witness* (New Haven, CT: Yale University Press, 1998), 153–240.

41. Heschel, *Man's Quest for God,* 94.

42. Ibid., 95.

43. Ibid.

44. Ibid.

45. Ibid.

46. Ibid. Emphasis in the original.

47. For a discussion of Heschel and the neo-Kantian tradition, see Robert Erlewine, "Reclaiming the Prophets."

48. Heschel, *God in Search of Man: A Philosophy of Judaism* (New York: Farrar, Straus and Giroux, 1955), 160.

49. One should be cautious in using Kaplan and Dresner's biography, *Abraham Joshua Heschel,* to understand Heschel's relationship to neo-Kantianism. For example, on p. 115, in an attempt to draw parallels with the neo-Kantian thinker Julius Guttmann, Kaplan and Dresner write, "Heschel shared Guttmann's neo-Kantian belief in a priori cognitive categories, for Heschel possessed a 'certainty' about the living God." Heschel's account of God is at odds with the neo-Kantian paradigm. His notion of certainty is existential and rooted in encounter and trust; it is not categorical or axiomatic.

50. Heschel, *Man's Quest for God,* 96.

51. Ibid.

52. Heschel, *God in Search of Man,* 163.

53. Heschel uses the term "Old Testament" frequently, which makes sense given the larger world religion discourse.

54. Heschel, *Die Prophetie*, 150.

55. For a more thorough discussion of Marcion, see the previous chapter; see also Lazier, *God Interrupted*, for background on the resurgence of heresies in German thought at the turn of the twentieth century. And see Adolf von Harnack, *Marcion: Das Evangelium vom Fremden Gott / Marcion: The Gospel of the Alien God*.

56. Heschel, *Die Prophetie*, 153. Emphasis in the original.

57. Ibid.

58. Ibid., 154.

59. Ibid.

60. Maimonides immediately comes to mind as a thinker in this anti-anthropomoporphic tradition. However, one must exercise great caution in making references to Maimonides when discussing Heschel's thought. In 1935, after the completion of his dissertation "Das prophetische Bewusstsein" but before the publication of *Die Prophetie*, Heschel wrote *Maimonides, Eine Biographie* (Neukrichen-Vluyn: Neukirchener Verlag: Hansen F. & Rosner F., 1992 [1935] / *Maimonides: A Biography*, trans. Joachim Neugroschel (New York: Farrar, Straus and Giroux, 1982). In his lifetime, Heschel also wrote other studies of Maimonides. His account of the great medieval philosopher differs in tone from standard accounts of him as a rationalist philosopher, insofar as Heschel emphasizes the Bible, particularly the *Schriftpropheten*, the yearning for prophecy, and the role of pathos. Heschel's account of Maimonides, given its complexity, demands a thorough treatment in itself, which cannot be undertaken here. Thus, it is best to minimize references to Maimonides in the present context.

61. Heschel is often—problematically or hastily—associated with Buber. This attempt has been made more complicated by the book by Alexander Even-Chen and Ephraim Meir, *Between Heschel and Buber*. In this vein, it is worth considering that Michael Wyschogrod charges Buber with possessing certain Maimonidean assumptions that prevent him from conceiving a personal notion of God. Wyschogrod, *The Body of Faith: God in the People of Israel* (San Francisco: Harper & Row, 1983), 86–91. Such a charge could not be applied to Heschel. Of course, it bears repeating that Wyschogrod is operating with a more standard notion of Maimonides as the great enemy of anthropomorphism.

62. Elliot Wolfson has illuminated areas where Heschel's thought overlaps with that of Rosenzweig, Wolfson, *Giving beyond the Gift*, 7–8, 58–59.

63. Heschel, *Die Prophetie*, 155.

64. Ibid., 156.

65. Heschel, *Die Prophetie*, 157.

66. On this point, see *Religion der Vernunft aus den Quellen des Judentums*, 157–166 / *Religion of Reason out of the Sources of Judaism*, 136–142. On the issue of the affects in Cohen, see Hartwig Wiedebach, "Physiology of the Pure Will: Concepts of Moral Energy in Hermann Cohen's *Ethics*," in *Hermann Cohen's Ethics*, 85–104.

67. Heschel, *Die Prophetie*, 159.

68. Ibid.

69. Eliezer Berkovits argues that Heschel willfully ignores—rather than attempts to reconfigure—the medieval tradition of Jewish philosophy. Berkovits thus fails to grasp that Heschel is grounding his investigation in a phenomenological/hermeneutical investigation into the subjectivity of the prophet, rather than offering metaphysics. Indeed, Heschel, thinks the exemplarity of the prophetic individual (and in later works, the pious individual) is the conduit for tradition, not timeless truths. Berkovits's critique, which attempts to read Heschel

as merely reiterating the tension between the God of Abraham, Isaac, and Jacob and the God of Aristotle completely misses this point. For example, in "Dr. A. J. Heschel's Theology of Pathos," in *Major Themes in Modern Philosophies of Judaism* (New York: KTAV, 1975), Berkovits writes, "The truth is that even though the bible calls perfect 'only' His work and it never refers to God as the Absolute, absoluteness is implied in the biblical concept of God as is perfection. If Dr. Heschel thinks otherwise, let him say so. The God of Abraham, Isaac, and Jacob is not the God of Aristotle, but certainly includes the philosopher's concept of absoluteness. The personal and living God of Israel is not so at the expense of perfection or true being; it is personal and living, even though it is perfect and all-transcendent" (202–203). Or later, Heschel "ought to realize that merely to contrast the personal aspect of the biblical concept with the philosophical concept of the absolute is no Jewish theology. Jewish theology begins when one realizes the implications of the presence of both aspects, that of the absolute and the personal, in the biblical concept of God" (203). Clearly, Berkovits has a normative notion of Judaism that he considers the only authentic one, and indeed he essentially criticizes Heschel for philosophizing about Judaism in a Christian manner. See Steven T. Katz's stinging criticism of Berkovits's account of Heschel in Steven T. Katz, "Eliezer Berkovits and Modern Jewish Philosophy," in *Post-Holocaust Dialogues: Critical Studies in Modern Jewish Thought,* eds. Steven Katz and Francis Gladstone (New York: New York University Press, 1983), 125–133.

70. Heschel, Die Prophetie, 159. This issue has been one of significant controversy in Heschel scholarship. As mentioned in n. 70, Eliezer Berkovits charges Heschel with going beyond the pale of Jewish theology. Berkovits's argument consists largely that, in deviating from Maimonides' critique of anthropomorphism, Heschel has strayed into Christian territory. Berkovits's critique was itself subject in turn to sharp critiques. See Katz, "Eliezer Berkovits and Modern Jewish Philosophy," 125–133; Perlman, *Abraham Heschel's Idea of Revelation,* 97–99, n 9–23; see also, Held, *Abraham Joshua Heschel,* 154–155.

71. Heschel, *Die Prophetie,* 131.

72. Ibid., 147.

73. Ibid., 159.

74. Ibid., 135.

75. Ibid., 136.

76. Again, we are not going to discuss whose account of Maimonides is more accurate, Berkovits's or Heschel's. I am merely pointing out Berkovits's use of Maimonides in his criticism (with no apparent attention to Heschel's own work on this figure).

77. Eliezer Berkovits, "Dr. A. J. Heschel's Theology of Pathos," 198.

78. Ibid., 199.

79. Ibid.

80. Held, *Abraham Joshua Heschel,* 149.

81. Berkovits, "Dr. A. J. Heschel's Theology of Pathos," 202.

82. Heschel, *Die Prophetie,* 102.

83. Ibid., 145.

84. Ibid., 67.

85. Ibid., 133.

86. Ibid., 148; Again, see the previous chapter for more on Marcion.

87. Ibid, 148.

88. Ibid., 145; Eliezer Berkovits, who in asserting a normative notion of Judaism in congruence with medieval Jewish philosophers' absolute notion of God, accuses Heschel of maintaining not only Christian sensibilities but also unorthodox or heretical ones. He claims that Heschel's emphasis on possibility and emotions puts him in the camp with the Patripassian

heresy. Berkovits, "Dr. A. J. Heschel's Theology of Pathos," 223. The irony here is that a Christian heresy does influence Heschel's thought, albeit negatively. Heschel, like Buber, is intensely worried about the Marcionite heresy and its resurgence, which undergird a great deal of theoretical and cultural antisemitism. It also, Heschel thinks, led Jews to misunderstand themselves.

89. Heschel, Die Prophetie, 104.

90. Ibid., 115.

91. Ibid., 121.

92. In *God in Search of Man*, Heschel discusses the Sinai event in terms complementary with his account of prophecy. The Sinai event, whatever else it is, is, to use the terminology of *Die Prophetie*, clearly a manifestation of theophany and thus is anthropotropic.

93. "Das theotropische Erlebnis hat seinen vollendeten Ausdruck im Psalm, das anthropotropische in der Prophetie und besonders in der prophetischen Vision gefunden. Wenn man die biblische Geistigkeit als Ganzheit ansehen will, so wird man eine Korrelation zwischen beiden Typen einsehen müssen." Heschel, *Die Prophetie*, 119. "The theotropic experience finds its fullest expression in the Psalm, while the anthropotropic is especially found in the prophetic vision. If one views biblical spirituality as a whole, one must realize a correlation between both types."

94. Ibid., 8.

95. Ibid., 9.

96. Ibid.

97. Ibid., 10, cited from Rohde, Erwin. *Psyche: Seelencult und Unsterblichkeitsglaube der Grieche II* (Tuebingen: Mohr, 1907), 311.

98. This is not to claim that Heschel equates the position of the philosophers with that of the ecstatics. On p. 28 of *Die Prophetie*, Heschel highlights an indirect connection between ecstasy and philosophy. "Ecstasy returns objectively to a theological representation that denies the highest being any immediate contact with the earthly, this world." The example Heschel offers in that of neo-Platonism, which following the denial of any relationship between the gods and earthly life by the Epicureans, used ecstasy as a means to "achieve a connection with transcendence." Of course, the Epicurean position, unlike the Platonic or the Aristotelian, was one that eschewed transcendence. Not all theotropism is ecstatic, but what all theotropic positions have in common is that the direction of movement is from the human being to God.

99. Heschel, *Die Prophetie*, 29.

100. Ibid.

101. Ibid., 130. In *Die Prophetie*, 175, n.1, Heschel, without referencing Cohen directly (but rather his student, Benzion Kellermann) makes a passing reference to the dispute between Cohen and Troeltsch that was discussed in chapter 1. For more on the dispute and Kellerman's role, see Schine, *Jewish Thought Adrift: Max Wiener (1882–1950)*, 54–67.

102. Heschel, *Die Prophetie*, 136.

103. Ibid., 137.

104. Ibid.

105. Ibid.

106. Although we would naturally assume Heschel would be familiar with Cohen's work based on the prominence of Cohen's thought in the environment in which Heschel was working, he also explicitly cites Cohen's *Ethik des reinen Willens* in n. 13, p. 100, in *God in Search of Man*.

107. See Erlewine, *Monotheism and Tolerance: Recovering a Religion of Reason*, 161.

108. Heschel, *Die Prophetie*, 120.

109. Ibid., 145.

110. Ibid., 165.

111. Much like Levinas's famous attempts to use phenomenology to describe the encounter with the human face—an enigma that presents itself *kath' hauto,* and thus defies intentionality—Heschel's account of revelation, also steeped in Husserlian phenomenology, seeks to describe that which exceeds or undercuts the intending subject's ability to grasp and intuit. For brief comparisons to Levinas, see Britton, *Abraham Heschel,* 231–252, and Even-Chen and Meir, *Between Heschel and Buber,* 121.

112. Heschel, *Die Prophetie,* 165.

113. Ibid., 36–37.

114. Ibid., 53.

115. Ibid., 70.

116. Ibid., 128.

117. Ibid., 95.

118. Ibid., 162.

119. Max Scheler, *The Nature of Sympathy,* trans. Peter Heath (New Brunswick, NJ: Transaction Publishers, 2009), 9.

120. Heschel, *Die Prophetie,* 128.

121. Ibid., 165; I use the masculine pronoun here because Heschel's investigations in *Die Prophetie* are limited to the *Schriftpropheten* who are all male.

122. Ibid., 162.

123. Ibid., 68.

124. Ibid., 100. Emphasis in original.

125. Ibid.

126. Ibid.

127. Ibid., 145.

128. Ibid., 163.

129. Heschel, *Die Prophetie,* 163. Emphasis in the original.

130. Ibid., 163; On the foundations of divine pathos in Heschel, see Rotenstreich, "On Prophetic Consciousness," 189; Perlman, *Abraham Heschel's Idea of Revelation,* 91–94; Held, *Abraham Joshua Heschel,* 154–155, Britton, *Abraham Heschel and the Phenomenon of Piety,* 286; cf. Berkovits, "Dr. A. J. Heschel's Theology of Pathos," 215–216.

131. Heschel, *Die Prophetie,* 34.

132. Ibid., 57.

133. Ibid., 57.

134. Ibid., 231.

135. Ibid., 143.

136. Heschel, *The Earth Is the Lord's and The Sabbath* (New York: Harper and Row, 1966 [1950]).

137. Aaron W. Hughes, "The 'Golden Age' of Muslim Spain: Religious Identity and the Invention of a Tradition in Modern Jewish Studies," in *Historicizing 'Tradition' in the Study of Religion,* ed. Steven Engler and Gregory P. Grieve (Berlin: Walter de Gruyter, 2005), 51–74, writes, "For these German-Jewish scholars, this romanticized and idealized fascination with Muslim Spain became the model for contemporary reform, which they thought would provide the key to acceptance and emancipation. In so doing, they constructed a dichotomy: whereas the growth of their unenlightened Eastern European Jewish compatriots was stunted by the casuistry of talmudic law, the great intellectuals of Muslim Spain engaged in philosophical, grammatical, and poetic studies. The 'golden age' of Spain thus held the key to a Jewish

renaissance in the modern world" (58). See also Ismar Shorsch, *From Text to Context: The Return to History in Modern Judaism* (Hanover: University Press of New England, 1994), 71–92, and Ivan Marcus, "Beyond the Sephardic Mystique," *Orim: A Jewish Journal at Yale* 1, no. 1 (Autumn 1985): 35–85.

138. Heschel, *The Earth Is the Lord's*, 24.

139. Ibid., 25. Given subsequent differences between Heschel and Rosenzweig, it is interesting to note that the language Heschel uses here is remarkably similar to Rosenzweig's account of authenticity in his now classic essay from 1923, "Apologetische Denken," in *Zweistromland: Kleinere Schriften zu Glauben und Denken*, ed. Reinhold Mayer and Annemarie Mayer (Dordrecht: Martinus Nijhoff, 1984), 677–686 / "Apologetic Thinking," in *Franz Rosenzweig: Philosophical and Theological Writings*, trans and ed. Paul W. Franks and Michael L. Morgan (Indianapolis: Hackett, 2000), 95–108. In this essay, Rosenzweig famously makes the distinction between apologetic thinking and systematic or authentic thinking. Whereas apologetic thinking "remains dependent on the cause, the adversary," systematic or authentic thinking "determines the circle of its objects itself," possessing, as it does, the truthfulness "of thought reacting to the occasion" (Rosenzweig, "Apologetische Denken," 679 / "Apologetic Thinking," 98). With this distinction, Rosenzweig instantiates a dichotomy between modes of thinking that take recourse to foreign terms and idioms in defining themselves and their tasks and those that proceed organically from within a tradition as it unfolds on the other.

140. Heschel, *The Earth Is the Lord's*, 24.

141. Ibid., 25.

142. Abraham Joshua Heschel, "No Religion Is an Island," in *Moral Grandeur and Spiritual Audacity: Essays,* ed. Susannah Heschel (New York: Farrar, Straus & Giroux, 1996), 235–250.

143. Ibid., 236.

144. For an interesting account of this essay in comparison to that of Soloveitchik's own response to this issue, see Reuven Kimmelman, "Rabbis Joseph B. Soloveitchik and Abraham Joshua Heschel on Jewish Christian Relations," *Modern Judaism*, 24, no. 3 (2004): 251–271.

145. Heschel, "No Religion Is An Island," 236.

146. On the relationship between Christianity and Nazism, see S. Heschel, *The Aryan Jesus.*

147. Even-Chen and Meir make this precise point in *Between Heschel and Buber*, 269.

148. Heschel, "No Religion Is An Island," 236.

149. Ibid. 242. Note, as published in *Moral Grandeur and Spiritual Audacity*, the text reads not "Marcionite trends" but "Anti-Marcionite trends." I have spoken with Susannah Heschel and confirmed that this is indeed a typographical error; the text should read "Marcionite." Email correspondence, 8/27/15.

150. Heschel, *God in Search of Man*, 15.

6. Cultivating Objectivity

1. Joseph Soloveitchik, *The Halakhic Mind: An Essay on Jewish Tradition and Modern Thought* (New York: Seth Press, 1986).

2. Ibid., 3.

3. Lawrence J. Kaplan, "Rabbi Joseph B. Soloveitchik's Philosophy of Halakhah," *Jewish Law Annual* 7 (1998): 194–195.

4. Jonathan Sacks, "Rabbi Joseph B. Soloveitchik's Early Epistemology," in *Tradition in an Untraditional Age: Essays on Modern Jewish Thought* (London: Vallentine, Mitchell, 1990), 288; see also Kaplan, "Rabbi Joseph B. Soloveitchik's Philosophy of Halakhah," 143–144, and idem,

"Joseph Soloveitchik and Halakhic Man," in *The Cambridge Companion to Modern Jewish Philosophy*, ed. Michael L. Morgan and Peter Eli Gordon (Cambridge: Cambridge University Press, 2007), 209–232.

5. Sacks, "Rabbi Joseph B. Soloveitchik's Early Epistemology," 296; See also William Kolbrenner, "Towards a Genuine Jewish Philosophy; Halakhic Mind's New Philosophy of Religion," in *Exploring the Thought of Rabbi Joseph B. Soloveitchik*, ed. Marc D. Angel (Hoboken, NJ: KTAV, 1997), 179–205. Like Sacks, Kolbrenner emphasizes this book's difference in tone from Solovietchik's other works, but also insists on its relevance for the rest of Soloveitchik's corpus. See also, Kaplan, "Joseph Soloveitchik and Halakhic Man," 212–214.

6. Joseph Soloveitchik, "Confrontation," *Tradition* 6, no. 2 (1964): 25–29.

7. Sacks claims, "There is a straight road from *The Halakhic Mind* to the argument in 'Confrontation.'" Sacks, "Rabbi Joseph B. Soloveitchik's Early Epistemology," 297. Note that although he does not explore Soloveitchik's link to the Marburg school, Daniel Rynhold also discusses the connection between *The Halakhic Mind* and "Confrontation." Rynhold, "The Philosophical Foundations of Soloveitchik's Critique of Interfaith Dialogue," *Harvard Theological Review* 96, No. 1 (January 2003): 101–120.

8. Whereas Dov Schwartz, *Religion or Halaka: The Philosophy of Rabbi B. Soloveitchik* (Leiden: Brill, 2007), tends to treat the works whose origins date back to the early 1940s as more or less complimentary, I tend to agree more with Moshe Sokol's statement that "however one judges the successes of the varying attempts to reconcile the underlying contradictions in R. Soloveitchik's writings, and I am bit skeptical about some of them, there can be very little doubt that there are serious differences amongst the writings, even if they do not in the end amount to actual contradictions." "'Ger ve-Toshav Anokhi': Modernity and Traditionalism in the Life and Thought of Rabbi Joseph B. Soloveitchik," *Tradition* 29, no. 1 (1994): 33. Similarly, in *The Rationale of the Halakhic Man: Joseph B. Soloveitchik's Conception of Jewish Thought* (Amsterdam: J. C. Gieben), 128–129, Reinier Munk writes,

> Soloveitchik's account of halakhic man's thought and acts is of an eclectic nature. In *The Halakhic Mind*, the line of reasoning is articulated against a wide variety of thinkers, among whom James Clerk Maxwell, Wolgang Koekler, Paul Natorp, Max Scheler, Rudolf Otto, and William James hold a central position. Next, the structure and content of "Ish haHalakha" bears the marks of Geisteswissenschaftler as Wilhelm Dilthey, Eduard Spranger, Henri Bergson, and again Scheler, Otto and James, in addition to *talmide hakhamim* like Maimonides, R. Shneur Zalman of Lyady, R Hayim of Volozhin, and others. And in the essay "U-viqqashtem mi-sham" the conjunction of man with God is articulated by means of the formula of the unity of intellect, intelligens, and intelligible which Maimonides adopted from al-Farabi or from Neo-Platonic sources.

9. See Lawrence Kaplan, "Revisionism and the Rav: The Struggle for the Soul of Modern Orthodoxy," *Judaism* 48, no. 3 (Summer 99): 290–311.

10. Josef Soloweijczyk, "Das reine Denken und die Seinskonstitutierung bei Hermann Cohen" (Inaugural-Dissertation, Friedrich-Wilhelms-Universität zu Berlin, 1932).

11. Munk, *The Rationale of the Halakhic Man*, 51.

12. Ibid., 128.

13. This is recounted in Kaplan, "Joseph B. Soloveitchik's Philosophy of Halakhah," 173. It should be noted that Kaplan disagrees with Taubes on this point.

14. For works that treat *The Halakhic Mind* yet pay little attention to the Cohenian legacy, see Sacks, "Rabbi Joseph B. Soloveitchik's Early Epistemology"; Kolbrenner, "Towards a Genuine Jewish Philosophy"; and Daniel Rynhold, "The Philosophical Foundations of Soloveitchik's

Critique of Interfaith Dialogue," *Harvard Theological Review* 96, no. 1 (Jan 2003), 101–120. To be sure, scholars such as Lawrence Kaplan, Dov Schwartz, Aviezer Ravitzky ("Rabbi J. B. Soloveitchik on Human Knowledge: Between Maimonidean and Neo-Kantian Philosophy," *Modern Judaism* 6, no. 2 (May 1986): 157–188), and others recognize the significance of this relationship. Sacks makes a passing reference, comparing Soloveitchik's rejection of Cohen to S. R. Hirsch's rejection of Moses Mendelssohn. Sacks, "Rabbi Joseph B. Soloveitchik's Early Epistemology," 295. Similarly, Kolbrenner focuses far more on Cohen's colleague Paul Natorp, whose method is frequently explicitly invoked in this chapter. However, ultimately, for Kolbrenner, Natorp and Marburg neo-Kantianism receive relatively marginal treatment given their importance to understanding Soloveitchik's work. Kaplan, Schwartz, and Ravitzky, in contrast, make the engagement with Cohen much more explicit in their accounts of Soloveitchik.

15. As Sacks puts it, "The central argument of *The Halakhic Mind* is that religion constitutes an autonomous cognitive domain" such that "the justification of religion" requires no "terms drawn from outside of itself." "Rabbi Joseph B. Soloveitchik's Early Epistemology," 290. See also Kaplan "Rabbi Joseph Soloveitchik's Philosophy of Halakhah," 144, and Kolbrenner, "Towards a Genuine Jewish Philosophy," 181.

16. Wayne Proudfoot, *Religious Experience* (London: University of California Press, 1985), 220.

17. Russell McCutcheon, *Manufacturing Religion* (New York: Oxford University Press, 1997), 61.

18. Of course, this is more than mere rhetoric. Indeed, this seems to be the heart of Jacob Taubes's claim that Soloveitchik should have followed Heidegger and Gadamer, rather than Cohen. Kaplan, "Rabbi Joseph Soloveitchik's Philosophy of Halakhah," 173.

19. Soloveitchik, *Halakhic Mind*, 3. A brief note on the term *homo religiosus*: As we saw with Heschel in the previous chapter, Soloveitchik invokes a typological notion of the religious human being, *homo religiosus*. This term, which occurs in other works by Soloveitchik, is rooted in the work of Scheler, Spranger, and others. Of course, in the current climate in religious studies, where there is a significant backlash against Mircea Eliade and his school, who made significant use of this notion, methods that seek to unify or highlight similarities through ideal types are viewed with great suspicion.

20. It is also noteworthy that Soloveitchik looks to much broader vistas of science and religion rather than simply Enlightenment and post-Enlightenment developments. No doubt this is a result not only of his knowledge of medieval philosophy but also his engagement with such luminaries of the Marburg School as Ernst Cassirer, who trace the history and development of science.

21. See Sacks, "Rabbi Joseph B. Soloveitchik's Early Epistemology," 292.

22. Soloveitchik, *The Halakhic Mind*, 16.

23. Cohen, *Einleitung mit kritischen Nachtrag zur F. A. Langes, 'Geschichte des Materialismus,'* 103. This text went through several editions. It offers a general overview of Cohen's system and its relationship to culture. I am utilizing the 1914 version, which has been included in the critical editions of Cohen's *Werke*. See discussion of this text in chapter 1.

24. Ibid., 13.

25. Ibid., 59.

26. Ursula Renz, "Critical Idealism and the Concept of Culture: Philosophy of Culture in Hermann Cohen and Ernst Cassirer," in *Hermann Cohen's Critical Idealism*, ed. Reinier Munk (Dordrecht: Springer, 2005), 336.

27. See Gregory B. Moynahan's instructive essay, "Hermann Cohen's 'Das Prinzip der Infinitesimalmethode,' Ernst Cassirer, and the Politics of Science in the Wilhemine Germany,"

Perspectives on Science 11, no. 1 (2003): 35–74, for an account of the social and political dimension to Cohen's philosophy of science and mathematics that is often missed in contemporary readings.

28. Zank, *The Idea of Atonement*, 242.

29. It is important therefore to recognize that Cohen's form of neo-Kantianism does not originate, as one commentator recently suggests, merely due to the environment of "scientism of the second half of the nineteenth century, when there was seemingly nothing left for philosophy to do apart from providing a foundation or explanatory basis for the activities of the positive sciences." Sebastian Luft, "Reconstruction and Reduction: Natorp and Husserl on Method and the Question of Subjectivity," in *Neo-Kantianism in Contemporary Philosophy*, ed. Rudolf A Makkreel and Sebastion Luft (Bloomington: Indiana University Press, 2010), 63. Such an account, unfortunately, reflects an uncritical Heideggerian assessment of the Marburg school that continues to operate too often unchecked in continental philosophy.

30. Soloveitchik, *Halakhic Mind*, 8.

31. Soloveitchik writes, "What is perhaps most striking in all these considerations is that the physicist himself, in expounding 'peculiar' epistemological theories concerning the physical world, has helped deliver the philosopher from his bondage to the mathematical sciences." *The Halakhic Mind*, 24. For a more contemporary critique of Cohen's transcendental philosophy that reaches similar conclusions—if by a somewhat different route—see Werner Flach, "Cohen's Urspründgsdenken," in *Hermann Cohen's Critical Idealism*, ed. Reinier Munk (Dordrecht: Springer, 2005), 41–67.

32. Munk, *The Rationale of the Halakhic Man*, 53 n. 6.

33. Here it is not unreasonable to suggest the influence of phenomenology, and in particular, the work of Max Scheler. Indeed, there are clear affinities to the position marked out by Scheler in his essay, "Idealism and Realism" (1927), which is not explicitly discussed in the dissertation but is cited in *The Halakhic Mind*. In this essay, Scheler critiques Cohen for failing to recognize that "the existence of an object is always and necessarily transcendent to every possible consciousness." Scheler, "Idealism and Realism," in *Selected Philosophical Essays*, trans. David R. Lachterman (Evanston, IL: Northwestern University Press, 1973), 290; for his specific critique of Cohen, see p. 308. See Munk, *The Rationale of the Halakhic Man*, 49.

34. See Munk, *The Rationale of The Halakhic Man*, 14–51, for an alternative account. Note that Munk does not refrain from assessing the adequacy of Soloveitchik's treatment to Cohen's thought—and indeed, he finds it wanting.

35. Solowiejczyk, *Das reine Denken und die Seinskonstitutierung bei Hermann Cohen*, 8.

36. Ibid.

37. Ibid., 16.

38. Soloveitchik frequently uses the term *mathematisch-naturwissenschaftliche* in the dissertation. *The Halakhic Mind* frequently uses the phrase "mathematico-scienctific," which presumably means the same thing.

39. This was not a particularly novel critique against Cohen. However, our concern is with the nature of Soloveitchik's critique, not with whether or not it was groundbreaking.

40. See Munk's critique of Soloveitchik's overly narrow definition of "pure" in Cohen's thought. *The Rationale of the Halakhic Man*, 45–46.

41. Solowiejczyk, *Das reine Denken und die Seinskonstitutierung bei Hermann Cohen*, 36.

42. Ibid., 39.

43. Ibid.

44. Ibid., 82.

45. Ibid., 84; my italics.

46. Ibid., 98.
47. Ibid., 99.
48. Ibid., 100.
49. Ibid. 31.
50. Ibid., 92.
51. Ibid., 30–31.
52. Ibid., 64.
53. Ibid., 80, n.2.
54. Ibid., 98.
55. As we see later, by psychology he means something along the lines of what Paul Natorp lays out in *Allgemeine Pyschologie nach kritischer Methode*. Thus we might say it is transcendental psychology, rather than applied psychology.
56. Solowiejczyk, *Das reine Denken und die Seinskonstituierung bei Hermann Cohen*, 98.
57. Ibid., 84.
58. Ibid., 107.
59. Ibid. As Munk points out, "According to Soloveitchik, consciousness is not to be conceived of as consciousness of the object, but can only be understood as selfconsciousness [sic] or consciousness of the knowing subject, containing ideas of objects instead of physical objects." *The Rationale of the Halakhic Man*, 41. Munk argues that, by excluding the interiority of the subject, the psyche, as a source of meaning, Cohen excludes the qualitative dimension of the interior, the *seelische*, leaving only the quantitative (44–45).
60. Ibid., 51.
61. Ibid., 50. This is clearly unavailable in Cohen's Idealism, although Soloveitchik seems to find the work of Cohen's colleague and co-founder of the Marburg school, Paul Natorp, more amenable to this outside world, a world external to thought. On the tensions between Cohen and Natorp, see Helmut Holzhey, esp. *Cohen und Natorp: Band 1:Ursprung und Einheit* (Basel: Schwabe, 1986).
62. Soloveitchik, *The Halakhic Mind*, 45.
63. Cohen, *Einleitung mit kritischen Nachtrag*, 101–103. See chapter 1.
64. To be sure, Cohen's philosophy of religion involves logic and aesthetics as well. However, Soloveitchik is not wrong to claim that the overwhelming emphasis is on its ethical expression.
65. Soloveitchik, *The Halakhic Mind*, 40.
66. Ibid., 5.
67. Ibid., 6.
68. Ibid., 64.
69. Ibid., 64.
70. Holzhey, *Cohen und Natorp*, 62.
71. Solovietchik, *The Halakhic Mind*, 65.
72. Ibid., 66.
73. Ibid., 6.
74. Ibid., 6–7.
75. Ibid., 33.
76. Ibid., 16.
77. Ibid., 15.
78. Ibid., 42.
79. Ibid., 51. Presumably, if we return to Lawrence Kaplan's "J. B. Soloveitchik's Philosophy of Halakhah," this is the road Jacob Taubes would have preferred that Soloveitchik take,

although he clearly would not have maintained such a negative view of the approach of the philosophers in question.

80. Soloveitchik, *The Halakhic Mind*, 52.

81. Ibid., 53.

82. Ibid., 54.

83. Ibid., 55.

84. McCutcheon, *Manufacturing Religion*, 68.

85. Ibid., xi.

86. Whether McCutcheon's claims here about all other disciplines in the university are true or not is beyond the scope of this discussion. For an important criticism of McCutcheon—and like-minded critics—in a larger discussion about the continued importance of philosophy of religion, see Kevin Schillbrack, *Philosophy and the Study of Religions: A Manifesto* (Malden, MA: Wiley Blackwell, 2014), esp 175–206.

87. Soloveitchik, *The Halakhic Mind*, 55.

88. Of course, such a distinction is a bit forced. There is definitely a genealogical dimension to McCutcheon's work, just as there are sociopolitical dimensions to the work of Smith and Masuzawa.

89. Soloveitchik, *The Halakhic Mind*, 61–62.

90. Ibid., 61.

91. Ibid., 62. According to Soloveitchik, his notion of reconstruction is modeled on Natorp's *Allgemeine Psychologie nach Kritischer Methode* (Tubingen: J. C. B. Mohr (Paul Siebeck), 1912). Natorp, of course, was Cohen's colleague at Marburg and, in many respects, was one of his disciples. Although recent scholarship has brought to light some interesting differences between their views, they remain, methodologically speaking, quite close. See Holzhey, *Cohen und Natorp*, and Wolfang Marx, "Die philosophische Entwicklung Paul Natorps in Hinblick auf das System Hermann Cohen," *Zeitschrift für philosophische Forschung* 18, no. 3 (1964): 486–500.

92. Soloveitchik, *The Halakhic Mind*, 53.

93. For an account of the respective positions of Cohen and Natorp regarding psychology, see Winrich de Schmidt, *Psychologie und Transzendentalphilosophie: Zur Psychologie-Rezeption bei Hermann Cohen und Paul Natorp* (Bonn: Bouvier Verlag Hermann Grundman, 1976).

94. Natorp, *Allgemeine Psychologie*, 191.

95. Ibid., 193.

96. See Natorp, *Allgemeine Psychologie*, 84.

97. Obviously, Soloveitchik sees Natorp's methodology as significantly in contrast with Husserl and especially his students. For a close and careful juxtaposition of Natorp's *Allgemeine Pyschologie* with Husserl's work, see Luft, "Reconstruction and Reduction: Natorp and Husserl on Method and the Question of Subjectivity."

98. Soloveitchik, *The Halakhic Mind*, 63

99. Ibid., 66–67.

100. Ibid., 67.

101. Ibid.

102. Ibid., 72–73.

103. Ibid., 71.

104. Ibid., 72.

105. Ibid., 72.

106. Ibid., 71–72.

107. Ibid., 73.

108. Ibid., 73–74.

109. Ibid., 74.

110. McCutcheon, *Manufacturing Religion*, 23.

111. On this, see Thomas A. Lewis, "On the Role of Normativity in Religious Studies," in *The Cambridge Companion to Religious Studies*, ed. Robert Orsi (New York: Cambridge University Press, 2012), 168–185.

112. Freidrich Schleiermacher, *On Religion: Speeches to its Cultured Despisers*, trans. and ed. Richard Crouter (Cambridge: Cambridge University Press, 1988), 22.

113. Ibid., 29.

114. Soloveitchik, *The Halakhic Mind*, 69.

115. Ibid., 67.

116. Ibid., 68.

117. Ibid., 102.

118. As is well known and widely discussed, Abraham Joshua Heschel famously played a prominent role in this process. For a discussion of Heschel's role in Vatican II, including some discussion of Soloveitchik, see Edward Kaplan, *Spiritual Radical: Abraham Joshua Heschel in America* (New Haven, CT: Yale University Press, 2007), 238–257. See also Reuven Kimelman, "Rabbis Joeph B. Soloveitchik and Abraham Joshua Heschel on Jewish-Christian Relations," *Modern Judaism* 24, no. 3 (2004): 251–271, and Angela West, "Soloveitchik's 'No' to Interfaith Dialogue," *European Judaism* 47, no. 2 (2014): 95–106.

119. For discussions about the nature and status of "Confrontation" in regard to religious discourse, see Kimelman, "Rabbis Joseph B. Soloveitchik and Abraham Joshua Heschel on Jewish-Christian Relations," 257; Eugene Korn, "The Man of Faith and Religious Dialogue: Revisiting Confrontation," *Modern Judaism* 25, no. 3 (2005): 290–292; and West, "Soloveitchik's 'No' to Interfaith Dialogue," 96.

120. Soloveitchik, "Confrontation," 23–24.

121. David Hartman, *Love and Terror in the God Encounter: The Theological Legacy of Joseph B. Soloveitchik* (Woodstock, VT: Jewish Lights Publishing, 2001), 131–167.

122. David Singer and Moshe Sokol, "Joseph Soloveitchik: Lonely Man of Faith," *Modern Judaism* 2 (1982): 227–272, quote from 255; others, such as Edward Kaplan, *Spiritual Radical: Abraham Joshua Heschel in America, 1940–1972*, have argued that Soloveitchik opposed Vatican II publicly but supported it, or at least was ambivalent about it, privately. It is not my intention to consider his personal state of mind, but to explore the methodological consistency of his position.

123. Rynhold, "The Philosophical Foundations of Soloveitchik's Critique of Interfaith Dialogue," 101–120, quote from 105. Although I tend to agree with Rynhold in spirit, he follows Dilthey and the hermeneutical tradition (along with some Anglo-American thinkers) in linking *Halakhic Mind* to "Confrontation," whereas I follow Soloveitchik's connection to the Marburg School in linking these texts.

124. Soloveitchik, "Confrontation," 24.

125. Joseph Soloveitchik, "Addendum to the Original Edition of 'Confrontation," in *A Treasury of Tradition*, ed. Walter S. Wurzburger and Norman Lamm (New York: Hebrew Publishing Company, 1980), 78–80.

126. Ibid., 79.

127. Ibid.

128. Eugene Borowitz offers a helpful point about much of Soloveitchik's writing, though he clearly does not take into account Soloveitchik's dissertation or *The Halakhic Mind* (which had not yet been published), when he states, "All of Soloveitchik's writing . . . takes place within a

fundamental structure of typology. That is to say, he does not deal with things as they are, or even with abstractions from things as they are, but rather with pure possibilities of existence." Borowitz, "The Typological Theology of Joseph B. Soloveitchik," *Judaism: A Quarterly Journal of Jewish Life and Thought* 15, no. 2 (1966): 205–206.

129. The two Adams are also pronounced in *Lonely Man of Faith* (Northvale, NJ: Jason Aronson, 1965). I would like to take this opportunity to thank Lawrence J. Kaplan for helping me clarify my thinking regarding the different levels of existence in "Confrontation," although, of course, all errors are my own.

130. Soloveitchik, "Confrontation," 6.

131. Ibid., 9.

132. Ibid., 11.

133. Ibid., 11 n5.

134. Ibid., 14.

135. Ibid., 16.

136. Ibid., 20.

137. Ibid., 19; Note Soloveitchik's reluctance to specifically name Christianity.

138. Ibid., 22.

139. Ibid., 16.

140. Ibid., 18.

141. Ibid., 19.

142. Ibid.

143. Ibid., 21.

144. Despite Soloveitchik's tone, as we have seen, Heschel's approach to Christianity can hardly be characterized as servile. See n 118 for discussions of their complex relationship to one another and to Vatican II.

145. Soloveitchik, "Confrontation," 21.

146. Ibid., 22.

147. Ibid., 28.

148. Ibid., 17.

149. Ibid., 26.

Conclusion

1. In Europe, one often finds many non-Jews actively engaged in Jewish Studies. This is a rather ironic outcome of the legacy of the world religions discourse. I would like to thank Aaron Hughes for pointing this out to me.

2. This is by no means to say its legacy does not live on in religious studies. The work of Daniel Dubuisson, Russell McCutcheon, Tomoko Masuzawa, and others explicitly problematize those aspects of its legacy that continue to shape the field of religious studies.

3. Novak emphasizes that "the Torah can never and, therefore, must never be justified by the world or anything in it." Because the "Torah comes from God, and it is for God's sake that it is given to us" it cannot be reduced to human reason, which is bound up with the world. David Novak, *The Election of Israel: The Idea of the Chosen People* (Cambridge: Cambridge University Press, 1995), 9.

4. Although conceivably works inspired by this impulse could take shape in a variety of disciplinary forms, for purposes of clarity, I focus on the form it takes (or can take) in religious studies and as a result of the dominant methodological sensibilities of this discipline. Note that

another alternative is to make the study of Jewish philosophy primarily an exercise of intellectual history rather than philosophy. However, because my focus is on the active engagement with the tradition rather than the descriptive study of it, I do not discuss this further. Nevertheless, it should be pointed out that this approach continues to exist as a productive avenue for scholarship.

5. Arnal and McCutcheon, *The Sacred Is the Profane: The Political Nature of Religion*.

6. Ibid., 7.

7. One need only look to Brill's s Library of Contemporary Jewish Philosophers series to see that, among many—though not all—of its subjects at least, this tendency is very much alive and well. Of course, the tendency to use such terminology must itself be historicized and examined within a broader ideological and cultural context.

8. Hughes, *Rethinking Jewish Philosophy*, 118.

9. Masuzawa, *The Invention of World Religions*, 282.

10. Given the debates about normativity in religious studies, I bracket questions about the place of constructive Jewish philosophy within the field of religious studies. However, I do want to again point to the important arguments about the inevitability of normativity by Schillbrack, *Philosophy and the Study of Religions: A Manifesto*, and Lewis, "On the Role of Normativity in Religious Studies," 168–185.

11. I use this rather cumbersome language because we must resist speaking of traditions in the singular now that we recognize the internal plurality of voices.

Index

ROBERT ERLEWINE is Associate Professor of Religion at Illinois Wesleyan University in Bloomington, IL. He is the author of *Monotheism and Tolerance: Recovering a Religion of Reason* (IUP, 2010). He has also written numerous articles and book chapters on modern Jewish philosophy and the philosophy of religion and was the former managing editor of *Journal of Jewish Thought and Philosophy*.

www.ingramcontent.com/pod-product-compliance
Lightning Source LLC
Chambersburg PA
CBHW030302100426
42812CB00002B/543